S|

EXACT ENGLISH USING AFFIXES

A Catalog of Signed Vocabulary Extended by Prefixes, Suffixes, Contractions and Tenses.

Compiled by
Billie McDavitt & Patrice Stephenson

International Standard Book Number: 0-916708-34-9

Library of Congress Catalog Number: 2002115219

Publisher

Modern Signs Press, Inc.
P.O. Box 1181
Los Alamitos, CA 90720
562/596-8548, 562/493-4168 V/TDD
FAX 562/795-6614
email: modsigns@modernsignspress.com

Illustrations and descriptions were taken from Signing Exact English.

First Printing 2003

Printed in the United States of America

Signing Exact English Using Affixes:

A Catalog of Signed Vocabulary Extended by Prefixes and Suffixes

A primary purpose for using Signing Exact English is to present a consistent and complete signed form of English. Signing "exact" English implies that English can be presented in a signed form with vocabulary altered using affixes. For this purpose, eighty-seven signed prefixes and suffixes are included in the 1993 Edition of Signing Exact English. Few are the English words that cannot be altered by the addition of a prefix or suffix. This catalog is consistent with the "Important Principles of Signing Exact English" in Section XIII in the Signing Exact English dictionary. Therefore, the base sign vocabulary of SEE can be expanded from 4400 signs to well over 60,000.

The question that frequently arises in sign language classes regarding the usage of affixes is, "How does a signer determine if a word to which an affix is applied is really the base word from SEE?" For example, does the word USUAL come from the base word USE? The answer is, "yes," since both words come to English from the Latin root word "usus," meaning "to use". This catalog is intended to provide a ready reference for signs that can be created from base signs using the affixes.

To create this catalog, a list of every word that can be produced from the base words by adding affixes was verified using standard English dictionaries. The resultant list contains words that are commonly used in spoken English as well as words primarily used only in written form. Under each base word there are two columns. The first column contains all the applicable affixes that can be applied. The second column presents the word that is created.

The notations used are the asterisk (*) and the caret (^). The asterisk indicates that the -s ending for a noun plural may be added. For example, *basement* is the word *base* plus the suffix *-ment.* Basement* means that *base* + *-ment* can also add the -s ending for the plural "basements". The caret appears following a verb such as *notify*, meaning that the base word *note* + the suffix *-ify* can then take the standard verb endings, *-s, -ed* and *-ing*, to produce *notifies, notified* and *notifying.* These two notations are used to conserve printing space. Sometimes you will see the following notation (2) after the blue printed word. This indicates that there are two alternative signs for that particular word in the S.E.E. dictionary. Use the sign most commonly used in your school or local area, or the sign most comfortable for you.

Bold type is used in column one when, consistent with "Important Principle Number Eight" in the Signing Exact English dictionary, an intervening affix may be dropped when there is no sacrifice of clarity. For example, under nature, these entries appear:

nature		
	+ -s	natures
	+ -al	natural
	+ **-ly**	naturally

"Naturally" can be signed *nature* + the suffix *-ly* because there is no word "naturely". The intervening -al ending may be dropped without sacrificing clarity. Reference to the preceding word in the list is required to determine the affix that has been dropped. Remember that ALL affixes may be signed to present the exact English word. For example, *naturally* may be signed *nature* + *-al* + *-ly.* This may be helpful until students have a firm understanding of English, or to assist in spelling, pronunciation and written work.

You will find that in some instances more than one affix may be dropped. The question then arises which affix should be dropped. There is no set rule for these occurrences. It is up to the individual signer to determine what seems to flow most naturally as the sign is produced. Again, it is important to make sure the person receiving the sign sees the whole word and clearly understands what it is before dropping any of the affixes. In some instances you may only want to drop one of the affixes and keep one of them.

Example:

	<u>visualization</u>
(using all the affixes)	vision + -al + -ize + -tion
(dropping one affix)	vision + -al + -**tion**
(dropping both middle affixes)	vision + -**tion**

Particular care should be taken in signing words with affixes. As stated in "Points to Remember for Clear, Expressive Signing" in Section XVII of the SEE book, "Affixes, and word-endings for tense, person, and the like, should not be made as signs separate from the sign for the basic word itself, but should flow from the base sign for the word. Similarly, signs for word endings should not be made with an emphasis equal to that for the sign of the basic word."

DISCLAIMER

Please note that there are very many words in the potential English vocabulary that are rarely used. Being in that category, however, does not automatically exclude them from this compilation. In fact, having them all here very well may add a bit of wonder and humor at the expansiveness of our English language's capability.

While many hours have been devoted to making this reference volume correct, it would be presumptuous to believe that no errors exist. So, you who are users have an opportunity to find words we have missed or words included incorrectly. Go to it!

AFFIXES

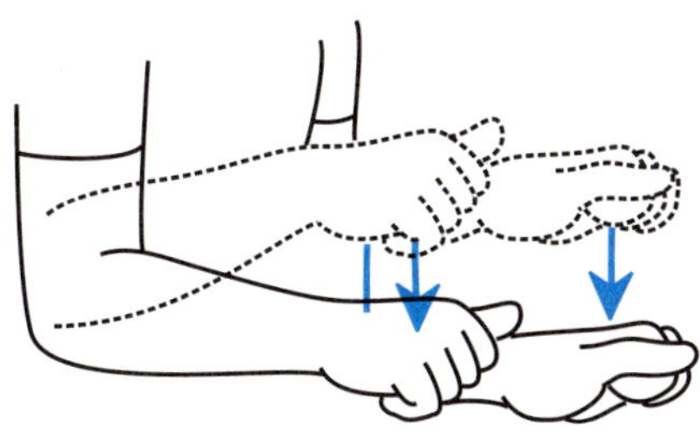

-ABLE, -IBLE
Palm-down A's drop slightly

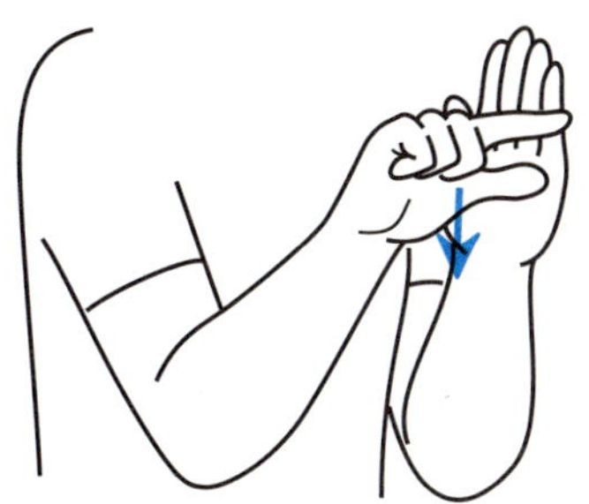

-AGE
Side of G slides down left fingers and palm

-AL
Palm-out L at end of preceding sign

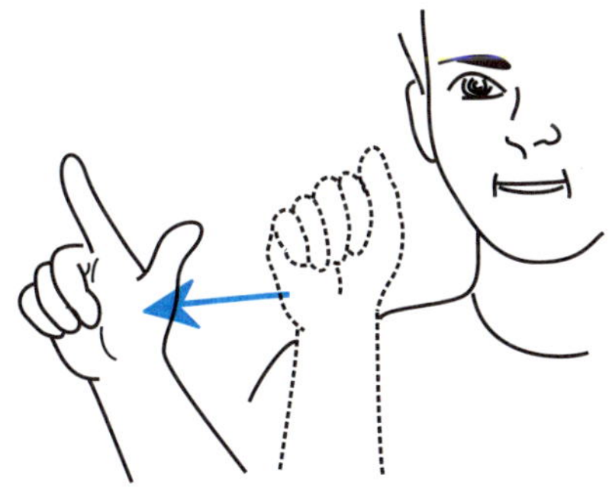

-AL, ALL-
Palm-out A slides right, changing to L

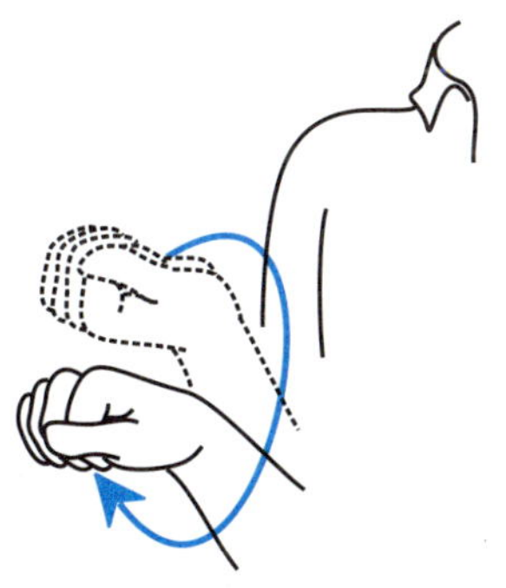

-AN, AN-
Palm-up A twists to palm down

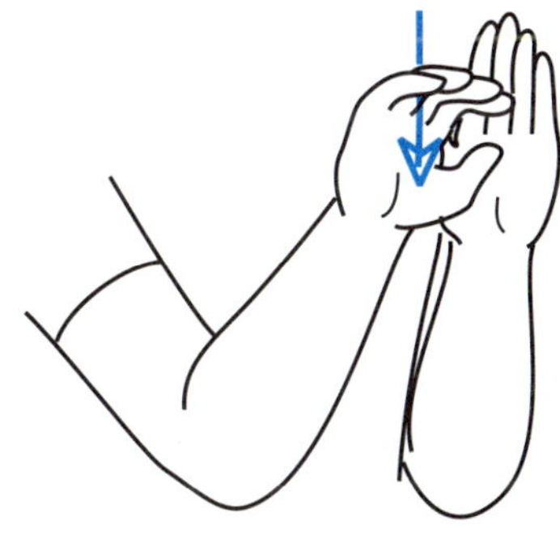

-ANCE, -ENCE
Side of C slides down left fingers and palm

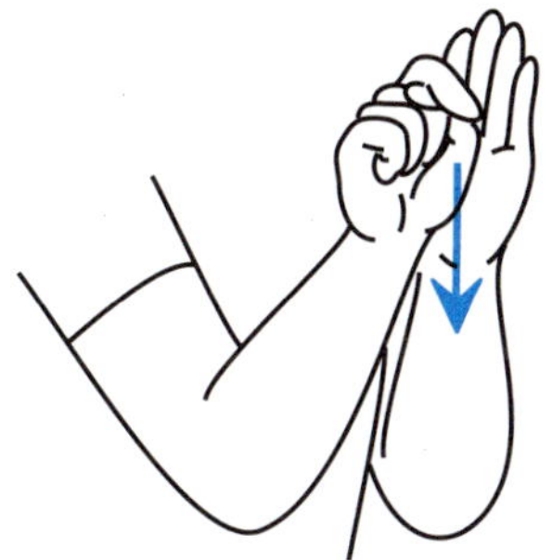

-ANT, -ENT
Side of T slides down left fingers and palm

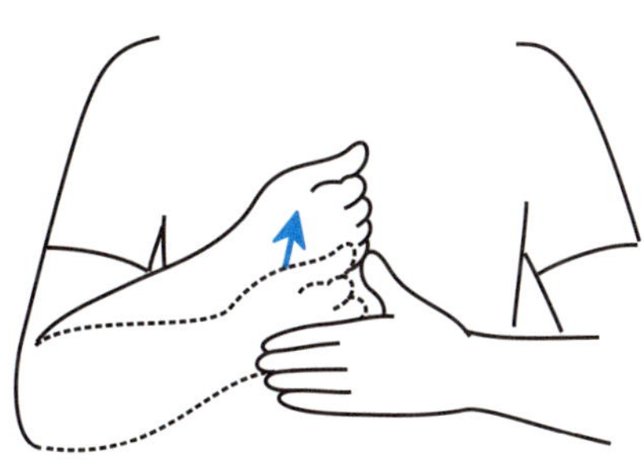

-ANTE
Palm-in A-hand moves toward body from left palm

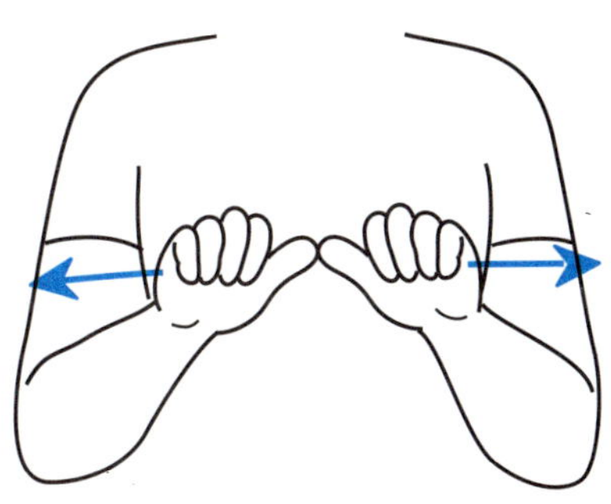

ANTI-
Thumbs of A's, touch; separate hands

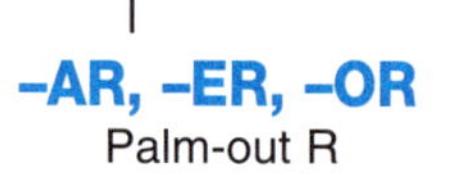

-AR, -ER, -OR
Palm-out R

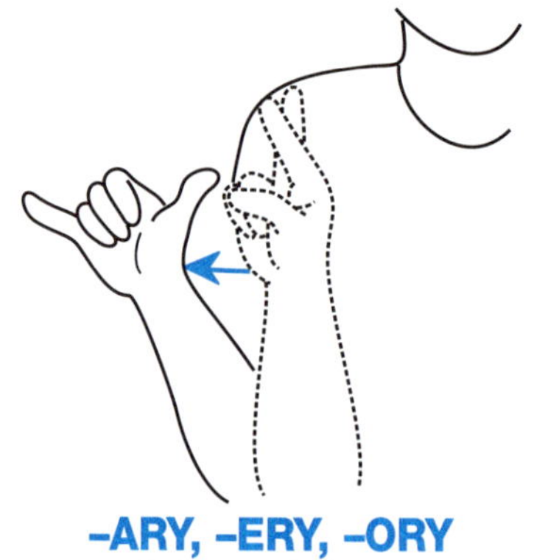

-ARY, -ERY, -ORY
Palm-out R and Y

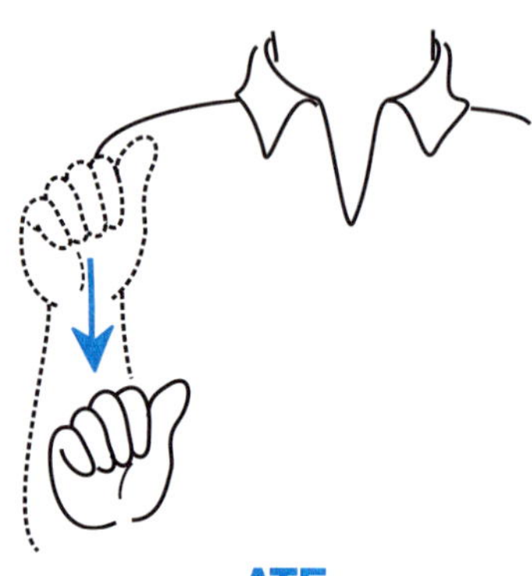

-ATE
Drop palm-out A down slightly

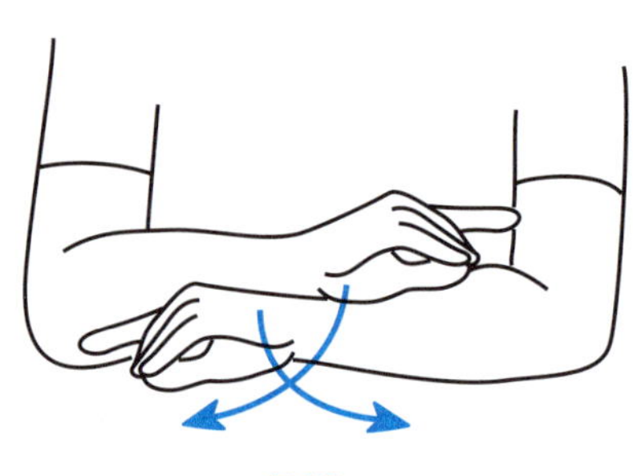

DIS-
Palm-down D's crossed at wrists separate sideways as in "not"

(see NOT)

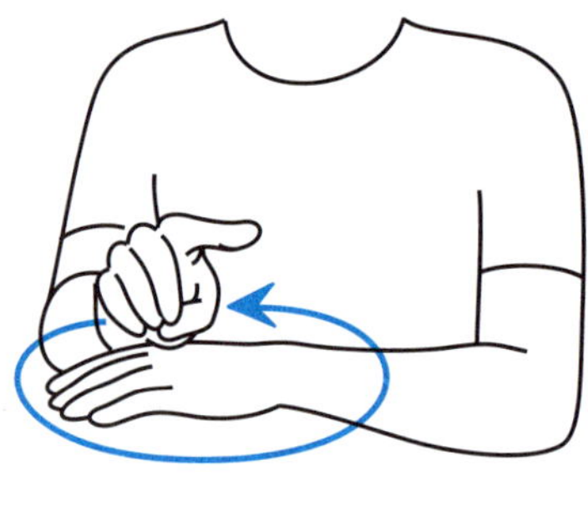

-DOM
D on back of hand circles out, left and back along left arm

(see GROUND)

-E
Palm-out E at end of word

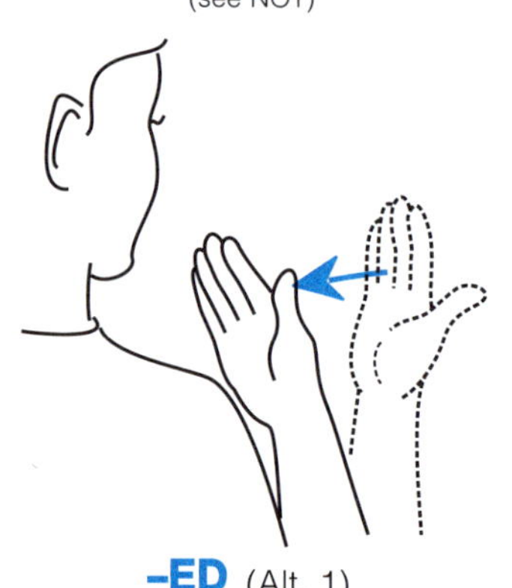

-ED (Alt. 1)
Palm of hand flips back toward shoulder (past tense)

-ED (Alt. 2)
For regular past tense (-ed), make a palm-out D at the end of the sign
(note: it is suggested that this alternate not be used with very young children)

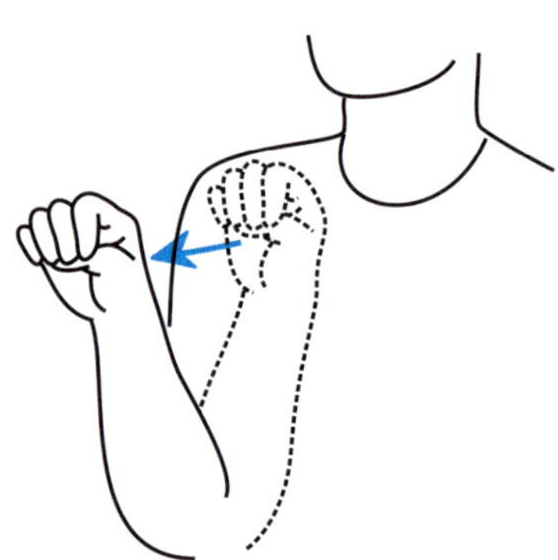

-EE
Move E slightly to the right

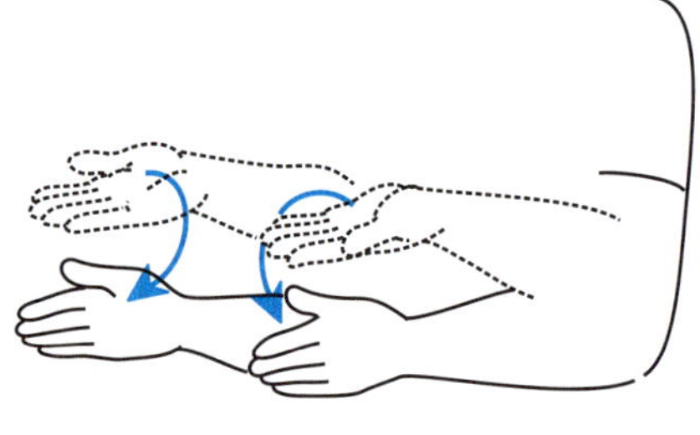

-EN (Alt. 1)
Flat hands twist from 5 palms-up to palms-facing *(past participle)*

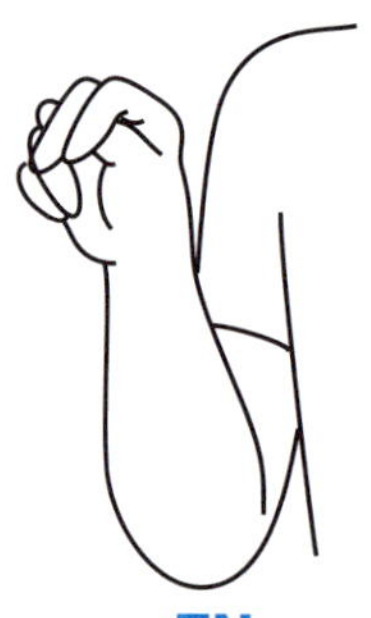

-EN (Alt. 2)
For regular past participle (-en) add N at completion of sign
(note: it is suggested that this alternate not be used with very young children)

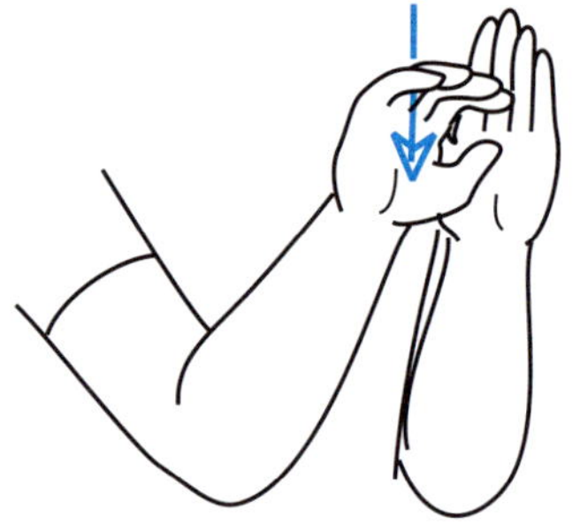

-ENCE, -ANCE
Side of C-hand slides down left fingers and palm

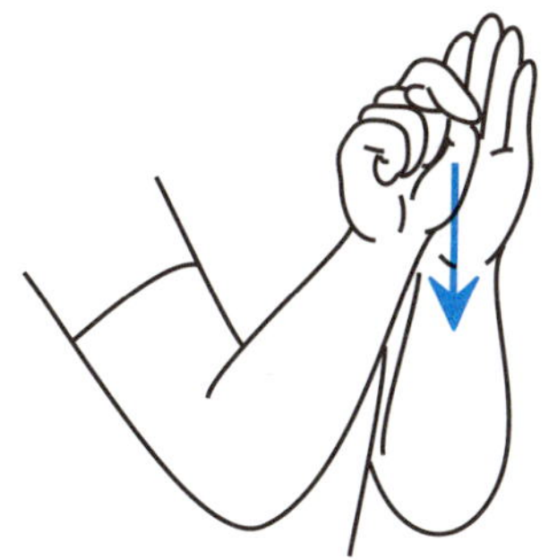

-ENT, -ANT
Side of T slides down left fingers and palm

-ER, -AR, -OR
Palm-out R

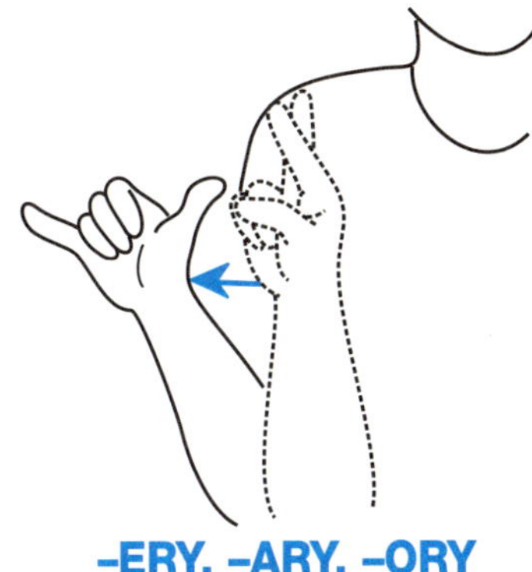

-ERY, -ARY, -ORY
Palm-out R and Y

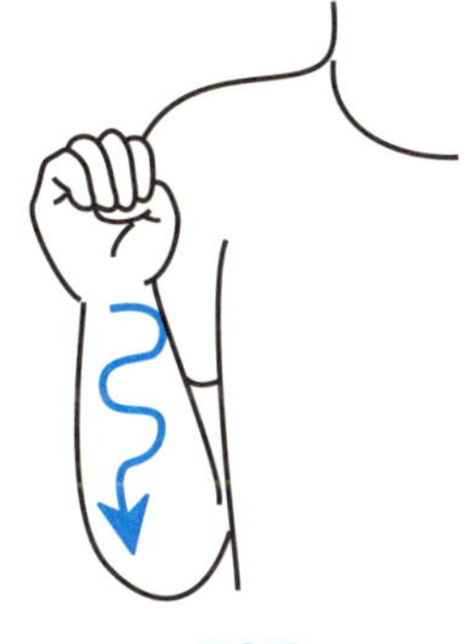

-ESE
E moves down in a wavy motion

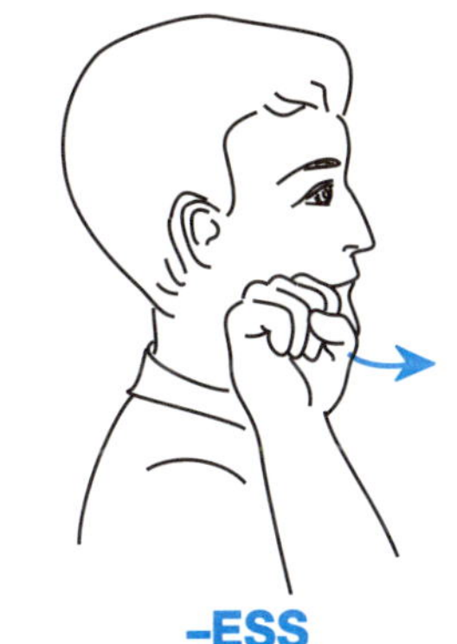

-ESS
Side of S slides along jaw forward

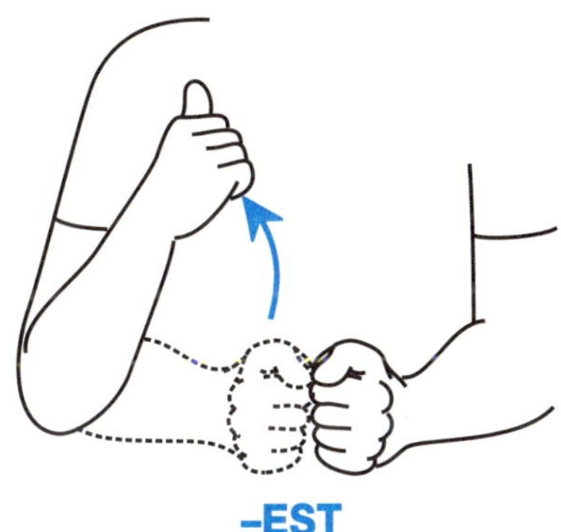

-EST
A-hands together; right A moves up

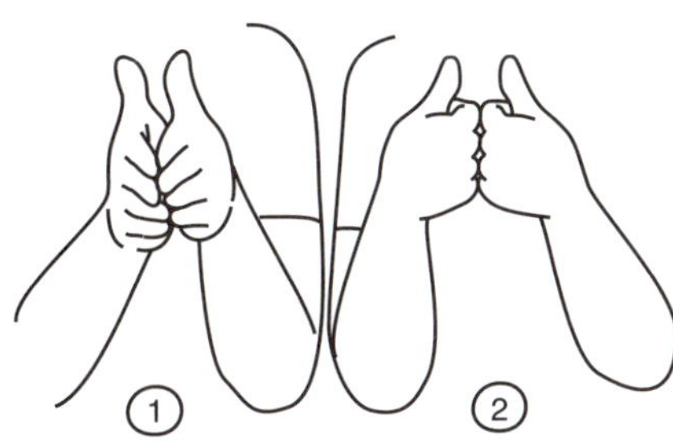

-FOLD
Palm-to-palm, keep fingertips together and bend hands back-to-back

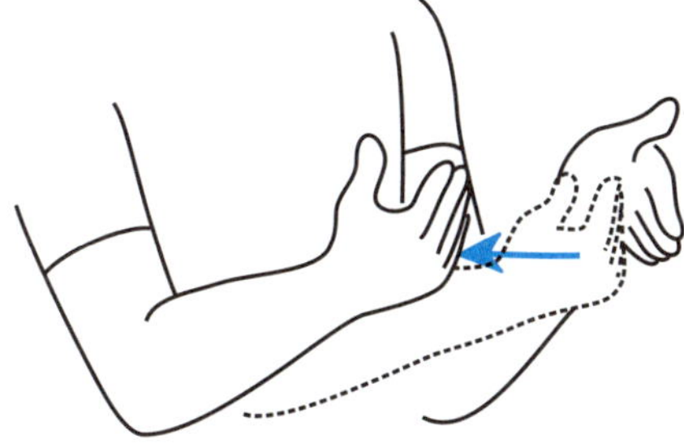

FORE-, -FORE
Bent right hand behind bent left; right moves back

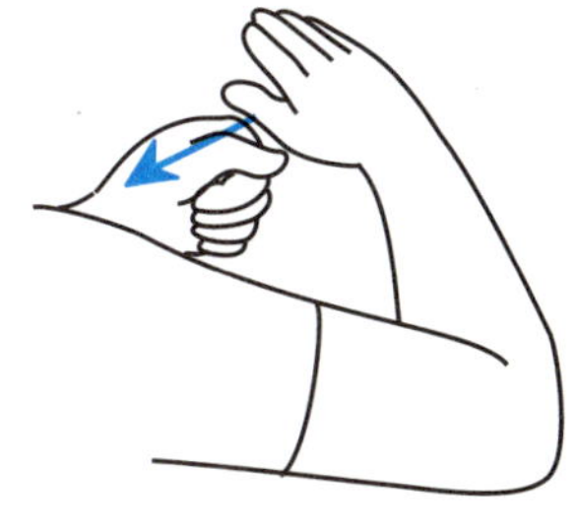

-FUL, FUL-
Palm-down hand brushes inward across top of left horizontal S

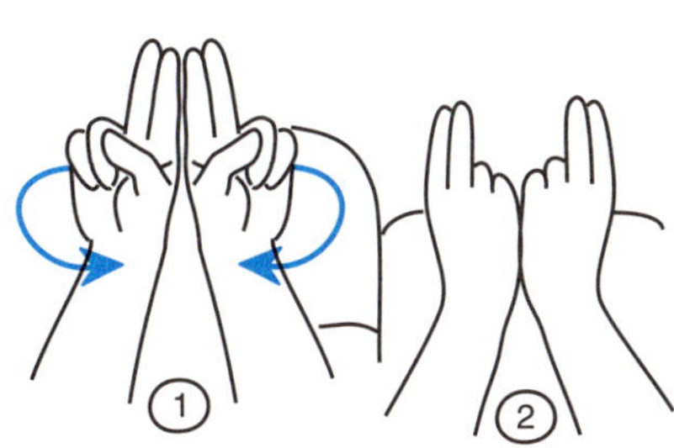

-HERD
Palm-out vertical H-hands circle horizontal to palm-in

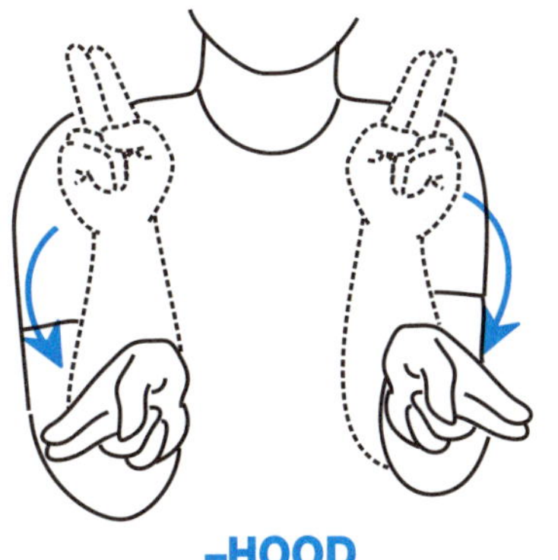

-HOOD
Vertical H to H-hands forward, as wrists cock

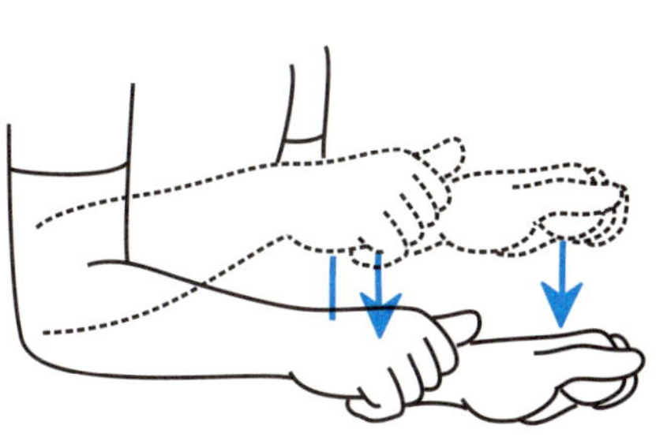

-IBLE, -ABLE
Palm-down A's drop slightly

-IC
Palm-out C

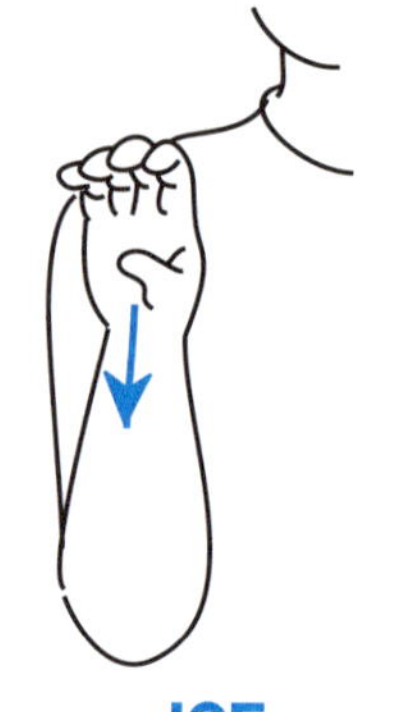

-ICE
Palm-out C moves slightly down

-ICITY, -ITY
Thumbtip of Y slides down left fingers and palm

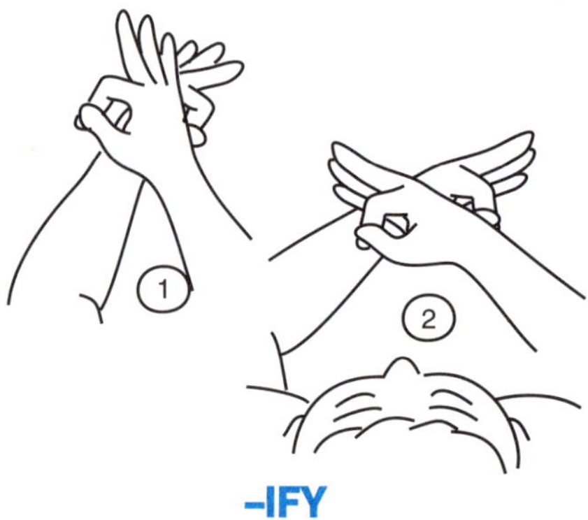

-IFY
F's, right on left, then pivot as in "make" and touch again

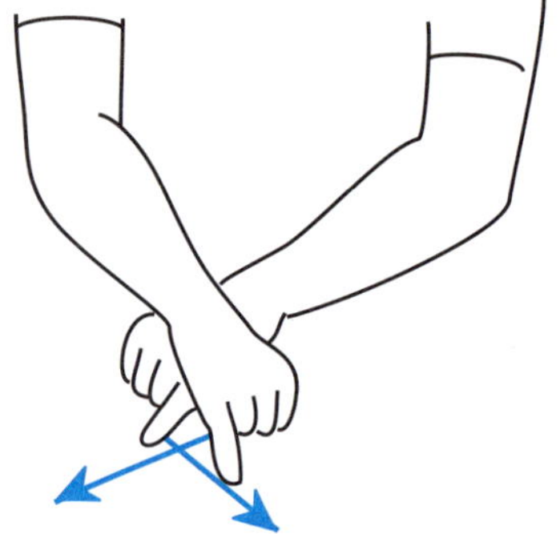

IL-, IM-, IR-, IN-
Palm-down I-hands, crossed at wrists, separate sideways
(see NOT)

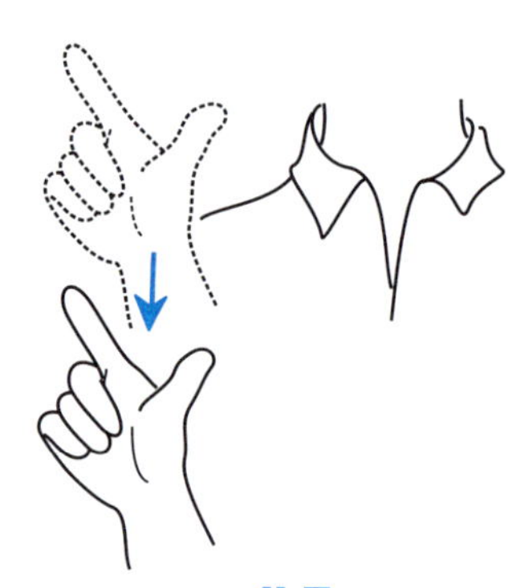

-ILE
L drops straight down

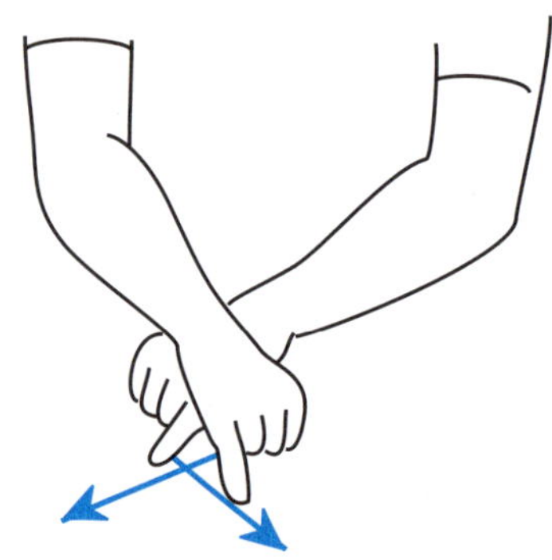

IM-, IR-, IN-, IL-
Palm-down I-hands, crossed at wrists, separate sideways
(see NOT)

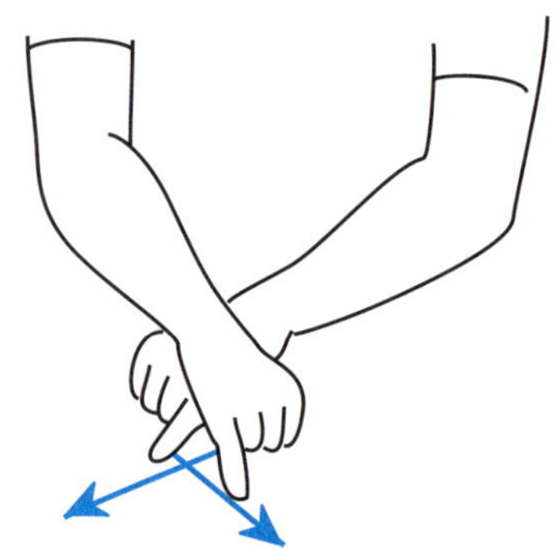

IN-, IR-, IM-, IL-
Palm-down I-hands, crossed at wrists, separate sideways
(see NOT)

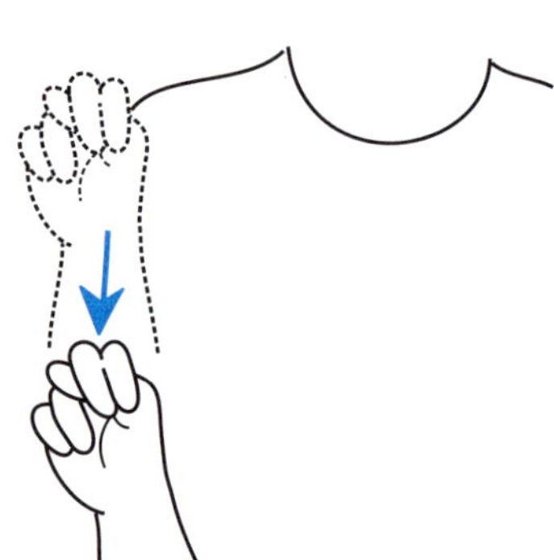

-INE
Palm-out N drops down slightly

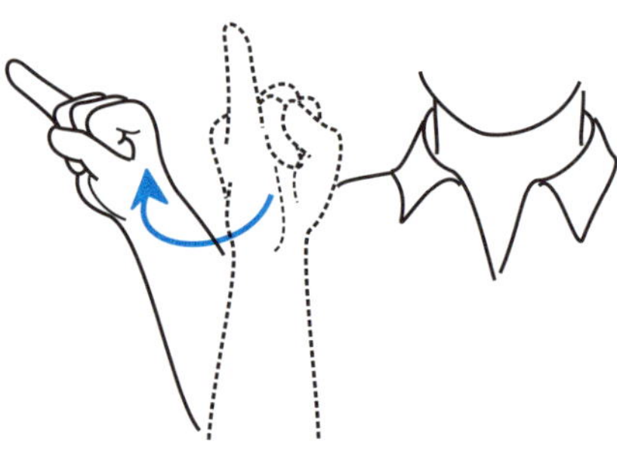

-ING
Palm-in, I-hand twists in slight downward arc to right, ending palm-out

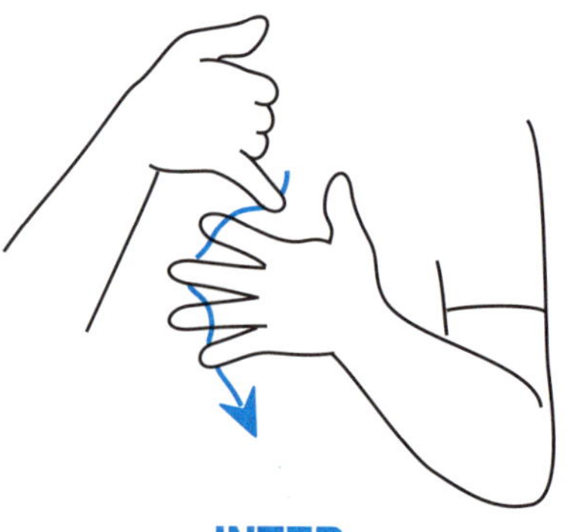

INTER-
Little finger of I weaves among fingers of left hand

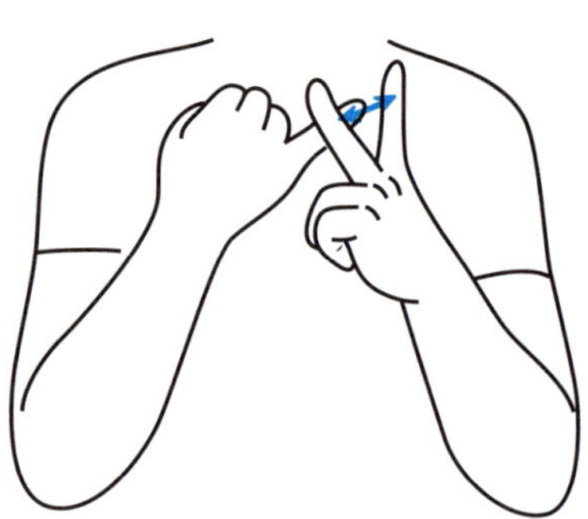

INTRA-
Little finger of I bounces between fingers of left hand

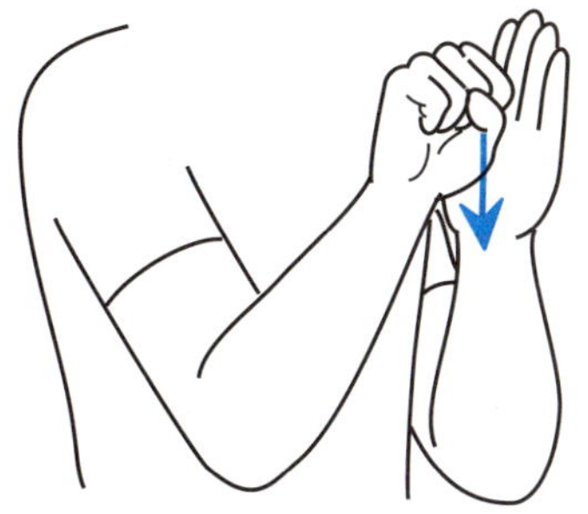

-ION, -TION, -SION
Side of S slides down fingers and palm

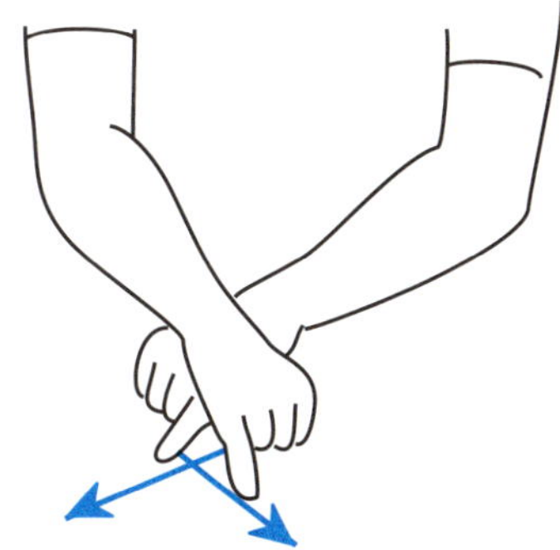

IR–, IM–, IN–, IL–
Palm-down I-hands, crossed at wrists, separate sideways
(see NOT)

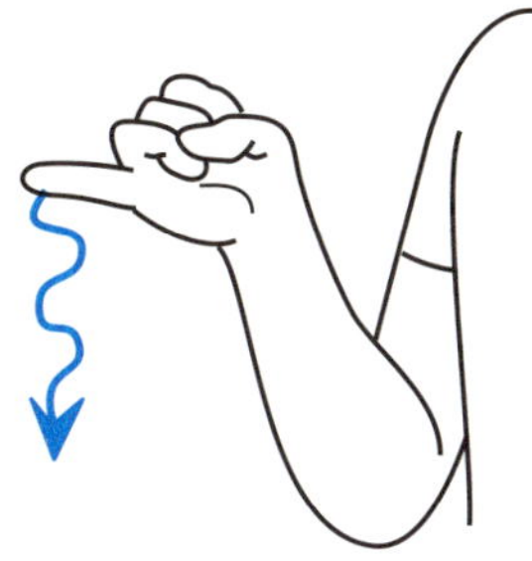

-ISH
I points forward and draws a wavy downward line

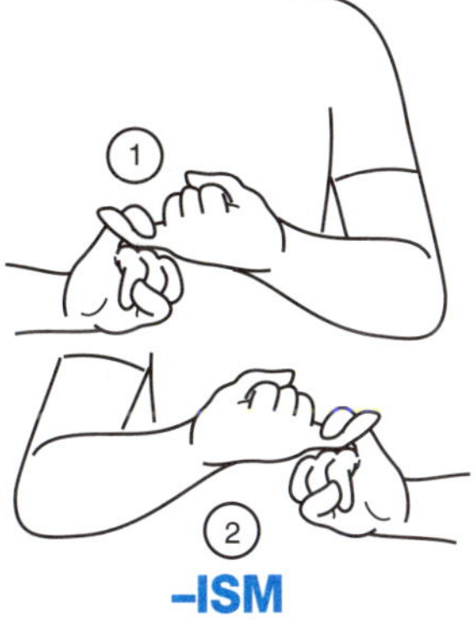

-ISM
Hook little fingers, one hand palm-up, the other palm-down, reverse
(see FRIEND)

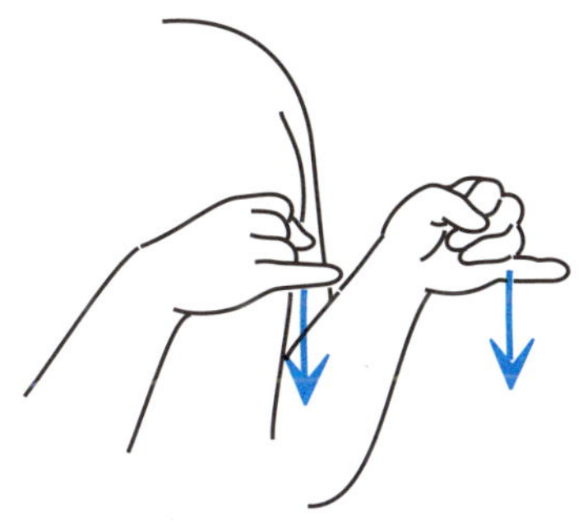

-IST
Drop palms-facing horizontal I's straight down near body
(see PERSON)

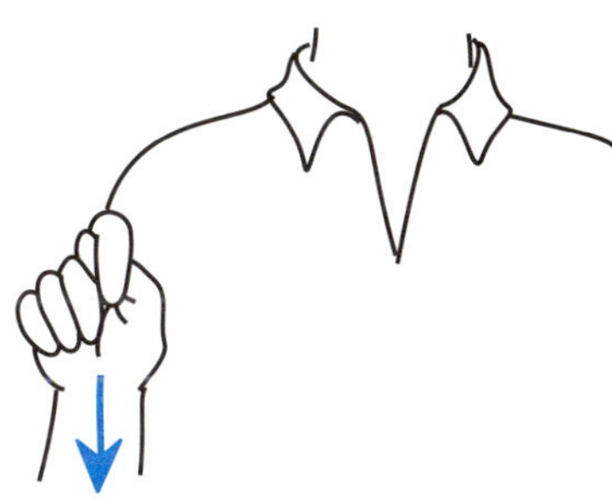

-ITE
Palm-out T moves slightly down

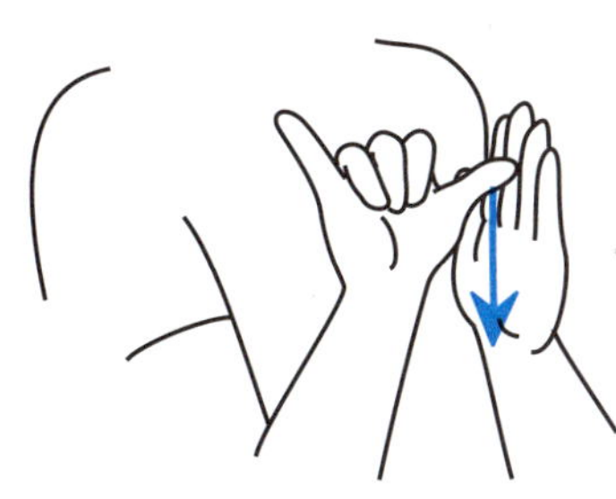

-ITY, -ICITY
Thumbtip of Y slides down left fingers and palm

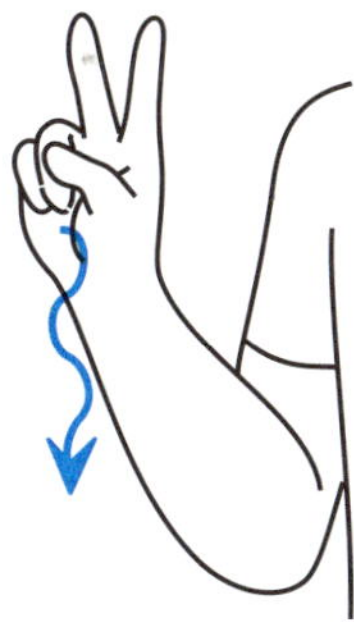

-IVE
Palm-out V moves downward in a wavy line

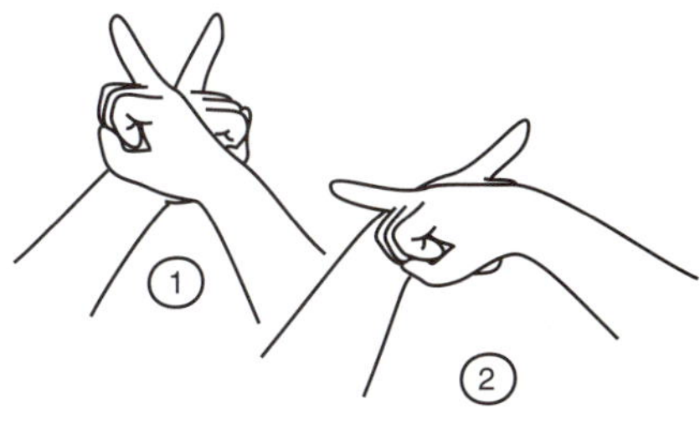

-IZE
I's, right on left, then pivot as in "make" and touch again

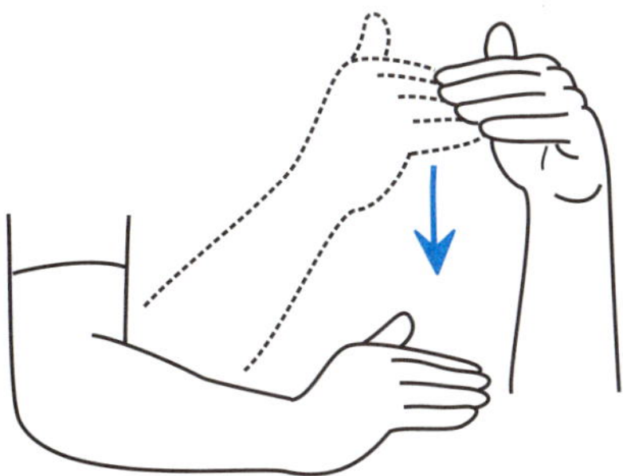

-LESS
Right bent hand under left bent hand; drop right hand downward

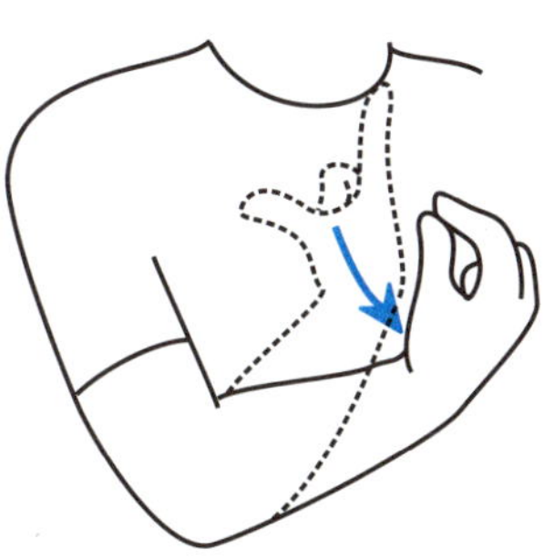

-LIKE
Palm-in L on chest moves forward, closing thumb and finger

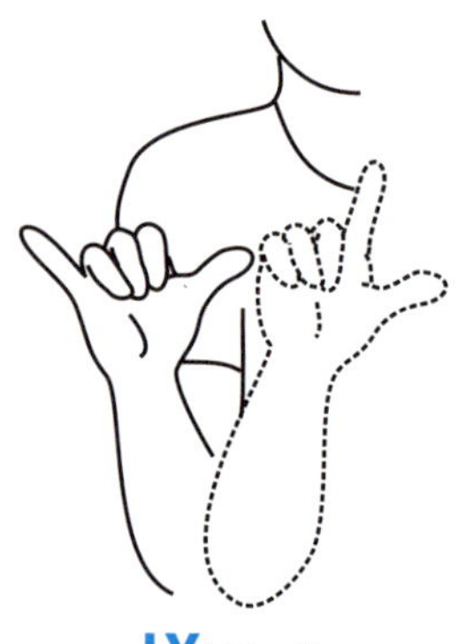

-LY (Alt. 1)
Form L and then Y

-LY (Alt. 2)
Palm-out I-L hand moves downward in a wavy line

-MENT
Side of right M slides down left fingers and palm

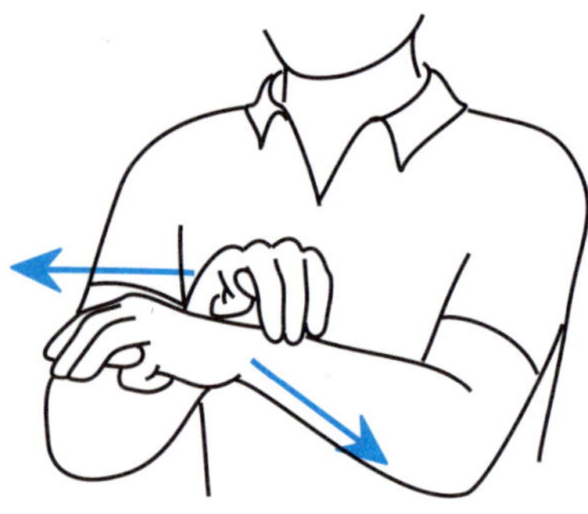

MIS-
Palm-down M's, crossed at wrists, separate

(see NOT)

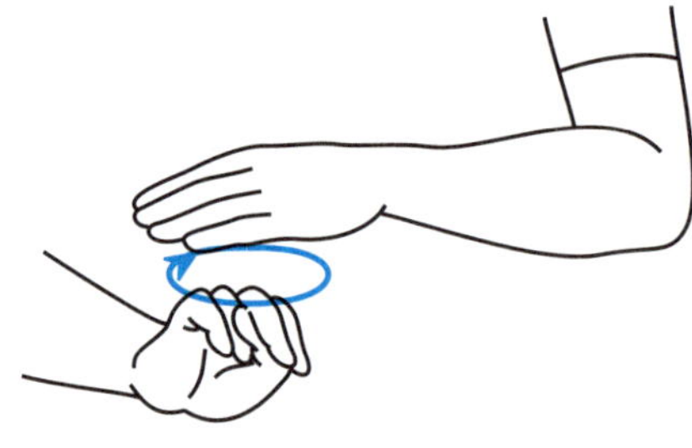

-NEATH
N circles below left palm

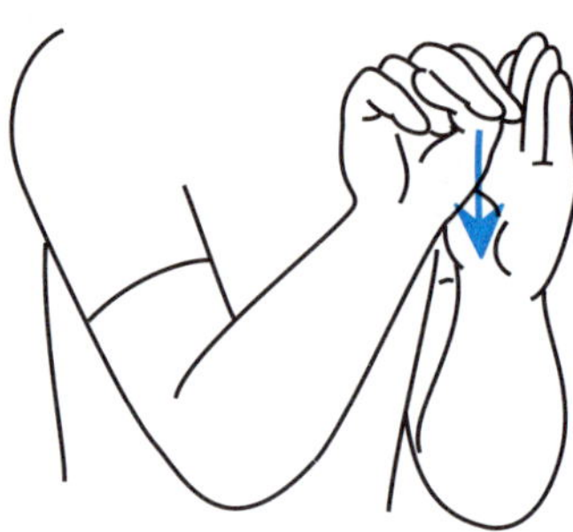

-NESS
Side of right N slides down left fingers and palm

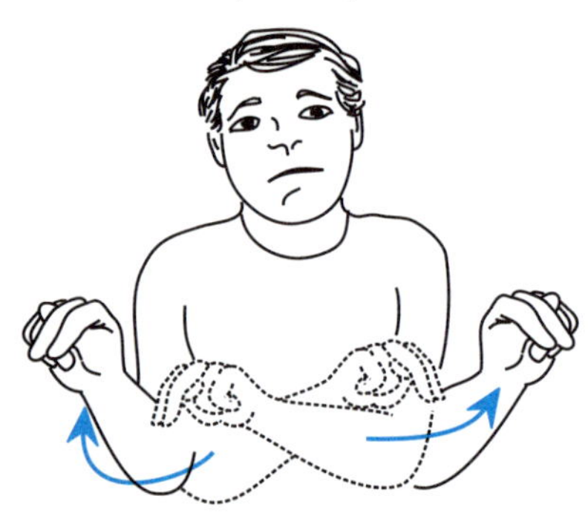

NON-
N-hands, crossed at wrists, separate hands to sides

(see NOT)

-OR, -ER, -AR
Palm-out R

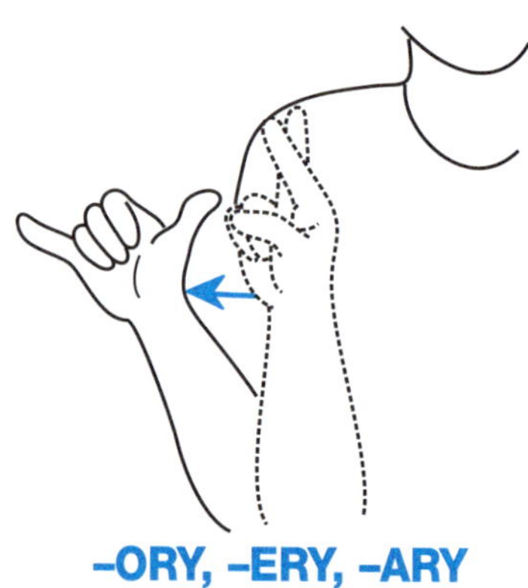

-ORY, -ERY, -ARY
Palm-out R and Y

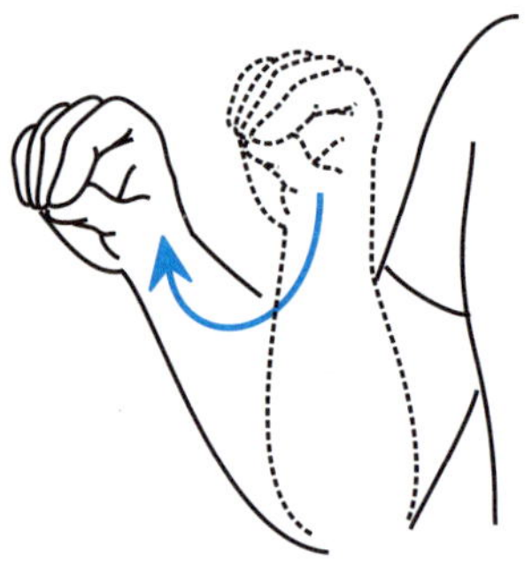

-OUS
Palm-out O draws a "U"

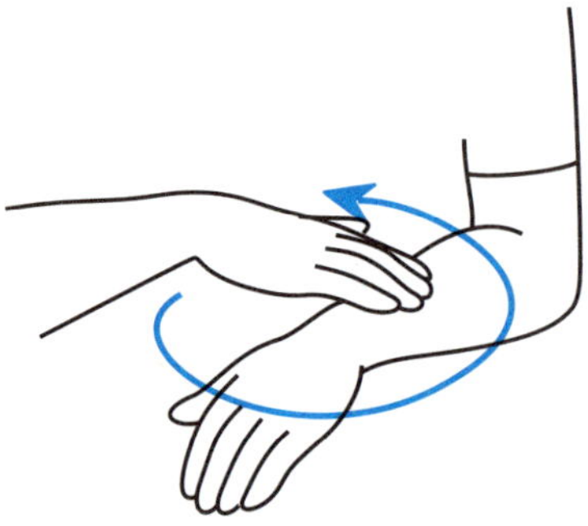

OVER-
Palm-down right hand circles over back of left hand

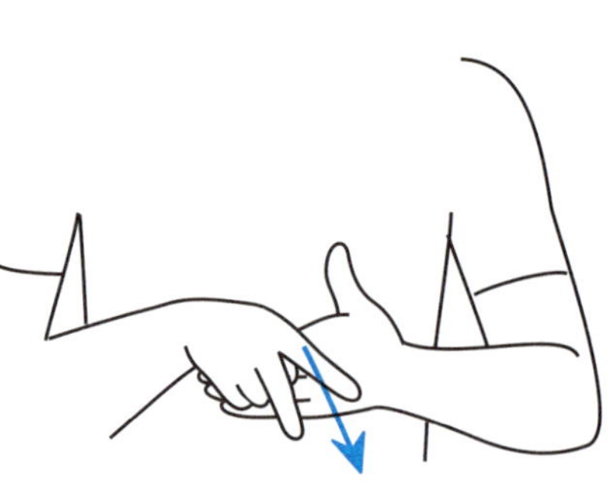

POST-
P moves from back of left hand straight forward

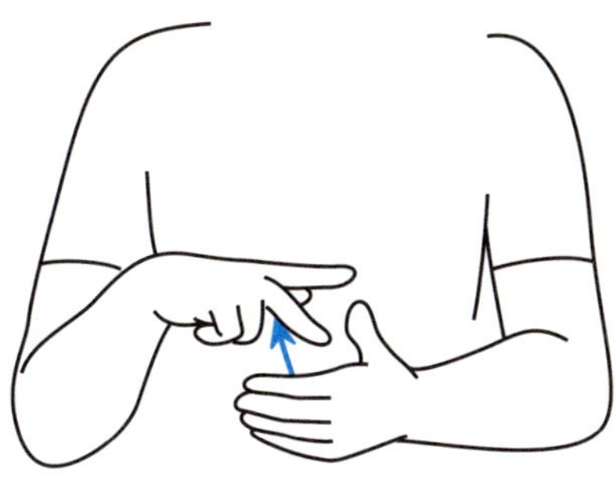

PRE–
P moves inward from behind left palm
(see FORE)

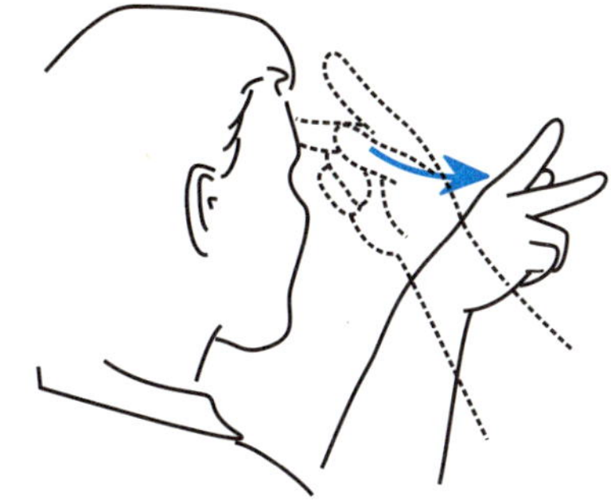

PRO–
Middle fingertip of P on forehead twists to palm-out
(see FOR)

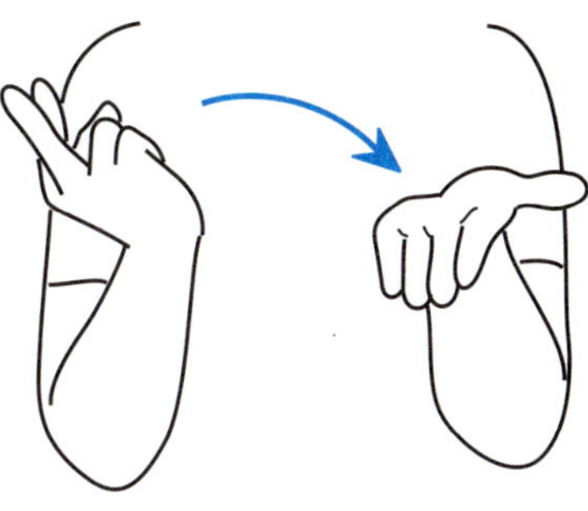

RE–
R fingertips hit left palm

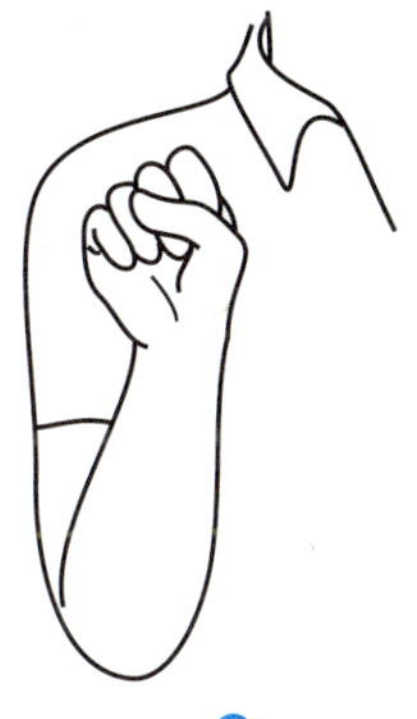

–S
Palm-out S

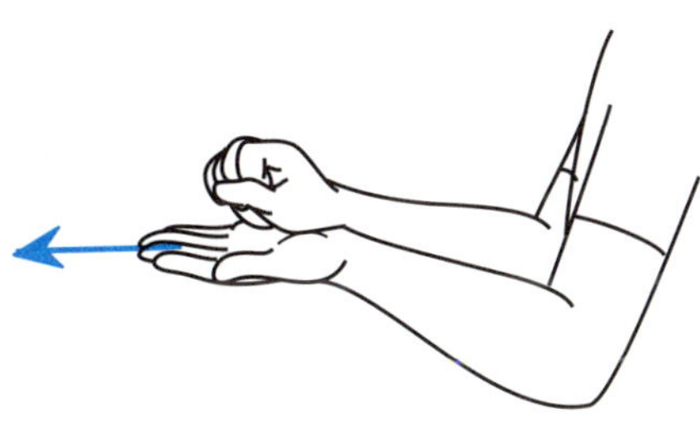

–SHIP
Palm-out S on left palm; both move forward together

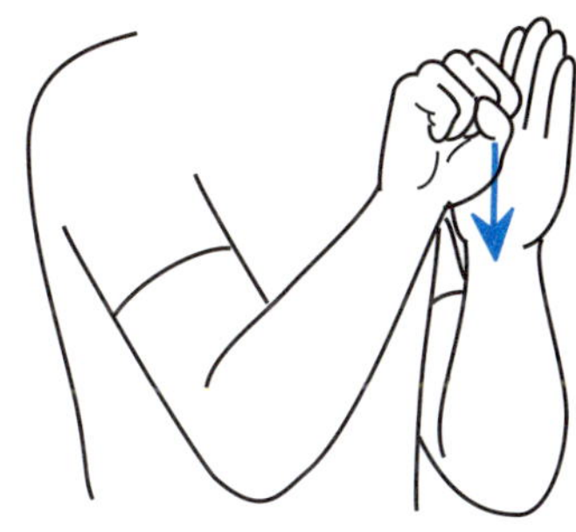

–SION, –ION, –TION
Side of right S slides down fingers and palm of left hand

–SOME, SOME–
Side of right hand draws small arc across left palm

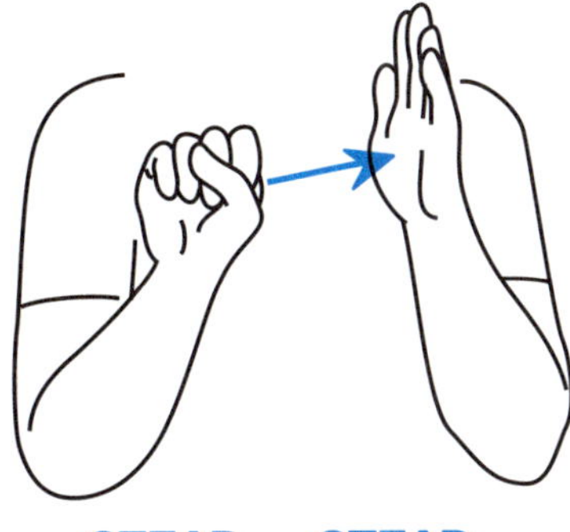

STEAD–, –STEAD
Side of S hits heel of left hand

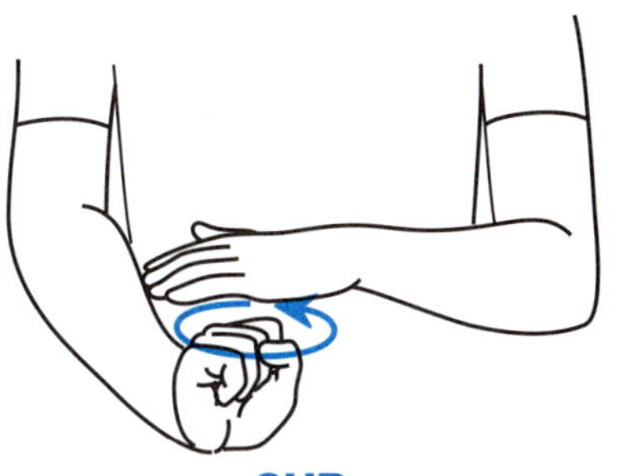

SUB–
S circles under palm
(see BASE)

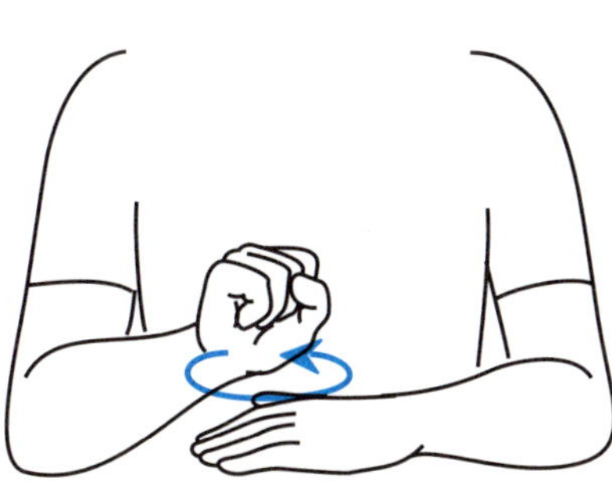

SUPER–
S circles over palm-down left hand

–T
Palm-out T

–TH
Make an H when you finish the sign for the word

-THING

Palm-up, arc hand slightly up and down to the right

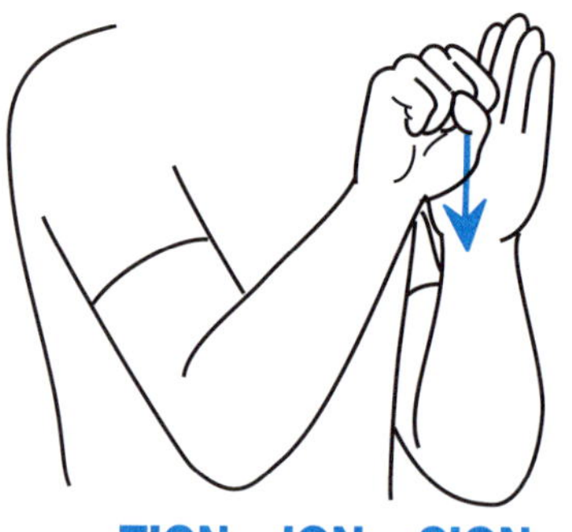

-TION, -ION, -SION

Side of right S slides down fingers and palm of left hand

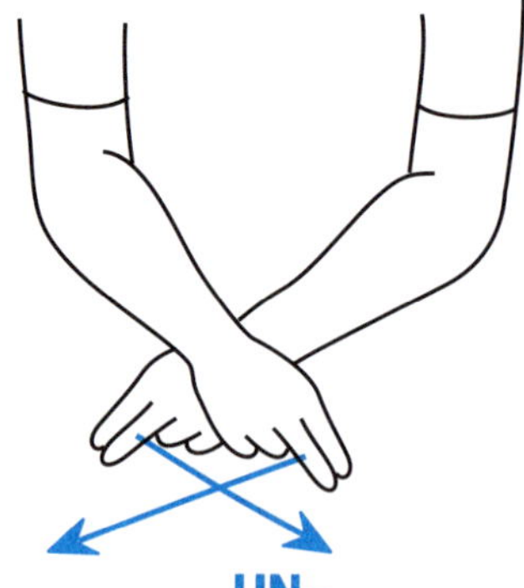

UN-

U hands, palm-down, cross at wrists; separate sideways

(see NOT)

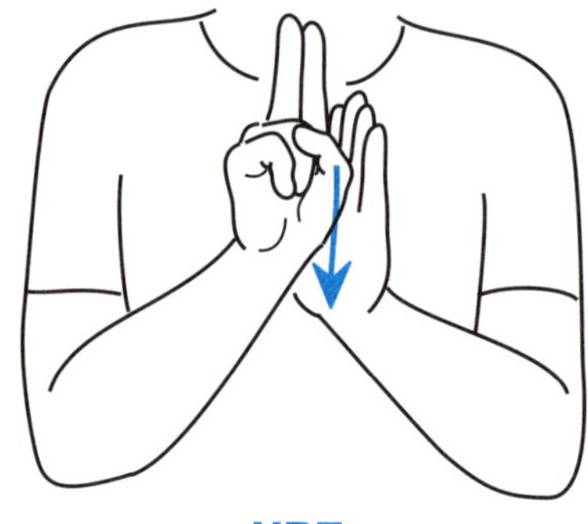

-URE

Side of right U slides down left fingers and palm

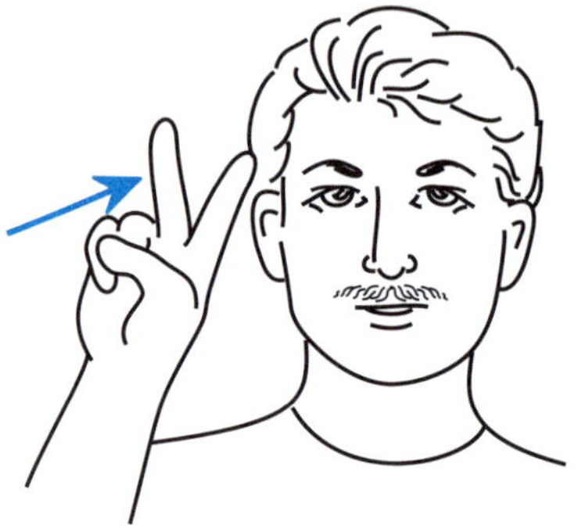

VICE-

Touch temple with index of V

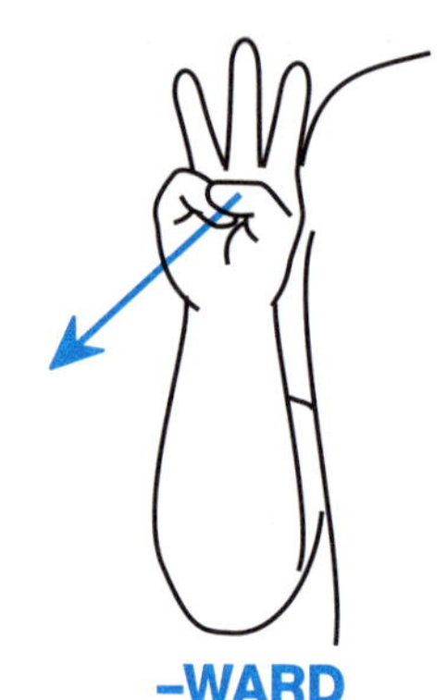

-WARD

Palm-out W moves forward

-Y

Palm-out Y

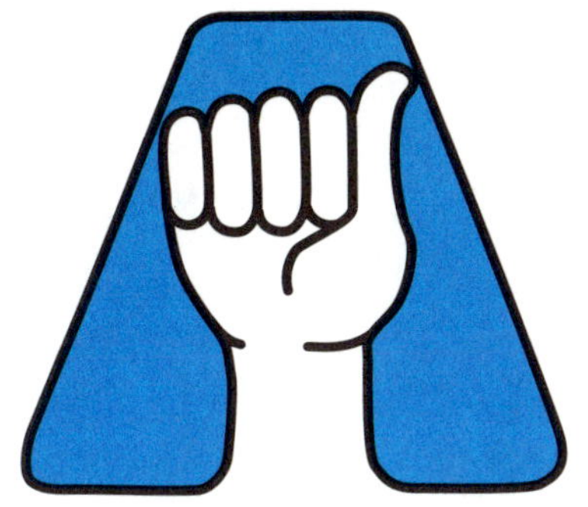

A

abbreviate	
+ s	abbreviates
+ ed	abbreviated
+ ing	abbreviating
+ ion	abbreviation*
+ or	abbreviator*
abdomen	
+ s	abdomens
+ al	abdomenal
+ ly	abdomenally
able	
+ er	abler
+ est	ablest
+ ly	ably
abort	
+ s	aborts
+ ed	aborted
+ ing	aborting
+ er	aborter
+ ion	abortion*
+ ist	abortionist*
+ ive	abortive
+ ly	abortively
+ ness	abortiveness
about	
above	
absent	
+ s	absents
+ ed	absented
+ ing	absenting
+ ly	absently
+ ence	absence*
+ ee	absentee*
+ ism	absenteeism
+ mind + ed	absentminded
abstract	
+ s	abstracts
+ ed	abstracted
+ ing	abstracting
+ able	abstractable
+ er	abstracter*
+ ly	abstractly
+ ness	abstractness
+ ed + ly	abstractedly
+ ed + ness	abstractedness
+ ion	abstraction*
+ al	abstractional
+ ism	abstractionism
+ ist	abstractionist*
+ ive	abstractive
abuse	
+ s	abuses
+ ed	abused
+ ing	abusing
+ able	abusable
+ er	abuser*
+ ive	abusive
+ ly	abusively
+ ness	abusiveness
academic	
+ s	academics
+ y	academy
+ y + s	academies
+ s	academics
+ al	academical
+ ly	academically
+ an	academician*
+ ism	academicism
accept	
+ s	accepts
+ ed	accepted
+ ing	accepting
+ able	acceptable
+ ity	acceptability
+ ness	acceptableness
+ ly	acceptably
+ ance	acceptance
+ ant	acceptant
+ ion	acceptation*
+ er, + or	accepter*,acceptor*
accident	
+ s	accidents
+ al	accidental*
+ ly	accidentally
+ ness	accidentalness

A

accompany

+ s	accompanies
+ ed	accompanied
+ ing	accompanying
+ ment	accompaniment*
+ ist	accompanist*

accomplish

+ s	accomplishes
+ ed	accomplished
+ ing	accomplishing
+ able	accomplishable
+ er	accomplisher*
+ ment	accomplishment*

account

+ s	accounts
+ ed	accounted
+ ing	accounting
+ able	accountable
+ ity	accountability
+ ness	accountableness
+ ly	accountably
+ ant	accountant*
+ y	accountancy
+ship	accountantship

accuse

+ s	accuses
+ ed	accused
+ ing	accusing
+ er	accuser*
+ ly	accusingly
+ al	accusal
+ ion	accusation*
+ ive	accusative
+ ive + ly	accusatively
+ ory	accusatory
+ ory + al	accusatorial

ache

+ s	aches
+ ed	ached
+ ing	aching
+ ly	achingly

achieve

+ s	achieves
+ ed	achieved
+ ing	achieving
+ able	achievable
+ er	achiever*
+ ment	achievement*

acquaint

+ s	acquaints
+ ed	acquainted
+ ing	acquainting
+ ance	acquaintance*
+ ship	acquaintanceship

acre

+ s	acres
+ age	acreage

across

act

+ s	acts
+ ed	acted
+ ing	acting
+ or	actor*
+ ess	actress*
+ able	actable
+ able + ity	actability
+ ion	action
+ ion + s	actions
+ ion + able	actionable
+ less	actionless
+ ate	activate
+ ate + s	activates
+ ate +ed	activated
+ ate + ing	activating
+ ate + ion	activation
+ ate + or	activator*
+ ive	active
+ ly	actively
+ ness	activeness
+ ism	activism
+ ist	activist*
+ ity	activity*
+ al	actual
+ al + ly	actually
+ al + ity	actuality
+ ize	actualize
+ ize + s	actualizes
+ ize + ed	actualized
+ ize + ing	actualizing
+ ize + ion	actualization*
+ ate	actuate
+ ate + s	actuates
+ ate + ed	actuated
+ ate + ing	actuating
+ ate + ion	actuation
+ ate + or	actuator*

acute

+ ly	acutely
+ ness	acuteness

adapt

+ s	adapts
+ ed	adapted
+ ing	adapting
+ ness	adaptedness
+ able	adaptable
+ ity	adaptability
+ ion	adaptation*
+ al	adaptational
+ ly	adaptationally

+ er	adapter*
+ ive	adaptive
+ ive + ly	adaptively
+ ive + ness	adaptiveness
+ ive + ity	adaptivity
add	
+ s	adds
+ ed	added
+ ing	adding
+ able	addable
+ er	adder
+ er + s	adders
+ ion	addition*
+ al	additional
+ ly	additionally
+ ive	additive*
+ ive + ly	additively
+ ity	additivity
address	
+ s	addresses
+ ed	addressed
+ ing	addressing
+ er	addresser*
+ able	addressable
+ ee	addressee*
adhesive	
+ s	adhesives
+ ly	adhesively
+ ness	adhesiveness
+ ion	adhesion*
+ al	adhesional
adjective	
+ s	adjectives
+ al	adjectival
+ ly	adjectively
adjust	
+ s	adjusts
+ ed	adjusted
+ ing	adjusting
+ able	adjustable
+ ity	adjustability
+ er	adjuster*
+ ive	adjustive
+ ment	adjustment*
+ al	adjustmental
admire	
+ s	admires
+ ed	admired
+ ing	admiring
+ able	admirable
+ ity	admirability
+ ness	admirableness
+ ly	admirably
+ er	admirer*
+ ing + ly	admiringly
+ ion	admiration
admit	
+ s	admits
+ ed	admitted
+ ing	admitting
+ ly	admittedly
+ ible	admissible
+ ity	admissability
+ ion	admission*
+ ive	admissive
+ ance	admittance*
adolescent	
+ s	adolescents
+ ly	adolescently
+ ence	adolescence
adopt	
+ s	adopts
+ ed	adopted
+ ing	adopting
+ able	adoptable
+ ity	adoptability
+ er	adopter*
+ ee	adoptee*
+ ion	adoption*
+ ism	adoptionism
+ ist	adoptionist*
+ ive	adoptive
+ ly	adoptively
adult	
+ s	adults
+ hood	adulthood
+ like	adultlike
+ ness	adultness
+ ly	adultly
advance	
+ s	advances
+ ed	advanced
+ ing	advancing
+ ment	advancement*
advantage	
+ s	advantages
+ ed	advantaged
+ ing	advantaging
+ ous	advantageous
adventure	
+ s	adventures
+ ed	adventured
+ ing	adventuring
+ er	adventurer*
+ ess	adventuress*
+ some	adventuresome
+ ness	adventuresomeness

A

	+ ism	adventurism
	+ ist	adventurist*
	+ ic	adventuristic
	+ ous	adventurous
	+ ly	adventurously
	+ ous + ness	adventurousness
adverb		
	+ s	adverbs
	+ al	adverbial
	+ ly	adverbially
advertise		
	+ s	advertises
	+ ed	advertised
	+ ing	advertising
	+ er	advertiser*
	+ ment	advertisement*
advice		
	+ s	advices
advise		
	+ s	advises
	+ ed	advised
	+ ing	advising
	+ er	adviser/or*
	+ ly	advisedly
	+ ee	advisee*
	+ ment	advisement
	+ ory	advisory*
	+ able	advisable
	+ ity	advisability
	+ ness	advisableness
	+ able + ly	advisably
affect		
	+ s	affects
	+ ed	affected
	+ ing	affecting
	+ able	affectable
	+ ity	affectability
	+ ate + ion	affectation*
	+ ion	affection*
	+ less	affectionless
	+ al	affectional
	+ ate	affectionate
	+ ly	affectionately
	+ ive	affective
	+ ive + ly	affectively
	+ ive + ity	affectivity
affiliate		
	+ s	affiliates
	+ ed	affiliated
	+ ing	affiliating
	+ ion	affiliation*
affirm		
	+ s	affirms
	+ ed	affirmed
	+ ing	affirming
	+ able	affirmable
	+ ance	affirmance
	+ tion	affirmation*
	+ ive	affirmative*
	+ ly	affirmatively
affix		
	+ s	affixes
	+ ed	affixed
	+ ing	affixing
	+ able	affixable
	+ tion	affixation*
	+ al	affixal, affixial
afraid		
Africa (2)		
	+ an	African*
	+ ness	Africaness
	+ ism	Africanism
	+ ist	Africanist*
	+ ize	Africanize
	+ ize + s	Africanizes
	+ ize + ed	Africanized
	+ tion	Africanization
after		
	+ birth	afterbirth
	+ burn + er	afterburner*
	+ care	aftercare
	+ clap	afterclap*
	+ deck	afterdeck*
	+ effect	aftereffect*
	+ glow	afterglow
	+ image	afterimage*
	+ life	afterlife
	+ more + est	aftermost
	+ piece	afterpiece
	+ taste	aftertaste
	+ tax	aftertax
	+ thought	afterthought*
	+ time	aftertime
	+ ward	afterward
	+ ward + s	afterwards
	+ word	afterword
	+ world	afterworld
afternoon*		
again		
against		
age		
	+ s	ages
	+ ed	aged
	+ ing	aging
	+ ness	agedness
	+ ism	ageism
	+ ist	ageist

+ less	ageless
+ ly	agelessly
+ less + ness	agelessness
+ long	agelong

agenda (singular is agendum)

+ less	agendaless

aggress

+ s	aggresses
+ ed	aggressed
+ ing	aggressing
+ or	aggressor*
+ ion	aggression
+ ive	aggressive
+ ly	aggressively
+ ness	aggressiveness
+ ity	aggressivity

aggression

+ s	aggressions

ago

agree

+ s	agrees
+ ed	agreed
+ ing	agreeing
+ able	agreeable
+ ness	agreeableness
+ ity	agreeability
+ ly	agreeably
+ ment	agreement*

agriculture

+ al	agricultural
+ al + ist	agriculturalist*
+ ly	agriculturally
+ ist	agriculturist*

ahead

aid

+ s	aids
+ ed	aided
+ ing	aiding
+ e	aide*
+ er	aider*

ail

+ s	ails
+ ed	ailed
+ ing	ailing
+ ment	ailment*

aim

+ s	aims
+ ed	aimed
+ ing	aiming
+ less	aimless
+ ly	aimlessly
+ ness	aimlessness

air

+ s	airs
+ ed	aired
+ ing	airing
+ less	airless
+ ness	airlessness
+ y	airy
+ er	airier
+ est	airiest
+ bear + en	airborne
+ brush	airbrush*^
+ bus	airbus*
+ craft	aircraft
+ crew	aircrew*
+ drop	airdrop*^
+ field	airfield*
+ flow	airflow*
+ frame	airframe*
+ freight	airfreight*
+ glow	airglow
+ head	airhead
+ lift	airlift*^
+ line	airline*
+ line + er	airliner*
+ mail	airmail
+ man	airman*
+ man + ship	airmanship
+ park	airpark
+ post	airpost
+ screw	airscrew
+ ship	airship*
+ sick	airsick
+ sick + ness	airsickness
+ space	airspace
+ speed	airspeed
+ stream	airstream
+ strip	airstrip*
+ tight	airtight
+ wave	airwave*
+ way	airway*
+ worth + y	airworthy
+ worthy + ness	airworthiness

air condition

+ s	air conditions
+ ed	air conditioned
+ ing	air conditioning
+ er	air conditioner*

airplane*

airport*

alarm

+ s	alarms
+ ed	alarmed
+ ing	alarming
+ ly	alarmingly

+ ism	alarmism
+ ist	alarmist*
Alaska	
+ an	Alaskan*
album*	
alcohol	
+ s	alcohols
+ ic	alcoholic*
+ ly	alcoholically
+ ism	alcoholism
+ ize	alcoholize
+ize + s	alcoholizes
+ ize + ed	alcoholized
+ize + ing	alcoholizing
alert	
+ s	alerts
+ ed	alerted
+ ing	alerting
+ ly	alertly
+ ness	alertness
alfalfa	
algae (singular is alga)	
+ al	algal
algebra	
+ ist	algebraist
+ s	algebraists
+ ic	algebraic
+ ly	algebraically
alike	
+ ness	alikeness
all	
allegiance	
+ ant	allegiant
allergy	
+ s	allergies
+ ic	allergic
+ ist	allergist*
+ an	allergen*
+ an + ic	allergenic
alligator*	
allow	
+ s	allows
+ ed	allowed
+ ing	allowing
+ able	allowable
+ ly	allowably
+ ness	allowableness
+ ance	allowance*
+ ance + ed	allowanced
+ ance + ing	allowancing
+ ed + ly	allowedly
all right	
allspice	
almost	
alone	
+ ness	aloneness
along	
+ shore	alongshore
+ side	alongside
alphabet	
+ s	alphabets
+ ic	alphabetic
+ al	alphabetical
+ ly	alphabetically
+ ize	alphabetize
+ ize + s	alphabetizes
+ ize + ed	alphabetized
+ ize + ing	alphabetizing
+ tion	alphabetization
already	
also	
altar	
+ s	altars
+ piece	altarpiece*
alter	
+ s	alters
+ ed	altered
+ ing	altering
+ able	alterable
+ ly	alterably
+ ity	alterability
+ er	alterer*
+ tion	alteration*
+ ive	alterative
alternate	
+ s	alternates
+ ed	alternated
+ ing	alternating
+ ly	alternately
+ tion	alternation*
+ ive	alternative*
+ ive + ly	alternatively
+ ness	alternativeness
+ or	alternator*
although	
aluminum	
+ ize	aluminize
+ ize + s	aluminizes
+ ize + ed	aluminized
+ ize + ing	aluminizing
+ ous	aluminous
always	
am	
amaze	
+ s	amazes
+ ed	amazed
+ ing	amazing
+ ly	amazingly
+ ment	amazement

ambition		
	+ s	ambitions
	+ less	ambitionless
	+ ous	ambitious
	+ ly	ambitiously
	+ness	ambitiousness
ambulance		
	+ s	ambulances
	+ ant	ambulant
	+ ory	ambulatory
	+ly	ambulatorily
	+ ate	ambulate
	+ ate + s	ambulates
	+ ate + ed	ambulated
	+ ate + ing	ambulating
amen		
amend (2)		
	+ s	amends
	+ ed	amended
	+ ing	amending
	+ able	amendable
	+ er	amender*
	+ ory	amendatory
	+ ment	amendment*
America		
	+ s	Americas
	+ an	American*
	+ ism	Americanism
	+ ist	Americanist
	+ tion	Americanization
	+ ize	Americanize
	+ ize + s	Americanizes
	+ ed	Americanized
	+ ing	Americanizing
among		
amount		
	+ s	amounts
	+ ed	amounted
	+ ing	amounting
amuse		
	+ s	amuses
	+ ed	amused
	+ ing	amusing
	+ ly	amusedly
	+ er	amuser*
	+ ment	amusement*
	+ ing + ly	amusingly
	+ ness	amusingness
	+ ive	amusive
an		
	+ y	any
analysis		
analyze		
	+ s	analyzes
	+ ed	analyzed
	+ ing	analyzing
	+ able	analyzable
	+ ity	analyzability
	+ ic	analytic*
	+ ist	analyst*
anatomy		
	+ s	anatomies
	+ ic	anatomic
	+ al	anatomical
	+ ly	anatomically
	+ ize	anatomize
	+ ize + s	anatomizes
	+ ed	anatomized
	+ ing	anatomizing
	+ ist	anatomist*
ancestor		
	+ s	ancestors
	+ ess	ancestress*
	+ al	ancestral
	+ ly	ancestrally
	+ y	ancestry*
anchor		
	+ s	anchors
	+ ed	anchored
	+ ing	anchoring
	+ age	anchorage*
	+ man	anchorman*
ancient		
	+ ness	ancientness
	+ ly	anciently
	+ ery	ancientry
and		
angel		
	+ s	angels
	+ ic	angelic
	+al	angelical
	+ ly	angelically
	+ fish	angelfish
anger		
	+ s	angers
	+ ed	angered
	+ ing	angering
	+ less	angerless
	+ y	angry
angle		
	+ s	angles
	+ ed	angled
	+ ing	angling
animal		
	+ s	animals
	+ ly	animally
	+ ism	animalism
	+ ist	animalist*

+ ity	animality
+ ic	animalistic
+ ize	animalize
+ ize + s	animalizes
+ ed	animalized
+ ing	animalizing
+ tion	animalization
+ ate	animate
+ ate + s	animates
+ ate + ed	animated
+ ate + ing	animating
+ ate + ly	animately
+ ness	animateness
+ ate + ed + ly	animatedly
+ or	animator*
ankle	
+ s	ankles
+ bone	anklebone*
anniversary*	
announce	
+ s	announces
+ ed	announced
+ ing	announcing
+ ment	announcement*
+ er	announcer*
annoy	
+ s	annoys
+ ed	annoyed
+ ing	annoying
+ ance	annoyance*
+ er	annoyer*
annual	
+ s	annuals
+ ly	annually
+ ity	annuity*
anonymous	
+ ly	anonymously
+ ness	anonymousness
+ ity	anonymity
+ s	anonymities
another	
answer	
+ s	answers
+ ed	answered
+ ing	answering
+ able	answerable
+ er	answerer
ant*	
antelope*	
antler	
+ s	antlers
+ ed	antlered

antonym	
+ s	antonyms
+ ic	antonymic
+ ous	antonymous
anxious	
+ ly	anxiously
+ ness	anxiousness
+ ity	anxiety
+ s	anxieties
any	
+ body	anybody
+ how	anyhow
+ more	anymore
+ one	anyone
+ place	anyplace
+ thing	anything
+ time	anytime
+ way	anyway
+ way + s	anyways
+ where	anywhere
+ wise	anywise
apart	
+ ness	apartness
apartment	
+ s	apartments
+ al	apartmental
apathy	
+ ic	apathic
+ ly	apathically
ape	
+ s	apes
+ ed	aped
+ ing	aping
+ er	aper*
+ like	apelike
aphasic*	
apologize	
+ s	apologizes
+ ed	apologized
+ ing	apologizing
+ y	apology*
+ ic	apologetic
+ ly	apologetically
+ ist	apologist*
apostrophe	
+ s	apostrophes
+ ic	apostrophic
+ ize	apostrophize
+ ize + s	apostrophizes
+ ed	apostrophized
+ ing	apostrophizing
appear	
+ s	appears
+ ed	appeared

+ ing appearing
+ ance appearance*

appetite
+ s appetites
+ ive appetitive
+ er appetizer*
+ ing appetizing
+ ly appetizingly

applaud
+ s applauds
+ ed applauded
+ ing applauding
+ able applaudable
+ ly applaudably
+ er applauder

applause

apple*

application*

apply
+ s applies
+ ed applied
+ ing applying
+ ance appliance*
+ able applicable
+ ity applicability
+ ant applicant*
+ tion application*
+ ive applicative
+ ly applicatively
+ or applicator*
+ ory applicatory

appoint
+ s appoints
+ ed appointed
+ ing appointing
+ ee appointee*
+ ive appointive
+ ment appointment*

appreciate
+ s appreciates
+ ed appreciated
+ ing appreciating
+ able appreciable
+ ly appreciably
+ tion appreciation
+ ive appreciative
+ ive + ly appreciatively
+ ness appreciativeness

approach
+ s approaches
+ ed approached
+ ing approaching
+ able approachable
+ ity approachability

appropriate
+ ly appropriately
+ ness appropriateness

approve (2)
+ s approves
+ ed approved
+ ing approving
+ ly approvingly
+ al approval
+ able approvable
+ able + ly approvably

approximate
+ s approximates
+ ed approximated
+ ing approximating
+ ly approximately
+ tion approximation*
+ ive approximative

apricot*

April (2)

apron*

architect
+ s architects
+ ure architecture
+ al architectural
+ ly architecturally
+ ic architectonic*

are
+ n't aren't

area
+ al areal
+ ly areally

argue
+ s argues
+ ed argued
+ ing arguing
+ er arguer*
+ ment argument*
+ tion argumentation
+ ive argumentative
+ ly argumentatively

arise
+ s arises
+ ed arose
+ ing arising
+ en arisen

arithmetic
+ al arithmetical
+ ly arithmetically
+ an arithmetician*

Arizona

arm
+ s arms
+ ed armed
+ ing arming

A

+ less	armless
+ like	armlike
+ chair	armchair*
+ ful	armful*
+ hole	armhole*
+ rest	armrest*
+ ment	armament*
+ y	army*
armadillo*	
armor	
+ s	armors
+ ed	armored
+ ing	armoring
+ er	armorer
+ less	armorless
+ al	armorial
+ly	armorially
+ y	armory*
+ ure	armature*
army*	
around (2)	
arrange	
+ s	arranges
+ ed	arranged
+ ing	arranging
+ ment	arrangement*
+ er	arranger*
arrest	
+ s	arrests
+ ed	arrested
+ ing	arresting
+ ly	arrestingly
+ er	arrester*
+ ment	arrestment
+ ee	arrestee*
+ ant	arrestant
arrive	
+ s	arrives
+ ed	arrived
+ ing	arriving
+ al	arrival*
+ er	arriver
arrogant	
+ ly	arrogantly
+ ance	arrogance
arrow	
+ s	arrows
+ y	arrowy
+ head	arrowhead*
+ root	arrowroot
+ wood	arrowwood
+ worm	arrowworm
art	
+ s	arts

+ ful	artful
+ ness	artfulness
+ ly	artfulnessly
+ ist	artist*
+ ic	artistic
+ ery	artistry
+ less	artless
+ less + ly	artlessly
+ less + ness	artlessness
artery	
+ s	arteries
+ al	arterial*
+ ly	arterially
+ ize	arterialize
+ ize + s	arterializes
+ ed	arterialized
+ ing	arterializing
+ tion	arterialization
+ gram	arteriogram*
+ graph	arteriograph*
+ y	arteriography
artichoke*	
article	
+ s	articles
+ ed	articled
+ ing	articling
+ able	articulable
+ ar	articular
+ ate	articulate
+ ate + s	articulates
+ ate + ed	articulated
+ ate + ing	articulating
+ ly	articulately
+ ness	articulateness
+ tion	articulation
+ ate + or	articulator
+ ory	articulatory
as	
ascend	
+ s	ascends
+ ed	ascended
+ ing	ascending
+ able	ascendable
+ ance	ascendance
+ y	ascendancy
+ ant	ascendant
+ ly	ascendantly
+ er	ascender*
+ sion	ascension
+ al	ascensional
+ ive	ascensive
+ t	ascent*
ashamed	
+ ly	ashamedly

Asia
+ an Asian*
+ ic Asiatic

ask
+ s asks
+ ed asked
+ ing asking
+ er asker

asleep

asparagus (2)

aspirin*

assassin
+ s assassins
+ ate assassinate
+ ate + s assassinates
+ ed assassinated
+ ing assassinating
+ tion assassination*
+ or assassinator*

assemble
+ s assembles
+ ed assembled
+ ing assembling
+ er assembler*
+ y assembly*
+ age assemblage*
+ ist assemblagist

assess
+ s assesses
+ ed assessed
+ ing assessing
+ able assessable
+ ment assessment*
+ or assessor*

assign
+ s assigns
+ ed assigned
+ ing assigning
+ able assignable
+ ity assignability
+ er assigner*
+ tion assignation*
+ al assignational
+ ee assignee*
+ ment assignment*

assist
+ s assists
+ ed assisted
+ ing assisting
+ ant assistant*
+ ship assistantship
+ ance assistance

associate
+ s associates
+ ed associated
+ ing associating
+ ion association*
+ ive associative
+ ly associatively
+ ship associateship

assort
+ s assorts
+ ed assorted
+ ing assorting
+ ment assortment*
+ ive assortative
+ er assorter*

assume
+ s assumes
+ ed assumed
+ ing assuming
+ tion assumption*
+ able assumable
+ ly assumably
+ ity assumability
+ ive assumptive

assure
+ s assures
+ ed assured
+ ing assuring
+ ly assuredly
+ ness assuredness
+ er assurer*

astonish
+ s astonishes
+ ed astonished
+ ing astonishing
+ ly astonishingly
+ ment astonishment

astronaut
+ s astronauts
+ ic astronautic*
+ al astronautical
+ ly astronautically

at

ate

athlete
+ s athletes
+ ic athletic*
+ ly athletically
+ ism athleticism

Atlanta

Atlantic
+ ism Atlanticism
+ ist Atlanticist

atmosphere
+ s atmospheres

+ ed atmosphered
+ ic atmospheric*
+ ly atmospherically

atom
+ s atoms
+ ic atomic*
+ ly atomically
+ ity atomicity
+ ism atomism
+ ist atomist
+ ist + ic atomistic
+ ize atomize
+ ize + s atomizes
+ ed atomized
+ ing atomizing
+ tion atomization
+ er atomizer*
+ y atomy*

attach
+ s attaches
+ ed attached
+ ing attaching
+ able attachable
+ ment attachment*

attack
+ s attacks
+ ed attacked
+ ing attacking
+ er attacker*
+ man attackman

attempt
+ s attempts
+ ed attempted
+ ing attempting
+ able attemptable

attend
+ s attends
+ ed attended
+ ing attending
+ er attender*
+ ance attendance
+ ant attendant*
+ ee attendee*
+ tion attention
+ al attentional
+ ive attentive
+ ly attentively
+ ness attentiveness

attention

attic*

attire
+ s attires
+ ed attired
+ ing attiring

attitude
+ s attitudes
+ al attitudinal
+ ize attitudinize
+ ize + s attitudinizes
+ ed attitudinized
+ ing attitudinizing

attract (2)
+ s attracts
+ ed attracted
+ ing attracting
+ able attractable
+ or attractor*
+ ant attractant*
+ ion attraction*
+ ive attractive
+ ness attractiveness

auction
+ s auctions
+ ed auctioned
+ ing auctioning
+ er auctioneer*

audience*

audio
+ meter audiometer*
+ vision + al audiovisual
+ tape audiotape*

audiogram*

audiology
+ al audiological
+ ist audiologist*

auditorium

August (2)

aunt
+ s aunts
+ like auntlike
+ ly auntly
+ hood aunthood

Australia (2)
+ an Australian*

author
+ s authors
+ ess authoress*
+ ship authorship
+ al authorial

authority
+ s authorities
+ ize authorize
+ ize + s authorizes
+ ed authorized
+ ing authorizing
+ tion authorization*
+ an authoritarian*

+ ism	authoritarianism
+ ive	authoritative
+ ly	authoritatively
+ ness	authoritativeness
autism	
+ ic	autistic
auto*	
automatic	
+ ly	automatically
+ ity	automaticity
+ tion	automation
automobile*	
autumn	
+ s	autumns
+ al	autumnal
+ ly	autumnally
avail	
+ s	avails
+ ed	availed
+ ing	availing
+ able	available
+ ity	availability
+ ness	availableness
+ ly	availably
avenue*	
average	
+ s	averages
+ ed	averaged
+ ing	averaging
+ ly	averagely
+ ness	averageness
avocado*	
avoid	
+ s	avoids
+ ed	avoided
+ ing	avoiding
+ able	avoidable
+ ly	avoidably
+ er	avoider*
+ ance	avoidance
awake	
+ s	awakes
+ ed	awoke/awaked
+ en	awoken
+ ing	awaking
+ en	awaken
+ en + s	awakens
+ en + ed	awakened
+ en + ing	awakening
+ er	awakener
award	
+ s	awards
+ ed	awarded
+ ing	awarding
+ able	awardable
+ er	awarder*
+ ee	awardee*
aware	
+ ness	awareness*
away	
+ ness	awayness
awful	
+ ly	awfully
+ ness	awfulness
awkward	
+ ly	awkwardly
+ ness	awkwardness
axe	
+ s	axes
+ ed	axed
+ ing	axing

A

B

babble
+ s babbles
+ ed babbled
+ ing babbling
+ ment babblement
+ er babbler*

baby
+ s babies
+ ed babied
+ ing babying
+ ish babyish
+ hood babyhood

bachelor
+ s bachelors
+ hood bachelorhood

back
+ s backs
+ ed backed
+ ing backing
+ er backer*
+ less backless
+ ache backache*
+ bite backbite
+ board backboard*
+ bone backbone*
+ country backcountry
+ court backcourt
+ cross backcross
+ drop backdrop*
+ field backfield
+ fire backfire*^
+ hand backhand
+ hand + ed backhanded
+ hand **+ ly** backhandedly
+ hoe backhoe*
+ house backhouse
+ lash backlash^
+ log backlog*^
+ pack backpack*^
+ rest backrest*
+ saw backsaw*
+ scatter backscatter^
+ seat backseat*
+ set backset
+ side backside
+ slap backslap
+ slide backslide^
+ spin backspin
+ stage backstage
+ stair + s backstairs
+ stay backstay
+ stitch backstitch^
+ stop backstop*
+ stretch backstretch
+ sweep + ed backswept
+ swing backswing
+ sword backsword*
+ track backtrack^
+ up backup
+ ward backward
+ ward + s backwards
+ ward + ly backwardly
+ ward + ness backwardness
+ wash backwash^
+ water backwater
+ wood + s backwoods
+ yard backyard*

background
+ s backgrounds
+ ed backgrounded
+ ing backgrounding

bacon

bacteria
+ al bacterial
+ ize bacterize
+ s bacterizes
+ ed bacterized
+ ing bacterizing
+ tion bacterization

bad
+ ly badly
+ ness badness
+ land badland*

badge
+ s badges
+ ed badged
+ ing badging

B

badminton

bag

+ s	bags
+ ed	bagged
+ ing	bagging
+ y	baggy
+ er	baggier
+ est	baggiest
+ ly	baggily
+ ness	bagginess
+ age	baggage
+ ful	bagful
+ man	bagman
+ pipe	bagpipe*
+ wig	bagwig
+ worm	bagworm*

bake

+ s	bakes
+ ed	baked
+ ing	baking
+ er	baker*
+ ery	bakery*
+ shop	bakeshop*

bakery*

balance

+ s	balances
+ ed	balanced
+ ing	balancing
+ er	balancer*

bald

+ s	balds
+ ed	balded
+ ing	balding
+ ish	baldish
+ ly	baldly
+ ness	baldness

ball

+ s	balls
+ ed	balled
+ ing	balling
+ carry + er	ballcarrier*
+ room	ballroom*

ballet

+ ic	balletic

balloon

+ s	balloons
+ ed	ballooned
+ ing	ballooning
+ ist	balloonist*

ballot

+ s	ballots
+ ed	balloted
+ ing	balloting
+ er	balloter*

baloney

Baltimore

+ an	Baltimorean*

ban

+ s	bans
+ ed	banned
+ ing	banning

banana*

band

+ s	bands
+ ed	banded
+ ing	banding
+ er	bander*

bandage

+ s	bandages
+ ed	bandaged
+ ing	bandaging
+ er	bandager*

band-aid*

bandana*

bang

+ s	bangs
+ ed	banged
+ ing	banging
+ er	banger*
+ tail	bangtail

banjo

+ s	banjos
+ ist	banjoist*

bank

+ s	banks
+ ed	banked
+ ing	banking
+ er	banker*
+ able	bankable
+ book	bankbook*
+ roll	bankroll
+ side	bankside

banner*

banquet

+ s	banquets
+ ed	banqueted
+ ing	banqueting
+ er	banqueter*

baptist*

baptize

+ s	baptizes
+ ed	baptized
+ ing	baptizing
+ er	baptizer*
+ ism	baptism*
+ al	baptismal
+ ly	baptismally
+ ist	baptist
+ ery	baptistry/baptistery*

bar

+ s	bars
+ ed	barred
+ ing	barring
+ er	barrister*
+ keep + er	barkeeper*
+ man	barman*
+ room	barroom*

Bar/Bat Mitzvah

barbecue

+ s	barbecues
+ ed	barbecued
+ ing	barbecuing
+ er	barbecuer*

barber

+ s	barbers
+ ed	barbered
+ ing	barbering
+ shop	barbershop*

bare

+ s	bares
+ ed	bared
+ ing	baring
+ er	barer
+ est	barest
+ ly	barely
+ ness	bareness
+ back	bareback
+ back + ed	barebacked
+ face	bareface
+ face + ed	barefaced
+ face + ed + ly	barefacedly
+ face + ed + ness	barefacedness
+ foot	barefoot
+ foot + ed	barefooted
+ head + ed	bareheaded
+ head + ed + ness	bareheadedness

bark

+ s	barks
+ ed	barked
+ ing	barking
+ er	barker*
+ less	barkless
+ y	barky
+ y + er	barkier
+ est	barkiest

barley

+ corn	barleycorn

barn

+ s	barns
+ y	barny
+ storm	barnstorm^
+ er	barnstormer*
+ yard	barnyard*

barometer

+ s	barometers
+ ic	barometric
+ al	barometrical
+ ly	barometrically
+ y	barometry

barrel

+ s	barrels
+ ed	barreled
+ ing	barreling
+ ful	barrelful*
+ house	barrelhouse*

barrier*

base

+ s	bases
+ ed	based
+ ing	basing
+ al	basal
+ al + ly	basally
+ al + ar	basilar
+ al + ary	basilary
+ ic	basic*
+ less	baseless
+ ly	basely
+ ment	basement*
+ ness	baseness
+ ify	basify
+ ify + s	basifies
+ ify + ed	basified
+ ify + ing	basifying
+ tion	basification
+ board	baseboard*
+ born	baseborn
+ level	baselevel
+ line	baseline*
+ ball	baseball*
+ ment	basement*

bashful

+ ly	bashfully
+ ness	bashfulness

basic

+ al + ly	basically

basil

basket

+ s	baskets
+ ery	basketry*
+ ful	basketful*
+ like	basketlike
+ work	basketwork

basketball*

bat

+ s	bats
+ ed	batted
+ ing	batting

B

+ er	batter*
+ boy	batboy*
+ fish	batfish
+ y	batty
+ y + er	battier
+ est	battiest
+ ness	battiness
batch	
+ s	batches
+ ed	batched
+ ing	batching
+ er	batcher*
bath	
+ s	baths
+ e	bathe
+ e + s	bathes
+ ed	bathed
+ ing	bathing
+ er	bather*
+ house	bathhouse*
+ robe	bathrobe*
+ room	bathroom*
+ tub	bathtub*
+ water	bathwater
batter	
+ s	batters
+ ed	battered
+ ing	battering
battery*	
battle	
+ s	battles
+ ed	battled
+ ing	battling
+ er	battler*
+ ment	battlement*
+ ment + ed	battlemented
+ field	battlefield*
+ front	battlefront*
+ ground	battleground*
+ ship	battleship*
+ wagon	battlewagon*
bawl	
+ s	bawls
+ ed	bawled
+ ing	bawling
+ er	bawler*
bay	
+ s	bays
+ ed	bayed
+ ing	baying
be	
+ en	been
+ ing	being*
+ cloud	becloud^
+ devil	bedevil^
+ dew	bedew^
+ fall	befall^
+ fit	befit^
+ fog	befog^
+ fool	befool^
+ friend	befriend^
+ gone	begone
+ half	behalf
+ head	behead^
+ hold	behold^
+ labor	belabor^
+ lie	belie^
+ little	belittle^
+ love + ed	beloved
+ medal + ed	bemedaled
+ moan	bemoan^
+ night + ed	benighted
+ set	beset
+ speak	bespeak^
+ sprinkle	besprinkle^
+ stir	bestir^
+ think	bethink
+ times	betimes
+ wail	bewail^
+ wig + ed	bewigged
+ witch	bewitch^
beach	
+ s	beaches
+ ed	beached
+ ing	beaching
+ y	beachy
+ boy	beachboy*
+ comb	beachcomb
+ comb + er	beachcomber*
+ front	beachfront*
+ head	beachhead*
+ side	beachside
+ wear	beachwear
bead	
+ s	beads
+ ed	beaded
+ ing	beading
+ y	beady
+ work	beadwork
beak	
+ s	beaks
+ ed	beaked
beam	
+ s	beams
+ ed	beamed
+ ing	beaming
+ ish	beamish
+ ly	beamishly
+ y	beamy

bean (2)

+ s	beans
+ ed	beaned
+ ing	beaning
+ y	beanie*
+ o	beano
+ bag	beanbag*
+ ball	beanball*
+ pole	beanpole*

bear

+ s	bears
+ ed	bore
+ en	born
+ ing	bearing
+ er	bearer*
+ able	bearable
+ ity	bearability
+ ly	bearably
+ ish	bearish
+ ish + ly	bearishly
+ ness	bearishness
+ skin	bearskin*

beard

+ s	beards
+ ed	bearded
+ ness	beardedness
+ less	beardless

beast

+ s	beasts
+ ly	beastly
+ er	beastlier
+ est	beastliest
+ ness	beastliness

beat

+ s	beats
+ en	beaten
+ ing	beating
+ er	beater*
+ less	beatless

beauty

+ s	beauties
+ ous	beauteous
+ ly	beauteously
+ ness	beauteousness
+ an	beautician*
+ ful	beautiful
+ ful + ly	beautifully
+ ful + ness	beautifulness
+ ify	beautify
+ ify + s	beautifies
+ ed	beautified
+ ing	beautifying
+ er	beautifier
+ tion	beautification

beaver

+ s	beavers
+ board	beaverboard

because

become

+ s	becomes
+ ed	became
+ ing	becoming
+ ly	becomingly

bed

+ s	beds
+ ed	bedded
+ ing	bedding*
+ bug	bedbug*
+ cloth + e + s	bedclothes
+ fellow	bedfellow*
+ mate	bedmate*
+ pan	bedpan*
+ plate	bedplate
+ post	bedpost
+ rock	bedrock
+ roll	bedroll*
+ room	bedroom*
+ side	bedside
+ sore	bedsore*
+ spread	bedspread*
+ spring	bedspring*
+ stead	bedstead*
+ straw	bedstraw
+ time	bedtime*

bee

+ s	bees
+ keep + er	beekeeper*
+ like	beelike
+ line	beeline*
+ s + wax	beeswax

beef

+ s	beefs (beeves)
+ y	beefy
+ er	beefier
+ est	beefiest
+ cake	beefcake
+ eat + er	beefeater*
+ steak	beefsteak*
+ wood	beefwood

been

beep

+ s	beeps
+ ed	beeped
+ ing	beeping
+ er	beeper*

beer

+ s	beers
+ y	beery
+ er	beerier

B

+ est	beeriest
beet*	
beetle	
+ s	beetles
+ ed	beetled
+ ing	beetling
before	
+ hand	beforehand
+ ness	beforehandedness
beg	
+ s	begs
+ ed	begged
+ ing	begging
+ ar	beggar*
+ ar + ed	beggared
+ ar + ing	beggaring
+ ly	beggarly
+ ness	beggarliness
+ y	beggary*
begin	
+ s	begins
+ ed	began
+ en	begun
+ ing	beginning*
+ er	beginner*
behave	
+ s	behaves
+ ed	behaved
+ ing	behaving
+ or	behavior*
+ al	behavioral
+ ly	behaviorally
+ ist	behaviorist*
behind	
+ hand	behindhand
beige	
+ s	beiges
+ y	beigy
believe	
+ s	believes
+ ed	believed
+ ing	believing
+ er	believer*
+ able	believable
+ ly	believably
+ ity	believability
bell	
+ s	bells
+ ed	belled
+ ing	belling
+ bird	bellbird
belly	
+ s	bellies
+ ed	bellied
+ ing	bellying
+ ful	bellyful*
+ ache	bellyache*
+ band	bellyband*
belong	
+ s	belongs
+ ed	belonged
+ ing	belonging*
below	
belt	
+ s	belts
+ ed	belted
+ ing	belting*
+ less	beltless
+ way	beltway*
bench	
+ s	benches
+ ed	benched
+ ing	benching
+ er	bencher*
bend	
+ s	bends
+ ed	bent
+ ing	bending
+ er	bender*
beneath	
benefit	
+ s	benefits
+ ed	benefitted
+ ing	benefitting
+ er	benefiter*
berry	
+ s	berries
+ ed	berried
+ ing	berrying
+ like	berrylike
beside*	
best	
+ s	bests
+ ed	bested
+ ing	besting
bet	
+ s	bets
+ ed	betted
+ ing	betting
+ or	bettor*
Bethlehem	
betray	
+ s	betrays
+ ed	betrayed
+ ing	betraying
+ er	betrayer*
+ al	betrayal*

better	
+ s	betters
+ ed	bettered
+ ing	bettering
+ ment	betterment
between	
+ brain	betweenbrain
+ ness	betweenness
+ time + s	betweentimes
+ while + s	betweenwhiles
beware	
bewilder	
+ s	bewilders
+ ed	bewildered
+ ing	bewildering
+ ly	bewilderedly
+ ness	bewilderedness
+ ing + ly	bewilderingly
+ ment	bewilderment
beyond*	
bib	
+ s	bibs
+ ed	bibbed
+ ing	bibbing
bible	
+ s	bibles
+ al	biblical
+ ly	biblically
+ ism	biblicism
+ ist	biblicist*
bibliography*	
bicycle	
+ s	bicycles
+ ed	bicycled
+ ing	bicycling
+ ist	bicyclist*
+ ic	bicyclic
bid	
+ s	bids
+ ed	bade (bid)
+ en	bidden (bid)
+ ing	bidding
+ er	bidder*
+ able	biddable
+ ly	biddably
big	
+ er	bigger
+ est	biggest
+ ly	bigly
+ ness	bigness
bike	
+ s	bikes
+ ed	biked
+ ing	biking
+ er	biker*
+ way	bikeway*

billion	
+ s	billions
+ th	billionth
bind	
+ s	binds
+ ed	bound
+ ing	binding*
+ er	binder*
+ ery	bindery*
+ ly	bindingly
+ ness	bindingness
binocular	
+ s	binoculars
+ ity	binocularity
+ ly	binocularly
biography	
+ s	biographies
+ ic	biographic
+ al	biographical
+ ly	biographically
+ er	biographer*
biology	
+ ic	biologic*
+ al	biological*
+ ly	biologically
+ ism	biologism
+ ist	biologist*
+ ist + ic	biologistic
bird	
+ s	birds
+ ed	birded
+ ing	birding
+ er	birder*
+ y	birdie*
+ like	birdlike
+ bath	birdbath*
+ brain	birdbrain
+ call	birdcall*
+ house	birdhouse*
+ man	birdman*
+ seed	birdseed*
birth	
+ s	births
+ en	born
+ day	birthday*
+ mark	birthmark*
+ place	birthplace*
+ rate	birthrate*
+ right	birthright*
+ root	birthroot
+ stone	birthstone*

B

birthday*
biscuit*
bishop

+ s	bishops
+ ic	bishopric*

bit (2)

+ s	bits
+ ed	bitted
+ ing	bitting

bite

+ s	bites
+ ed	bit
+ en	bitten
+ ing	biting
+ er	biter*
+ ly	bitingly

bitter

+ ish	bitterish
+ ly	bitterly
+ ness	bitterness
+ brush	bitterbrush
+ root	bitterroot
+ weed	bitterweed
+ sweet	bittersweet
+ sweet + ly	bittersweetly
+ sweet + ness	bittersweetness

black

+ s	blacks
+ ed	blacked
+ en	blacken
+ en + s	blackens
+ en + ed	blackened
+ en + ing	blackening
+ en + er	blackener
+ ing	blacking
+ ish	blackish
+ ly	blackly
+ ness	blackness
+ ball	blackball^
+ berry	blackberry*
+ bird	blackbird*
+ bird + er	blackbirder
+ board	blackboard*
+ body	blackbody
+ cap	blackcap*
+ face	blackface
+ fish	blackfish
+ fly	blackfly*
+ guard	blackguard*
+ head	blackhead*
+ heart	blackheart
+ land	blackland
+ leg	blackleg
+ list	blacklist^
+ mail	blackmail
+ out	blackout*
+ snake	blacksnake
+ tail	blacktail
+ thorn	blackthorn
+ top	blacktop
+ wash	blackwash
+ water	blackwater

blade

+ s	blades
+ ed	bladed

blame

+ s	blames
+ ed	blamed
+ ing	blaming
+ er	blamer*
+ ful	blameful
+ ly	blamefully
+ worth + y	blameworthy
+ worth **+ ness**	blameworthiness

blank

+ s	blanks
+ ed	blanked
+ ing	blanking
+ ly	blankly
+ ness	blankness

blanket

+ s	blankets
+ ed	blanketed
+ ing	blanketing
+ like	blanketlike

blaze

+ s	blazes
+ ed	blazed
+ ing	blazing
+ ly	blazingly
+ er	blazer*

bleed

+ s	bleeds
+ ed	bled
+ ing	bleeding
+ er	bleeder*

blend

+ s	blends
+ ed	blended
+ ing	blending
+ er	blender*

bless

+ s	blesses
+ ed	blessed
+ ing	blessing
+ ly	blessedly
+ ness	blessedness

blind

+ s	blinds
+ ed	blinded
+ ing	blinding
+ er	blinder*
+ ly	blindly
+ ness	blindness
+ ing + ly	blindingly
+ fish	blindfish
+ fold	blindfold
+ worm	blindworm

blink

+ s	blinks
+ ed	blinked
+ ing	blinking
+ er	blinker*

blister

+ s	blisters
+ ed	blistered
+ ing	blistering
+ y	blistery
+ ly	blisteringly

block

+ s	blocks
+ ed	blocked
+ ing	blocking
+ er	blocker*
+ age	blockage*
+ ish	blockish
+ ly	blockishly
+ y	blocky
+ y + er	blockier
+ est	blockiest
+ head	blockhead
+ house	blockhouse

blond

+ s	blonds
+ e	blonde*
+ ish	blondish

blood

+ s	bloods
+ ed	blooded
+ ing	blooding
+ y	bloody
+ y + ed	bloodied
+ y + ing	bloodying
+ ly	bloodily
+ ness	bloodiness
+ less	bloodless
+ less + ly	bloodlessly
+ less + ness	bloodlessness
+ bath	bloodbath
+ guilt	bloodguilt
+ guilt + y	bloodguilty
+ guilt + y + ness	bloodguiltiness
+ let + ing	bloodletting
+ line	bloodline
+ red	bloodred
+ root	bloodroot
+ shot	bloodshot
+ stone	bloodstone*
+ stream	bloodstream
+ sucker	bloodsucker*
+ suck + ing	bloodsucking
+ thirst + y	bloodthirsty
+ thirst **+ ly**	bloodthirstily
+ thirst **+ ness**	bloodthirstiness
+ worm	bloodworm*

bloom

+ s	blooms
+ ed	bloomed
+ ing	blooming
+ er	bloomer*
+ y	bloomy

blossom

+ s	blossoms
+ ed	blossomed
+ ing	blossoming

blouse

+ s	blouses
+ ed	bloused
+ ing	blousing

blow

+ s	blows
+ ed	blew
+ en	blown
+ ing	blowing
+ er	blower
+ er + s	blowers
+ fish	blowfish
+ fly	blowfly*
+ gun	blowgun*
+ hard	blowhard*
+ hole	blowhole*
+ out	blowout*
+ pipe	blowpipe*
+ torch	blowtorch*

blue

+ s	blues
+ ed	blued
+ ing	blueing
+ ly	bluely
+ ness	blueness
+ er	bluer
+ est	bluest
+ s + y	bluesy
+ y	bluey
+ beard	bluebeard*

+ bell	bluebell*
+ berry	blueberry*
+ bird	bluebird*
+ bonnet	bluebonnet*
+ bottle	bluebottle*
+ coat	bluecoat*
+ fish	bluefish
+ grass	bluegrass
+ jacket	bluejacket*
+ nose	bluenose
+ point	bluepoint
+ print	blueprint*
+ s + man	bluesman*
+ stocking	bluestocking*
+ stone	bluestone*
+ tongue	bluetongue*
+ weed	blueweed*
blush	
+ s	blushes
+ ed	blushed
+ ing	blushing
+ er	blusher*
+ ly	blushingly
+ ful	blushful
board	
+ s	boards
+ ed	boarded
+ ing	boarding
+ er	boarder*
+ like	boardlike
+ house	boardinghouse*
+ man	boardman*
+ room	boardroom*
+ walk	boardwalk*
boast	
+ s	boasts
+ ed	boasted
+ ing	boasting
+ er	boaster*
+ ful	boastful
+ ly	boastfully
+ ness	boastfulness
boat	
+ s	boats
+ ed	boated
+ ing	boating
+ er	boater*
+ man	boatman*
+ man + ship	boatmanship
body	
+ s	bodies
+ ed	bodied
+ ing	bodying
+ ly	bodily
+ less	bodiless
+ guard	bodyguard*
+ work	bodywork
boil	
+ s	boils
+ ed	boiled
+ ing	boiling
+ er	boiler*
+ er + make + er	boilermaker*
bold	
+ er	bolder
+ est	boldest
+ ly	boldly
+ ness	boldness
+ face	boldface
+ face + ed	boldfaced
bomb	
+ s	bombs
+ ed	bombed
+ ing	bombing
+ er	bomber*
+ proof	bombproof
+ shell	bombshell*
+ sight	bombsight*
bone	
+ s	bones
+ ed	boned
+ ing	boning
+ er	boner*
+ less	boneless
+ y	boney
+ fish	bonefish
+ head	bonehead
+ head + ed	boneheaded
+ set	boneset
+ set + er	bonesetter
+ yard	boneyard*
bonfire*	
bonnet	
+ s	bonnets
+ ed	bonneted
+ ing	bonneting
book	
+ s	books
+ ed	booked
+ ing	booking
+ er	booker*
+ ish	bookish
+ ly	bookishly
+ ness	bookishness
+ y	bookie*
+ bind + ing	bookbinding
+ bind + er	bookbinder*
+ bind + ery	bookbindery

+ case	bookcase*
+ end	bookend*
+ keep + er	bookkeeper*
+ keep + ing	bookkeeping
+ make + er	bookmaker*
+ man	bookman*
+ mark	bookmark*
+ plate	bookplate*
+ sell + er	bookseller*
+ shelf	bookshelf*
+ store	bookstore*
+ worm	bookworm*
boost	
+ s	boosts
+ ed	boosted
+ ing	boosting
+ er	booster*
+ ism	boosterism
boot	
+ s	boots
+ ed	booted
+ ing	booting
+ ee	bootee*
+ less	bootless
+ ly	bootlessly
+ ness	bootlessness
+ black	bootblack
+ leg	bootleg
+ lick	booklick
+ lick + er	bootlicker
+ print	bootprint
border	
+ s	borders
+ ed	bordered
+ ing	bordering
+ er	borderer*
+ land	borderland*
+ line	bordlerline*
bore	
+ s	bores
+ ed	bored
+ ing	boring
+ er	borer*
+ dom	boredom
+ ly	boringly
+ ness	boringness
born	
borrow	
+ s	borrows
+ ed	borrowed
+ ing	borrowing
+ er	borrower*
boss	
+ s	bosses
+ ed	bossed
+ ing	bossing
+ dom	bossdom
+ ism	bossism
+ y	bossy
+ er	bossier
+ est	bossiest
+ ness	bossiness
both	
bother	
+ s	bothers
+ ed	bothered
+ ing	bothering
+ tion	botheration
+ some	bothersome
bottle	
+ s	bottles
+ ed	bottled
+ ing	bottling
+ er	bottler*
+ neck	bottleneck*
bottom	
+ s	bottoms
+ ed	bottomed
+ ing	bottoming
+ er	bottomer*
+ less	bottomless
+ ly	bottomlessly
+ ness	bottomlessness
+ more + est	bottommost
bought	
boulevard	
+ s	boulevards
+ er	boulevardier*
bounce	
+ s	bounces
+ ed	bounced
+ ing	bouncing
+ er	bouncer*
+ y	bouncy
+ y + er	bouncier
+ est	bounciest
bound	
+ s	bounds
+ ed	bounded
+ ing	bounding
+ er	bounder*
+ ish	bounderish
+ ly	bounderishly
+ less	boundless
+ less + ly	boundlessly
+ ness	boundlessness
+ ary	boundary*
bow (noun)	
+ s	bows
+ ed	bowed

+ ing	bowing
+ man	bowman*
bow (verb)	
+ s	bows
+ ed	bowed
+ ing	bowing
bowel movement*	
bowl	
+ s	bowls
+ ed	bowled
+ ing	bowling
+ er	bowler*
box	
+ s	boxes
+ ed	boxed
+ ing	boxing
+ er	boxer*
+ y	boxy
+ y + er	boxier
+ est	boxiest
+ ness	boxiness
+ like	boxlike
+ car	boxcar*
+ thorn	boxthorn
+ wood	boxwood
boy	
+ s	boys
+ hood	boyhood*
+ ish	boyish
+ ly	boyishly
+ ness	boyishness
+ friend	boyfriend*
bra*	
bracelet*	
brag	
+ s	brags
+ ed	bragged
+ ing	bragging
+ er	bragger*
braid	
+ s	braids
+ ed	braided
+ ing	braiding
+ er	braider*
braille	
+ s	brailles
+ ed	brailled
+ ing	brailling
+ ist	braillist*
+ write + er	braillewriter*
brain	
+ s	brains
+ ed	brained
+ ing	braining
+ y	brainy
+ er	brainier
+ est	brainiest
+ ness	braininess
+ ish	brainish
+ less	brainless
+ ly	brainlessly
+ less + ness	brainlessness
+ case	braincase*
+ child	brainchild*
+ pan	brainpan*
+ power	brainpower
+ sick	brainsick
+ storm	brainstorm^
+ storm + ing	brainstorming
+ tease + er	brainteaser*
+ wash	brainwash^
+ wash + ing	brainwashing
brake	
+ s	brakes
+ ed	braked
+ ing	braking
+ y	braky
+ man	brakeman
branch	
+ s	branches
+ ed	branched
+ ing	branching
+ less	branchless
+ y	branchy
brand	
+ s	brands
+ ed	branded
+ ing	branding
+ er	brander*
brass	
+ y	brassy
+ er	brassier
+ est	brassiest
+ ly	brassily
+ ness	brassiness
brat	
+ s	brats
+ y	bratty
+ ness	brattiness
+ ish	brattish
brave	
+ er	braver
+ est	bravest
+ s	braves
+ ed	braved
+ ing	braving
+ ery	bravery*
+ ly	bravely
+ ness	braveness

bread

+ s	breads
+ ed	breaded
+ ing	breading
+ basket	breadbasket*
+ board	breadboard*
+ fruit	breadfruit
+ stuff	breadstuff
+ win + er	breadwinner*

break

+ s	breaks
+ ed	broke
+ en	broken
+ ing	breaking
+ er	breaker*
+ able	breakable
+ age	breakage*
+ away	breakaway
+ down	breakdown*
+ front	breakfront*
+ neck	breakneck
+ out	breakout*
+ point	breakpoint
+ through	breakthrough*
+ up	breakup*
+ water	breakwater*

breakfast

+ s	breakfasts
+ ed	breakfasted
+ ing	breakfasting
+ er	breakfaster*

breast

+ s	breasts
+ ed	breasted
+ ing	breasting
+ bone	breastbone*
+ plate	breastplate*
+ work	breastwork*

breath

+ s	breaths
+ e	breathe
+ e + s	breathes
+ ed	breathed
+ ing	breathing
+ able	breathable
+ ity	breathability
+ er	breather*
+ less	breathless
+ ly	breathlessly
+ ness	breathlessness
+ take + ing	breathtaking
+ take + ing + ly	breathtakingly
+ y	breathy
+ y + er	breathier
+ est	breathiest

breed

+ s	breeds
+ ed	bred
+ ing	breeding
+ er	breeder*

breeze

+ s	breezes
+ ed	breezed
+ ing	breezing
+ y	breezy
+ er	breezier
+ est	breeziest
+ ly	breezily
+ ness	breeziness

bribe

+ s	bribes
+ ed	bribed
+ ing	bribing
+ er	briber*
+ ery	bribery
+ able	bribable

brick

+ s	bricks
+ ed	bricked
+ ing	bricking
+ field	brickfield*
+ lay + er	bricklayer*
+ lay + ing	bricklaying
+ work	brickwork*
+ yard	brickyard*

bride

+ s	brides
+ al	bridal

bridegroom*

bridge

+ s	bridges
+ ed	bridged
+ ing	bridging
+ able	bridgeable
+ board	bridgeboard*
+ head	bridgehead*
+ work	bridgework*

brief

+ s	briefs
+ ed	briefed
+ ing	briefing
+ er	briefer
+ est	briefest
+ ly	briefly
+ ness	briefness
+ less	briefless
+ case	briefcase*

bright

+ s	brights
+ en	brighten

B

+ en + s	brightens
+ ed	brightened
+ ing	brightening
+ en + er	brightener*
+ er	brighter
+ est	brightest
+ ly	brightly
+ ness	brightness
+ work	brightwork
brilliant	
+ s	brilliants
+ ance	brilliance
+ ly	brilliantly
+ ness	brilliantness
bring	
+ s	brings
+ ed	brought
+ ing	bringing
Britain	
+ ish	British
+ ic	Britannic
+ er	Britisher*
+ ism	Briticism*
British	
broad	
+ er	broader
+ est	broadest
+ s	broads
+ en	broaden
+ en + s	broadens
+ en + ed	broadened
+ **ing**	broadening
+ ly	broadly
+ ness	broadness
+ ax	broadax*
+ band	broadband*
+ cloth	broadcloth*
+ leaf	broadleaf*
+ side	broadside*
+ sword	broadsword*
+ tail	broadtail*
+ wife	broadwife*
broccoli	
brochure*	
broil	
+ s	broils
+ ed	broiled
+ ing	broiling
+ er	broiler*
broke	
broken	
Brontosaurus	
bronze	
+ s	bronzes
+ ed	bronzed
+ ing	bronzing
+ er	bronzer*
+ y	bronzy
brooch*	
brook	
+ s	brooks
+ ed	brooked
+ ing	brooking
broom	
+ s	brooms
+ ed	broomed
+ ing	brooming
+ ball	broomball*
+ corn	broomcorn
+ stick	broomstick*
broth*	
brother	
+ s	brothers
+ hood	brotherhood
+ ly	brotherly
+ ness	brotherliness
brought	
brow	
+ s	brows
+ ed	browed
brown	
+ s	browns
+ ed	browned
+ ing	browning
+ ish	brownish
+ y	brownie*
+ out	brownout*
+ shirt	brownshirt*
bruise	
+ s	bruises
+ ed	bruised
+ ing	bruising
+ er	bruiser
+ er + s	bruisers
brush	
+ s	brushes
+ ed	brushed
+ ing	brushing
+ er	brusher*
+ ity	brushability
+ y	brushy
+ y + er	brushier
+ est	brushiest
+ back	brushback*
+ firs	brushfire*
+ land	brushland*
+ wood	brushwood
+ work	brushwork

bubble	
+ s	bubbles
+ ed	bubbled
+ ing	bubbling
+ er	bubbler*
+ ly	bubbly
+ ly + er	bubblier
+ est	bubbliest
bucket	
+ s	buckets
+ ed	bucketed
+ ing	bucketing
+ ful	bucketful*
buckle	
+ s	buckles
+ ed	buckled
+ ing	buckling
+ er	buckler*
bud	
+ s	buds
+ ed	budded
+ ing	budding
buffalo	
+ s	buffalos
+ ed	buffaloed
+ ing	buffaloing
buffet*	
bug	
+ s	bugs
+ ed	bugged
+ ing	bugging
+ er	bugger*^
+ y	buggy
+ y + er	buggier
+ est	buggiest
buggy*	
build	
+ s	builds
+ ed	built
+ ing	building
+ er	builder*
+ up	buildup
bulb	
+ s	bulbs
+ ed	bulbed
+ ous	bulbaceous
bull	
+ s	bulls
+ ed	bulled
+ ing	bulling
+ y	bully
+ y + s	bullies
+ y + ed	bullied
+ y + ing	bullying
+ y + boy	bullyboy*
+ rag	bullyrag*
+ dog	bulldog*
+ fight	bullfight*
+ fight + er	bullfighter*
+ frog	bullfrog*
+ head	bullhead*
+ head + ed	bullheaded*
+ horn	bullhorn*
+ ring	bullring*
+ whip	bullwhip*
bulldozer	
+ s	bulldozers
+ ed	bulldozered
+ ing	bulldozing
bulletin*	
bump	
+ s	bumps
+ ed	bumped
+ ing	bumping
+ er	bumper*
+ y	bumpy
+ y + er	bumpier
+ est	bumpiest
+ ly	bumpily
+ ness	bumpiness
bun*	
bunch	
+ s	bunches
+ ed	bunched
+ ing	bunching
+ y	bunchy
+ ly	bunchily
bundle	
+ s	bundles
+ ed	bundled
+ ing	bundling
+ er	bundler*
bunny*	
burden	
+ s	burdens
+ ed	burdened
+ ing	burdening
+ some	burdensome
+ some + ly	burdensomely
+ some + ness	burdensomeness
burn	
+ s	burns
+ ed	burned
+ ing	burning
+ er	burner*
+ able	burnable
+ ly	burningly
+ out	burnout

B

B

burp

+ s	burps
+ ed	burped
+ ing	burping

bury (2)

+ s	buries
+ ed	buried
+ ing	burying
+ al	burial*

bus

+ s	buses
+ ed	bused
+ ing	busing

bush

+ s	bushes
+ ed	bushed
+ ing	bushing
+ y	bushy
+ er	bushier
+ est	bushiest
+ ness	bushiness
+ ly	bushily
+ fire	bushfire*
+ man	bushman*
+ master	bushmaster*
+ ranger	bushranger*

business

+ s	businesses
+ like	businesslike

busy

+ s	busies
+ ed	busied
+ ing	busying
+ er	busier
+ est	busiest
+ work	busywork
+ body	busybody

but

butcher

+ s	butchers
+ ed	butchered
+ ing	butchering
+ y	butchery
+ er	butcherer*

butter

+ s	butters
+ ed	buttered
+ ing	buttering
+ y	buttery*

butterfly*

button

+ s	buttons
+ ed	buttoned
+ ing	buttoning
+ er	buttoner*
+ less	buttonless
+ y	buttony
+ hole	buttonhole*

buy

+ s	buys
+ ed	bought
+ ing	buying
+ er	buyer*

buzz

+ s	buzzes
+ ed	buzzed
+ ing	buzzing
+ er	buzzer*
+ word	buzzword*

by

bye-bye

cabbage		
	+ s	cabbages
	+ ed	cabbaged
	+ ing	cabbaging
cabin		
cabinet		
	+ s	cabinets
	+ make + er	cabinetmaker*
	+ work	cabinetwork
cable		
	+ s	cables
	+ ed	cabled
	+ ing	cabling
caboose*		
cactus		
cafe*		
cafeteria* (2)		
cage		
	+ s	cages
	+ ed	caged
	+ ing	caging
cake		
	+ s	cakes
	+ ed	caked
	+ ing	caking
calculate		
	+ s	calculates
	+ ed	calculated
	+ ing	calculating
	+ or	calculator*
	+ ion	calculation*
calculus		
calendar		
	+ s	calendars
	+ ed	calendared
	+ ing	calendaring
calf		
	+ s	calves
	+ like	calflike
	+ skin	calfskin*
California		
	+ an	Californian*
call		
	+ s	calls
	+ ed	called
	+ ing	calling
	+ er	caller*
calm		
	+ er	calmer
	+ est	calmest
	+ s	calms
	+ ed	calmed
	+ ing	calming
	+ ly	calmly
	+ ness	calmness
	+ ive	calmative*
calorie		
	+ s	calories
	+ ic	caloric
	+ ly	calorically
camel		
	+ s	camels
	+ back	camelback
camera		
	+ s	cameras
	+ man	cameraman*
camp		
	+ s	camps
	+ ed	camped
	+ ing	camping
	+ er	camper*
	+ y	campy
	+ ly	campily
	+ ness	campiness
	+ ground	campground*
can (2)		
	+ en	could
	+ n't	can't
	+ en + n't	couldn't
	+ s	cans
	+ ed	canned
	+ ing	canning
	+ er	canner*

Canada		
	+ an	Canadian*
	+ ism	Canadianism
canal		
	+ s	canals
	+ ed	canaled
	+ ing	canaling
	+ ize	canalize
	+ ize + s	canalizes
	+ ize + ed	canalized
	+ ize + ing	canalizing
	+ tion	canalization*
	+ boat	canalboat*
cancel		
	+ s	cancels
	+ ed	cancelled
	+ ing	cancelling
	+ able	cancelable
	+ er	canceler*
	+ tion	cancelation*
cancer		
	+ s	cancers
	+ ous	cancerous
	+ ly	cancerously
candle		
	+ s	candles
	+ ed	candled
	+ ing	candling
	+ er	candler*
	+ hold + er	candleholder*
	+ light	candlelight
	+ light + er	candlelighter*
	+ berry	candleberry*
	+ fish	candlefish
	+ nut	candlenut*
	+ pin	candlepin
	+ power	candlepower
	+ stick	candlestick*
candy		
	+ s	candies
	+ ed	candied
	+ ing	candying
cane		
	+ s	canes
	+ ed	caned
	+ ing	caning
	+ er	caner*
cannon		
	+ s	cannons
	+ er	cannoneer*
	+ ery	cannonry
	+ ball	cannonball*
canoe		
	+ s	canoes
	+ ed	canoed
	+ ing	canoeing
	+ ist	canoeist*
can't		
cantaloupe*		
canyon*		
cap		
	+ s	caps
	+ ed	capped
	+ ing	capping
capacity		
	+ s	capacities
	+ ance	capacitance
	+ or	capacitor*
capital		
	+ s	capitals
	+ ism	capitalism
	+ ist	capitalist*
	+ ic	capitalistic
	+ ic + ly	capitalistically
	+ ize	capitalize
	+ ize + s	capitalizes
	+ ed	capitalized
	+ ing	capitalizing
	+ tion	capitalization*
	+ ly	capitally
capitol		
	+ s	capitols
	+ ine	Capitoline
captain		
	+ s	captains
	+ y	captaincy
	+ ship	captainship
caption		
	+ s	captions
	+ ed	captioned
	+ ing	captioning
	+ er	captioner*
	+ less	captionless
capture		
	+ s	captures
	+ ed	captured
	+ ing	capturing
	+ or	captor*
	+ ive	captive*
	+ ate	captivate
	+ ate + s	captivates
	+ ate + ed	captivated
	+ ate + ing	captivating
	+ tion	captivation*
	+ ity	captivity*
car		
	+ s	cars
	+ sick	carsick

+ sick + ness	carsickness
+ top	cartop
+ top + er	cartopper*
caramel	
+ s	caramels
+ ize	caramelize
+ ize + s	caramelizes
+ ed	caramelized
+ ing	caramelizing
card	
+ s	cards
+ ed	carded
+ ing	carding
+ er	carder*
+ board	cardboard
care	
+ s	cares
+ ed	cared
+ ing	caring
+ er	carer*
+ ful	careful
+ ful + er	carefuller
+ est	carefullest
+ ly	carefully
+ ness	carefullness
+ free	carefree
+ take + er	caretaker*
+ wear + en	careworn
career	
+ s	careers
+ ed	careered
+ ing	careering
+ ism	careerism
+ ist	careerist*
careless	
+ ly	carelessly
+ ness	carelessness
cargo*	
carnival*	
carol	
+ s	carols
+ ed	caroled
+ ing	caroling
+ er	caroler*
carpenter	
+ s	carpenters
+ ed	carpentered
+ ery	carpentry
carpet	
+ s	carpets
+ ed	carpeted
+ ing	carpeting
+ bag	carpetbag*
+ bag + er	carpetbagger*

carrot	
+ s	carrots
+ y	carroty
carry	
+ s	carries
+ ed	carried
+ ing	carrying
+ er	carrier*
+ all	carryall
+ on	carryon
+ out	carryout
cart	
+ s	carts
+ ed	carted
+ ing	carting
+ er	carter*
+ load	cartload*
+ wheel	cartwheel*
carton	
+ s	cartons
+ ed	cartoned
+ ing	cartoning
cartoon	
+ s	cartoons
+ ed	cartooned
+ ing	cartooning
+ ist	cartoonist*
carve	
+ s	carves
+ ed	carved
+ ing	carving
+ en	carven
+ er	carver*
case	
+ s	cases
+ ed	cased
+ ing	casing*
+ ment	casement*
+ bear + er	casebearer
+ book	casebook*
+ mate	casemate
+ work	casework
cash	
+ s	cashes
+ ed	cashed
+ ing	cashing
+ able	cashable
+ er	cashier*
+ less	cashless
+ book	cashbook*
casserole*	
cassette*	
castle	
+ s	castles

C

+ ed	castled
+ ing	castling
cat	
+ s	cats
+ ed	catted
+ ing	catting
+ y	catty
+ er	cattier
+ est	cattiest
+ like	catlike
+ nap	catnap*
+ walk	catwalk*
catalogue	
+ s	catalogues
+ ed	catalogued
+ ing	cataloguing
catch	
+ s	catches
+ ed	caught
+ ing	catching
+ er	catcher*
+ ment	catchment
+ y	catchy
+ y + er	catchier
+ est	catchiest
+ all	catchall
+ up	catchup
+ word	catchword*
category*	
caterpillar*	
Catholic	
+ s	Catholics
+ ly	catholically
+ ize	catholicize
+ ize + s	catholicizes
+ ed	catholicized
+ ing	catholicizing
+ ism	catholicism
+ ity	catholicity*
catsup	
cattle	
+ man	cattleman*
cauliflower*	
cause	
+ s	causes
+ ed	caused
+ ing	causing
+ al	causal
+ ity	causality*
+ tion	causation
+ ive	causative
+ ly	causatively
+ less	causeless
caution	
+ s	cautions
+ ed	cautioned
+ ing	cautioning
+ ous	cautious
+ ly	cautiously
+ ness	cautiousness
cave	
+ s	caves
+ ed	caved
+ ing	caving
+ er	caver*
+ ity	cavity*
+ man	caveman*
cease	
+ s	ceases
+ ed	ceased
+ ing	ceasing
+ tion	cessation
+ less	ceaseless
+ ly	ceaselessly
+ ness	ceaselessness
ceiling	
+ s	ceilings
+ ed	ceilinged
celebrate	
+ s	celebrates
+ ed	celebrated
+ ing	celebrating
+ ant	celebrant*
+ tion	celebration*
+ or	celebrator*
+ ory	celebratory
+ ness	celebratedness
+ ity	celebrity*
celery*	
cell	
+ s	cells
+ ed	celled
+ ar	cellular
cellar	
+ s	cellars
+ age	cellarage
+ er	cellarer
cemetery*	
cent*	
center	
+ s	centers
+ ed	centered
+ ing	centering
+ al	central
+ ly	centrally
+ al + ism	centralism
+ al + ist	centralist*

+ ist + ic	centralistic
+ ity	centrality*
+ ize	centralize
+ ize + s	centralizes
+ ize + ed	centralized
+ ize + ing	centralizing
+ tion	centralization
+ ize + er	centralizer*
+ ism	centrism
+ ic	centric
+ ic + al + ly	centrically
+ ic + al + ity	centricality
+ ist	centrist*
centigrade	
centigram*	
centimeter*	
century*	
cereal (2)*	
ceremony	
+ s	ceremonies
+ al	ceremonial
+ ous	ceremonious
+ ly	ceremoniously
+ ness	ceremoniousness
certain	
+ ly	certainly
+ y	certainty
+ y + s	certainties
certify	
+ s	certifies
+ ed	certified
+ ing	certifying
+ able	certifiable
+ ly	certifiably
+ ate	certificate*
+ ate + ed	certificated
+ ate + ing	certificating
+ er	certifier*
+ ory	certificatory
+ tion	certification*
chain	
+ s	chains
+ ed	chained
+ ing	chaining
chair	
+ s	chairs
+ ed	chaired
+ ing	chairing
+ man	chairman*
+ person	chairperson
+ woman	chairwoman*
chalk	
+ s	chalks
+ ed	chalked
+ ing	chalking

+ y	chalky
+ board	chalkboard*
challenge	
+ s	challenges
+ ed	challenged
+ ing	challenging
+ ly	challengingly
+ er	challenger*
champ	
+ s	champs
+ ed	champed
champion	
+ s	champions
+ ed	championed
+ ing	championing
+ ship	championship*
chance	
+ s	chances
+ ed	chanced
+ ing	chancing
change	
+ s	changes
+ ed	changed
+ ing	changing
+ able	changeable
+ ity	changeability
+ ness	changeableness
+ ly	changeably
+ er	changer*
+ ful	changeful
+ ful + ly	changefully
+ ful + ness	changefulness
+ less	changeless
+ less + ly	changelessly
+ less + ness	changelessness
channel	
+ s	channels
+ ed	channeled
+ ing	channeling
+ ion	channelion
chant	
+ s	chants
+ ed	chanted
+ ing	chanting
+ er	chanter*
+ ess	chanteress*
chapter*	
character	
+ s	characters
+ ful	characterful
+ ic	characteristic
+ ly	charactistically
+ ize	characterize
+ ize + s	characterizes
+ ed	characterized

+ ing	characterizing
+ tion	characterization*
+ y	charactery*
charity*	
charm	
+ s	charms
+ ed	charmed
+ ing	charming
+ er	charmer*
+ less	charmless
chart	
+ s	charts
+ ed	charted
+ ing	charting
+ er	charter*
+ er + ed	chartered
+ er + ing	chartering
+ ist	chartist*
chase	
+ s	chases
+ ed	chased
+ ing	chasing
+ er	chaser*
chat	
+ s	chats
+ ed	chatted
+ ing	chatting
chatter	
+ s	chatters
+ ed	chattered
+ ing	chattering
+ er	chatterer*
+ box	chatterbox*
cheap	
+ en	cheapen
+ s	cheapens
+ ed	cheapened
+ ing	cheapening
+ er	cheaper
+ est	cheapest
+ ish	cheapish
+ ish + ly	cheapishly
+ ly	cheaply
+ ness	cheapness
+ y	cheapie*
cheat (2)	
+ s	cheats
+ ed	cheated
+ ing	cheating
+ er	cheater*
check	
+ s	checks
+ ed	checked
+ ing	checking

+ able	checkable
+ er	checker*
+ er + ed	checkered
+ er + ing	checkering
+ board	checkerboard*
+ less	checkless
+ list	checklist*
+ off	checkoff
+ out	checkout
+ point	checkpoint*
+ room	checkroom*
+ row	checkrow*
+ up	checkup*
cheek	
+ s	cheeks
+ ed	cheeked
+ ing	cheeking
+ y	cheeky
+ er	cheekier
+ est	cheekiest
+ ly	cheekily
+ ness	cheekiness
+ bone	cheekbone*
cheer	
+ s	cheers
+ ed	cheered
+ ing	cheering
+ ful	cheerful
+ ly	cheerfully
+ ness	cheerfulness
+ less	cheerless
+ less + ly	cheerlessly
+ less + ness	cheerlessness
+ y	cheery
+ er	cheerier
+ est	cheeriest
+ y + ness	cheeriness
+ lead	cheerlead^
+ lead + er	cheerleader*
cheese	
+ s	cheeses
+ ed	cheesed
+ ing	cheesing
+ y	cheesy
+ er	cheesier
+ est	cheesiest
+ ness	cheesiness
+ cake	cheesecake*
+ cloth	cheesecloth*
+ make + ing	cheesemaking
+ make + er	cheesemaker*
chemistry	
+ s	chemistries
+ ist	chemist*

+ al	chemical
+ ly	chemically
cherry	
+ s	cherries
+ like	cherrylike
+ stone	cherrystone*
chess	
+ board	chessboard*
+ man	chessman*
chest	
+ s	chests
+ ed	chested
+ ful	chestful*
+ y	chesty
+ er	chestier
+ est	chestiest
chew	
+ s	chews
+ ed	chewed
+ ing	chewing
+ able	chewable
+ er	chewer*
+ y	chewy
+ y + er	chewier
+ est	chewiest
Chicago	
+ an	Chicagoan*
chick*	
chicken	
+ s	chickens
+ heart + ed	chickenhearted
+ liver + ed	chickenlivered
chief	
+ s	chiefs
+ dom	chiefdom*
+ ly	chiefly
+ ship	chiefship
child	
+ hood	childhood*
+ ish	childish
+ ly	childishly
+ ness	childishness
+ like	childlike
+ less	childless
+ less + ness	childlessness
+ bear + ing	childbearing
+ bed	childbed
+ birth	childbirth
children	
chill	
+ s	chills
+ ed	chilled
+ ing	chilling
+ er	chiller*
+ ly	chillingly

+ ness	chillness
+ y	chilly
+ y + er	chillier
+ est	chilliest
+ est + ly	chilliestly
chime	
+ s	chimes
+ ed	chimed
+ ing	chiming
chimney	
+ s	chimneys
+ piece	chimneypiece*
chin	
+ s	chins
+ ed	chinned
+ ing	chinning
+ less	chinless
China (china)	
+ ese	Chinese
+ man	Chinaman*
+ town	Chinatown*
+ s	chinas
+ berry	chinaberry*
+ ware	chinaware
chip	
+ s	chips
+ ed	chipped
+ ing	chipping
+ er	chipper*
+ board	chipboard
chipmunk*	
chiropractor	
+ s	chiropractors
+ ic	chiropractic
chocolate	
+ y	chocolaty
choice	
+ s	choices
+ er	choicer
+ est	choicest
+ ly	choicely
+ ness	choiceness
choir	
+ s	choirs
+ boy	choirboy*
+ master	choirmaster*
choke	
+ s	chokes
+ ed	choked
+ ing	choking
+ er	choker*
+ ly	chokingly
+ y	choky
choose	
+ s	chooses

+ ed	chose
+ en	chosen
+ ing	choosing
+ er	chooser*
+ y	choosey
+ y + er	choosier
+ est	choosiest
chop	
+ s	chops
+ ed	chopped
+ ing	chopping
+ er	chopper*
+ y	choppy
+ y + er	choppier
+ est	choppiest
+ ness	choppiness
+ house	chophouse*
+ stick	chopstick*
chord	
+ s	chords
+ ed	chorded
+ ing	chording
+ al	chordal
chore*	
chorus*	
Christ	
+ s	Christs
+ an	Christian*
+ ity	Christianity
+ en	christen
+ en + s	christens
+ ed	christened
+ ing	christening
+ ize	Christianize
+ ize + s	Christianizes
+ ize + ed	Christianized
+ ize + ing	Christianizing
+ er	Christianizer
+ tion	Christianization
+ like	Christlike
+ ly	Christly
Christmas* (2)	
chubby	
+ er	chubbier
+ est	chubbiest
+ ly	chubbily
chuckle	
+ s	chuckles
+ ed	chuckled
+ ing	chuckling
+ ing + ly	chucklingly
+ some	chucklesome
church	
+ s	churches
+ ed	churched
+ ing	churching
+ less	churchless
+ ly	churchly
+ ness	churchliness
+ y	churchy
+ er	churchier
+ est	churchiest
+ go + er	churchgoer*
+ go + ing	churchgoing
+ man	churchman*
+ man + ship	churchmanship
+ woman	churchwoman*
+ yard	churchyard*
cider*	
cigar*	
cigarette*	
cinnamon	
+ ic	cinnamonic
circle	
+ s	circles
+ ed	circled
+ ing	circling
+ er	circler*
+ ity	circuity*
+ al + ar	circular
+ ly	circularly
+ ness	circularness
+ ity	circularity
+ ize	circularize^
+ ate	circulate^
+ tion	circulation
+ ory	circulatory
circuit	
+ s	circuits
+ al	circuital
+ ous	circuitous
+ ly	circuitously
+ ness	circuitousness
+ ery	circuitry*
circumstance	
+ s	circumstances
+ ed	circumstanced
+ al	circumstantial
+ ity	circumstantiality
+ ly	circumstantially
+ ate	circumstantiate^
circus	
+ s	circuses
+ y	circusy
cite	
+ s	cites
+ ed	cited
+ ing	citing
+ able	citeable

citizen	
+ s	citizens
+ ess	citizeness*
+ ly	citizenly
+ ery	citizenry
+ ship	citizenship
city*	
civil	
+ an	civilian*
+ an + ize	civilianize^
+ an **+ tion**	civilianization*
+ ity	civility
+ ize	civilize^
+ able	civilizable
+ er	civilizer*
+ tion	civilization*
+ ly	civilly
claim	
+ s	claims
+ ed	claimed
+ ing	claiming
+ able	claimable
+ er	claimer*
+ ant	claimant*
clam	
+ s	clams
+ ed	clammed
+ ing	clamming
+ bake	clambake*
clap	
+ s	claps
+ ed	clapped
+ ing	clapping
+ er	clapper*
clash	
+ s	clashes
+ ed	clashed
+ ing	clashing
+ er	clasher*
class	
+ s	classes
+ ed	classed
+ ing	classing
+ ic	classic
+ ism	classicism
+ ist	classicist*
+ ist + ic	classicistic
+ ize	classicize^
+ al	classical
+ ly	classically
+ al + ism	classicalism
+ al + ist	classicalist*
+ ity	classicality
+ ify	classify^
+ ify + er	classifier*
+ able	classifiable
+ able + ly	classifiably
+ ory	classificatory
+ tion	classification*
+ less	classless
+ ness	classlessness
+ y	classy
+ er	classier
+ est	classiest
+ mate	classmate*
+ room	classroom*
clause	
+ s	clauses
+ al	clausal
claw	
+ s	claws
+ ed	clawed
+ ing	clawing
clay	
+ s	clays
+ ish	clayish
+ y	clayey
+ pan	claypan
+ ware	clayware
clean	
+ s	cleans
+ ed	cleaned
+ ing	cleaning
+ able	cleanable
+ er	cleaner*
+ est	cleanest
+ ly	cleanly
+ ly + ness	cleanliness
+ ly + er	cleanlier
+ ly + est	cleanliest
+ ness	cleanness
+ up	cleanup
clear	
+ s	clears
+ ed	cleared
+ ing	clearing*
+ able	clearable
+ ance	clearance*
+ er	clearer*
+ ly	clearly
+ ness	clearness
+ head + ed	clearheaded
clever	
+ ly	cleverly
+ ness	cleverness
+ ish	cleverish
client	
+ s	clients

C

+ age	clientage
+ al	cliental
climate	
+ s	climates
+ ic	climatic
+ ly	climatically
climax	
+ s	climaxes
+ ed	climaxed
+ ing	climaxing
+ ic	climactic
+ er + ic	climacteric
climb	
+ s	climbs
+ ed	climbed
+ ing	climbing
+ able	climbable
+ er	climber*
clinic	
+ s	clinics
+ al	clinical
+ ly	clinically
+ an	clinician*
clip	
+ s	clips
+ ed	clipped
+ ing	clipping
+ er	clipper*
+ board	clipboard*
clock	
+ s	clocks
+ ed	clocked
+ ing	clocking
+ er	clocker*
+ like	clocklike
+ wise	clockwise
+ work	clockwork
close	
+ ly	closely
+ er	closer
+ est	closest
+ ness	closeness
close (verb)	
+ s	closes
+ ed	closed
+ ing	closing*
+ er	closer*
+ able	closeable
+ ure	closure*
+ out	closeout*
closet	
+ s	closets
+ ful	closetful*
cloth	
+ s	cloths
+ e	clothe
+ e + s	clothes
+ ed	clothed
+ ing	clothing
+ horse	clotheshorse*
+ line	clothesline*
+ pin	clothespin*
+ press	clothespress*
+ er	clothier*
cloud	
+ s	clouds
+ ed	clouded
+ ing	clouding
+ less	cloudless
+ less + ly	cloudlessly
+ less + ness	cloudlessness
+ y	cloudy
+ er	cloudier
+ est	cloudiest
+ y + ly	cloudily
+ y + ness	cloudiness
clover*	
clown	
+ s	clowns
+ ed	clowned
+ ing	clowning
+ ery	clownery
+ ish	clownish
+ ly	clownishly
+ ness	clownishness
club	
+ s	clubs
+ ed	clubbed
+ ing	clubbing
+ able	clubable
+ er	clubber*
+ y	clubby
+ y + er	clubbier
+ est	clubbiest
+ ness	clubbiness
clue	
+ s	clues
+ ed	clued
+ ing	clueing
clumsy	
+ er	clumsier
+ est	clumsiest
+ ly	clumsily
+ ness	clumsiness
cluster	
+ s	clusters
+ ed	clustered
+ ing	clustering

clutch

+ s	clutches
+ ed	clutched
+ ing	clutching

coach

+ s	coaches
+ ed	coached
+ ing	coaching
+ er	coacher*
+ man	coachman*

coal

+ s	coals
+ ed	coaled
+ ing	coaling
+ er	coaler*
+ ify	coalify^
+ tion	coalification
+ field	coalfield*
+ hole	coalhole*

coarse

+ en	coarsen
+ s	coarsens
+ ed	coarsened
+ ing	coarsening
+ er	coarser
+ est	coarsest
+ ly	coarsely
+ ness	coarseness

coast

+ s	coasts
+ ed	coasted
+ ing	coasting
+ al	coastal
+ er	coaster*
+ guard	coastguard*
+ line	coastline*
+ land	coastland*
+ ward	coastward
+ wise	coastwise

coat

+ s	coats
+ ed	coated
+ ing	coating
+ er	coater*
+ dress	coatdress*
+ room	coatroom*
+ tail	coattail*

coax

+ s	coaxes
+ ed	coaxed
+ ing	coaxing

cocoa

coconut*

cocoon

+ s	cocoons
+ ed	cocooned
+ ing	cocooning

code

+ s	codes
+ ed	coded
+ ing	coding
+ able	codeable
+ er	coder*
+ less	codeless

coffee

+ s	coffees
+ house	coffeehouse*
+ pot	coffeepot*

cohesive

+ ion	cohesion
+ less	cohesiveless
+ ly	cohesively
+ ness	cohesiveness
+ s	coheres
+ ed	cohered
+ ing	cohering
+ ent	coherent
+ ent + ly	coherently
+ ence	coherence
+ ency + y	coherency

coin

+ s	coins
+ ed	coined
+ ing	coining
+ age	coinage
+ er	coiner*

coincide

+ s	coincides
+ ed	coincided
+ ing	coinciding
+ ence	coincidence*
+ ent	coincident
+ ly	coincidently
+ al	coincidental
+ al + ly	coincidentally

coke*

cold

+ s	colds
+ er	colder
+ est	coldest
+ ish	coldish
+ ly	coldly
+ ness	coldness
+ heart + ed	coldhearted

cole slaw

collapse

+ s	collapses

C

+ ed	collapsed
+ ing	collapsing
+ ible	collapsible
+ ity	collapsibility
collar	
+ s	collars
+ ed	collared
+ ing	collaring
+ less	collarless
+ bone	collarbone*
colleague	
+ s	colleagues
+ ship	colleagueship
collect	
+ s	collects
+ ed	collected
+ ing	collecting
+ ed + ly	collectedly
+ ness	collectedness
+ ible	collectible*
+ ion	collection*
+ ive	collective*
+ ive + ly	collectively
+ ity	collectivity
+ ism	collectivism
+ ist	collectivist*
+ ic	collectivistic
+ al + ly	collectivistically
+ ize	collectivize^
+ ive + tion	collectivization
+ or	collector*
college	
+ s	colleges
+ al	collegial
+ al + ly	collegially
+ ity	collegiality
+ an	collegian*
+ ate	collegiate
+ ate + ly	collegiately
colony	
+ s	colonies
+ al	colonial
+ ism	colonialism
+ al + ist	colonialist*
+ ic	colonialistic
+ ly	colonially
+ ness	colonialness
+ al + ize	colonialize^
+ ize	colonize^
+ er	colonizer*
+ tion	colonization*
+ ist	colonist*
color	
+ s	colors
+ ed	colored
+ ing	coloring
+ er	colorer*
+ tion	coloration*
+ able	colorable
+ able + ly	colorably
+ ful	colorful
+ ful + ly	colorfully
+ ful + ness	colorfulness
+ ism	colorism
+ ist	colorist*
+ ic	coloristic
+ ic + ly	coloristically
+ less	colorless
+ less + ness	colorlessness
Colorado	
+ an	Coloradoan*
colt	
+ s	colts
+ ish	coltish
+ ness	coltishness
+ ly	coltishly
column	
+ s	columns
+ ed	columned
+ ar	columnar
+ ist	columnist*
+ ic	columnistic
+ tion	columniation
comb	
+ s	combs
+ ed	combed
+ ing	combing
+ er	comber*
+ like	comblike
combine	
+ s	combines
+ ed	combined
+ ing	combining
+ able	combinable
+ ity	combinability
+ ate	combinate^
+ tion	combination*
+ tion + al	combinational
+ ive	combinative
+ ory	combinatory
+ ory + al	combinatorial
+ ic + s	combinatorics
come	
+ s	comes
+ ed	came
+ ing	coming
+ er	comer*
+ ly	comely
+ back	comeback*
+ down	comedown*

comfort	
+ s	comforts
+ ed	comforted
+ ing	comforting
+ able	comfortable
+ ly	comfortably
+ ness	comfortableness
+ er	comforter*
comic	
+ al	comical
+ ly	comically
+ s	comics
comma*	
command	
+ s	commands
+ ed	commanded
+ ing	commanding
+ ly	commandingly
+ able	commandable
+ ant	commandant*
+ er	commander*
+ ery	commandery*
+ ship	commandership*
+ ee + er	commandeer^
+ ment	commandment*
+ o	commando*
commandment*	
commence	
+ s	commences
+ ed	commenced
+ ing	commencing
+ er	commencer*
+ ment	commencement*
commerce	
commercial	
+ s	commercials
+ ly	commercially
+ ism	commercialism
+ ist	commercialist*
+ ic	commercialistic
+ ize	commercialize^
+ tion	commercialization
commission	
+ s	commissions
+ ed	commissioned
+ ing	commissioning
+ er	commissioner*
commit	
+ s	commits
+ ed	committed
+ ing	committing
+ able	committable
+ al	commital*
+ ment	commitment*

committee	
+ s	committees
+ man*	committeeman
+ woman	committeewoman*
common	
+ s	commons
+ age	commonage*
+ ity	commonality*
+ er	commoner*
+ ly	commonly
+ ness	commonness
+ place	commonplace
communicate	
+ s	communicates
+ ed	communicated
+ ing	communicating
+ able	communicable
+ able + ness	communicableness
+ ity	communicability
+ able + ly	communicably
+ ant	communicant*
+ ee	communicatee*
+ tion	communication*
+ tive	communicative
+ tive + ly	communicatively
+ tive + ness	communicativeness
+ or	coommunicator*
+ ory	communicatory
communist	
+ s	communists
+ ic	communistic
+ ism	communism
+ ly	communistically
+ ize	communize*
+ tion	communization
community	
+ s	community
+ wide	communitywide
commute	
+ s	commutes
+ ed	commuted
+ ing	commuting
+ able	commutable
+ er	commuter*
+ ate	commutate*
+ tion	commutation*
+ ive	commutative
+ ity	commutativity
+ ate + or	commutator*
compact	
+ s	compacts
+ ed	compacted
+ ing	compacting
+ er	compacter*

+ ible	compactible
+ ly	compactly
+ ness	compactness
+ tion	compaction
company*	
compare	
+ s	compares
+ ed	compared
+ ing	comparing
+ able	comparable
+ ity	comparability
+ able + ly	comparably
+ able + ness	comparableness
+ ist	comparatist*
+ ate + or	comparator*
+ sion	comparison*
+ ive	comparative
+ ive + ly	comparatively
+ ive + ness	comparativeness
+ ive + ist	comparativist*
compass	
+ s	compasses
+ ed	compassed
+ ing	compassing
+ able	compassable
compassion	
+ ate	compassionate^
+ ly	compassionately
+ ate + less	compassionateless
+ ness	compassionateness
+ less	compassionless
compel	
+ s	compels
+ ed	compelled
+ ing	compelling
+ er	compeller*
+ able	compellable
compete	
+ s	competes
+ ed	competed
+ ing	competing
+ ence	competence
+ y	competency*
+ tion	competition*
+ ive	competitive
+ ly	competitively
+ ness	competitiveness
+ or	competitor*
+ ory	competitory
competent	
+ ly	competently
complain	
+ s	complains
+ ed	complained
+ ing	complaining
+ ly	complainingly
+ ant	complainant*
+ er	complainer*
+ t	complaint*
complete	
+ s	completes
+ ed	completed
+ ing	completing
+ er	completer*
+ ly	completely
+ ness	completeness
+ ive	completive
+ tion	completion*
complex	
+ ly	complexly
+ ness	complexness
+ ity	complexity*
+ ion	complexion
+ al	complexional
+ ed	complexioned
+ ate + tion	complexation
complicate	
+ s	complicates
+ ed	complicated
+ ing	complicating
+ ly	complicatedly
+ ness	complicatedness
+ tion	complication*
+ y	complicacy*
compliment	
+ s	compliments
+ ed	complimented
+ ing	complimenting
+ ary	complimentary
+ ly	complimentarily
component	
+ s	components
+ al	componential
compose	
+ s	composes
+ ed	composed
+ ing	composing
+ ed + ly	composedly
+ ness	composedness
+ er	composer*
+ ite	composite*^
+ ite + ly	compositely
+ tion	composition*
+ al	compositional
+ al + ly	compositionally
+ ite + or	compositor*
+ ure	composure*

compound	
+ s	compounds
+ ed	compounded
+ ing	compounding
+ er	compounder*
comprehend	
+ s	comprehends
+ ed	comprehended
+ ing	comprehending
+ ible	comprehensible
+ ity	comprehensibility
+ ible + ly	comprehensibly
+ ible + ness	comprehensibleness
+ sion	comprehension*
+ ive	comprehensive
+ ive + ly	comprehensively
+ ive + ness	comprehensiveness
compromise	
+ s	compromises
+ ed	compromised
+ ing	compromising
+ er	compromiser*
compute	
+ s	computes
+ ed	computed
+ ing	computing
+ able	computable
+ ity	computability
+ ate + tion	computation*
+ al	computational
+ er	computer*
+ ese	computerese
+ ize	computerize
+ ize + able	computerizable
+ ize + tion	computerization
con	
+ s	cons
+ ed	conned
+ ing	conning
conceal	
+ s	conceals
+ ed	concealed
+ ing	concealing
+ able	concealable
+ er	concealer*
+ ly	concealingly
+ ment	concealment*
concede	
+ s	concedes
+ ed	conceded
+ ing	conceding
+ ed + ly	concededly
+ er	conceder*
+ sion	concession*
+ al	concessional
+ ary	concessionary
+ sion + er	concessioner*
+ ive	concessive
+ ive + ly	concessively
conceit	
+ s	conceits
+ ed	conceited
+ ly	conceitedly
+ ness	conceitedness
concentrate	
+ s	concentrates
+ ed	concentrated
+ ing	concentrating
+ ive	concentrative
+ or	concentrator*
+ tion	concentration*
concept	
+ s	concepts
+ tion	conception*
+ tion + al	conceptional
+ ive	conceptive
+ al	conceptual
+ ity	conceptuality
+ ly	conceptually
+ ism	conceptualism
+ ist	conceptualist
+ ic	conceptualistic
+ ize	conceptualize^
+ er	conceptualizer*
+ ize + tion	conceptualization*
concern	
+ s	concerns
+ ed	concerned
+ ing	concerning
+ ment	concernment*
concrete	
+ s	concretes
+ ed	concreted
+ ing	concreting
+ ly	concretely
+ ness	concreteness
+ ion	concretion*
+ ary	concretionary
+ ism	concretism
+ ist	concretist*
+ ize	concretize^
+ ize + tion	concretization*
condense	
+ s	condenses
+ ed	condensed
+ ing	condensing
+ able	condenseable
+ ate	condensate*

C

+ er	condenser*
+ tion	condensation
+ al	condensational
condition	
+ s	conditions
+ ed	conditioned
+ ing	conditioning
+ able	conditionable
+ al	conditional*
+ ity	conditionality
+ ly	conditionally
+ er	conditioner*
condominium (2)	
+ s	condominiums
+ al	condominial
conduct	
+ s	conducts
+ ed	conducted
+ ing	conducting
+ ible	conductible
+ ible + ity	conductibility
+ ance	conductance
+ tion	conduction
+ ive	conductive
+ ive + ity	conductivity*
+ or	conductor*
+ al	conductorial
+ ess	conductress*
cone	
+ s	cones
+ ed	coned
+ ing	coning
+ ic	conic
+ al	conical
+ ly	conically
+ ness	conicalness
+ ity	conicity
confederate	
+ s	confederates
+ ed	confederated
+ ing	confederating
+ y	confederacy*
+ al	confederal
+ ist	confederalist*
+ tion	confederation*
confess	
+ s	confesses
+ ed	confessed
+ ing	confessing
+ ed + ly	confessedly
+ able	confessable
+ ion	confession*
+ al	confessional*
+ ism	confessionalism
+ ist	confessionalist
+ al + ly	confessionally
+ or	confessor*
confident	
+ al	confidential
+ ity	confidentiality*
+ al + ly	confidentially
+ ness	confidentialness
+ ly	confidently
+ ence	confidence*
confirm	
+ s	confirms
+ ed	confirmed
+ ing	confirming
+ ly	confirmedly
+ ness	confirmedness
+ able	confirmable
+ ity	confirmability
+ tion	confirmation*
+ al	confirmational
+ ory	confirmatory
conflict	
+ s	conflicts
+ ed	conflicted
+ ing	conflicting
+ ly	conflictingly
+ ful	conflictful
+ less	conflictless
+ al	conflictual
+ ion	confliction
+ ive	conflictive
confront	
+ s	confronts
+ ed	confronted
+ ing	confronting
+ al	confrontal
+ er	confronter*
+ tion	confrontation*
+ tion + al	confrontational
+ ism	confrontationism
+ ist	confrontationist*
confuse	
+ s	confuses
+ ed	confused
+ ing	confusing
+ ed + ly	confusedly
+ ing + ly	confusingly
+ ness	confusedness
+ ion	confusion*
congratulate	
+ s	congratulates
+ ed	congratulated
+ ing	congratulating
+ or	congratulator*
+ ory	congratulatory
+ tion	congratulation*

congress	
+ s	congresses
+ al	congressional
+ ly	congressionally
+ man	congressman*
+ woman	congresswoman*
conjunction	
+ s	conjunctions
+ al	conjunctional
+ al + ly	conjunctionally
+ ive	conjunctive
+ ive + ly	conjunctively
+ ure	conjuncture*
connect	
+ s	connects
+ ed	connected
+ ing	connecting
+ ed + ly	connectedly
+ **ness**	connectedness
+ ion	connection*
+ al	connectional
+ ive	connective
+ ive + ly	connectively
+ ity	connectivity
conquer	
+ s	conquers
+ ed	conquered
+ ing	conquering
+ or	conqueror*
+ t	conquest*
conscience	
+ s	consciences
+ less	conscienceless
+ ous	conscientious
+ ly	conscientiously
+ ness	conscienctousness
conscious	
+ ly	consciously
+ ness	consciousness
conserve	
+ s	conserves
+ ed	conserved
+ ing	conserving
+ y	conservancy
+ tion	conservation
+ tion + al	conservational
+ ist	conservationist
+ ism	conservatism
+ ive	conservative*
+ ly	conservatively
+ ness	conservativeness
+ ize	conservatize^
+ or	conservator*
+ ory	conservatory*
+ ory + al	conservatorial

consider	
+ s	considers
+ ed	considered
+ ing	considering
+ able	considerable
+ able + ly	considerably
+ ate	considerate
+ ate + ly	considerately
+ ness	considerateness
+ tion	consideration*
consistent	
+ ly	consistently
console	
+ s	consoles
+ ed	consoled
+ ing	consoling
+ ly	consolingly
+ tion	consolation
+ ory	concilatory
consonant	
+ s	consonants
+ al	consonantal
+ ly	consonantly
+ ance	consonance
+ y	consonancy
constant	
+ ly	constantly
+ y	constancy
constellation	
+ s	constellations
+ ory	constellatory
constipate	
+ s	constipates
+ ed	constipated
+ ing	constipating
+ ion	constipation
constitute	
+ s	constitutes
+ ed	constituted
+ ing	constituting
+ ent	constituent*
+ ent + ly	constituently
+ y	constituency*
+ tion	constitution*
+ al	constitutional
+ ism	constitutionalism
+ ist	constitutionalist*
+ ity	constitutionality
+ ize	constitutionalize^
+ al + ly	constitutionally
+ less	constitutionless
+ ive	constitutive
+ ive + ly	constitutively
construct	
+ s	constructs

+ ed	constructed
+ ing	constructing
+ ible	constructible
+ ion	construction*
+ al	constructional
+ al + ly	constructionally
+ ist	constructionist*
+ ive	constructive
+ ive + ly	constructively
+ ness	constructiveness
+ ism	constructivism
+ ive + ist	constructivist*
+ or	constructor
consult	
+ s	consults
+ ed	consulted
+ ing	consulting
+ y	consultancy
+ ant	consultant*
+ ship	consultantship
+ er	consulter*
+ tion	consultation*
+ ive	consultative
consume	
+ s	consumes
+ ed	consumed
+ ing	consuming
+ ed + ly	consumedly
+ ing + ly	consumingly
+ er	consumer*
+ ism	consumerism
+ ist	consumerist
contact	
+ s	contacts
+ ed	contacted
+ ing	contacting
contagious	
+ ion	contagion
+ ly	contagiously
+ ness	contagiousness
contain	
+ s	contains
+ ed	contained
+ ing	containing
+ able	containable
+ er	container*
+ ize	containerize^
+ tion	containerization
+ ment	containment
+ ship	containership*
content	
+ s	contents
+ ed	contented
+ ing	contenting

+ ly	contentedly
+ ness	contentedness
+ ment	contentment
contest	
+ s	contests
+ ed	contested
+ ing	contesting
+ able	contestable
+ ant	contestant*
+ er	contester
+ tion	contestation
continent	
+ s	continents
+ al	continental
+ al + ly	continentally
+ ly	continently
+ ence	continence
continue	
+ s	continues
+ ed	continued
+ ing	continuing
+ al	continual
+ al + ly	continually
+ ance	continuance
+ ant	continuant
+ ate	continuate
+ tion	continuation*
+ ive	continuative
+ ate + or	continuator
+ er	continuer
+ ity	continuity*
+ ous	continuous
+ ous + ly	continuously
+ ness	continuousness
contour	
+ s	contours
+ ed	contoured
+ ing	contouring
contract	
+ s	contracts
+ ed	contracted
+ ing	contracting
+ ible	contractible
+ ible + ity	contractibility
+ ile	contractile
+ ile + ity	contractility
+ ion	contraction*
+ ion + al	contractional
+ ive	contractive
+ or	contractor*
+ al	contractual
+ ly	contractually
+ ure	contracture*

contrast	
+ s	contrasts
+ ed	contrasted
+ ing	contrasting
+ able	contrastable
+ ive	contrastive
+ ly	contrastively
+ y	constrasty
contribute	
+ s	contributes
+ ed	contributed
+ ing	contributing
+ ion	contribution*
+ ive	contributive
+ ly	contributively
+ or	contributor*
+ ory	contributory
control	
+ s	controls
+ ed	controlled
+ ing	controlling
+ able	controllable
+ er	controller*
+ ship	controllership
+ ment	controlment
controversy	
+ s	controversies
+ al	controversial
+ ism	controversialism
+ ist	controversialist*
+ ly	controversially
convene	
+ s	convenes
+ ed	convened
+ ing	convening
+ er	convener*
+ tion	convention*
+ al	conventional
+ ism	conventionalism
+ ist	conventionalist*
+ ity	conventionality
+ ize	conventionalize^
+ ize + tion	conventionalization
+ ly	conventionally
+ tion + er	conventioneer*
convenient	
+ ly	conveniently
+ ence	convenience*
convention*	
converse	
+ s	converses
+ ed	conversed
+ ing	conversing
+ able	conversable
+ ant	conversant
+ ant + ly	conversantly
+ ance	conversance
+ er	converser*
+ ly	conversely
+ tion	conversation*
+ al	conversational
+ ist	conversationalist*
+ al + ly	conversationally
convert	
+ s	converts
+ ed	converted
+ ing	converting
+ er	converter*
+ ible	convertible
+ ily	convertibility
+ ness	convertibleness
+ ly	convertibly
+ sion	conversion*
+ al	conversional
convince	
+ s	convinces
+ ed	convinced
+ ing	convincing
+ ly	convincingly
+ ness	convincingness
+ er	convincer*
cook	
+ s	cooks
+ ed	cooked
+ ing	cooking
+ er	cooker*
+ ery	cookery
+ book	cookbook*
+ out	cookout*
+ shop	cookshop*
+ ware	cookware
cookie*	
cool	
+ s	cools
+ ed	cooled
+ ing	cooling
+ er	cooler
+ est	coolest
+ ant	coolant*
+ ish	coolish
+ ly	coolly
+ ness	coolness
+ head + ed	coolheaded
cooperate	
+ s	cooperates
+ ed	cooperated
+ ing	cooperating
+ er	cooperator

+ tion	cooperation
+ ive	cooperative
+ ly	cooperatively
+ ness	cooperativeness
copper	
+ s	coppers
+ ed	coppered
+ ing	coppering
+ y	coppery
+ head	copperhead*
+ plate	copperplate^
copy	
+ s	copies
+ ed	copied
+ ing	copying
+ er	copier*
+ ist	copyist*
+ book	copybook*
+ boy	copyboy*
+ cat	copycat*
+ desk	copydesk*
+ read + er	copyreader*
+ right	copyright*
+ write + er	copywriter*
cord	
+ s	cords
+ ed	corded
+ ing	cording
+ age	cordage
+ less	cordless
corduroy	
+ s	corduroys
+ ed	corduroyed
+ ing	corduroying
core	
+ s	cores
+ ed	cored
+ ing	coring
cork	
+ s	corks
+ ed	corked
+ ing	corking
+ er	corker*
+ y	corky
+ y + er	corkier
+ est	corkiest
+ board	corkboard*
+ screw	corkscrew*
corn	
+ s	corns
+ ed	corned
+ ing	corning
+ y	corny
+ er	cornier
+ est	corniest
+ ly	cornily
+ ness	corniness
+ ball	cornball*
+ field	cornfield*
+ flakes + s	cornflakes
+ flower	cornflower*
+ meal	cornmeal
corner	
+ s	corners
+ ed	cornered
+ ing	cornering
+ wise	cornerwise
+ way + s	cornerways
correct	
+ s	corrects
+ ed	corrected
+ ing	correcting
+ able	correctable
+ tion	correction*
+ al	correctional
+ ive	corrective
+ ive + ly	correctively
+ ive + ness	correctiveness
+ ly	correctly
+ ness	correctness
+ or	corrector*
correlate	
+ s	correlates
+ ed	correlated
+ ing	correlating
+ able	correlatable
+ tion	correlation
+ al	correlational
+ ive	correlative
+ ly	correlatively
correspond	
+ s	corresponds
+ ed	corresponded
+ ing	corresponding
+ ly	correspondingly
+ ence	correspondence
+ y	correspondency
+ ent	correspondent*
+ ive	corresponsive
cosmetic	
+ s	cosmetics
+ an	cosmetician*
cost	
+ s	costs
+ ing	costing
+ less	costless
+ less + ly	costlessly
+ ly	costly
+ er	costlier
+ est	costliest

+ ness	costliness
costume	
+ s	costumes
+ ed	costumed
+ ing	costuming
+ er	costumer*
+ ery	costumery
cotton	
+ s	cottons
+ ed	cottoned
+ ing	cottoning
+ y	cottony
+ mouth	cottonmouth*
+ seed	cottonseed*
+ tail	cottontail*
+ weed	cottonweed*
+ wood	cottonwood*
couch	
+ s	couches
+ ed	couched
+ ing	couching
+ ant	couchant
cough	
+ s	coughs
+ ed	coughed
+ ing	coughing
could (2)	
council	
+ s	councils
+ man	councilman*
+ woman	councilwoman*
+ or	councilor*
+ ship	councilorship
counsel	
+ s	counsels
+ ed	counseled
+ ing	counseling
+ or	counselor*
+ ship	counselorship
+ ee	counselee*
count	
+ s	counts
+ ed	counted
+ ing	counting
+ able	countable
+ ity	countability
+ able + ly	countably
+ er	counter*
+ ess	countess*
+ less	countless
+ less + ly	countlessly
counter	
+ s	counters
+ top	countertop*

country	
+ s	countries
+ ish	countryish
+ ed	countrified
+ man	countryman*
+ seat	countryseat*
+ side	countryside
+ woman	countrywoman*
county	
+ s	counties
+ an	countian*
couple	
+ s	couples
+ ed	coupled
+ ing	coupling
+ er	coupler*
+ ment	couplement
coupon*	
courage	
+ ous	courageous
+ ly	courageously
+ ness	courageousness
course	
+ s	courses
+ ed	coursed
+ ing	coursing
+ er	courser*
court	
+ s	courts
+ ed	courted
+ ing	courting
+ er	courtier*
+ ly	courtly
+ ly + er	courtlier
+ est	courtliest
+ room	courtroom*
+ ship	courtship
+ side	courtside
+ yard	courtyard*
courtesy*	
+ s	courtesies
+ ous	courteous
+ ous + ly	courteously
+ ness	courteousness
cousin	
+ s	cousins
+ age	cousinage
+ hood	cousinhood
+ ship	cousinship
cove	
+ s	coves
+ ed	coved
+ ing	coving

cover

+ s	covers
+ ed	covered
+ ing	covering
+ able	coverable
+ age	coverage
+ er	coverer*
+ less	coverless
+ ure	coverture
+ all	coverall*

C

cow

+ s	cows
+ ed	cowed
+ ing	cowing
+ bell	cowbell*
+ berry	cowberry*
+ bird	cowbird*
+ boy	cowboy*
+ catch + er	cowcatcher*
+ fish	cowfish
+ girl	cowgirl*
+ hand	cowhand*
+ herd	cowherd*
+ hide	cowhide*
+ lick	cowlick*
+ pony	cowpony*
+ pox	cowpox

coward

+ s	cowards
+ ice	cowardice
+ ly	cowardly
+ ness	cowardliness

cozy

+ s	cozies up
+ ed	cozied up
+ ing	cozying up
+ er	cozier
+ est	coziest
+ ly	cozily
+ ness	coziness

crab

+ s	crabs
+ ed	crabbed
+ ing	crabbing
+ ly	crabbedly
+ ness	crabbedness
+ er	crabber*
+ y	crabby
+ y + er	crabbier
+ est	crabbiest
+ grass	crabgrass
+stick	crabstick
+ wise	crabwise

crack

+ s	cracks
+ ed	cracked
+ ing	cracking
+ s + man	cracksman
+ back	crackback
+ brain	crackbrain
+ brain + ed	crackbrained
+ down	crackdown*
+ pot	crackpot*

cracker*

crackerjack*

cradle

+ s	cradles
+ ed	cradled
+ ing	cradling
+ song	cradlesong*

craft

+ s	crafts
+ ed	crafted
+ ing	crafting
+ y	crafty
+ er	craftier
+ est	craftiest
+ ly	craftily
+ ness	craftiness
+ s + man	craftsman*
+ s + woman	craftswoman*

crank

+ s	cranks
+ ed	cranked
+ ing	cranking
+ y	cranky
+ er	crankier
+ est	crankiest
+ ly	crankily
+ ness	crankiness

crash

+ s	crashes
+ ed	crashed
+ ing	crashing
+ worth + y	crashworthy
+ worth **+ ness**	crashworthiness

crawl

+ s	crawls
+ ed	crawled
+ ing	crawling
+ er	crawler*
+ y	crawly
+ way	crawlway*

crayon*

craze

+ s	crazes
+ ed	crazed
+ ing	crazing
+ y	crazy
+ er	crazier

+ est	craziest
+ ly	crazily
+ ness	craziness
+ weed	crazyweed
cream	
+ s	creams
+ ed	creamed
+ ing	creaming
+ er	creamer*
+ ery	creamery*
+ y	creamy
+ y + er	creamier
+ est	creamiest
+ ly	creamily
+ ness	creaminess
create	
+ s	creates
+ ed	created
+ ing	creating
+ ion	creation*
+ ive	creative
+ ive+ ly	creatively
+ ive + ness	creativeness
+ ity	creativity
+ or	creator*
+ ure	creature*
+ al	creatural
+ hood	creaturehood
+ ure + ly	creaturely
+ ure + ly + ness	creatureliness
credential*	
credit	
+ s	credits
+ ed	credited
+ ing	crediting
+ able	creditable
+ ness	creditableness
+ ity	creditability
+ ly	creditably
+ or	creditor*
creek*	
creep	
+ s	creeps
+ ed	crept
+ ing	creeping
+ age	creepage
+ er	creeper*
+ y	creepy
+ y + er	creepier
+ est	creepiest
+ ness	creepiness
crew	
+ s	crews
+ ed	crewed
+ ing	crewing
+ less	crewless
+ man	crewman*
crib	
+ s	cribs
+ ed	cribbed
+ ing	cribbing
+ age	cribbage
+ er	cribber*
cricket	
+ s	crickets
+ ed	cricketed
+ ing	cricketing
+ er	cricketer*
cried (2)	
crime	
+ s	crimes
+ al	criminal*
+ ate	criminate^
+ tion	crimination
+ ous	criminous
cripple	
+ s	cripples
+ ed	crippled
+ ing	crippling
+ er	crippler*
crisis*	
criteria	
critic	
+ s	critics
+ al	critical
+ ity	criticality
+ ly	critically
+ ness	criticalness
+ ism	criticism*
+ ize	criticize^
+ able	criticizable
+ er	criticizer*
crochet	
+ s	crochets
+ ed	crocheted
+ ing	crocheting
+ er	crocheter*
crocodile	
+ s	crocodiles
+ an	crocodilian
croissant*	
crooked	
+ ly	crookedly
+ ness	crookedness
crop	
+ s	crops

C

+ ed	cropped
+ ing	cropping
+ er	cropper*

croquet^

cross

+ s	crosses
+ ed	crossed
+ ing	crossing
+ ing + s	crossings
+ er	crosser*
+ able	crossable
+ ity	crossability
+ ly	crossly
+ ness	crossness
+ bar	crossbar*
+ bear + er	crossbearer*
+ bone + s	crossbones
+ bow	crossbow*
+ bow + man	crossbowman*
+ breed + ed	crossbred
+ breed	crossbreed*
+ court	crosscourt
+ current	crosscurrent*
+ cut	crosscut*^
+ hatch	crosshatch^
+ head	crosshead*
+ over	crossover*
+ patch	crosspatch*
+ piece	crosspiece*
+ road	crossroad*
+ town	crosstown
+ walk	crosswalk*
+ way	crossway*
+ way + s	crossways
+ wind	crosswind*
+ wise	crosswise
+ word	crossword*

crow^

crowd

+ s	crowds
+ ed	crowded
+ ing	crowding
+ ness	crowdedness

crown^

crucify

+ s	crucifies
+ ed	crucified
+ ing	crucifying
+ ion	crucifixion*

cruel

+ er	crueler
+ est	cruelest
+ ly	cruelly
+ ness	cruelness
+ y	cruelty*

crumb

+ s	crumbs
+ ed	crumbed
+ ing	crumbing
+ y	crumby
+ er	crumbier
+ est	crumbiest

crumble

+ s	crumbles
+ ed	crumbled
+ ing	crumbling
+ ing + s	crumblings
+ y	crumbly
+ er	crumblier
+ est	crumbliest
+ ness	crumbliness

crunch

+ s	crunches
+ ed	crunched
+ ing	crunching
+ er	cruncher
+ y	crunchy
+ y + er	crunchier
+ est	crunchiest
+ ness	crunchiness

crusade

+ s	crusades
+ ed	crusaded
+ ing	crusading
+ er	crusader*

crush

+ s	crushes
+ ed	crushed
+ ing	crushing
+ able	crushable
+ er	crusher*

crust

+ s	crusts
+ ed	crusted
+ ing	crusting
+ al	crustal
+ tion	crustification
+ y	crusty
+ er	crustier
+ est	crustiest
+ ly	crustily
+ ness	crustiness
+ an	crustacean

crutch*^

cry

+ s	cries
+ ed	cried
+ ing	crying
+ baby	crybaby*

crystal	
+ s	crystals
+ ine	crystaline
+ ity	crystalinity
+ ite	crystallite
+ ic	crystallitic
+ ize	crystalize^
+ able	crystalizable
+ tion	crystalization
+ er	crystalizer
+ ous	crystaliferous
cub*	
cube	
+ s	cubes
+ ed	cubed
+ ing	cubing
+ age	cubage
+ ic	cubic
+ ic + ly	cubicly
+ al	cubical*
+ al + ly	cubically
+ ism	cubism
+ ist	cubist*
+ ist + ic	cubistic
+ ure	cubature
cucumber*	
cuff	
+ s	cuffs
+ ed	cuffed
+ ing	cuffing
+ less	cuffless
culture	
+ s	cultures
+ ed	cultured
+ ing	culturing
+ al	cultural
+ ly	culturally
cup	
+ s	cups
+ ed	cupped
+ ing	cupping
+ ful	cupful*
+ like	cuplike
+ y	cuppy
+ er	cuppier
+ est	cuppiest
+ bear + er	cupbearer*
+ cake	cupcake*
cupboard*	
cupid*	
curb	
+ s	curbs
+ ed	curbed
+ ing	curbing
+ stone	curbstone*

cure	
+ s	cures
+ ed	cured
+ ing	curing
+ er	curer*
+ less	cureless
curious	
+ a	curiosa
+ ity	curiosity
+ ness	curiousness
+ ly	curiously
curl	
+ s	curls
+ ed	curled
+ ing	curling
+ er	curler*
+ y	curly
+ y + er	curlier
+ est	curliest
+ ness	curliness
+ paper	curlpaper*
current	
+ s	currents
+ ly	currently
+ ness	currentness
+ y	currency*
curriculum	
+ s	curriculums
+ ar	curricular
curse (2)	
+ s	curses
+ ed	cursed
+ ing	cursing
+ t	curst
+ ly	cursedly
+ ness	cursedness
curtain*^	
curve	
+ s	curves
+ ed	curved
+ ing	curving
+ ous	curvaceous
+ ure	curvature*
+ y	curvy
+ line + al	curvilineal
+ ball	curveball*
custard*	
custody	
+ s	custodies
+ al	custodial
+ an	custodian*
+ ship	custodianship
custom	
+ s	customs
+ ary	customary

+ ly	customarily
+ ness	customariness
+ er	customer*
+ ize	customize^
cut	
+ s	cuts
cute	
+ er	cuter
+ est	cutest
+ ly	cutely
+ ness	cuteness
+ y	cutesy
cycle	
+ s	cycles
+ ed	cycled
+ ing	cycling
+ ic	cyclic
+ al	cyclical
+ ly	cyclically
+ ist	cyclist*
+ ize	cyclize^
+ tion	cyclization
cyclone	
+ s	cyclones
+ ic	cyclonic
+ ly	cyclonically
cylinder	
+ s	cylinders
+ ed	cylindered
+ al	cylinderical
+ ly	cylinderically
cymbal	
+ s	cymbals
+ ist	cymbalist*

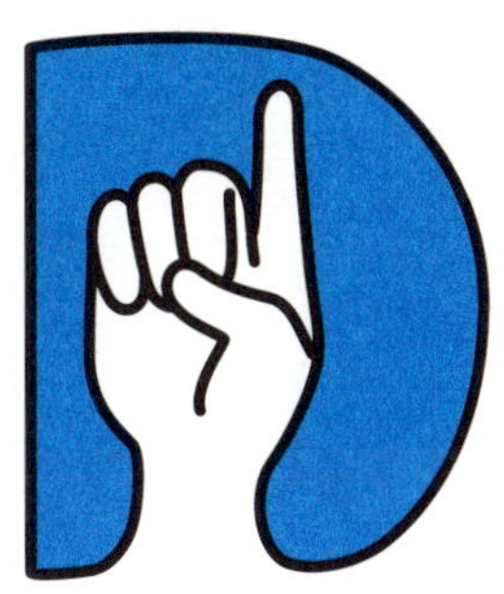

D

dad		
	+ s	dads
	+ y	daddy*
daffodil*		
daily*		
daisy*		
dam^		
damage		
	+ s	damages
	+ ed	damaged
	+ ing	damaging
	+ er	damager*
	+ ly	damagingly
damn		
	+ s	damns
	+ ed	damned
	+ ing	damning
	+ able	damnable
	+ ness	damnableness
	+ able + ly	damnably
	+ ify	damnify^
	+ tion	damnation
	+ ory	damnatory
	+ er	damneder
	+ est	damnedest
	+ ing + ly	damningly
damp		
	+ s	damps
	+ ed	damped
	+ ing	damping
	+ en	dampen*
	+ er	damper*
	+ ish	dampish
	+ ly	damply
	+ ness	dampness
dance		
	+ s	dances
	+ ed	danced
	+ ing	dancing
	+ able	danceable
	+ er	dancer*
dandelion*		

dandy		
	+ s	dandies
	+ er	dandier
	+ est	dandiest
	+ ify	dandify*
	+ tion	dandification
	+ ish	dandyish
	+ ly	dandyishly
	+ ism	dandism
danger		
	+ s	dangers
	+ ous	dangerous
	+ ly	dangerously
	+ ness	dangerousness
dare		
	+ s	dares
	+ ed	dared
	+ ing	daring
	+ er	darer*
	+ ly	daringly
	+ ness	daringness
	+ devil	daredevil*
	+ devil + ery	daredevilry
	+ say	daresay
dark		
	+ er	darker
	+ est	darkest
	+ ish	darkish
	+ ly	darkly
	+ ness	darkness
	+ en	darken^
	+ en + er	darkener
	+ y	darky*
	+ room	darkroom*
darling		
	+ s	darlings
	+ ly	darlingly
	+ ness	darlingness
dart		
	+ s	darts
	+ ed	darted
	+ ing	darting
	+ er	darter*

dash	
+ s	dashes
+ ed	dashed
+ ing	dashing
+ ly	dashingly
+ er	dasher*
date	
+ s	dates
+ ed	dated
+ ing	dating
+ able	dateable
+ ly	datedly
+ ness	datedness
+ er	dater
+ ive	dative
+ less	dateless
+ line	dateline*
daughter	
+ s	daughters
+ less	daughterless
+ in + law	daughter-in-law
dawn^	
day	
+ s	days
+ ly	daily*
+ bed	daybed*
+ book	daybook*
+ break	daybreak
+ dream	daydream*^
+ glow	dayglow
+ light	daylight
+ long	daylong
+ room	dayroom
+ star	daystar
+ time	daytime
dead	
+ en	deaden^
+ en + er	deadener*
+ ing + ly	deadeningly
+ ly	deadly
+ ly + er	deadlier
+ est	deadliest
+ ly + ness	deadliness
+ ness	deadness
+ beat	deadbeat*
+ eye	deadeye*
+ fall	deadfall*
+ head	deadhead*^
+ line	deadline*
+ lock	deadlock*^
+ pan	deadpan^
+ weight	deadweight
+ wood	deadwood
deaf (2)	
+ en	deafen^
+ ed	deafened
+ ing + ly	deafeningly
+ ly	deafly
+ ness	deafness
deal	
+ s	deals
+ ed	dealt
+ ing	dealing
+ er	dealer*
+ ship	dealership*
dear	
+ ly	dearly
+ ness	dearness
death	
+ less	deathless
+ less + ly	deathlessly
+ ness	deathlessness
+ ly	deathly
+ bed	deathbed
+ blow	deathblow
+ watch	deathwatch
debate	
+ s	debates
+ ed	debated
+ ing	debating
+ able	debatable
+ er	debater*
+ ment	debatement
debt	
+ s	debts
+ less	debtless
+ or	debtor*
decade*	
deceive	
+ s	deceives
+ ed	deceived
+ ing	deceiving
+ ing + ly	deceivingly
+ t	deceit*
+ ful	deceitful
+ ful + ly	deceitfully
+ ful + ness	deceitfulness
+ tion	deception*
+ al	deceptional
+ ive	deceptive
+ ive + ly	deceptively
+ ive + ness	deceptiveness
December (2)	
+ ist	Decemberist*
decent	
+ ly	decently
decide	
+ s	decides
+ ed	decided
+ ing	deciding

+ able	decidable
+ ity	decidability
+ ed + ly	decidedly
+ ed + ness	decidedness
+ er	decider*
+ ion	decision*
+ ive	decisive
+ ive + ly	decisively
+ ive + ness	decisiveness
decimal	
+ s	decimals
+ ly	decimally
+ ize	decimalize^
+ tion	decimalization
deck	
+ s	decks
+ ed	decked
+ ing	decking
+ er	decker*
+ hand	deckhand*
+ house	deckhouse*
declare	
+ s	declares
+ ed	declared
+ ing	declaring
+ able	declarable
+ ant	declarant*
+ er	declarer*
+ ory	declaratory
+ tion	declaration*
decode^	
decoder*	
decorate	
+ s	decorates
+ ed	decorated
+ ing	decorating
+ ion	decoration*
+ ive	decorative
+ ive + ly	decoratively
+ ive + ness	decorativeness
+ or	decorator*
+ ous	decorous
+ ous + ly	decorously
+ ous + ness	decorousness
decrease	
+ s	decreases
+ ed	decreased
+ ing	decreasing
+ ly	decreasingly
dedicate	
+ s	dedicates
+ ed	dedicated
+ ing	dedicating
+ ly	dedicatedly
+ ion	dedication*
+ ive	dedicative
+ or	dedicator*
+ ory	dedicatory
deduce	
+ s	deduces
+ ed	deduced
+ ing	deducing
+ ible	deducible
+ t	deduct^
+ t + ible	deductible
+ t **+ ity**	deductibility
+ ion	deduction*
+ ive	deductive
+ ly	deductively
deep	
+ ly	deeply
+ ness	deepness
+ en	deepen^
+ th	depth*
+ less	depthless
deer	
+ s	deers
+ skin	deerskin*
+ yard	deeryard
defeat	
+ s	defeats
+ ed	defeated
+ ing	defeating
+ ism	defeatism
+ ist	defeatist*
+ ance	defeasance
+ ible	defeasible
+ ity	defeasibility
defend	
+ s	defends
+ ed	defended
+ ing	defending
+ able	defendable
+ ant	defendant*
+ er	defender*
defense	
+ s	defenses
+ ed	defensed
+ ing	defensing
+ less	defenseless
+ less + ly	defenselessly
+ less + ness	defenselessness
+ ible	defensible
+ ity	defensibility
+ ible + ly	defensibly
+ ive	defensive
+ ive + ly	defensively
+ ive + ness	defensiveness
deficit	
+ s	deficits

D

+ ent	deficient*
+ ly	deficiently
+ y	deficiency*
define	
+ s	defines
+ ed	defined
+ ing	defining
+ able	definable
+ able + ly	definably
+ er	definer*
+ ment	definement
+ tion	definition*
+ al	definitional
definite	
+ ly	definitely
+ ness	definiteness
+ ive	definitive*
+ ive + ly	definitively
+ ive + ness	definitiveness
+ ize	definitize*
deflate	
+ s	deflates
+ ed	deflated
+ ing	deflating
+ or	deflator*
+ ion	deflation
+ ary	deflationary
defy	
+ s	defies
+ ed	defied
+ ing	defying
+ er	defier*
degenerate	
+ s	degenerates
+ ed	degenerated
+ ing	degenerating
+ ly	degenerately
+ ness	degenerateness
+ y	degeneracy*
+ ion	degeneration
+ ive	degenerative
degree	
+ s	degrees
+ ed	degreed
delay	
+ s	delays
+ ed	delayed
+ ing	delaying
+ er	delayer*
delegate (2)	
+ s	delegates
+ ed	delegated
+ ing	delegating
+ able	delegable

+ y	delegacy*
delicate	
+ y	delicacy*
+ ly	delicately
+ ness	delicateness
delicious	
+ ly	deliciously
+ ness	deliciousness
delight	
+ s	delights
+ ed	delighted
+ ing	delighting
+ er	delighter*
+ ed + ly	delightedly
+ ed + ness	delightedness
+ ful	delightful
+ ful + ly	delightfully
+ ful + ness	delightfulness
+ some	delightsome
+ some + ly	delightsomely
delinquent	
+ s	delinquents
+ y	delinquency*
+ ly	delinquently
deliver	
+ s	delivers
+ ed	delivered
+ ing	delivering
+ able	deliverable
+ ity	deliverability
+ er	deliverer*
+ ance	deliverance
+ y	delivery*
+ man	deliveryman*
demand	
+ s	demands
+ ed	demanded
+ ing	demanding
+ able	demandable
+ er	demander*
+ ant	demandant*
+ ly	demandingly
democrat	
+ s	democrats
+ y	democracy*
+ ic	democratic
+ ly	democratically
+ ize	democratize^
+ er	democratizer*
+ tion	democratization
demolish	
+ s	demolishes
+ ed	demolished
+ ing	demolishing
+ er	demolisher*

+ ment	demolishment
+ tion	demolition*
+ ist	demolitionist*
demon	
+ s	demons
+ ess	demoness*
+ an	demonian
+ ize	demonize^
+ tion	demonization
+ ic	demonic
+ al	demonical
+ ly	demonically
demonstrate	
+ s	demonstrates
+ ed	demonstrated
+ ing	demonstrating
+ able	demonstrable
+ ity	demonstrability
+ able + ness	demonstrableness
+ ion	demonstration*
+ al	demonstrational
+ ist	demonstrationist*
+ ive	demonstrative
+ ly	demonstratively
+ ive + ness	demonstrativeness
+ or	demonstrator*
demote	
+ s	demotes
+ ed	demoted
+ ing	demoting
+ tion	demotion*
den^	
Denmark (2)	
denominator*	
dentist	
+ s	dentists
+ al	dental
+ al + ly	dentally
+ y	dentistry
+ tion	dentition
+ ous	dentulous
+ ure	denture*
+ ate	dentate
+ ed	dentated
+ ate + ly	dentately
+ ate + tion	dentation
deny	
+ s	denies
+ ed	denied
+ ing	denying
+ ly	denyingly
deodorant	
+ s	deodorants
+ ize	deodorize^

depart	
+ s	departs
+ ed	departed
+ ing	departing
+ ure	departure*
department	
+ s	departments
+ al	departmental
+ ly	departmentally
+ ize	departmentalize*
+ tion	departmentalization
depend	
+ s	depends
+ ed	depended
+ ing	depending
+ able	dependable
+ ity	dependability
+ ness	dependableness
+ able + ly	dependably
+ ence	dependence
+ y	dependency*
+ ent	dependent*
+ ent + ly	dependently
deplete	
+ s	depletes
+ ed	depleted
+ ing	depleting
+ able	depletable
+ tion	depletion
+ ive	depletive
deposit	
+ s	deposits
+ ed	deposited
+ ing	depositing
+ or	depositor*
+ ary *or* + ory	depositary*, depository*
depreciate	
+ s	depreciates
+ ed	depreciated
+ ing	depreciating
+ able	depreciable
+ ly	depreciatingly
+ tion	depreciation
+ ive	depreciative
+ or	depreciator
+ ory	depreciatory
depress	
+ s	depresses
+ ed	depressed
+ ing	depressing
+ ing + ly	depressingly
+ ible	depressible
+ ant	depressant*
+ ion	depression*
+ ive	depressive

+ ive + ly	depressively
+ or	depressor*

describe

+ s	describes
+ ed	described
+ ing	describing
+ able	describable
+ er	describer*
+ tion	description*
+ ive	descriptive
+ ly	descriptively
+ ness	descriptiveness

desert

+ s	deserts
+ ic	desertic

deserve

+ s	deserves
+ ed	deserved
+ ing	deserving
+ er	deserver*
+ ly	deservedly
+ ness	deservedness

design

+ s	designs
+ ed	designed
+ ing	designing
+ ly	designedly
+ er	designer*
+ ee	designee*
+ ment	designment

designate

+ s	designates
+ ed	designated
+ ing	designating
+ ive	designative
+ or	designator*
+ ory	designatory
+ tion	designation

desire

+ s	desires
+ ed	desired
+ ing	desiring
+ able	desirable
+ able + ly	desirably
+ ity	desirability
+ ous	desirous
+ ous + ly	desirously
+ ous + ness	desirousness

desk

+ s	desks
+ man	deskman*

desperate

+ ly	desperately
+ ness	desperateness
+ tion	desperation

dessert (2)

+ s	desserts
+ spoon	dessertspoon
+ spoon + ful	dessertspoonful*

destine

+ s	destines
+ ed	destined
+ ing	destining
+ tion	destination*
+ y	destiny*

destroy

+ s	destroys
+ ed	destroyed
+ ing	destroying
+ er	destroyer*

destruct

+ ible	destructible
+ ible + ity	destructibility
+ ion	destruction
+ ist	destructionist
+ ive	destructive
+ ly	destructively
+ ness	destructiveness
+ ive + ity	destructivity
+ or	destructor*

detail

+ s	details
+ ed	detailed
+ ing	detailing
+ er	detailer
+ ness	detailedness
+ ly	detailedly

detain

+ s	detains
+ ed	detained
+ ing	detaining
+ ment	detainment
+ ee	detainee*
+ er	detainer*
+ tion	detention*

detect

+ s	detects
+ ed	detected
+ ing	detecting
+ able	detectable
+ ity	detectability
+ ion	detection
+ ive	detective*
+ or	detector*

deteriorate

+ s	deteriorates
+ ed	deteriorated
+ ing	deteriorating
+ ion	deterioration
+ ive	deteriorative

D

determine	
+ s	determines
+ ed	determined
+ ing	determining
+ ed + ly	determinedly
+ ed + ness	determinedness
+ able	determinable
+ able + ly	determinably
+ able + ness	determinableness
+ y	determinacy*
+ ant	determinant*
+ al	determinantal
+ ate	determinate
+ ate + ly	determinately
+ ate + ness	determinateness
+ ate + or	determinator^
+ tion	determination
+ ive	determinative
+ ive + ly	determinatively
+ ive + ness	determinativeness
+ er	determiner*
+ ism	determinism
+ ist	determinist*
+ ic	deterministic
+ al + ly	deterministically
Detroit	
develop	
+ s	develops
+ ed	developed
+ ing	developing
+ able	developable
+ er	developer*
+ ment	development*
+ al	developmental
+ ly	developmentally
deviate	
+ s	deviates
+ ed	deviated
+ ing	deviating
+ or	deviator*
+ ory	deviatory
+ tion	deviation*
+ ism	deviationism
+ ist	deviationist*
+ ant	deviant*
+ ance	deviance*
+ y	deviancy*
device*	
devil	
+ s	devils
+ ed	deviled
+ ing	deviling
+ ish	devilish
+ ly	devilishly
+ ness	devilishness
+ ment	devilment
+ y	devilry*
+ fish	devilfish
+ ic	diabolic
devise	
+ s	devises
+ ed	devised
+ ing	devising
+ able	devisable
+ al	devisal
+ ee	devisee*
+ er, + or	deviser*, devisor*
devote	
+ s	devotes
+ ed	devoted
+ ing	devoting
+ ed + ly	devotedly
+ ness	devotedness
+ ee	devotee*
+ ment	devotement
+ ion	devotion*
+ al	devotional
+ al + ly	devotionally
dew	
+ s	dews
+ ed	dewed
+ ing	dewing
+ less	dewless
+ y	dewy
+ er	dewier
+ est	dewiest
+ ly	dewily
+ ness	dewiness
+ berry	dewberry*
+ claw	dewclaw*
+ drop	dewdrop*
+ fall	dewfall
+ lap	dewlap*
diabetes	
+ ic	diabetic*
diagnose	
+ s	diagnoses
+ ed	diagnosed
+ ing	diagnosing
+ able	diagnosable
+ ic	diagnostic
+ al	diagnostical
+ ly	diagnostically
+ an	diagnostician*
diagnosis	
diagonal	
+ s	diagonals
+ ize	diagonalize^
+ able	diagonalizable
+ tion	diagonalization

D

+ ly diagonally

diagram

+ s diagrams
+ ed diagramed
+ ing diagraming
+ able diagrammable
+ ic diagrammatic
+ al diagrammatical
+ ly diagrammatically

dialect (2)

+ s dialects
+ al dialectal
+ al + ly dialectally
+ ic dialectic*
+ ic + al dialectical
+ ic + al + ly dialectically
+ an dialectician*

dialogue

+ s dialogues
+ ed dialogued
+ ing dialoguing
+ ic dialogic
+ al dialogical
+ ly dialogically
+ ist dialogist*
+ ist + ic dialogistic

diameter

+ s diameters
+ al diametral
+ ic diametric
+ ic + al diametrical
+ ly diametrically

diamond

+ s diamonds
+ ous diamondiferous
+ back diamondback*

diaper^

diarrhea

+ al diarrheal
+ ic diarrhetic

dice

+ s dices
+ ed diced
+ ing dicing
+ er dicer*
+ y dicey
+ y + er dicier
+ est diciest

dictionary*

did

die

+ s dies
+ ed died
+ ing dying
+ d dead
+ th death
+ back dieback
+ hard diehard*

diet

+ s diets
+ ed dieted
+ ing dieting
+ ary dietary*
+ ary + ly dietarily
+ ic dietetic*
+ al + ly dietetically
+ an dietician*

differ

+ s differs
+ ed differed
+ ing differing
+ ence difference*^
+ ent different
+ able differentiable
+ ity differentiability
+ al differential
+ al + ly differentially
+ ate differentiate^
+ ion differentiation*
+ ly differently
+ ness differentness

different

difficult

+ y difficulty*
+ ly difficultly

dig

+ s digs
+ ed dug
+ ing digging*
+ er digger*

digest

+ s digests
+ ed digested
+ ing digesting
+ er digester
+ ible digestible
+ ity digestibility*
+ ion digestion
+ ive digestive*
+ ly digestively
+ ness digestiveness

digit

+ s digits
+ al digital
+ al + ly digitally
+ ate digitate
+ ate + ly digitately
+ ate + ion digitation

+ ize	digitize^
+ ize + tion	digitization
+ er	digitizer*
dim	
+ s	dims
+ ed	dimmed
+ ing	dimming
+ er	dimmer*
+ est	dimmest
+ able	dimmable
+ ly	dimly
+ ness	dimness
+ wit	dimwit
dime*	
diminish	
+ s	diminishes
+ ed	diminished
+ ing	diminishing
+ able	diminishable
+ ment	diminishment
+ tion	diminution
+ al	diminutional
+ ive	diminutive
+ ly	diminutively
+ ness	diminutiveness
dimple	
+ s	dimples
+ ed	dimpled
+ ing	dimpling
+ ly	dimply
dine	
+ s	dines
+ ed	dined
+ ing	dining
+ er	diner*
dinner	
+ s	dinners
+ less	dinnerless
+ ware	dinnerware
dinosaur	
+ s	dinosaurs
+ ic	dinosauric
+ an	dinosaurian
dip	
+ s	dips
+ ed	dipped
+ ing	dipping
+ able	dippable
+ er	dipper*
+ ful	dipperful*
+ stick	dipstick*
diplodocus	
diploma	
+ s	diplomas
+ t	diplomat*
+ y	diplomacy
+ ate	diplomate*
+ ic	diplomatic
+ ly	diplomatically
+ ist	diplomatist
direct	
+ s	directs
+ ed	directed
+ ing	directing
+ ion	direction*
+ ion + al	directional
+ al + ity	directionality
+ less	directionless
+ ive	directive*
+ ive + ity	directivity
+ ly	directly
+ ness	directness
+ or	director*
+ ate	directorate*
+ ship	directorship*
+ ory	directory*
+ ory + al	directorial
dirt	
+ y	dirty^
+ er	dirtier
+ est	dirtiest
+ ness	dirtiness
+ ly	dirtily
disagree	
+ s	disagrees
+ ed	disagreed
+ ing	disagreeing
+ able	disagreeable
+ ity	disagreeability
+ ly	disagreeably
+ ness	disagreeableness
+ ment	disagreement*
disappear	
+ s	disappears
+ ed	disappeared
+ ing	disappearing
+ ance	disappearance*
disappoint	
+ s	disappoints
+ ed	disappointed
+ ing	disappointing
+ ed + ly	disappointedly
+ ing + ly	disappointingly
+ ment	disappointment *
discount	
+ s	discounts
+ ed	discounted
+ ing	discounting

D

+ able	discountable
+ er	discounter
discourage	
+ s	discourages
+ ing	discouraging
+ ed	discouraged
+ ly	discouragingly
+ able	discouragable
+ er	discourager
+ ment	discouragement
discover	
+ s	discovers
+ ed	discovered
+ ing	discovering
+ able	discoverable
+ er	discoverer*
+ y	discovery*
discriminate	
+ s	discriminates
+ ed	discriminated
+ ing	discriminating
+ ing + ly	discriminatingly
+ able	discriminable
+ ity	discriminability
+ ion	discrimination
+ al	discriminational
+ ive	discriminative
+ or	discriminator
+ ory	discriminatory
+ ory + ly	discriminatorily
discuss	
+ s	discusses
+ ed	discussed
+ ing	discussing
+ able	discussable
+ ant	discussant*
+ er	discusser*
+ ion	discussion*
disease	
+ s	diseases
+ ed	diseased
disguise	
+ s	disguises
+ ed	disguised
+ ing	disguising
+ ly	disguisedly
+ er	disguiser*
+ ment	disguisement
disgust	
+ s	disgusts
+ ed	disgusted
+ ing	disgusting
+ ed + ly	disgustedly
+ ing + ly	disgustingly

+ ful	disgustful
+ ful + ly	disgustfullly
dish	
+ s	dishes
+ ed	dished
+ ing	dishing
+ y	dishy
+ cloth	dishcloth
+ pan	dishpan*
+ rag	dishrag*
+ ware	dishware
+ wash + er	dishwasher*
+ water	dishwater
disk or disc	
+ s	disks
+ ed	disked
+ ing	disking
+ like	disklike
dismiss	
+ s	dismisses
+ ed	dismissed
+ ing	dismissing
+ al	dismissal*
+ ion	dismission*
+ ive	dismissive
display^	
dispose	
+ s	disposes
+ ed	disposed
+ ing	disposing
+ al	disposal*
+ able	disposable
+ er	disposer
+ tion	disposition*
+ ive	dispositive
dissect	
+ s	dissects
+ ed	dissected
+ ing	dissecting
+ or	dissector*
+ ion	dissection*
disseminate	
+ s	disseminates
+ ed	disseminated
+ ing	disseminating
+ ion	dissemination*
+ or	disseminator
dissolve	
+ s	dissolves
+ ed	dissolved
+ ing	dissolving
+ able	dissolveable
+ er	dissolver*
+ ent	dissolvent*

distant	
+ ance	distance^
+ ly	distantly
+ ness	distantness
distinguish	
+ s	distinguishes
+ ed	distinguished
+ ing	distinguishing
+ able	distinguishable
+ ity	distinguishability
+ ly	distinguishably
distort	
+ s	distorts
+ ed	distorted
+ ing	distorting
+ er	distortioner
+ ion	distortion*
+ al	distortional
distract	
+ s	distracts
+ ed	distracted
+ ing	distracting
+ ed + ly	distractedly
+ ing + ly	distractingly
+ ible	distractible
+ ity	distractibility
+ ion	distraction*
+ ive	distractive
distribute	
+ s	distributes
+ ed	distributed
+ ing	distributing
+ or	distributor*
+ ee	distributee*
+ ion	distribution*
+ al	distributional
+ ive	distributive
+ ly	distributively
+ ness	distributiveness
+ ity	distributivity
district^	
disturb	
+ s	disturbs
+ ed	disturbed
+ ing	disturbing
+ ly	disturbingly
+ ance	disturbance*
+ er	disturber*
dive	
+ s	dives
+ ed	dived
+ en	dove
+ ing	diving
+ er	diver*

diverge	
+ s	diverges
+ ed	diverged
+ ing	diverging
+ ent	divergent
+ ly	divergently
+ ence	divergence
+ y	divergency*
divide	
+ s	divides
+ ed	divided
+ ing	dividing
+ er, + or	divider*, divisor*
+ able, + ible	dividable, divisible
+ ent	dividend*
+ ity	divisibility
+ sion	division*
+ ism	divisionism
+ ist	divisionist*
+ al	divisional
+ ive	divisive
+ ly	divisively
+ ness	divisiveness
divine	
+ s	divines
+ ed	divined
+ ing	divining
+ er	diviner*
+ est	divinest
+ ity	divinity*
+ ly	divinely
+ tion	divination
+ ory	divinatory
divorce	
+ s	divorces
+ ed	divorced
+ ing	divorcing
+ ee	divorcee*
+ ment	divorcement
dizzy	
+ er	dizzier
+ est	dizziest
+ ing	dizzying
+ ly	dizzily
+ ness	dizziness
+ ing + ly	dizzyingly
do	
+ s	does
+ ed	did
+ en	done
+ ing	doing
dock	
+ s	docks
+ ed	docked
+ ing	docking

+ age	dockage
+ er	docker*
+ hand	dockhand*
+ land	dockland
+ side	dockside
+ work + er	dockworker*
+ yard	dockyard*
doctor	
+ s	doctors
+ ed	doctored
+ ing	doctoring
+ al	doctoral
+ ate	doctorate*
+ less	doctorless
+ ship	doctorship
doctrine	
+ s	doctrines
+ al	doctrinal
dodge	
+ s	dodges
+ ed	dodged
+ ing	dodging
+ er	dodger*
+ ery	dodgery*
+ y	dodgy
dog	
+ s	dogs
+ ed	dogged
+ ing	dogging
+ y	doggy*
+ er	doggier
+ est	doggiest
+ dom	dogdom
+ ish	doggish
+ ly	doggishly
+ ness	doggishness
+ like	doglike
+ berry	dogberry*
+ cart	dogcart*
+ catch + er	dogcatcher*
+ fight	dogfight
+ fish	dogfish
+ house	doghouse*
+ leg	dogleg*
+ s + body	dogsbody
+ sled	dogsled*
+ tooth	dogtooth
+ watch	dogwatch
+ wood	dogwood
doll	
+ s	dolls
+ ed	dolled
+ ing	dolling
+ ish	dollish
+ ly	dollishly
+ ness	dollishness
+ y	dolly*
+ house	dollhouse*
dollar*	
dolphin*	
dominate	
+ s	dominates
+ ed	dominated
+ ing	dominating
+ ance	dominance
+ ant	dominant
+ ly	dominantly
+ er	dominator
+ ion	domination
+ ive	dominative
domino*	
done (2)	
donkey	
+ s	donkeys
+ work	donkeywork
door	
+ s	doors
+ keep + er	doorkeeper*
+ man	doorman*
+ mat	doormat*
+ nail	doornail*
+ plate	doorplate*
+ post	doorpost*
+ step	doorstep*
+ stop	doorstop*
+ way	doorway*
+ yard	dooryard*
+ knob	doorknob*
dormitory*	
dot	
+ s	dots
+ ed	dotted
+ ing	dotting
+ er	dotter*
+ y	dotty
double	
+ s	doubles
+ ed	doubled
+ ing	doubling
+ er	doubler
+ ly	doubly
+ ness	doubleness
doubt	
+ s	doubts
+ ed	doubted
+ ing	doubting
+ ing + ly	doubtingly
+ able	doubtable
+ er	doubter*

+ ful	doubtful
+ ful + ly	doubtfully
+ ful + ness	doubtfulness
+ less	doubtless
+ less + ly	doubtlessly
+ ness	doubtlessness
dough	
+ s	doughs
+ like	doughlike
+ y	doughy
+ er	doughier
+ est	doughiest
+ nut	doughnut*
down	
+ s	downs
+ ed	downed
+ ing	downing
+ er	downer*
+ y	downy
+ y + er	downier
+ est	downiest
+ ward	downward
+ ward + ly	downwardly
+ ward + ness	downwardness
+ beat	downbeat*
+ court	downcourt
+ fall	downfall*
+ fall + en	downfallen
+ field	downfield
+ grade	downgrade^
+ haul	downhaul
+ heart + ed	downhearted
+ heart + ed + ly	downheartedly
+ heart + ed + ness	downheartedness
+ hill	downhill*
+ play	downplay^
+ pour	downpour*
+ range	downrange
+ right	downright
+ river	downriver
+ stage	downstage
+ stair + s	downstairs
+ state	downstate
+ stream	downstream
+ swing	downswing
+ time	downtime
+ town	downtown
+ turn	downturn*^
+ wind	downwind
dozen	
+ s	dozens
+ th	dozenth
drag	
+ s	drags
+ ed	dragged
+ ing	dragging
+ ly	draggingly
+ er	dragger
+ y	draggy
+ y + er	draggier
+ est	draggiest
+ line	dragline*
+ net	dragnet*
+ rope	dragrope*
dragon	
+ s	dragons
+ ish	dragonish
+ fly	dragonfly*
+ head	dragonhead*
drain	
+ s	drains
+ ed	drained
+ ing	draining
+ age	drainage
+ er	drainer*
+ pipe	drainpipe*
drama	
+ s	dramas
+ ic	dramatic*
+ ly	dramatically
+ ist	dramatist*
+ ize	dramatize^
+ tion	dramatization*
+ able	dramatizable
drape	
+ s	drapes
+ ed	draped
+ ing	draping
+ able	drapeable
+ ity	drapeability
+ er	draper*
+ ery	drapery*
draw	
+ s	draws
+ ed	drew
+ en	drawn
+ ing	drawing
+ able	drawable
+ ee	drawee*
+ back	drawback*
+ bar	drawbar*
+ bridge	drawbridge*
+ down	drawdown
+ knife	drawknife
+ plate	drawplate
+ shave	drawshave
+ string	drawstring*
+ tube	drawtube*
+ en + work	drawnwork

drawer
+ s | drawers
+ ful | drawerful*

dream
+ s | dreams
+ ed | dreamed
+ ing | dreaming
+ er | dreamer*
+ ful | dreamful
+ ful + ly | dreamfully
+ ful + ness | dreamfulness
+ less | dreamless
+ less + ly | dreamlessly
+ less + ness | dreamlessness
+ like | dreamlike
+ y | dreamy
+ y + er | dreamier
+ est | dreamiest
+ y + ly | dreamily
+ y + ness | dreaminess
+ land | dreamland
+ world | dreamworld

dress
+ s | dresses
+ ed | dressed
+ ing | dressing
+ age | dressage
+ er | dresser*
+ y | dressy
+ y + er | dressier
+ est | dressiest
+ ness | dressiness
+ make + er | dressmaker*
+ make + ing | dressmaking

drift
+ s | drifts
+ ed | drifted
+ ing | drifting
+ ly | driftingly
+ age | driftage
+ er | drifter*
+ y | drifty
+ y + er | driftier
+ est | driftiest
+ weed | driftweed
+ wood | driftwood

drill
+ s | drills
+ ed | drilled
+ ing | drilling
+ master | drillmaster

drink
+ s | drinks
+ ed | drank
+ en | drunk
+ ing | drinking
+ able | drinkable
+ ity | drinkability
+ er | drinker*

drip
+ s | drips
+ ed | dripped
+ ing | dripping
+ er | dripper*
+ less | dripless
+ y | drippy
+ y + er | drippier
+ est | drippiest
+ stone | dripstone

drive
+ s | drives
+ ed | drove
+ en | driven
+ ing | driving
+ able | drivable
+ er | driver*
+ ness | drivenness
+ line | driveline
+ way | driveway*

drizzle
+ s | drizzles
+ ed | drizzled
+ ing | drizzling
+ ing + ly | drizzlingly
+ ly | drizzly

drool^

drop
+ s | drops
+ ed | dropped
+ ing | dropping
+ er | dropper*
+ kick | dropkick*
+ light | droplight*
+ out | dropout*
+ shot | dropshot*

drown^

drug
+ s | drugs
+ ed | drugged
+ ing | drugging
+ ist | druggist*
+ make + er | drugmaker*
+ store | drugstore*

drum
+ s | drums
+ ed | drummed
+ ing | drumming
+ er | drummer*

+ like	drumlike
+ beat	drumbeat
+ fire	drumfire
+ head	drumhead*
+ roll	drumroll*
+ stick	drumstick*
drunk	
+ en	drunken
+ ly	drunkenly
+ ness	drunkenness
dry	
+ s	dries
+ ed	dried
+ ing	drying
+ able	dryable
+ er	drier*
+ est	driest
+ ly	dryly / drily
+ ness	dryness
duck	
+ s	ducks
+ ed	ducked
+ ing	ducking
+ er	ducker
+ y	ducky
+ y + er	duckier
+ est	duckiest
+ foot + ed	duckfooted
+ weed	duckweed
duckling*	
duke	
+ s	dukes
+ ess	duchess*
+ dom	dukedom
+ y	duchy*
dull	
+ s	dulls
+ ed	dulled
+ ing	dulling
+ ish	dullish
+ ly	dullishly
+ ness	dullness
+ y	dully
dumb	
+ ly	dumbly
+ ness	dumbness
+ y	dummy*^
+ bell	dumbbell*
+ strike + ed	dumbstruck
+ wait + er	dumbwaiter*
dump	
+ s	dumps
+ ed	dumped
+ ing	dumping
+ er	dumper*
+ ish	dumpish
+ y	dumpy
+ y + er	dumpier
+ est	dumpiest
+ ly	dumpily
+ ness	dumpiness
duplicate	
+ s	duplicates
+ ed	duplicated
+ ing	duplicating
+ ion	duplication*
+ ive	duplicative
+ or	duplicator*
+ ity	duplicity
+ ous	duplicitous
+ ly	duplicitously
during	
dusk	
+ y	dusky
+ er	duskier
+ est	duskiest
dust	
+ s	dusts
+ ed	dusted
+ ing	dusting
+ er	duster*
+ less	dustless
+ like	dustlike
+ y	dusty
+ ly	dustily
+ ness	dustiness
+ cover	dustcover*
+ heap	dustheap*
+ man	dustman*
+ pan	dustpan*
Dutch	
+ ly	Dutchly
duty	
+ s	duties
+ ous	duteous
+ able	dutiable
+ ful	dutiful
+ ly	dutifully
+ ness	dutifulness
dwarf	
+ s	dwarfs
+ ed	dwarfed
+ ing	dwarfing
+ ish	dwarfish
+ ly	dwarfishly
+ ish + ness	dwarfishness
+ like	dwarflike
+ ness	dwarfness
+ ism	dwarfism

dwell

+ s	dwells
+ t	dwelt
+ ed	dwelled
+ ing	dwelling*
+ er	dweller*

dwindle*

dye

+ s	dyes
+ ed	dyed
+ ing	dyeing
+ able	dyeable
+ ity	dyeability
+ er	dyer

dynamite

+ s	dynamites
+ ed	dynamited
+ ing	dynamiting
+ er	dynamiter

D

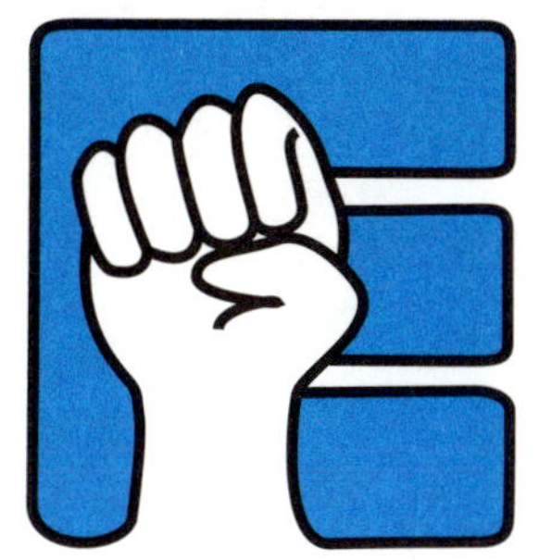

E

each
eager
+ ly eagerly
+ ness eagerness
eagle
+ s eagles
ear
+ s ears
+ ed eared
+ ing earing
+ ful earful
+ less earless
+ ache earache*
+ drop eardrop*
+ drum eardrum*
+ flap earflap*
+ mold earmold
+ mark earmark*
+ muff earmuff*
+ phone earphone*
+ piece earpiece*
+ plug earplug*
+ shot earshot
+ split + ing earsplitting
+ wax earwax
+ worm earworm
early (2)
+ er earlier
+ est earliest
+ ness earliness
earn
+ s earns
+ ed earned
+ ing earning*
+ er earner*
earnest
+ ly earnestly
+ ness earnestness
earphone*
earring*
earth
+ s earths
+ ed earthed
+ ing earthing
+ en earthen
+ like earthlike
+ ly earthly
+ ly + ness earthliness
+ y earthy
+ er earthier
+ est earthiest
+ y + ly earthily
+ y + ness earthiness
+ birth + en earthborn
+ bind + ed earthbound
+ en + ware earthenware
+ nut earthnut*
+ shake + er earthshaker*
+ shake + ing earthshaking
+ shine earthshine
+ star earthstar
+ ward earthward*
+ work earthwork*
+ worm earthworm*
earthquake*
ease
+ s eases
+ ed eased
+ ing easing
+ ful easeful
+ ly easefully
+ ful + ness easefulness
+ ment easement*
easel*
east
+ bound eastbound
+ er easterner*
+ ly easterly
+ ize easternize^
+ more + est easternmost
+ ing easting
+ ward eastward
+ ward + s eastwards
Easter
+ tide Eastertide
easy
+ ly easily
+ er easier

+ est	easiest
+ ness	easiness
+ go + ing	easygoing
+ go + ing + ness	easygoingness

eat

+ s	eats
+ ed	ate
+ en	eaten
+ ing	eating
+ er	eater
+ able	eatable
+ ery	eatery*

echo

+ s	echoes
+ ed	echoed
+ ing	echoing
+ y	echoey
+ ic	echoic
+ locate + tion	echolocation

eclipse

+ s	eclipses
+ ed	eclipsed
+ ing	eclipsing
+ ic	ecliptic

ecology

+ s	ecologies
+ ic	ecologic
+ al	ecological
+ ly	ecologically
+ ist	ecologist*

economy

+ s	economies
+ meter + ic + s	econometrics
+ meter **+ ly**	econometrically
+ meter **+ an**	econometrician*
+ ic	economic*
+ al	economical
+ ly	economically
+ ist	economist*
+ ize	economize^
+ ize + er	economizer*

edge

+ s	edges
+ ed	edged
+ ing	edging
+ er	edger*
+ less	edgeless
+ way + s	edgeways
+ wise	edgewise
+ y	edgy
+ y + er	edgier
+ est	edgiest
+ ly	edgily
+ ness	edginess

edit

+ s	edits
+ ed	edited
+ ing	editing
+ ion	edition*
+ or	editor*
+ al	editorial*
+ ly	editorially
+ ist	editorialist*
+ ize	editorialize^
+ ize + tion	editorialization*
+ ize + er	editorializer*
+ ship	editorship
+ ess	editress*

educate

+ s	educates
+ ed	educated
+ ing	educating
+ ed + ly	educatedly
+ ness	educatedness
+ able	educable
+ ity	educability
+ ion	education*
+ al	educational
+ al + ly	educationally
+ al + ist	educationalist*
+ ist	educationist*
+ ive	educative
+ or	educator*

effect

+ s	effects
+ ed	effected
+ ing	effecting
+ ive	effective*
+ ive + ly	effectively
+ ive + ness	effectiveness
+ ive + ity	effectivity
+ or	effector
+ al	effectual
+ al + ness	effectualness
+ al + ity	effectuality
+ al + ly	effectually
+ ate	effectuate*
+ tion	effectuation

effort

+ s	efforts
+ ful	effortful
+ ful + ly	effortfully
+ less	effortless
+ less + ly	effortlessly
+ ness	effortlessness

egg

+ s	eggs
+ less	eggless

+ beat + er	eggbeater*
+ cup	eggcup*
+ head	egghead*
+ head + ed	eggheaded
+ head **+ ness**	eggheadedness
+ plant	eggplant*
+ shell	eggshell*
Egypt	
+ an	Egyptian*
either	
eject	
+ s	ejects
+ ed	ejected
+ ing	ejecting
+ able	ejectable
+ ion	ejection
+ ive	ejective
+ ment	ejectment
+ or	ejector*
elaborate	
+ s	elaborates
+ ed	elaborated
+ ing	elaborating
+ ly	elaborately
+ ness	elaborateness
+ ion	elaboration*
+ ive	elaborative
elastic	
+ ly	elastically
+ ity	elasticity*
+ ize	elasticize^
elbow* ^	
elder	
+ s	elders
+ est	eldest
+ ly	elderly
+ ness	elderliness
+ ship	eldership
elect	
+ s	elects
+ ed	elected
+ ing	electing
+ able	electable
+ ity	electability
+ ion	election*
+ ion + er	electioneer*
+ ive	elective
+ ness	electiveness
+ ly	electively
+ or	elector*
+ al	electoral
+ ate	electorate
electric	
+ al	electrical

+ ly	electrically
+ ness	electricalness
+ an	electrician*
+ ify	electrify^
+ tion	electrification
+ ity	electricity*
electron	
+ s	electrons
+ ic	electronic*
elegant	
+ ance	elegance
+ y	elegancy
+ ly	elegantly
element	
+ s	elements
+ al	elemental
+ ly	elementally
elementary	
+ s	elementaries
+ ly	elementarily
+ ness	elementariness
elephant	
+ s	elephants
+ ine	elephantine
elevate	
+ s	elevates
+ ed	elevated
+ ing	elevating
+ or	elevator*
+ ion	elevation*
elf	
+ s	elves
+ ish	elfish
+ ly	elfishly
eliminate	
+ s	eliminates
+ ed	eliminated
+ ing	eliminating
+ ion	elimination*
+ ive	eliminative
+ or	eliminator*
elk*	
elope	
+ s	elopes
+ ed	eloped
+ ing	eloping
+ er	eloper*
+ ment	elopement
else	
+ where	elsewhere
embarrass	
+ s	embarrasses
+ ed	embarrassed
+ ing	embarrassing

E

+ able	embarrassable
+ ed + ly	embarrassedly
+ ing + ly	embarrassingly
+ ment	embarrassment*
emblem	
+ s	emblems
+ ic	emblematic
+ al	emblematical
+ ly	emblematically
+ ize	emblematize^
embroider	
+ s	embroiders
+ ed	embroidered
+ ing	embroidering
+ er	embroiderer*
+ y	embroidery*
embryo	
+ s	embryos
+ al	embryonal
+ al + ly	embryonally
+ ed	embryonated
+ ic	embryonic
+ ic + al + ly	embryonically
emerge	
+ s	emerges
+ ed	emerged
+ ing	emerging
+ ent	emergent*
+ ence	emergence*
+ y	emergency*
emit	
+ s	emits
+ ed	emitted
+ ing	emitting
+ er	emitter*
+ sion	emission*
+ ive	emissive
+ ity	emissivity*
+ ary	emissary*
emotion	
+ s	emotions
+ al	emotional
+ al + ly	emotionally
+ ist	emotionalist*
+ al + ity	emotionality
+ ize	emotionalize^
+ less	emotionless
+ ness	emotionlessness
+ ive	emotive
+ ive + ly	emotively
+ ive + ity	emotivity
emphasis	
+ ize	emphasize^
+ ic	emphatic
+ ly	emphatically
emperor*	
+ y	empery*
empire*	
employ	
+ s	employs
+ ed	employed
+ ing	employing
+ er	employer*
+ ee	employee*
+ able	employable
+ ity	employability
+ ment	employment
empress*	
empty	
+ s	empties
+ ed	emptied
+ ing	emptying
+ er	emptier
+ est	emptiest
+ ly	emptily
+ ness	emptiness
enchilada*	
encourage	
+ s	encourages
+ ed	encouraged
+ ing	encouraging
+ er	encourager
+ ly	encouragingly
+ ment	encouragement
encyclopedia	
+ ic	encyclopedic
+ al	encyclopedical
+ ly	encyclopedically
+ ism	encyclopedism
+ ist	encyclopedist*
end	
+ s	ends
+ ed	ended
+ ing	ending
+ less	endless
+ ly	endlessly
+ ness	endlessness
+ more + est	endmost
+ way + s	endways
+ wise	endwise
enemy*	
energy	
+ s	energies
+ ic	energetic*
+ ly	energetically
+ ize	energize^
+ er	energizer*
enforce	
+ s	enforces

+ ed	enforced
+ ing	enforcing
+ er	enforcer*
+ able	enforceable
+ ity	enforceability
+ ment	enforcement
engage	
+ s	engages
+ ed	engaged
+ ing	engaging
+ ly	engagingly
+ ment	engagement*
engine	
+ s	engines
+ ed	engined
+ ing	engining
+ ee + r	engineer*
+ ee + r + ing	engineering
+ ery	enginery
England	
English^	
+ ism	Englishism
+ ness	Englishness
+ man	Englishman*
+ woman	Englishwoman*
engross	
+ s	engrosses
+ ed	engrossed
+ ing	engrossing
+ er	engrosser
+ ed + ly	engrossedly
+ ing + ly	engrossingly
+ ment	engrossment
enjoy	
+ s	enjoys
+ ed	enjoyed
+ ing	enjoying
+ able	enjoyable
+ ly	enjoyably
+ ness	enjoyableness
+ er	enjoyer*
+ ment	enjoyment*
enormous	
+ ity	enormity*
+ ly	enormously
+ ness	enormousness
enough	
enter	
+ s	enters
+ ed	entered
+ ing	entering
+ able	enterable
+ ance	entrance*
+ ant	entrant*
+ y	entry*

+ y + way	entryway*
entertain	
+ s	entertains
+ ed	entertained
+ ing	entertaining
+ er	entertainer
+ ly	entertainingly
+ ment	entertainment*
enthuse	
+ s	enthuses
+ ed	enthused
+ ing	enthusing
+ ism	enthusiasm
+ ist	enthusiast*
+ ic	enthusiastic
+ ly	enthusiastically
entire	
+ ly	entirely
+ ness	entireness
+ t + y	entirety*
envelope*	
environment	
+ al	environmental
+ ly	environmentally
+ ism	environmentalism
+ ist	environmentalist*
envy	
+ s	envies
+ ed	envied
+ ing	envying
+ ing + ly	envyingly
+ ous	envious
+ ous + ly	enviously
+ ness	enviousness
epidemic	
+ s	epidemics
+ al	epidemical
+ ly	epidemically
+ ity	epidemicity
episcopal	
+ ly	episcopally
+ an	Episcopalian*
+ ism	episcopalianism
+ ate	episcopate
+ y	episcopacy*
equal	
+ s	equals
+ ed	equaled
+ ing	equalling
+ able	equable
+ able + ity	equability
+ able + ly	equably
+ ness	equableness
+ ly	equally
+ ity	equality*

+ ize	equalize^
+ tion	equalization
+ er	equalizer
equate	
+ s	equates
+ ed	equated
+ ing	equating
+ ion	equation*
+ al	equational
+ ly	equationally
equator	
+ al	equatorial
+ ly	equatorially
+ ward	equatorward
equip	
+ s	equips
+ ed	equipped
+ ing	equipping
+ age	equipage
+ ment	equipment
equivalent	
+ ence	equivalence
+ y	equivalency*
+ ly	equivalently
era*	
erase	
+ s	erases
+ ed	erased
+ ing	erasing
+ able	erasable
+ ity	erasability
+ er	eraser*
+ ion	erasion
+ ure	erasure*
erect	
+ s	erects
+ ed	erected
+ ing	erecting
+ able	erectable
+ ile	erectile
+ ity	erectility
+ ion	erection*
+ ly	erectly
+ ness	erectness
+ or	erector*
error	
+ s	errors
+ ous	erroneous
+ ly	erroneously
+ ness	erroneousness
+ less	errorless
escalate	
+ s	escalates
+ ed	escalated
+ ing	escalating
+ ion	escalation
+ or	escalator*
+ ory	escalatory
escape	
+ s	escapes
+ ed	escaped
+ ing	escaping
+ er	escaper*
+ ee	escapee*
+ ism	escapism
+ ist	escapist
+ ment	escapement
escort^	
Eskimo	
+ s	Eskimos
+ an	Eskimoan
especially	
essay	
+ s	essays
+ ed	essayed
+ ing	essaying
+ er	essayer*
+ ist	essayist*
+ ic	essayistic
essence	
+ al	essential
+ ly	essentially
+ ness	essentialness
+ ity	essentiality
+ ism	essentialism
+ ist	essentialist
establish	
+ s	establishes
+ ed	established
+ ing	establishing
+ able	establishable
+ er	establisher
+ ment	establishment
+ an	establishmentarian
+ ism	establishmentarianism
esteem	
+ s	esteems
+ ed	esteemed
+ ing	esteeming
+ able	estimable
estimate	
+ s	estimates
+ ed	estimated
+ ing	estimating
+ able	estimable
+ ive	estimative
+ ion	estimation*
+ or	estimator*
etch	
+ s	etches

+ ed	etched
+ ing	etching
+ ing + s	etchings
eternal	
+ ize	eternalize*
+ ly	eternally
+ ness	eternalness
eternity	
+ s	eternities
+ ize	eternize^
Europe	
+ an	European*
+ ize	Europeanize
+ tion	Europeanization
evacuate	
+ s	evacuates
+ ed	evacuated
+ ing	evacuating
+ ant	evacuant*
+ ion	evacuation*
+ ee	evacuee*
evade	
+ s	evades
+ ed	evaded
+ ing	evading
+ er	evader
+ able	evadable
+ sion	evasion*
+ ive	evasive
+ ly	evasively
+ ness	evasiveness
evaluate	
+ s	evaluates
+ ed	evaluated
+ ing	evaluating
+ ion	evaluation*
+ ive	evaluative
+ or	evaluator*
evaporate	
+ s	evaporates
+ ed	evaporated
+ ing	evaporating
+ able	evaporable
+ able + ity	evaporability
+ ion	evaporation
+ ive	evaporative
+ ly	evaporatively
+ ive + ity	evaporativity
+ or	evaporator*
eve	
+ ing	evening*
+ fall	evenfall
+ song	evensong
+ tide	eventide
even	
+ s	evens
+ ed	evened
+ ing	evening
+ er	evener
+ ly	evenly
+ ness	evenness
+ hand + ed	evenhanded
+ hand **+ ly**	evenhandedly
+ hand **+ ness**	evenhandedness
event	
+ s	events^
+ ful	eventful
+ ful + ly	eventfully
+ ness	eventfulness
+ less	eventless
+ al	eventual
+ al + ly	eventually
+ ity	eventuality*
+ ate	eventuate^
ever	
+ bloom + ing	everblooming
+ last + ing	everlasting
+ last **+ ly**	everlastingly
+ last **+ ness**	everlastingness
+ more	evermore
+ green	evergreen*
every	
+ body	everybody
+ day	everyday
+ man	everyman
+ one	everyone
+ place	everyplace
+ thing	everything
+ where	everywhere
evident	
+ al	evidential
+ al + ly	evidentially
+ ary	evidentiary
+ ly	evidently
+ ence	evidence^
evil	
+ er	eviler
+ est	evilest
+ ly	evilly
+ ness	evilness
+ do + er	evildoer*
+ do + ing	evildoing
evolve	
+ s	evolves
+ ed	evolved
+ ing	evolving
+ able	evolvable
+ ment	evolvement

E

+ tion	evolution
+ al	evolutional
+ ary	evolutionary
+ ly	evolutionarily
+ ism	evolutionism
+ ist	evolutionist
exact	
+ s	exacts
+ ed	exacted
+ ing	exacting
+ er, or	exacter, exactor
+ able	exactable
+ ly	exactly
+ ness	exactness
+ ing + ly	exactingly
+ ing + ness	exactingness
+ ion	exaction
exaggerate	
+ s	exaggerates
+ ed	exaggerated
+ ing	exaggerating
+ or	exaggerator*
+ ory	exaggeratory
+ ly	exaggeratedly
+ ness	exaggeratedness
+ ion	exaggeration*
+ ive	exaggerative
exam	
+ s	exams
+ ine	examine
+ ine + s	examines
+ ed	examined
+ ing	examining
+ able	examinable
+ ant	examinant*
+ er	examiner*
+ ee	examinee*
+ tion	examination*
+ al	examinatorial
example^	
excavate	
+ s	excavates
+ ed	excavated
+ ing	excavating
+ ion	excavation*
+ al	excavational
+ or	excavator*
exceed	
+ s	exceeds
+ ed	exceeded
+ ing	exceeding
+ ly	exceedingly
excel	
+ s	excels
+ ed	excelled
+ ing	excelling
+ ence	excellence
+ y	excellency*
+ ent	excellent
+ ly	excellently
except	
+ s	excepts
+ ed	excepted
+ ing	excepting
+ ion	exception*
+ able	exceptionable
+ ity	exceptionability
+ able + ly	exceptionably
+ al	exceptional
+ al + ly	exceptionally
+ ness	exceptionalness
+ ive	exceptive
excess*	
excessive	
+ ly	excessively
+ ness	excessiveness
exchange	
+ s	exchanges
+ ed	exchanged
+ ing	exchanging
+ able	exchangeable
+ ity	exchangeability
+ er	exchanger*
+ ee	exchangee*
excite	
+ s	excites
+ ed	excited
+ ing	exciting
+ ed + ly	excitedly
+ ing + ly	excitingly
+ able	excitable
+ ness	excitableness
+ able + ly	excitably
+ ity	excitability
+ ant	excitant*
+ tion	excitation*
+ ive	excitative
+ ory	excitatory
+ ment	excitement*
+ er	exciter
exclaim	
+ s	exclaims
+ ed	exclaimed
+ ing	exclaiming
+ tion	exclamation*
+ ory	exclamatory
+ er	exclaimer

exclude

+ s	excludes
+ ed	excluded
+ ing	excluding
+ able	excludable
+ able + ity	excludability
+ er	excluder
+ ion	exclusion*
+ ary	exclusionary
+ ist	exclusionist

exclusive

+ ity	exclusivity
+ ly	exclusively
+ ness	exclusiveness

excuse

+ s	excuses
+ ed	excused
+ ing	excusing
+ able	excusable
+ ly	excusably
+ ness	excusableness
+ ory	excusatory
+ er	excuser

exercise

+ s	exercises
+ ed	exercised
+ ing	exercising
+ able	exercisable
+ er	exerciser*
+ tion	exercitation*

exhaust

+ s	exhausts
+ ed	exhausted
+ ing	exhausting
+ er	exhauster*
+ ible	exhaustible
+ ity	exhaustibility
+ ion	exhaustion
+ ive	exhaustive
+ ly	exhaustively
+ ive + ness	exhaustiveness
+ less	exhaustless
+ less + ness	exhaustlessness

exhibit

+ s	exhibits
+ ed	exhibited
+ ing	exhibiting
+ ion	exhibition*
+ ion + er	exhibitioner*
+ ism	exhibitionism
+ ist	exhibitionist*
+ ic	exhibitionistic
+ ive	exhibitive
+ ly	exhibitively
+ or	exhibitor*
+ ory	exhibitory

exist

+ s	exists
+ ed	existed
+ ing	existing
+ ence	existence*
+ ent	existent
+ al	existential
+ al + ly	existentially
+ ism	existentialism
+ ist	existentialist*
+ ic	existentialistic
+ ic + al + ly	existentialistically

exit^

expand

+ s	expands
+ ed	expanded
+ ing	expanding
+ er	expander
+ able	expandable
+ e	expanse
+ e + ible	expansible
+ ible + ity	expansibility
+ ile	expansile
+ ion	expansion*
+ al	expansional
+ ism	expansionism
+ ist	expansionist*
+ ary	expansionary
+ ive	expansive
+ ly	expansively
+ ness	expansiveness
+ ive + ity	expansivity

expect

+ s	expects
+ ed	expected
+ ing	expecting
+ ed + ly	expectedly
+ ed + ness	expectedness
+ able	expectable
+ ance	expectance
+ y	expectancy
+ ant	expectant
+ ly	expectantly
+ tion	expectation*
+ ive	expectative

expense

+ s	expenses
+ ed	expensed
+ ing	expensing
+ ive	expensive
+ ly	expensively
+ ness	expensiveness

experience

+ s	experiences
+ ed	experienced
+ ing	experiencing
+ al	experiential
+ ly	experientially

experiment

+ s	experiments
+ ed	experimented
+ ing	experimenting
+ al	experimental
+ ly	experimentally
+ ism	experimentalism
+ ist	experimentalist*
+ tion	experimentation*
+ er	experimenter*

expert

+ s	experts
+ ed	experted
+ ing	experting
+ ly	expertly
+ ness	expertness
+ ism	expertism
+ ize	expertize^

expire

+ s	expires
+ ed	expired
+ ing	expiring
+ tion	expiration
+ ory	expiratory

explain

+ s	explains
+ ed	explained
+ ing	explaining
+ able	explainable
+ tion	explanation*
+ ive	explanative
+ ory	explanatory
+ er	explainer

explode

+ s	explodes
+ ed	exploded
+ ing	exploding
+ er	exploder
+ ent	explodent
+ ible	explosible
+ ity	explosibility
+ sion	explosion*
+ ive	explosive*
+ ly	explosively
+ ness	explosiveness

explore

+ s	explores
+ ed	explored
+ ing	exploring
+ er	explorer*
+ tion	exploration
+ ive	explorative
+ ly	exploratively
+ ory	exploratory

export

+ s	exports
+ ed	exported
+ ing	exporting
+ er	exporter*
+ able	exportable
+ ity	exportability
+ tion	exportation*

expose

+ s	exposes
+ ed	exposed
+ ing	exposing
+ er	exposer
+ tion	exposition
+ ive	expositive
+ ory	expository

express

+ s	expresses
+ ed	expressed
+ ing	expressing
+ age	expressage
+ er	expresser
+ ible	expressible
+ ion	expression*
+ al	expressional
+ al + ly	expressionally
+ ism	expressionism
+ ist	expressionist
+ ic	expressionistic
+ ly	expressly

expressive

+ ive + ly	expressively
+ ness	expressiveness
+ ity	expressivity

extend

+ s	extends
+ ed	extended
+ ing	extending
+ er	extender*
+ ible	extensible
+ ible + ity	extensibility
+ sion	extension*
+ al	extensional
+ al + ity	extensionality
+ al + ly	extensionally
+ ile	extensile
+ ive	extensive
+ ive + ly	extensively
+ ness	extensiveness

+ ity	extensity
+ t	extent
extinct	
+ ion	extinction
+ ive	extinctive
+ able	extinctable
+ ment	extinctment
extinguish	
+ s	extinguishes
+ ed	extinguished
+ er	extinguisher
+ ing	extinguishing
extra*	
extract	
+ s	extracts
+ ed	extracted
+ ing	extracting
+ or	extractor*
+ able	extractable
+ ity	extractability
+ ion	extraction*
+ ive	extractive
+ ly	extractively
extreme	
+ s	extremes
+ ly	extremely
+ ness	extremeness
+ ism	extremism
+ ist	extremist*
+ ity	extremity*
eye	
+ s	eyes
+ ed	eyed
+ ing	eying
+ ness	eyedness
+ er	eyer
+ ball	eyeball*
+ cup	eyecup*
+ drop + s	eyedrops
+ drop + er	eyedropper*
+ ful	eyeful
+ glass	eyeglass*
+ hole	eyehole
+ less	eyeless
+ lid	eyelid*
+ like	eyelike
+ line + er	eyeliner*
+ piece	eyepiece*
+ point	eyepoint
+ pop + er	eyepopper*
+ pop + ing	eyepopping
+ shade	eyeshade*
+ shot	eyeshot
+ sight	eyesight
+ sore	eyesore*
+ spot	eyespot
+ tooth	eyetooth
+ wash	eyewash
+ wink	eyewink
+ witness	eyewitness*
eyebrow*	
eyelash*	

fable	
+ s	fables
+ ed	fabled
+ ing	fabling
+ er	fabler
fabric	
+ s	fabrics
+ ant	fabricant*
+ ate	fabricate^
+ tion	fabrication*
+ or	fabricator*
fabulous	
+ ly	fabulously
+ ness	fabulousness
face	
+ s	faces
+ ed	faced
+ ing	facing
+ er	facer
+ less	faceless
+ ness	facelessness
+ al	facial*
+ cloth	facecloth*
+ down	facedown
+ plate	faceplate*
+ up	faceup
facilitate	
+ s	facilitates
+ ed	facilitated
+ ing	facilitating
+ or	facilitator*
+ ion	facilitation
+ ive	facilitative
+ ity	facility*
fact	
+ s	facts
+ ity	facticity
+ ous	factitious
+ ous + ly	factitiously
+ ous + ness	factitiousness
+ al	factual
+ al + ly	factually
+ al + ness	factualness
+ ism	factualism
+ ist	factualist
+ ure	facture
factor	
+ s	factors
+ ed	factored
+ ing	factoring
+ able	factorable
+ age	factorage
+ al	factorial*
+ ize	factorize^
+ tion	factorization
+ ship	factorship
factory*	
faculty*	
fade	
+ s	fades
+ ed	faded
+ ing	fading
+ ed + ly	fadedly
+ ness	fadedness
+ less	fadeless
+ less + ly	fadelessly
+ away	fadeaway
Fahrenheit	
fail	
+ s	fails
+ ed	failed
+ ing	failing
+ ly	failingly
+ ure	failure*
faint	
+ s	faints
+ ed	fainted
+ ing	fainting
+ ish	faintish
+ ish + ness	faintishness
+ ly	faintly
+ ness	faintness
+ heart + ed	fainthearted
+ heart **+ ly**	faintheartedly
+ heart **+ ness**	faintheartedness
fair	
+ s	fairs
+ ly	fairly

+ ish	fairish
+ ish + ly	fairishly
+ ness	fairness
+ ground	fairground*
+ way	fairway*

fairy

+ s	fairies
+ hood	fairyhood
+ ism	fairyism
+ land	fairyland*

faith

+ s	faiths
+ ful	faithful
+ ful + ly	faithfully
+ ful + ness	faithfulness*
+ less	faithless
+ less + ly	faithlessly
+ less + ness	faithlessness

fake

+ s	fakes
+ ed	faked
+ ing	faking
+ er	faker
+ ery	fakery

fall

+ s	falls
+ ed	fell
+ en	fallen
+ ing	falling
+ er	faller*
+ back	fallback
+ off	falloff
+ out	fallout

false

+ er	falser
+ est	falsest
+ ly	falsely
+ hood	falsehood*
+ ness	falseness
+ ify	falsify^
+ tion	falsification*
+ ify + er	falsifier
+ ity	falsity*
+ y	falsie*

fame

+ ed	famed
+ ous	famous
+ ly	famously
+ ness	famousness

familiar

+ ly	familiarly
+ ness	familiarness
+ ity	familiarity*
+ ize	familiarize^
+ tion	familiarization

family

+ s	families
+ al	familial
+ ism	familism

fan

+ s	fans
+ ed	fanned
+ ing	fanning
+ er	fanner
+ dom	fandom
+ like	fanlike

fancy

+ s	fancies
+ ed	fancied
+ ing	fancying
+ er	fancier*
+ est	fanciest
+ ful	fanciful
+ ful + ly	fancifully
+ ful + ness	fancifulness
+ ly	fancily
+ ness	fanciness
+ work	fancywork

fang

+ s	fangs
+ ed	fanged

fantastic

+ al	fantastical
+ ity	fantasticality
+ ly	fantastically
+ ness	fantasticalness
+ ate	fantasticate^
+ tion	fantastication

fantasy

+ s	fantasies
+ ed	fantasied
+ ing	fantasying
+ ist	fantasist*
+ ize	fantasize^

far

+ er	farther
+ est	farthest
+ more + est	farthermost
+ see + ing	farseeing
+ sight + ed	farsighted
+ sight **+ ly**	farsightedly
+ sight **+ ness**	farsightedness

farewell*

farm

+ s	farms
+ ed	farmed
+ ing	farming
+ er	farmer*
+ hand	farmhand*

+ house	farmhouse*
+ land	farmland*
+ stead	farmstead*
+ stead + ing	farmsteading
+ yard	farmyard*
fascinate	
+ s	fascinates
+ ed	fascinated
+ ing	fascinating
+ ly	fascinatingly
+ tion	fascination*
+ or	fascinator
fashion	
+ s	fashions
+ ed	fashioned
+ ing	fashioning
+ er	fashioner
+ able	fashionable
+ ity	fashionability
+ ly	fashionably
+ ness	fashionableness
fast	
+ s	fasts
+ ed	fasted
+ ing	fasting
+ er	faster
+ est	fastest
+ ness	fastness
+ back	fastback*
+ ball	fastball*
fat	
+ s	fats
+ ed	fatted
+ ing	fatting
+ ly	fatly
+ ness	fatness
+ er	fatter
+ est	fattest
+ en	fatten^
+ en + er	fattener
+ ish	fattish
+ y	fatty*
+ y + er	fattier
+ y + est	fattiest
+ y + ness	fattiness
+ back	fatback
+ head	fathead*
+ head + ed	fatheaded
+ head **+ ly**	fatheadedly
+ head **+ ness**	fatheadedness
fate (2)	
+ s	fates
+ ed	fated
+ ing	fating
+ al	fatal
+ ism	fatalism
+ ist	fatalist*
+ ic	fatalistic
+ ic + al + ly	fatalistically
+ ity	fatality*
+ al + ly	fatally
+ ful	fateful
+ ful + ly	fatefully
+ ness	fatefulness
father	
+ s	fathers
+ ed	fathered
+ ing	fathering
+ ly	fatherly
+ ness	fatherliness
+ hood	fatherhood
+ less	fatherless
+ like	fatherlike
+ land	fatherland
fatigue	
+ s	fatigues
+ ed	fatigued
+ ing	fatiguing
+ able	fatigable
+ ity	fatigability
+ ly	fatiguingly
faucet*	
fault	
+ s	faults
+ ed	faulted
+ ing	faulting
+ less	faultless
+ less + ly	faultlessly
+ less + ness	faultlessness
+ y	faulty
+ er	faultier
+ est	faultiest
+ y + ness	faultiness
+ y + ly	faultily
+ find + er	faultfinder
+ find + ing	faultfinding
favor	
+ s	favors
+ ed	favored
+ ing	favoring
+ er	favorer
+ able	favorable
+ ness	favorableness
+ ly	favorably
favorite	
+ s	favorites
+ ism	favoritism

fear		
	+ s	fears
	+ d	feared
	+ ing	fearing
	+ er	fearer
	+ ful	fearful
	+ ful + ly	fearfully
	+ ful + ness	fearfulness
	+ less	fearless
	+ less + ly	fearlessly
	+ less + ness	fearlessness
	+ some	fearsome
	+ some + ly	fearsomely
	+ some + ness	fearsomeness
feast		
	+ s	feasts
	+ ed	feasted
	+ ing	feasting
	+ er	feaster
feather		
	+ s	feathers
	+ ed	feathered
	+ ing	feathering
	+ less	featherless
	+ y	feathery
	+ bed	featherbed*
	+ bed + ing	featherbedding
	+ brain	featherbrain
	+ brain + ed	featherbrained
	+ edge	featheredge
	+ edge + ed	featheredged
	+ head	featherhead
	+ stitch	featherstitch
	+ weigh + t	featherweight*
feature		
	+ s	features
	+ ed	featured
	+ ing	featuring
	+ less	featureless
February (2)		
federal		
	+ ly	federally
	+ ism	federalism
	+ ist	federalist*
	+ ize	federalize^
	+ ize + tion	federalization
	+ ate	federate^
	+ ate + tion	federation*
	+ ive	federative
	+ ive + ly	federatively
fee^		
feed		
	+ s	feeds
	+ ed	fed
	+ ing	feeding*
	+ er	feeder*
	+ lot	feedlot*
	+ stock	feedstock
	+ stuff	feedstuff
feedback		
feel		
	+ s	feels
	+ ed	felt
	+ ing	feeling*
	+ ly	feelingly
	+ ness	feelingness
feet		
	+ first	feetfirst
fell		
fellow		
	+ s	fellows
	+ ly	fellowly
	+ man	fellowman
	+ ship	fellowship*^
female		
	+ s	females
	+ ness	femaleness
	+ ine	feminine
	+ ly	femininely
	+ ine + ness	feminineness
	+ ity	femininity
	+ ism	feminism
	+ ist	feminist*
	+ ic	feministic
	+ ize	feminize^
	+ tion	feminization
fence		
	+ s	fences
	+ ed	fenced
	+ ing	fencing
	+ er	fencer*
	+ less	fenceless
	+ ness	fencelessness
	+ row	fencerow*
ferris wheel*		
fertile		
	+ ly	fertilely
	+ ness	fertileness
	+ ity	fertility
	+ ize	fertilize^
	+ able	fertilizable
	+ tion	fertilization
	+ al	fertilizational
	+ er	fertilizer*
festival		
	+ s	festivals
	+ ive	festive
	+ ly	festively

+ ness	festiveness
+ ity	festivity*
+ go + er	festivalgoer*
fever	
+ s	fevers
+ ed	fevered
+ ing	fevering
+ ish	feverish
+ ish + ly	feverishly
+ ish + ness	feverishness
+ ous	feverous
+ ous + ly	feverously
few	
+ er	fewer
+ est	fewest
+ ness	fewness
fib	
+ s	fibs
+ ed	fibbed
+ ing	fibbing
+ er	fibber*
fiber	
+ s	fibers
+ ed	fibered
+ ize	fiberize^
+ tion	fiberization
+ ous	fibrous
+ ly	fibrously
+ ness	fibrousness
+ board	fiberboard
fiction	
+ s	fictions
+ al	fictional
+ al + ize	fictionalize^
+ al + ize + tion	fictionalization
+ al + ly	fictionally
+ ee + er	fictioneer*
+ ee + er + ing	fictioneering
+ ist	fictionist*
+ ize	fictionize^
+ ize + tion	fictionization
+ ous	fictitious
+ ous + ly	fictitiously
+ ness	fictitiousness
+ ive	fictive
+ ive + ly	fictively
+ ive + ness	fictiveness
field	
+ s	fields
+ ed	fielded
+ ing	fielding
+ er	fielder*
+ piece	fieldpiece
+ stone	fieldstone
+ strip	fieldstrip^
+ work	fieldwork
fierce	
+ er	fiercer
+ est	fiercest
+ ly	fiercely
+ ness	fierceness
fig	
+ s	figs
+ y	figgy
fight	
+ s	fights
+ ed	fought
+ ing	fighting
+ er	fighter*
figure	
+ s	figures
+ ed	figured
+ ing	figuring
+ al	figural
+ tion	figuration
+ ive	figurative
+ ly	figuratively
+ ness	figurativeness
+ er	figurer
+ ine	figurine*
+ head	figurehead*
file^	
fill	
+ s	fills
+ ed	filled
+ ing	filling
+ er	filler*
film	
+ s	films
+ ed	filmed
+ ing	filming
+ dom	filmdom
+ ic	filmic
+ al + ly	filmically
+ y	filmy
+ er	filmier
+ est	filmiest
+ y + ly	filmily
+ ness	filminess
+ card	filmcard
+ make + er	filmmaker*
+ make + ing	filmmaking
+ set	filmset^
+ strip	filmstrip*
filth	
+ y	filthy
+ er	filthier
+ est	filthiest

F

+ ly	filthily
+ ness	filthiness
final	
+ s	finals
+ e	finale*
+ ist	finalist*
+ ity	finality
+ ize	finalize^
+ tion	finalization
+ ly	finally
finance	
+ s	finances
+ ed	financed
+ ing	financing
+ al	financial
+ ly	financially
+ er	financier*
find	
+ s	finds
+ ed	found
+ ing	finding*
+ er	finder
fine	
+ s	fines
+ ed	fined
+ ing	fining
+ er	finer
+ est	finest
+ ery	finery*
finger	
+ s	fingers
+ ed	fingered
+ ing	fingering
+ like	fingerlike
+ board	fingerboard*
+ nail	fingernail*
+ post	fingerpost*
+ print	fingerprint*^
+ tip	fingertip*
finish	
+ s	finishes
+ ed	finished
+ ing	finishing
+ er	finisher*
Finland	
+ ic	Finnic
+ ish	Finnish
+ tion	Finlandization
fire	
+ s	fires
+ ed	fired
+ ing	firing
+ er	firer
+ less	fireless
+ y	fiery
+ y + er	fierier
+ est	fieriest
+ arm	firearm*
+ ball	fireball*
+ boat	fireboat*
+ bomb	firebomb
+ box	firebox
+ brand	firebrand
+ break	firebreak
+ brick	firebrick
+ bug	firebug
+ clay	fireclay
+ crack + er	firecracker
+ damp	firedamp
+ dog	firedog
+ fight	firefight
+ fly	firefly
+ guard	fireguard
+ house	firehouse
+ light	firelight
+ lock	firelock
+ man	fireman*
+ place	fireplace
+ plug	fireplug
+ power	firepower
+ proof	fireproof^
+ room	fireroom
+ side	fireside
+ stone	firestone
+ trap	firetrap
+ water	firewater
+ weed	fireweed
+ wood	firewood
+ work	firework*
firm	
+ s	firms
+ ed	firmed
+ ing	firming
+ er	firmer
+ est	firmest
+ ly	firmly
+ ness	firmness
first	
+ ly	firstly
+ birth + en	firstborn
+ fruit + s	firstfruits
+ hand	firsthand
fish	
+ s	fishes
+ ed	fished
+ ing	fishing
+ able	fishable
+ ity	fishability

+ er	fisher*
+ er + man	fisherman*
+ ery	fishery*
+ less	fishless
+ like	fishlike
+ y	fishy
+ y + er	fishier
+ est	fishiest
+ ness	fishiness
+ bone	fishbone
+ bowl	fishbowl
+ hook	fishhook
+ net	fishnet
+ tail	fishtail*^
+ way	fishway
+ wife	fishwife
+ y + back	fishyback
fit	
+ s	fits
+ ed	fitted
+ ing	fitting
+ er	fitter
+ est	fittest
+ ly	fitly
+ ness	fitness
+ ing + ly	fittingly
+ ing + ness	fittingness
+ ful	fitful
+ ful + ly	fitfully
+ ful + ness	fitfulness
+ ment	fitment
fix	
+ s	fixes
+ ed	fixed
+ ing	fixing
+ able	fixable
+ ate	fixate^
+ tion	fixation
+ ive	fixative*
+ ly	fixedly
+ ness	fixedness
+ er	fixer*
+ ity	fixity*
+ ure	fixture*
flabbergast	
+ s	flabbergasts
+ ed	flabbergasted
+ ing	flabbergasting
+ ly	flabbergastingly
flag	
+ s	flags
+ ed	flagged
+ ing	flagging
+ ly	flaggingly
+ man	flagman*
+ pole	flagpole
+ ship	flagship
+ staff	flagstaff
+ stick	flagstick
+ stone	flagstone
flake	
+ s	flakes
+ ed	flaked
+ ing	flaking
+ er	flaker
+ y	flaky
+ y + er	flakier
+ est	flakiest
+ ness	flakiness
flame	
+ s	flames
+ ed	flamed
+ ing	flaming
+ er	flamer
+ ing + ly	flamingly
+ able	flammable
+ ity	flammability
+ able + ly	flammably
+ out	flameout
+ proof	flameproof^
+ proof + er	flameproofer
+ throw + er	flamethrower*
flannel (2)	
+ ly	flannelly
flap	
+ s	flaps
+ ed	flapped
+ ing	flapping
+ able	flappable
+ er	flapper*
+ y	flappy
flapjack*	
flare	
+ s	flares
+ ed	flared
+ ing	flaring
+ ly	flaringly
+ back	flareback
flash	
+ s	flashes
+ ed	flashed
+ ing	flashing
+ er	flasher*
+ y	flashy
+ y + er	flashier
+ est	flashiest
+ ly	flashily
+ ness	flashiness
+ back	flashback*
+ board	flashboard*

F

+ bulb flashbulb*
+ cube flashcube*
+ gun flashgun*
+ over flashover*

flashlight*

flat

+ s flats
+ ly flatly
+ ness flatness
+ en flatten^
+ en + er flattener*
+ er flatter
+ est flattest
+ ish flattish
+ bed flatbed
+ boat flatboat
+ cap flatcap
+ car flatcar
+ fish flatfish
+ foot flatfoot*
+ feet flatfeet
+ iron flatiron
+ land flatland*
+ land + er flatlander*
+ top flattop
+ ware flatware
+ worm flatworm
+ way + s flatways
+ wise flatwise
+ work flatwork

flatter

+ s flatters
+ ed flattered
+ ing flattering
+ ly flatteringly
+ y flattery*

flavor

+ s flavors
+ ed flavored
+ ing flavoring*
+ ful flavorful
+ ly flavorfully
+ less flavorless
+ some flavorsome

flee^

flesh

+ s fleshes
+ ed fleshed
+ ing fleshing*
+ y fleshy
+ er fleshier
+ est fleshiest
+ ness fleshiness
+ ly fleshly
+ ment fleshment
+ color fleshcolor
+ hook fleshhook
+ pot fleshpot
+ wound fleshwound

flew

flex

+ s flexes
+ ed flexed
+ ing flexing
+ ible flexible
+ ity flexibility
+ ible + ly flexibly
+ ile flexile
+ ion flexion
+ or flexor*
+ ous flexuous
+ ous + ly flexuously
+ ure flexure
+ al flexural

fling

+ s flings
+ ed flung
+ ing flinging
+ er flinger

flirt

+ s flirts
+ ed flirted
+ ing flirting
+ er flirter
+ ous flirtatious
+ ly flirtatiously
+ ness flirtatiousness
+ y flirty

float

+ s floats
+ ed floated
+ ing floating
+ er floater*
+ age floatage
+ tion floatation
+ y floaty
+ plane floatplane*

flock^

flood

+ s floods
+ ed flooded
+ ing flooding
+ er flooder
+ gate floodgate*
+ light floodlight*
+ plain floodplain*
+ wall floodwall*
+ water floodwater*
+ way floodway*

floor	
+ s	floors
+ ed	floored
+ ing	flooring
+ er	floorer
+ age	floorage
+ board	floorboard*
+ walk + er	floorwalker*
flour	
+ s	flours
+ ed	floured
+ ing	flouring
+ less	flourless
+ y	floury
flow	
+ s	flows
+ ed	flowed
+ ing	flowing
+ ly	flowingly
+ age	flowage
+ chart	flowchart*
+ chart + ing	flowcharting
flower	
+ s	flowers
+ ed	flowered
+ ing	flowering
+ age	flowerage
+ less	flowerless
+ like	flowerlike
+ y	flowery
+ ness	floweriness
+ pot	flowerpot*
flu	
+ like	flulike
fluid	
+ t	fluent
+ s	fluids
+ ly	fluidly
+ ness	fluidness
+ al	fluidal
+ al + ly	fluidally
+ ic	fluidic*
+ ity	fluidity
+ ize	fluidize^
+ er	fluidizer
+ tion	fluidization
flunk	
+ s	flunks
+ ed	flunked
+ ing	flunking
+ er	flunker
flush	
+ s	flushes
+ ed	flushed
+ ing	flushing
+ ness	flushness
flute	
+ s	flutes
+ ed	fluted
+ ing	fluting
+ like	flutelike
+ er	fluter
+ ist	flutist*
+ y	fluty
flutter	
+ s	flutters
+ ed	fluttered
+ ing	fluttering
+ er	fluttoror
+ y	fluttery
+ board	flutterboard*
fly	
+ s	flies
+ ed	flew
+ en	flown
+ ing	flying
+ er	flier*
+ able	flyable
+ t	flight*
+ less	flightless
+ y	flighty
+ y + er	flightier
+ est	flightiest
+ ly	flightily
+ ness	flightiness
+ away	flyaway
+ belt	flybelt
+ blow	flyblow^
+ boat	flyboat*
+ by	flyby*
+ catch + er	flycatcher*
+ leaf	flyleaf
+ man	flyman*
+ over	flyover
+ paper	flypaper
+ pass + t	flypast
+ way	flyway
+ weigh + t	flyweight
+ wheel	flywheel
foam	
+ s	foams
+ ed	foamed
+ ing	foaming
+ er	foamer
+ able	foamable
+ y	foamy

+ y + er	foamier
+ est	foamiest
+ ly	foamily
+ ness	foaminess
+ less	foamless
focus	
+ s	focuses
+ ed	focused
+ ing	focusing
+ er	focuser
+ able	focusable
+ al	focal
+ ly	focally
+ ize	focalize^
+ tion	focalization
foe*	
fog	
+ s	fogs
+ ed	fogged
+ ing	fogging
+ er	fogger*
+ less	fogless
+ y	foggy
+ y + er	foggier
+ est	foggiest
+ ly	foggily
+ ness	fogginess
+ bind + ed	fogbound
+ bow	fogbow*
+ dog	fogdog*
+ horn	foghorn*
fold (2)	
+ s	folds
+ ed	folded
+ ing	folding
+ er	folder*
+ able	foldable
+ away	foldaway
+ boat	foldboat*
+ boat + er	foldboater
+ out	foldout
folk	
+ s	folks
+ ish	folkish
+ ish + ness	folkishness
+ like	folklike
+ s + y	folksy
+ er	folksier
+ est	folksiest
+ ly	folksily
+ y + ness	folksiness
+ y	folkie*
+ sing + er	folksinger*
+ sing + ing	folksinging

+ tale	folktale*
+ way	folkway*
follow	
+ s	follows
+ ed	followed
+ ing	following
+ er	follower*
+ ship	followship
fond	
+ er	fonder
+ est	fondest
+ ly	fondly
+ ness	fondness
food	
+ s	foods
+ less	foodless
+ ness	foodlessness
+ stuff	foodstuff*
fool	
+ s	fools
+ ed	fooled
+ ing	fooling
+ er	fooler
+ ish	foolish
+ ish + ness	foolishness
+ ish + ly	foolishly
+ ery	foolery*
+ hard + y	foolhardy
+ hard + y + ly	foolhardily
+ hard + y + ness	foolhardiness
+ proof	foolproof
foot	
foot signed twice	feet
+ s	foots
+ ed	footed
+ ing	footing
+ age	footage
+ less	footless
+ like	footlike
+ bath	footbath
+ board	footboard
+ boy	footboy
+ bridge	footbridge
+ candle	footcandle
+ cloth	footcloth
+ fall	footfall
+ hill	foothill
+ hold	foothold
+ light	footlight*
+ lock + er	footlocker
+ loose	footloose
+ man	footman
+ mark	footmark
+ note	footnote

+ pad	footpad
+ path	footpath
+ print	footprint
+ race	footrace
+ rest	footrest
+ rope	footrope
+ sore	footsore
+ sore + ness	footsoreness
+ step	footstep
+ stone	footstone
+ wall	footwall
+ way	footway
+ wear	footwear
+ work	footwork

football

+ s	footballs
+ er	footballer*

for

+ ever	forever
+ ever + more	forevermore
+ ever + ness	foreverness

forbid

+ s	forbids
+ ed	forbade
+ en	forbidden
+ ing	forbidding
+ er	forbidder
+ ance	forbiddance
+ ly	forbiddingly
+ ness	forbiddingness

force

+ s	forces
+ ed	forced
+ ing	forcing
+ er	forcer
+ ed + ly	forcedly
+ ful	forceful
+ ful + ly	forcefully
+ ful + ness	forcefulness
+ ible	forcible
+ ible + ly	forcibly
+ ible + ness	forcibleness
+ less	forceless

fore -

+ arm	forearm*^
+ bay	forebay
+ bear	forebear*
+ brain	forebrain
+ castle	forecastle
+ close	foreclose^
+ close + ure	foreclosure*
+ deck	foredeck
+ face	foreface
+ father	forefather
+ feel	forefeel
+ finger	forefinger
+ foot	forefoot
+ front	forefront
+ gather	foregather
+ go	forego^
+ ground	foreground
+ hand	forehand
+ hand + ed	forehanded
+ hand + ed + ly	forehandedly
+ hand + ed + ness	forehandedness
+ head	forehead
+ hoof	forehoof
+ judge	forejudge
+ know	foreknow^
+ know + edge	foreknowledge
+ lady	forelady
+ land	foreland
+ leg	foreleg
+ limb	forelimb
+ lock	forelock
+ man	foreman
+ man + ship	foremanship
+ mast	foremast
+ milk	foremilk
+ more + est	foremost
+ mother	foremother
+ name	forename
+ noon	forenoon
+ part	forepart
+ pass + ed	forepassed
+ paw	forepaw
+ peak	forepeak
+ play	foreplay
+ quarter	forequarter
+ reach	forereach
+ run	forerun
+ run + er	forerunner
+ saddle	foresaddle
+ say + ed	foresaid
+ sail	foresail
+ see	foresee^
+ see + able	foreseeable
+ shade + w	foreshadow^
+ sheet	foresheet
+ shore	foreshore
+ short + en	foreshorten^
+ show	foreshow
+ side	foreside
+ sight	foresight
+ sight + ed	foresighted
+ sight + ed + ly	foresightedly
+ sight + ed + ness	foresightedness
+ sight + ful	foresightful

F

+ skin	foreskin
+ speak	forespeak^
+ stage	forestage
+ stall	forestall
+ stall + ment	forestallment
+ stay	forestay
+ swear	foreswear
+ taste	foretaste
+ tell	foretell^
+ thought	forethought
+ thought + ful	forethoughtful
+ thought + ful + ly	forethoughtfully
+ thought + ful + ness	forethoughtfulness
+ time	foretime
+ top	foretop
+ warn	forewarn^
+ wing	forewing
+ woman	forewoman
+ word	foreword
+ yard	foreyard
foreign	
+ er	foreigner*
+ ness	foreignness
+ ism	foreignism*
forest	
+ s	forests
+ ed	forested
+ ing	foresting
+ al	forestal
+ er	forester*
+ r + y	forestry
+ tion	forestation
forget	
+ s	forgets
+ ed	forgot
+ en	forgotten
+ ing	forgetting
+ er	forgetter
+ able	forgetable
+ ful	forgetful
+ ly	forgetfully
+ ness	forgetfulness
forgive	
+ s	forgives
+ ed	forgave
+ en	forgiven
+ ing	forgiving
+ able	forgivable
+ able + ly	forgivably
+ ness	forgiveness
+ ing + ly	forgivingly
+ ing + ness	forgivingness
fork	
+ s	forks
+ ed	forked
+ ing	forking
+ er	forker
+ ful	forkful
+ y	forky
+ y + er	forkier
+ est	forkiest
form	
+ s	forms
+ ed	formed
+ ing	forming
+ er	former
+ able	formable
+ able + ity	formability
+ al	formal
+ al + ly	formally
+ al + ness	formalness
+ in + form + al	informal
+ in + form + **ly**	informally
+ in + form + al + ity	informality
+ ism	formalism
+ al + ity	formality*
+ ist	formalist
+ ic	formalistic
+ ic + al + ly	formalistically
+ ful	formful
+ less	formless
+ less + ly	formlessly
+ less + ness	formlessness
+ ize	formalize^
+ ize + able	formalizable
+ ize + tion	formalization
+ ize + er	formalizer
+ tion	formation*
+ tion + al	formational
+ ive	formative
+ ive + ly	formatively
+ ive + ness	formativeness
+ fit + ing	formfitting
former	
+ ly	formerly
formula	
+ s	formulas
+ ar + ize	formularize^
+ ar + ize + tion	formularization
+ ar + ize + er	formularizer
+ ate	formulate^
+ ate + or	formulator
+ ate + tion	formulation
+ ic	formulaic
+ ly	formulaically
+ r + y	formulary
+ ize	formulize^
+ ize + tion	formulization
fort	
+ s	forts

+ e	forte
+ ify	fortify^
+ er	fortifier*
+ tion	fortification*
+ ess	fortress*
forth	
+ come + ing	forthcoming
+ right	forthright
+ with	forthwith
fortunate	
+ ly	fortunately
+ ness	fortunateness
fortune^	
forward	
+ s	forwards
+ ed	forwarded
+ ing	forwarding
+ er	forwarder
+ ly	forwardly
+ ness	forwardness
fossil (2)	
+ s	fossils
+ ize	fossilize^
+ tion	fossilization
+ ous	fossiliferous
foster	
+ s	fosters
+ ed	fostered
+ ing	fostering
+ er	fosterer
+ age	fosterage
found	
+ s	founds
+ ed	founded
+ ing	founding
+ er	founder*
+ tion	foundation*
+ al	foundational
+ ly	foundationally
+ less	foundationless
fountain	
+ s	fountains
+ ed	fountained
+ ing	fountaining
+ head	fountainhead
fox	
+ s	foxes
+ ed	foxed
+ ing	foxing
+ y	foxy
+ er	foxier
+ est	foxiest
+ ly	foxily
+ ness	foxiness

+ hole	foxhole
+ tail	foxtail
fraction	
+ s	fractions
+ al	fractional
+ ize	fractionalize^
+ ize + tion	fractionalization
+ ly	fractionally
+ ate	fractionate^
+ ate + tion	fractionation
+ or	fractionator
fragile	
+ ity	fragility
fragment	
+ s	fragments
+ ed	fragmented
+ ing	fragmenting
+ al	fragmental
+ al + ly	fragmentally
+ ary	fragmentary
+ ary + ly	fragmentarily
+ ness	fragmentariness
+ ate	fragmentate^
+ tion	fragmentation
+ ize	fragmentize^
+ er	fragmentizer
fragrant	
+ ance	fragrance*
+ y	fragrancy*
+ ly	fragrantly
frame	
+ s	frames
+ ed	framed
+ ing	framing
+ able	framable
+ er	framer
+ work	framework
France (2)	
frank	
+ s	franks
+ ed	franked
+ ing	franking
+ able	frankable
+ er	franker
+ ly	frankly
+ ness	frankness
frankfurter*	
freak	
+ s	freaks
+ ed	freaked
+ ing	freaking
+ y	freaky
+ er	freakier
+ est	freakiest

F

+ ish	freakish
+ ly	freakishly
+ ness	freakishness
freckle	
+ s	freckles
+ ed	freckled
+ ing	freckling
+ ly	freckly
free	
+ s	frees
+ ed	freed
+ ing	freeing
+ er	freer
+ est	freest
+ dom	freedom
+ ly	freely
+ ness	freeness
+ board	freeboard
+ boot	freeboot
+ boot + er	freebooter
+ birth + en	freeborn
+ ed + man	freedman
+ ed + woman	freedwoman
+ hold	freehold
+ load	freeload
+ stand + ing	freestanding
+ stone	freestone
+ style	freestyle
+ think + er	freethinker
+ wheel	freewheel^
+ will	freewill
freeway*	
freeze	
+ s	freezes
+ ed	froze
+ en	frozen
+ ing	freezing
+ ing + ly	freezingly
+ er	freezer
+ en + ly	frozenly
+ ness	frozenness
freight	
+ s	freights
+ ed	freighted
+ ing	freighting
+ er	freighter*
+ age	freightage
french fry^	
frequent	
+ s	frequents
+ ed	frequented
+ ing	frequenting
+ er	frequenter
+ tion	frequentation
+ ive	frequentative

+ ence	frequence
+ y	frequency*
+ ly	frequently
+ ness	frequentness
fresh	
+ en	freshen^
+ en + er	freshener
+ ly	freshly
+ ness	freshness
+ water	freshwater
freshman*	
Friday	
friend	
+ s	friends
+ ed	friended
+ ing	friending
+ ly	friendly
+ ly + ness	friendliness
+ er	friendlier
+ est	friendliest
+ less	friendless
+ less + ness	friendlessness
+ ship	friendship
fright	
+ en	frighten^
+ ful	frightful
+ ly	frightfully
+ ness	frightfulness
fringe	
+ s	fringes
+ ed	fringed
+ ing	fringing
+ y	fringy
frisbee*	
frisk	
+ s	frisks
+ ed	frisked
+ ing	frisking
+ er	frisker
+ y	frisky
+ y + er	friskier
+ est	friskiest
+ ly	friskily
+ ness	friskiness
frog	
+ s	frogs
+ man	frogman*
from	
front	
+ s	fronts
+ ed	fronted
+ ing	fronting
+ age	frontage
+ al	frontal
+ ity	frontality

+ er	frontier*
+ er + s + man	frontiersman*
+ court	frontcourt
+ line	frontline*
+ ward	frontward
frost	
+ s	frosts
+ ed	frosted
+ ing	frosting
+ y	frosty
+ er	frostier
+ est	frostiest
+ ly	frostily
+ ness	frostiness
+ bite	frostbite^
+ work	frostwork
frown	
+ s	frowns
+ ed	frowned
+ ing	frowning
+ er	frowner
+ ly	frowningly
fruit	
+ s	fruits
+ age	fruitage
+ ful	fruitful
+ ion	fruition
+ less	fruitless
+ ly	fruitlessly
+ less + ness	fruitlessness
+ y	fruity
+ er	fruitier
+ est	fruitiest
+ ness	fruitiness
+ ify	fructify^
+ ify + tion	fructification
+ ous	fructuous
+ cake	fruitcake
frustrate	
+ s	frustrates
+ ed	frustrated
+ ing	frustrating
+ ly	frustratingly
+ ion	frustration*
fry	
+ s	fries
+ ed	fried
+ ing	frying
+ er	fryer
fudge^	
fudgesicle*	
fuel	
+ s	fuels
+ ed	fueled
+ ing	fueling
+ er	fueler
full	
+ y	fully
+ ness	fullness
+ fill	fulfill^
+ fill + ment	fulfillment*
fun (2)	
+ s	funs
+ ed	funned
+ ing	funning
+ y	funny*
+ er	funnier
+ est	funniest
+ ly	funnily
+ ness	funniness
function	
+ s	functions
+ ed	functioned
+ ing	functioning
+ al	functional
+ ly	functionally
+ ism	functionalism
+ ist	functionalist
+ ic	functionalistic
+ ity	functionality
+ ary	functionary
+ less	functionless
+ or	functor*
fundamental	
+ ly	fundamentally
+ ism	fundamentalism
+ ist	fundamentalist
+ ic	fundamentalistic
funeral	
+ s	funerals
+ al	funereal
+ ly	funereally
+ ary	funerary
fungus	
+ al	fungal
funnel^	
fur	
+ s	furs
+ ed	furred
+ ing	furring
+ less	furless
+ y	furry
+ er	furrier*
+ est	furriest
+ ery	furriery
+ bear + er	furbearer*
+ bear + ing	furbearing

furnace*
furnish

+ s	furnishes
+ ed	furnished
+ ing	furnishing*
+ er	furnisher

furniture
fury

+ s	furies
+ ous	furious
+ ly	furiously
+ or	furor

fuss

+ s	fusses
+ ed	fussed
+ ing	fussing
+ y	fussy
+ ly	fussily
+ ness	fussiness

future

+ s	futures
+ less	futureless
+ ism	futurism
+ ist	futurist
+ ic	futuristic
+ ly	futuristically
+ ity	futurity

gain

+ s	gains
+ ed	gained
+ ing	gaining
+ er	gainer*
+ ful	gainful
+ ful + ly	gainfully
+ ful + ness	gainfulness
+ less	gainless
+ less + ness	gainlessness
+ ly	gainly

galaxy

+ s	galaxies
+ ic	galactic

Gallaudet

gallery

+ s	galleries
+ ed	galleried
+ ite	galleryite
+ go + er	gallerygoer*

gallon

+ s	gallons
+ age	gallonage

gallop

+ s	gallops
+ ed	galloped
+ ing	galloping
+ er	galloper

gamble

+ s	gambles
+ ed	gambled
+ ing	gambling
+ er	gambler*

game (2)

+ s	games
+ ed	gamed
+ ing	gaming
+ ly	gamely
+ ness	gameness
+ keep + er	gamekeeper
+ ship	gamesmanship
+ some	gamesome
+ some + ly	gamesomely
+ some + ness	gamesomeness

gang

+ s	gangs
+ ed	ganged
+ ing	ganging
+ er	ganger*
+ land	gangland

garage

+ s	garages
+ ed	garaged
+ ing	garaging
+ man	garageman

garbage

+ man	garbageman

garden

+ s	gardens
+ ed	gardened
+ ing	gardening
+ er	gardener

gas

+ s	gases
+ ed	gassed
+ ing	gassing
+ er	gasser*
+ ous	gaseous
+ ous + ness	gaseousness
+ ify	gasify^
+ ify + er	gasifier
+ tion	gasification
+ y	gassy
+ y + er	gassier
+ est	gassiest
+ y + ness	gassiness
+ bag	gasbag*
+ hold + er	gasholder
+ house	gashouse
+ light	gaslight
+ light + ed	gaslit
+ tight	gastight
+ tight + ness	gastightness
+ work + s	gasworks

gasoline

gate (2)

+ s	gates
+ ed	gated

+ ing	gating
+ fold	gatefold
+ keep + er	gatekeeper*
+ leg	gateleg
+ post	gatepost*
+ way	gateway*
gather	
+ s	gathers
+ ed	gathered
+ ing	gathering
+ er	gatherer*
gay	
+ er	gayer
+ est	gayest
+ ness	gayness
+ ly	gaily
+ ity	gaiety
gaze	
+ s	gazes
+ ed	gazed
+ ing	gazing
+ er	gazer*
geese	
gem^	
+ s	gems
+ ed	gemmed
+ ing	gemming
+ stone	gemstone*
gender^	
gene	
+ s	genes
+ ic	genic
+ ly	genically
general	
+ s	generals
+ ly	generally
+ ist	generalist
+ ity	generality*
+ ize	generalize^
+ able	generalizable
+ tion	generalization*
+ er	generalizer
+ ship	generalship
generate	
+ s	generates
+ ed	generated
+ ing	generating
+ tion	generation*
+ al	generational
+ ive	generative
+ or	generator*
generous	
+ ly	generously
+ ness	generousness
+ ity	generosity*

genius*	
gentle	
+ s	gentles
+ ed	gentled
+ ing	gentling
+ er	gentler
+ est	gentlest
+ ly	gently
+ folk	gentlefolk*
+ person	gentleperson
+ woman	gentlewoman*
gentleman	
+ ly	gentlemanly
gentlemen	
genuine	
+ ly	genuinely
+ ness	genuineness
geography	
+ er	geographer*
+ ic	geographic
+ al	geographical
+ ly	geographically
geometry	
+ s	geometries
+ ic	geometric
+ al	geometrical
+ ly	geometrically
+ an	geometrician*
+ ize	geometrize^
+ tion	geometrization
+ er	geometer
gerbil*	
germ	
+ s	germs
+ an	german
+ y	germy
+ er	germier
+ est	germiest
+ al	germinal
+ ly	germinally
+ ate	germinate^
+ ity	germinability
+ tion	germination
+ ive	germinative
+ free	germfree
+ proof	germproof
German (2)	
+ ic	Germanic
+ ism	Germanism
+ ist	Germanist
+ ize	germanize^
+ tion	germanization
Germany	
gesture	
+ s	gestures

+ ed	gestured
+ ing	gesturing
+ ic	gestic
+ al	gestural
+ ant	gesticulant
+ ate	gesticulate^
+ tion	gesticulation
+ ive	gesticulative
+ or	gesticulator
+ ory	gesticulatory
get	
+ s	gets
+ ed	got
+ en	gotten
+ ing	getting
ghost	
+ s	ghosts
+ ed	ghosted
+ ing	ghosting
+ ly	ghostly
+ er	ghostlier
+ est	ghostliest
+ ness	ghostliness
+ like	ghostlike
+ y	ghosty
+ write	ghostwrite^
+ write + er	ghostwriter
giant	
+ s	giants
+ ess	giantess
+ ism	giantism
+ like	giantlike
gift	
+ s	gifts
+ ed	gifted
+ ing	gifting
+ ly	giftedly
+ ness	giftedness
+ ware	giftware
gigantic	
+ ly	gigantically
+ ism	gigantism
giggle	
+ s	giggles
+ ed	giggled
+ ing	giggling
+ er	giggler
+ ly	giggly
+ ing + ly	gigglingly
gill	
+ s	gills
+ ed	gilled
+ ing	gilling
+ y	gilly
ginger	
+ s	gingers
+ ed	gingered
+ ing	gingering
+ ly	gingerly
+ ness	gingerliness
+ y	gingery
+ bread	gingerbread
+ root	gingerroot*
+ snap	gingersnap*
giraffe*	
girl	
+ s	girls
+ hood	girlhood
+ ish	girlish
+ ly	girlishly
+ ness	girlishness
+ y	girly
+ friend	girlfriend*
give	
+ s	gives
+ ed	gave
+ en	given
+ ing	giving
+ er	giver
+ away	giveaway*
glacier	
+ s	glaciers
+ al	glacial
+ ly	glacially
+ ate	glaciate^
+ tion	glaciation
glad	
+ en	gladden^
+ er	gladder
+ est	gladdest
+ ly	gladly
+ ness	gladness
+ some	gladsome
+ some + ly	gladsomely
+ some + ness	gladsomeness
glance	
+ s	glances
+ ed	glanced
+ ing	glancing
+ er	glancer
+ ly	glancingly
glass	
+ s	glasses
+ ed	glassed
+ ing	glassing
+ ful	glassful
+ ine	glassine
+ less	glassless

+ y	glassy*
+ y + er	glassier
+ est	glassiest
+ er	glazier
+ ery	glaziery
+ blow + er	glassblower*
+ blow + ing	glassblowing
+ house	glasshouse
+ make + er	glassmaker*
+ make + ing	glassmaking
+ ware	glassware
+ work	glasswork
+ work + er	glassworker
glaze	
+ s	glazes
+ ed	glazed
+ ing	glazing
+ er	glazer
glide	
+ s	glides
+ ed	glided
+ ing	gliding
+ er	glider
glimpse	
+ s	glimpses
+ ed	glimpsed
+ ing	glimpsing
+ er	glimpser
glisten^	
globe	
+ s	globes
+ ed	globed
+ ing	globing
+ al	global
+ ly	globally
+ ism	globalism
+ ist	globalist
+ ize	globalize^
+ tion	globalization
+ fish	globefish
+ flower	globeflower
glory	
+ s	glories
+ ed	gloried
+ ing	glorying
+ ify	glorify^
+ tion	glorification
+ er	glorifier
+ ous	glorious
+ ly	gloriously
+ ness	gloriousness
glove	
+ s	gloves
+ ed	gloved

+ ing	gloving
+ er	glover
glow	
+ s	glows
+ ed	glowed
+ ing	glowing
+ ly	glowingly
+ worm	glowworm
glue	
+ s	glues
+ ed	glued
+ ing	glueing
+ y	gluey
+ y + ly	gluily
+ ous	glutinous
+ ous + ly	glutinously
go	
+ s	goes
+ ed	went
+ en	gone
+ ing	going
+ er	goer*
+ en + er	goner*
goal	
+ s	goals
+ y	goalie*
+ keep + er	goalkeeper*
+ post	goalpost*
+ tend + er	goaltender*
+ tend + ing	goaltending
goat	
+ s	goats
+ ee	goatee*
+ ish	goatish
+ like	goatlike
+ fish	goatfish
+ herd	goatherd*
+ skin	goatskin*
+ suck + er	goatsucker*
gobble	
+ s	gobbles
+ ed	gobbled
+ ing	gobbling
+ er	gobbler*
goblet*	
goblin*	
god	
+ s	gods
+ ed	godded
+ ing	godding
+ ess	goddess*
+ hood	godhood
+ less	godless
+ less + ness	godlessness

+ like	godlike
+ like + ness	godlikeness
+ ly	godly
+ er	godlier
+ est	godliest
+ ly + ness	godliness
+ child	godchild
+ daughter	goddaughter
+ father	godfather
+ mother	godmother
+ son	godson
+ head	godhead
+ send	godsend
+ speed	Godspeed
gold	
+ en	golden
+ ly	goldenly
+ ness	goldenness
+ brick	goldbrick*^
+ bug	goldbug
+ eye	goldeneye
+ field	goldfield
+ fish	goldfish
+ stone	goldstone
golf	
+ s	golfs
+ ed	golfed
+ ing	golfing
+ er	golfer*
good	
+ s	goods
+ ish	goodish
+ ly	goodly
+ ly + er	goodlier
+ ly + est	goodliest
+ ness	goodness
+ y	goody*
+ will	goodwill
+ will + ed	goodwilled
goof	
+ s	goofs
+ ed	goofed
+ ing	goofing
+ er	goofer
+ y	goofy
+ y + er	goofier
+ est	goofiest
+ ly	goofily
+ ness	goofiness
+ ball	goofball*
goose	
+ s	gooses
+ ed	goosed
+ ing	goosing
+ y	goosey
+ er	goosier
+ est	goosiest
+ berry	gooseberry*
+ flesh	gooseflesh
+ neck	gooseneck*
gopher*	
gorgeous	
+ ly	gorgeously
+ ness	gorgeousness
gorilla*	
gospel	
+ er	gospeler
gossip	
+ s	gossips
+ ed	gossiped
+ ing	gossiping
+ er	gossiper
+ r + y	gossipry
+ y	gossipy
govern	
+ s	governs
+ ed	governed
+ ing	governing
+ able	governable
+ ance	governance
+ ess	governess*
+ y	governessy
+ ment	government*
+ al	governmental
+ ly	governmentally
+ ism	governmentalism
+ ist	governmentalist
+ ize	governmentalize^
+ or	governor*
+ ate	governorate
+ ship	governorship
+ ate + or	gubernator
+ or + al	gubernatorial
gown	
+ s	gowns
+ s + man	gownsman
grab	
+ s	grabs
+ ed	grabbed
+ ing	grabbing
+ er	grabber
+ y	grabby
+ y + er	grabbier
+ est	grabbiest
grace	
+ s	graces
+ ed	graced
+ ing	gracing
+ ful	graceful

G

+ ful + ness	gracefulness
+ ful + ly	gracefully
+ less	graceless
+ less + ness	gracelessness
+ less + ly	gracelessly
+ ile	gracile
+ ity	gracility
+ **ness**	gracileness
+ ous	gracious
+ ous + ness	graciousness
+ ous + ly	graciously
grade	
+ s	grades
+ ed	graded
+ ing	grading
+ er	grader*
+ able	gradable
+ ate	gradate^
+ tion	gradation
+ al	gradational
+ ly	gradationally
+ less	gradeless
+ ent	gradient*
gradual	
+ ism	gradualism
+ ist	gradualist
+ ly	gradually
+ ness	gradualness
graduate	
+ s	graduates
+ ed	graduated
+ ing	graduating
+ or	graduator
+ ion	graduation*
graham	
grain	
+ s	grains
+ ed	grained
+ ing	graining
+ er	grainer
+ ary	granary*
+ y	grainy
+ y + er	grainier
+ est	grainiest
+ ness	graininess
+ ile	granule*
+ ile + ar	granular
+ ate	granulate^
+ tion	granulation
+ ive	granulative
+ or	granulator
gram*	
grammar	
+ s	grammars
+ an	grammarian*
+ al	grammatical
+ ity	grammaticality
+ ly	grammatically
+ ness	grammaticalness
grand	
+ er	grander
+ est	grandest
+ ly	grandly
+ ness	grandness
+ ee	grandee*
+ aunt	grandaunt*
+ baby	grandbaby*
+ child	grandchild*
+ dad	granddad
+ dad + y	granddaddy*
+ nephew	grandnephew*
+ niece	grandniece*
+ parent	grandparent*
+ parent + al	grandparental
+ parent + hood	grandparenthood
+ stand	grandstand^
+ stand + er	grandstander
+ uncle	granduncle*
granddaughter*	
grandfather	
+ s	grandfathers
+ ly	grandfatherly
grandmother	
+ s	grandmothers
+ ly	grandmotherly
grandson*	
granola	
grant (2)	
+ s	grants
+ ed	granted
+ ing	granting
+ er, + or	granter, grantor
+ able	grantable
+ ee	grantee
+ s + man	grantsman
+ ship	grantsmanship
grape	
+ s	grapes
+ y	grapey
+ er	grapier
+ est	grapiest
+ shot	grapeshot
+ vine	grapevine
grapefruit	
graph	
+ s	graphs
+ ed	graphed
+ ing	graphing

G

+ ic	graphic*
+ al	graphical
+ ly	graphically
+ ness	graphicness
+ ite	graphite
+ ite + ic	graphitic
+ ize	graphitize^
+ able	graphitizable
+ tion	graphitization
grasp	
+ s	grasps
+ ed	grasped
+ ing	grasping
+ er	grasper
+ able	graspable
+ ly	graspingly
+ ness	graspingness
grass (2)	
+ s	grasses
+ ed	grassed
+ ing	grassing
+ like	grasslike
+ y	grassy
+ er	grassier
+ est	grassiest
+ land	grassland*
grasshopper*	
grate	
+ s	grates
+ ed	grated
+ ing	grating
+ er	grater*
grateful	
+ ly	gratefully
+ ness	gratefulness
gratitude	
grave	
+ s	graves
+ ed	graved
+ ing	graving
+ less	graveless
+ ly	gravely
+ ness	graveness
+ ure	gravure
+ ity	gravity
+ ate	gravitate^
+ tion	gravitation
+ al	gravitational
+ al + ly	gravitationally
+ ive	gravitative
+ yard	graveyard*
gravel^	
+ s	gravels
+ ed	graveled
+ ing	graveling
+ ly	gravelly
gravy*	
gray (2)	
+ s	grays
+ ed	grayed
+ ing	graying
+ ish	grayish
+ ly	grayly
+ ness	grayness
graze	
+ s	grazes
+ ed	grazed
+ ing	grazing
+ er	grazier
grease	
+ s	greases
+ ed	greased
+ ing	greasing
+ er	greaser
+ less	greaseless
+ y	greasy
+ y + er	greasier
+ est	greasiest
+ ly	greasily
+ ness	greasiness
+ paint	greasepaint
+ wood	greasewood
great	
+ s	greats
+ en	greaten^
+ er	greater
+ est	greatest
+ ly	greatly
+ ness	greatness
+ coat	greatcoat*
+ heart + ed	greathearted
+ heart **+ ly**	greatheartedly
+ heart **+ ness**	greatheartedness
Greece	
+ an	Grecian
+ an + ize	Grecianize^
+ ism	Grecism
+ ize	grecize^
greed	
+ y	greedy
+ er	greedier
+ est	greediest
+ ly	greedily
+ ness	greediness
green	
+ s	greens
+ ed	greened
+ ing	greening
+ er	greener

G

+ est greenest
+ ery greenery
+ ish greenish
+ ish + ness greenishness
+ ly greenly
+ ness greenness
+ y greeny
+ back greenback
+ belt greenbelt
+ bug greenbug
+ grocer greengrocer
+ horn greenhorn
+ house greenhouse
+ room greenroom
+ sick greensick
+ stuff greenstuff
+ wing greenwing
+ wood greenwood

gremlin*

grey (see gray)

grief

+ less griefless

grieve

+ s grieves
+ ed grieved
+ ing grieving
+ er griever
+ ance grievance*
+ ant grievant
+ ous grievous
+ ly grievously
+ ness grievousness

grill

+ s grills
+ ed grilled
+ ing grilling
+ er griller
+ room grillroom

grim

+ er grimmer
+ est grimmest
+ ly grimly
+ ness grimness

grin

+ s grins
+ ed grinned
+ ing grinning
+ er grinner
+ ly grinningly

grind

+ s grinds
+ ed ground
+ ing grinding
+ er grinder
+ ly grindingly
+ stone grindstone*

grip (2)

+ s grips
+ ed gripped
+ ing gripping
+ er gripper*
+ ly grippingly
+ sack gripsack*

gripe

+ s gripes
+ ed griped
+ ing griping
+ er griper*

groan

+ s groans
+ ed groaned
+ ing groaning
+ er groaner

grocer

+ s grocers
+ y grocery*

gross

+ ly grossly
+ ness grossness
+ er grosser

grouch

+ s grouches
+ ed grouched
+ ing grouching
+ y grouchy
+ er grouchier
+ est grouchiest
+ ly grouchily
+ ness grouchiness

ground

+ s grounds
+ ed grounded
+ ing grounding
+ er grounder*
+ less groundless
+ ly groundlessly
+ ness groundlessness
+ fish groundfish
+ hog groundhog
+ nut groundnut
+ out groundout
+ sheet groundsheet
+ water groundwater
+ wood groundwood
+ work groundwork

group

+ s groups
+ ed grouped

+ ing	grouping*
+ able	groupable
+ y	groupie*
+ think	groupthink
grove*	
grow	
+ s	grows
+ ed	grew
+ en	grown
+ ing	growing
+ er	grower*
+ ly	growingly
+ th	growth
growl	
+ s	growls
+ ed	growled
+ ing	growling
+ er	growler*
+ ly	growlingly
+ y	growly
+ y + er	growlier
+ est	growliest
+ ness	growliness
grumble	
+ s	grumbles
+ ed	grumbled
+ ing	grumbling
+ er	grumbler
+ ly	grumblingly
+ y	grumbly
guarantee	
+ s	guarantees
+ ed	guaranteed
+ ing	guaranteeing
+ or	guarantor*
+ y	guaranty^
guard	
+ s	guards
+ ed	guarded
+ ing	guarding
+ an	guardian*
+ ship	guardianship
+ ant	guardant
+ ly	guardedly
+ ness	guardedness
+ house	guardhouse
+ rail	guardrail*
+ room	guardroom*
+ man	guardsman*
guess	
+ s	guesses
+ ed	guessed
+ ing	guessing
+ er	guesser
+ work	guesswork
guest^	
guide	
+ s	guides
+ ed	guided
+ ing	guiding
+ er	guider
+ able	guidable
+ ance	guidance
+ book	guidebook*
+ line	guideline*
+ post	guidepost*
+ way	guideway
guilt	
+ less	guiltless
+ less + ly	guiltlessly
+ less + ness	guiltlessness
+ y	guilty
+ er	guiltier
+ est	guiltiest
+ y + ly	guiltily
+ y + ness	guiltiness
guinea pig*	
guitar	
+ s	guitars
+ ist	guitarist*
gulf*	
gull	
+ s	gulls
+ ed	gulled
+ ing	gulling
+ ible	gullible
+ ity	gullibility
+ ly	gullibly
gulp	
+ s	gulps
+ ed	gulped
+ ing	gulping
+ er	gulper
gum	
+ s	gums
+ ed	gummed
+ ing	gumming
+ er	gummer
+ ous	gummous
+ y	gummy
+ y + er	gummier
+ est	gummiest
+ ness	gumminess
+ boil	gumboil
+ drop	gumdrop*
+ shoe	gumshoe
gun	
+ s	guns
+ ed	gunned

+ ing	gunning
+ er	gunner*
+ ery	gunnery*
+ boat	gunboat*
+ cotton	guncotton
+ dog	gundog*
+ fight	gunfight*
+ fire	gunfire
+ man	gunman*
+ metal	gunmetal
+ play	gunplay
+ point	gunpoint
+ powder	gunpowder
+ run + er	gunrunner*
+ run + ing	gunrunning
+ ship	gunship*
+ shot	gunshot*
guy^	
gym	
+ s	gyms
+ ist	gymnast*
gymnastic*	
+ ly	gymnastically
gypsy*	

G

H

habilitate	
+ s	habilitates
+ ed	habilitated
+ ing	habilitating
+ tion	habilitation
habit	
+ s	habits
+ able	habitable
+ ity	habitability
+ able + ness	habitableness
+ able + ly	habitably
+ ant	habitant*
+ t	habitat*
+ tion	habitation*
+ al	habitual
+ al + ly	habitually
+ al + ness	habitualness
+ ate	habituate^
+ ate + tion	habituation
had (2)	
+ n't	hadn't
hail	
+ s	hails
+ ed	hailed
+ ing	hailing
+ er	hailer
+ stone	hailstone*
+ storm	hailstorm*
hair	
+ s	hairs
+ ed	haired
+ less	hairless
+ less + ness	hairlessness
+ like	hairlike
+ y	hairy
+ er	hairier
+ est	hairiest
+ y + ness	hairiness
+ brush	hairbrush*
+ cloth	haircloth
+ cut	haircut*
+ do	hairdo*
+ dress + er	hairdresser*
+ dress + ing	hairdressing
+ line	hairline*
+ piece	hairpiece*
+ pin	hairpin*
+ split + er	hairsplitter*
+ split + ing	hairsplitting
+ spring	hairspring
+ style	hairstyle
+ style + ing	hairstyling
+ style + ist	hairstylist
half	
+ s	halves
+ ed	halved
+ ing	halving
+ er + s	halvers
+ ness	halfness
+ penny	halfpenny
+ time	halftime
+ way	halfway
hall	
+ way	hallway*
Halloween	
hallucinate	
+ s	hallucinates
+ ed	hallucinated
+ ing	hallucinating
+ ion	hallucination*
+ al	hallucinational
+ ive	hallucinative
+ or	hallucinator*
+ ory	hallucinatory
halo^	
halt	
+ s	halts
+ ed	halted
+ ing	halting
+ ly	haltingly
ham	
+ s	hams
+ ed	hammed
+ ing	hamming
+ y	hammy
+ er	hammier

+ est hammiest
+ ly hammily
+ ness hamminess

hamburger*

hammer
+ s hammers
+ ed hammered
+ ing hammering
+ er hammerer
+ less hammerless
+ head hammerhead*
+ lock hammerlock*
+ toe hammertoe*

hamper^

hamster*

hand
+ s hands
+ ed handed
+ ing handing
+ less handless
+ y handy
+ er handier
+ est handiest
+ ly handily
+ y + ness handiness
+ ed + ness handedness
+ ful handful*
+ bag handbag*
+ ball handball
+ book handbook
+ car handcar
+ cart handcart
+ craft handcraft
+ y + craft handicraft
+ cuff handcuff
+ grip handgrip
+ gun handgun
+ list handlist
+ make + ed handmade
+ out handout
+ pick handpick^
+ press handpress
+ print handprint
+ rail handrail
+ saw handsaw
+ set handset
+ shake handshake
+ spring handspring
+ stand handstand
+ wheel handwheel
+ work handwork
+ y + work handiwork
+ write handwrite^
+ y + man handyman

handicap
+ s handicaps
+ ed handicapped
+ ing handicapping
+ er handicapper

handkerchief*

handle
+ s handles
+ ed handled
+ ing handling
+ er handler*
+ able handleable
+ less handleless
+ bar handlebar*

handsome
+ ly handsomely
+ ness handsomeness

hang
+ s hangs
+ ed hanged
+ en hung
+ ing hanging*
+ able hangable
+ man hangman
+ nail hangnail
+ out hangout
+ over hangover
+ tag hangtag

hangar*

hanger*

Hanukkah

happen
+ s happens
+ ed happened
+ ing happening*
+ chance happenchance

happy
+ er happier
+ est happiest
+ ly happily
+ ness happiness

harbor
+ s harbors
+ ed harbored
+ ing harboring
+ age harborage
+ er harborer
+ ful harborful
+ less harborless
+ master harbormaster

hard
+ er harder
+ est hardest
+ ly hardly

+ ness hardness
+ y hardy
+ y + er hardier
+ y + est hardiest
+ hood hardihood
+ y + ly hardily
+ y + ness hardiness
+ y + ly hardily
+ en harden^
+ en + er hardener*
+ back hardback*
+ ball hardball
+ board hardboard
+ boot hardboot
+ bind + ed hardbound
+ case hardcase
+ cover hardcover
+ hand + ed hardhanded
+ hand + ed + ness hardhandedness
+ head hardhead
+ head + ed hardheaded
+ head + ed + ness hardheadedness
+ head + ed + ly hardheadedly
+ heart + ed hardhearted
+ heart + ed + ly hardheartedly
+ heart + ed + ness hardheartedness
+ mouth + ed hardmouthed
+ pan hardpan
+ ship hardship*
+ stand hardstand
+ top hardtop
+ ware hardware
+ wood hardwood
+ work + ing hardworking

hare

+ s hares
+ ed hared
+ ing haring
+ bell harebell
+ brain + ed harebrained
+ lip harelip*
+ lip + ed harelipped

harm

+ s harms
+ ed harmed
+ ing harming
+ er harmer
+ ful harmful
+ less harmless
+ ly harmlessly
+ ness harmlessness

harmonica*

harmony

+ s harmonies
+ ic harmonic*
+ ic + al + ly harmonically
+ ic + al + ness harmonicalness
+ ous harmonious
+ ous + ly harmoniously
+ ous + ness harmoniousness
+ ist harmonist*
+ ist + ic harmonistic
+ ist + ic + al + ly harmonistically
+ ize harmonize^
+ er harmonizer*

harp

+ s harps
+ ed harped
+ ing harping
+ er harper
+ ist harpist*

harsh

+ ly harshly
+ ness harshness
+ er harsher
+ est harshest
+ en harshen^

harvest

+ s harvests
+ ed harvested
+ ing harvesting
+ er harvester*
+ able harvestable
+ man harvestman
+ time harvesttime

has (2)

+ n't hasn't

hassle^

hat

+ s hats
+ ed hatted
+ ing hatting
+ er hatter*
+ less hatless
+ band hatband
+ box hatbox
+ check hatcheck
+ make + er hatmaker

hatch

+ s hatches
+ ed hatched
+ ing hatching*
+ ery hatchery*
+ able hatchable
+ ity hatchability
+ back hatchback*
+ way hatchway

hatchet*

hate

+ s hates

+ ed	hated
+ ing	hating
+ er	hater
+ ful	hateful
+ ly	hatefully
+ ness	hatefulness
haul	
+ s	hauls
+ ed	hauled
+ ing	hauling
+ er	hauler
+ age	haulage
+ age + way	haulageway
haunt	
+ s	haunts
+ ed	haunted
+ ing	haunting
+ er	haunter
+ ly	hauntingly
have (2)	
+ s	has
+ ed	had
+ ing	having
+ n't	haven't
Hawaii	
+ an	Hawaiian*
hay	
+ s	hays
+ ed	hayed
+ ing	haying
+ fork	hayfork
+ make + er	haymaker
+ ride	hayride
+ seed	hayseed
+ stack	haystack
+ wire	haywire
haze	
+ s	hazes
+ ed	hazed
+ ing	hazing
+ er	hazer
+ y	hazy
+ y + er	hazier
+ est	haziest
+ ly	hazily
+ ness	haziness
he	
head	
+ s	heads
+ ed	headed
+ ing	heading
+ er	header*
+ less	headless
+ less + ness	headlessness
+ y	heady
+ y + er	headier
+ est	headiest
+ ly	headily
+ y + ness	headiness
+ ache	headache*
+ ache + y	headachy
+ band	headband*
+ board	headboard*
+ cheese	headcheese
+ dress	headdress*
+ first	headfirst
+ fore + more + est	headforemost
+ gate	headgate
+ hunt + er	headhunter
+ lamp	headlamp*
+ land	headland*
+ light	headlight*
+ line	headline*
+ line + er	headliner
+ lock	headlock
+ long	headlong
+ man	headman
+ s + man	headsman
+ master	headmaster
+ miss + ess	headmistress
+ more + est	headmost
+ note	headnote
+ phone	headphone
+ piece	headpiece
+ pin	headpin
+ quarter	headquarter*^
+ rest	headrest
+ room	headroom
+ sail	headsail
+ set	headset
+ ship	headship
+ shrink + er	headshrinker
+ space	headspace
+ spring	headspring
+ stone	headstone
+ stream	headstream
+ strong	headstrong
+ wait + er	headwaiter
+ water	headwater
+ way	headway
+ word	headword
+ work	headwork
heal	
+ s	heals
+ ed	healed
+ ing	healing
+ er	healer*

health	
+ ful	healthful
+ y	healthy
+ er	healthier
+ est	healthiest
+ ly	healthily
+ ness	healthiness
heap^	
hear	
+ s	hears
+ ed	heard
+ ing	hearing
+ er	hearer
+ say	hearsay
hearing aid*	
heart (2)	
+ s	hearts
+ ed	hearted
+ y	hearty*
+ er	heartier
+ est	heartiest
+ y + ly	heartily
+ y + ness	heartiness
+ less	heartless
+ less + ly	heartlessly
+ less + ness	heartlessness
+ en	hearten^
+ en + ing + ly	hearteningly
+ ache	heartache*
+ beat	heartbeat
+ break	heartbreak
+ break + ing	heartbreaking
+ break + ing + ly	heartbreakingly
+ break + en	heartbroken
+ burn	heartburn
+ burn + ing	heartburning
+ feel + ed	heartfelt
+ land	heartland
+ s + ease	heartsease
+ sick	heartsick
+ sick + ness	heartsickness
+ some	heartsome
+ some + ly	heartsomely
+ sore	heartsore
+ string	heartstring
+ warm + ing	heartwarming
+ wood	heartwood
+ worm	heartworm
heat	
+ s	heats
+ ed	heated
+ ing	heating
+ able	heatable
+ ly	heatedly

+ er	heater*
+ less	heatless
+ proof	heatproof
heaven	
+ s	heavens
+ ly	heavenly
+ ness	heavenliness
+ ward	heavenward*
heavy	
+ s	heavies
+ er	heavier
+ est	heaviest
+ ly	heavily
+ ness	heaviness
+ heart + ed	heavyhearted
+ heart + ed + ly	heavyheartedly
+ heart + ed + ness	heavyheartedness
+ set	heavyset
+ weigh + t	heavyweight
Hebrew	
+ s	hebrews
+ ic	Hebraic
+ ly	Hebraically
+ ist	Hebraist
+ ist + ic	Hebraistic
+ ism	Hebraism
+ ize	hebraize^
+ tion	hebraization
heel	
+ s	heels
+ ed	heeled
+ ing	heeling
+ er	heeler*
+ less	heelless
+ ball	heelball
+ piece	heelpiece
+ tap	heeltap
height	
+ s	heights
+ en	heighten^
helicopter^	
hell	
+ er	heller*
+ ion	hellion*
+ ish	hellish
+ ly	hellishly
+ ness	hellishness
+ box	hellbox
+ broth	hellbroth
+ cat	hellcat
+ fire	hellfire
+ hole	hellhole
hello*	

helmet

+ s	helmets
+ ed	helmeted
+ like	helmetlike

help

+ s	helps
+ ed	helped
+ ing	helping
+ er	helper*
+ ful	helpful
+ ful + ly	helpfully
+ ful + ness	helpfulness
+ less	helpless
+ less + ly	helplessly
+ less + ness	helplessness
+ mate	helpmate

hem

+ s	hems
+ ed	hemmed
+ ing	hemming
+ er	hemmer
+ line	hemline
+ stitch	hemstitch

hen (2)

+ s	hens
+ ery	hennery*
+ peck	henpeck^

her

+ s	hers
+ self	herself

herb

+ s	herbs
+ ous	herbaceous
+ age	herbage
+ al	herbal
+ ist	herbalist
+ like	herblike
+ y	herby

herd

+ s	herds
+ ed	herded
+ ing	herding
+ er	herder*
+ s + man	herdsman*

here

+ about	hereabout*
+ after	hereafter
+ by	hereby
+ in	herein
+ in + above	hereinabove
+ in + after	hereinafter
+ in + before	hereinbefore
+ in + below	hereinbelow
+ of	hereof
+ on	hereon
+ to	hereto
+ to + fore	heretofore
+ under	hereunder
+ up + on	hereupon
+ with	herewith

heredity

+ able	heritable
+ age	heritage
+ ary	hereditary
+ an	hereditarian*
+ ism	hereditarianism
+ ly	hereditarily

hero

+ s	heroes
+ ic	heroic
+ al	heroical
+ ly	heroically
+ ine	heroine*
+ ism	heroism
+ ize	heroize^

hesitate

+ s	hesitates
+ ed	hesitated
+ ing	hesitating
+ ing + ly	hesitatingly
+ er	hesitater
+ ance	hesitance
+ y	hesitancy
+ ant	hesitant
+ ant + ly	hesitantly
+ ion	hesitation*

hiccup^

hide

+ s	hides
+ ed	hid
+ en	hidden
+ ing	hiding
+ er	hider
+ away	hideaway
+ bind + ed	hidebound
+ out	hideout*

high

+ er	higher
+ est	highest
+ ly	highly
+ ness	highness
+ t	height
+ ball	highball*
+ bind + er	highbinder*
+ birth + en	highborn
+ boy	highboy
+ breed + ed	highbred
+ brow	highbrow

+ brow + ed	highbrowed
+ fly + er	highflier
+ land	highland
+ land + er	highlander
+ light	highlight^
+ road	highroad
+ tail	hightail^
+ way	highway*
+ way + man	highwayman
high school	
+ s	high schools
+ er	high schooler
highway (2)*	
hike	
+ s	hikes
+ ed	hiked
+ ing	hiking
+ er	hiker
hill	
+ s	hills
+ ed	hilled
+ ing	hilling
+ er	hiller
+ y	hilly
+ y + er	hillier
+ est	hilliest
+ side	hillside*
+ top	hilltop*
him	
+ self	himself
hind	
+ s	hinds
+ brain	hindbrain
+ more + est	hindmost
+ quarter	hindquarter
+ sight	hindsight
hinge (2)^	
hint	
+ s	hints
+ ed	hinted
+ ing	hinting
+ er	hinter
hip	
+ s	hips
+ ed	hipped
+ ing	hipping
+ er	hipper
+ est	hippest
+ ness	hipness
+ y	hippy*
+ y + er	hippier
+ y + est	hippiest
+ dom	hippiedom
+ hood	hippiehood
+ y + ness	hippieness
hippopotamus*	
hire	
+ s	hires
+ ed	hired
+ ing	hiring
+ er	hirer
his	
Hispanic	
+ ism	Hispanicism
+ ist	Hispanicist
+ ize	Hispanicize^
history (2)	
+ s	histories
+ an	historian*
+ ic	historic
+ al	historical
+ ly	historically
+ ness	historicalness
+ ism	historicism
+ ist	historicist
+ ize	historicize^
+ ity	historicity
hit	
+ s	hits
+ ed	hit
+ ing	hitting
+ er	hitter*
+ less	hitless
hitch	
+ s	hitches
+ ed	hitched
+ ing	hitching
+ er	hitcher
+ hike	hitchhike^
+ hike + er	hitchhiker*
hoarse	
+ en	hoarsen^
+ er	hoarser
+ est	hoarsest
+ ly	hoarsely
+ ness	hoarseness
hockey	
hoe (2)	
+ s	hoes
+ ed	hoed
+ ing	hoeing
+ er	hoer
+ cake	hoecake*
+ down	hoedown*
hog	
+ s	hogs
+ ed	hogged
+ ing	hogging
+ ish	hoggish
+ ly	hoggishly

H

+ ness	hoggishness
+ back	hogback
+ fish	hogfish
+ nose	hognose
+ s + head	hogshead
+ wash	hogwash
hold	
+ s	holds
+ ed	held
+ ing	holding*
+ er	holder
+ all	holdall
+ back	holdback
+ fast	holdfast
+ out	holdout*
+ over	holdover*
+ up	holdup*
hole^	
holiday	
+ s	holidays
+ ed	holidayed
+ ing	holidaying
+ er	holidayer*
+ make + er	holidaymaker
Holland	
holler^	
hollow	
+ er	hollower
+ est	hollowest
+ ly	hollowly
+ ness	hollowness
+ ware	holloware
holly*	
holster^	
holy	
+ s	holies
+ er	holier
+ est	holiest
+ ly	holily
+ ness	holiness
home	
+ s	homes
+ ed	homed
+ ing	homing
+ er	homer^
+ less	homeless
+ less + ness	homelessness
+ like	homelike
+ ly	homely
+ ly + er	homelier
+ ly + est	homeliest
+ ly + ness	homeliness
+ y	homey
+ y + er	homier
+ y + est	homiest
+ y + ness	hominess
+ body	homebody
+ bind + ed	homebound
+ bound	homebound
+ breed + ed	homebred
+ build + ed	homebuilt
+ come + ing	homecoming
+ grow + en	homegrown
+ land	homeland
+ make + ed	homemade
+ make + er	homemaker*
+ make + ing	homemaking
+ room	homeroom
+ sick	homesick
+ sick + ness	homesickness
+ site	homesite
+ spin + en	homespun
+ stay	homestay
+ stead	homestead
+ stead + er	homesteader*
+ stead + ing	homesteading
+ stretch	homestretch
+ town	hometown
+ ward	homeward
+ work	homework
homonym	
+ s	homonyms
+ ic	homonymic
+ ous	homonymous
+ ly	homonymously
+ y	homonymy
honest	
+ ly	honestly
+ y	honesty*
honey	
+ s	honeys
+ ed	honeyed
+ ing	honeying
+ bee	honeybee*
+ comb	honeycomb^
+ creep + er	honeycreeper
+ dew	honeydew
+ moon	honeymoon^
+ moon + er	honeymooner*
honor	
+ s	honors
+ ed	honored
+ ing	honoring
+ able	honorable
+ ity	honorability
+ ness	honorableness
+ able + ly	honorably
+ ary	honorary

+ ary + ly honorarily
+ ee honoree*
+ er honorer
+ ic honorific
+ al + ly honorifically

hood
+ s hoods
+ ed hooded
+ ing hooding
+ ness hoodedness
+ like hoodlike
+ y hoody*
+ wink hoodwink^

hoof
+ s hooves, hoofs
+ ed hoofed
+ ing hoofing
+ er hoofer*
+ beat hoofbeat*
+ print hoofprint*

hook
+ s hooks
+ ed hooked
+ ing hooking
+ er hooker*
+ let hooklet*
+ y hooky
+ up hookup*
+ worm hookworm*

hoop
+ s hoops
+ ed hooped
+ ing hooping
+ er hooper
+ like hooplike
+ skirt hoopskirt

hop
+ s hops
+ ed hopped
+ ing hopping
+ er hopper
+ head hophead*
+ sack hopsack*

hope
+ s hopes
+ ed hoped
+ ing hoping
+ er hoper
+ ful hopeful
+ ful + ly hopefully
+ ful + ness hopefulness
+ less hopeless
+ less + ly hopelessly
+ less + ness hopelessness

hopscotch

horizon
+ s horizons
+ al horizontal
+ ly horizontally

horn
+ s horns
+ ed horned
+ ing horning
+ ed + ness hornedness
+ ist hornist
+ less hornless
+ less + ness hornlessness
+ like hornlike
+ y horny
+ er hornier
+ est horniest
+ y + ness horniness
+ book hornbook
+ pipe hornpipe
+ stone hornstone
+ tail horntail
+ worm hornworm

horror
+ s horrors
+ ible horrible
+ ness horribleness
+ ible + ly horribly
+ ify horrify^
+ ic horrific
+ ing + ly horrifyingly
+ ous horrendous
+ ous + ly horrendously

horse
+ s horses
+ ed horsed
+ ing horsing
+ less horseless
+ y horsey
+ er horsier
+ est horsiest
+ ly horsily
+ ness horsiness
+ back horseback
+ car horsecar
+ feather + s horsefeathers
+ flesh horseflesh
+ fly horsefly
+ hair horsehair
+ hide horsehide
+ laugh horselaugh
+ man horseman*
+ man + ship horsemanship
+ play horseplay

+ power	horsepower
+ radish	horseradish
+ shoe	horseshoe^
+ tail	horsetail
+ weed	horseweed
+ whip	horsewhip^
+ woman	horsewoman*
hose	
+ s	hoses
+ ed	hosed
+ ing	hosing
+ ery	hosiery
hospital	
+ s	hospitals
+ ize	hospitalize^
+ tion	hospitalization*
hospitality	
+ able	hospitable
+ ly	hospitably
hostage*	
hostile	
+ ly	hostilely
+ ity	hostility
hot	
+ er	hotter
+ est	hottest
+ ish	hottish
+ ly	hotly
+ ness	hotness
+ s	hots
+ bed	hotbed
+ box	hotbox
+ cake	hotcake
+ dog	hotdog^
+ foot	hotfoot^
+ head	hothead*
+ head + ed	hotheaded
+ head **+ ly**	hotheadedly
+ head **+ ness**	hotheadedness
+ house	hothouse*
+ shot	hotshot*
hotel (2)	
+ s	hotels
+ man	hotelman*
hour	
+ s	hours
+ ly	hourly
+ glass	hourglass
house	
+ s	houses
+ ed	housed
+ ing	housing
+ ful	houseful
+ less	houseless
+ ness	houselessness
+ boat	houseboat*
+ bind + ed	housebound
+ boy	houseboy*
+ break	housebreak^
+ break + er	housebreaker
+ clean	houseclean^
+ clean + er	housecleaner*
+ coat	housecoat*
+ dress	housedress*
+ fly	housefly*
+ front	housefront
+ guest	houseguest*
+ hold	household
+ hold + er	householder*
+ keep	housekeep^
+ keep + er	housekeeper*
+ light + s	houselights
+ man	houseman*
+ mate	housemate*
+ mother	housemother*
+ plant	houseplant*
+ top	housetop*
+ ware + s	housewares
+ warm + ing	housewarming
+ wife	housewife*
+ work	housework
how	
+ s	hows
+ be + it	howbeit
+ ever	however
+ so + ever	howsoever
howl	
+ s	howls
+ ed	howled
+ ing	howling
+ ly	howlingly
+ er	howler*
hug	
+ s	hugs
+ ed	hugged
+ ing	hugging
+ able	huggable
huge	
+ er	huger
+ est	hugest
+ ly	hugely
+ ness	hugeness
+ ous	hugeous
+ ous + ly	hugeously
hula	
human	
+ s	humans
+ e	humane
+ e + ly	humanely
+ e + ness	humaneness

+ ism	humanism
+ ist	humanist
+ ic	humanistic
+ al + ly	humanistically
+ an	humanitarian*
+ an + ism	humanitarianism
+ ity	humanity*
+ ize	humanize^
+ er	humanizer
+ tion	humanization
+ kind	humankind
+ like	humanlike
+ ly	humanly
+ ness	humanness
humble	
+ s	humbles
+ ed	humbled
+ ing	humbling
+ er	humbler
+ est	humblest
+ ness	humbleness
+ y	humbly
+ ate	humiliate^
+ tion	humiliation
+ ly	humiliatingly
+ ity	humility
humid	
+ ify	humidify^
+ ify + er	humidifier*
+ tion	humidification
+ ity	humidity
+ ly	humidly
+ or	humidor*
humor	
+ s	humors
+ ed	humored
+ ing	humoring
+ al	humoral
+ ist	humorist*
+ ic	humoristic
+ less	humorless
+ less + ness	humorlessness
+ ous	humorous
+ ly	humorously
+ ous + ness	humorousness
hundred	
+ fold	hundredfold
+ s	hundreds
+ th	hundredth
+ weigh + t	hundredweight*
hung	
hunger^	
hungry	
+ er	hungrier
+ est	hungriest
+ ly	hungrily
+ ness	hungriness
hunt	
+ s	hunts
+ ed	hunted
+ ing	hunting
+ er	hunter*
+ ess	huntress*
+ s + man	huntsman*
hurricane*	
hurry	
+ s	hurries
+ ed	hurried
+ ing	hurrying
+ er	hurrier
+ ly	hurriedly
+ ness	hurriedness
hurt	
+ s	hurts
+ ed	hurt
+ ing	hurting
+ er	hurter
+ ful	hurtful
+ ly	hurtfully
+ ness	hurtfulness
+ less	hurtless
husband	
+ s	husbands
+ ed	husbanded
+ ing	husbanding
+ er	husbander
+ ly	husbandly
+ r + y	husbandry
+ man	husbandman
hush^	
hut*	
hybrid	
+ s	hybrids
+ ity	hybridity
+ ism	hybridism
+ ize	hybridize^
+ tion	hybridization
+ er	hybridizer*
hydrant*	
hymn	
+ s	hymns
+ al	hymnal*
+ book	hymnbook*
hypnosis	
+ s	hypnoses
hypnotize	
+ s	hypnotizes
+ ed	hypnotized
+ ing	hypnotizing
+ er	hypnotizer

H

+ able	hypnotizable
+ tion	hypnotization
+ ic	hypnotic
+ ly	hypnotically
+ ism	hypnotism
+ ist	hypnotist*
hypocrite	
+ al	hypocritical
+ ly	hypocritically
+ y	hypocrisy*
hypothesis	
+ s	hypotheses
+ al	hypothetical
+ ly	hypothetically
+ ize	hypothesize^
hysteric	
+ s	hysterics
+ al	hysterical
+ ly	hysterically

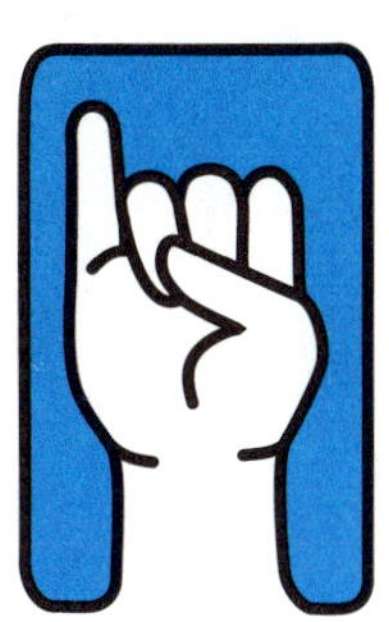

I
+ 've — I've
+ 'm — I'm
+ 'll — I'll

ice
+ s — ices
+ ed — iced
+ ing — icing*
+ er — icer
+ y — icey
+ y + er — icier
+ est — iciest
+ ly — icily
+ ness — iciness
+ blink — iceblink
+ boat — iceboat
+ boat + er — iceboater
+ boat + ing — iceboating
+ bind + ed — icebound
+ box — icebox
+ break + er — icebreaker*
+ fall — icefall
+ house — icehouse
+ man — iceman

ice cream

icicle*

idea
+ s — ideas
+ less — idealess
+ al — ideal
+ al + less — idealless
+ ism — idealism
+ ist — idealist*
+ ic — idealistic
+ ic + ly — idealistically
+ ity — ideality*
+ ize — idealize^
+ ize + tion — idealization
+ ize + er — idealizer
+ ly — ideally
+ ate — ideate^
+ ate + ion — ideation
+ ion + al — ideational

identify
+ s — identifies
+ ed — identified
+ ing — identifying
+ ic — identic
+ al — identical
+ al + ly — identically
+ ness — identicalness
+ able — identifiable
+ able + ly — identifiably
+ tion — identification*
+ er — identifier*
+ ity — identity*

idiom
+ s — idioms
+ ic — idiomatic
+ ly — idiomatically
+ ness — idiomaticness

idiot
+ s — idiots
+ y — idiocy
+ ic — idiotic
+ al — idiotical
+ ly — idiotically
+ ness — idioticalness

idle
+ s — idles
+ ed — idled
+ ing — idling
+ er — idler*
+ est — idlest
+ ly — idly
+ ness — idleness

if
+ y — iffy
+ ness — iffiness

igloo*

ignorance

ignorant
+ ly — ignorantly
+ ness — ignorantness

ignore
+ s — ignores

I

+ ed	ignored
+ ing	ignoring
+ able	ignorable
+ er	ignorer
ill	
+ s	ills
+ ness	illness*
illusion	
+ s	illusions
+ al	illusional
+ ism	illusionism
+ ist	illusionist
+ ic	illusionistic
+ al + ly	illusionistically
+ ive	illusive
+ ive + ly	illusively
+ ive + ness	illusiveness
+ ory	illusory
+ ory + ly	illusorily
+ ory + ness	illusoriness
illustrate	
+ s	illustrates
+ ed	illustrated
+ ing	illustrating
+ or	illustrator*
+ ion	illustration*
+ al	illustrational
+ ive	illustrative
+ ive + ly	illustratively
+ ous	illustrious
+ ous + ly	illustriously
+ ness	illustriousness
image	
+ s	images
+ ed	imaged
+ ing	imaging
+ er	imager
+ ery	imagery*
+ ism	imagism
+ ist	imagist
+ ic	imagistic
+ ly	imagistically
imagine	
+ s	imagines
+ ed	imagined
+ ing	imagining
+ able	imaginable
+ able + ly	imaginably
+ able + ness	imaginableness
+ al	imaginal
+ ary	imaginary
+ ary + ly	imaginarily
+ ary + ness	imaginariness
+ tion	imagination*

+ ive	imaginative
+ ive + ly	imaginatively
+ ive + ness	imaginativeness
imitate	
+ s	imitates
+ ed	imitated
+ ing	imitating
+ ion	imitation*
+ ive	imitative
+ ly	imitatively
+ ness	imitativeness
+ or	imitator*
immaculate	
+ ly	immaculately
+ y	immaculacy
immediate	
+ ly	immediately
+ ness	immediateness
+ y	immediacy
immense	
+ ly	immensely
+ ness	immenseness
+ ity	immensity*
impair	
+ s	impairs
+ ed	impaired
+ ing	impairing
+ er	impairer
+ ment	impairment*
imply	
+ s	implies
+ ed	implied
+ ing	implying
+ ate	implicate^
+ ion	implication*
+ ive	implicative
+ ive + ly	implicatively
+ ive + ness	implicativeness
+ t	implicit
+ t + ly	implicitly
+ t + ness	implicitness
import	
+ s	imports
+ ed	imported
+ ing	importing
+ able	importable
+ er	importer*
+ tion	importation*
important	
+ ance	importance
+ y	importancy
+ ly	importantly
impossible	
+ ity	impossibility*

+ ness	impossibleness
+ ly	impossibly
impress	
+ s	impresses
+ ed	impressed
+ ing	impressing
+ ible	impressible
+ ity	impressibility
+ ible + ly	impressibly
+ ion	impression*
+ ion + able	impressionable
+ ion **+ ity**	impressionability
+ able + ness	impressionableness
+ al	impressional
+ ism	impressionism
+ ist	impressionist*
+ ic	impressionistic
+ ic + ly	impressionistically
+ ive	impressive
+ ive + ly	impressively
+ ive + ness	impressiveness
+ ment	impressment
+ ure	impressure
imprint^	
improve	
+ s	improves
+ ed	improved
+ ing	improving
+ er	improver
+ ment	improvement*
in	
+ er	inner
+ ly	innerly
+ er + more + est	innermost
+ er + spring	innerspring
+ ing	inning*
+ board	inboard
+ birth + en	inborn
+ bound	inbound*
+ more + est	inmost
+ put	input
+ set	inset^
+ step	instep
+ ward	inward
inch	
+ s	inches
+ ed	inched
+ ing	inching
+ er	incher*
+ worm	inchworm*
incident	
+ al	incidental*
+ ly	incidentally
+ s	incidents
+ ence	incidence*
include	
+ s	includes
+ ed	included
+ ing	including
+ able	includable
+ sion	inclusion*
+ ive	inclusive
+ ly	inclusively
+ ness	inclusiveness
increase	
+ s	increases
+ ed	increased
+ ing	increasing
+ ly	increasingly
+ able	increasable
+ er	increaser
indeed	
indent	
+ s	indents
+ ed	indented
+ ing	indenting
+ er	indenter
+ ion	indention*
+ ate + tion	indentation*
+ ure	indenture^
independent	
+ ence	independence
+ y	independency
+ ly	independently
India	
+ an	Indian
Indian	
+ ism	Indianism
+ ist	Indianist
+ ness	Indianness
indicate	
+ s	indicates
+ ed	indicated
+ ing	indicating
+ ion	indication*
+ al	indicational
+ ive	indicative
+ ly	indicatively
+ or	indicator*
+ ory	indicatory
individual	
+ s	individuals
+ ly	individually
+ ism	individualism
+ ist	individualist
+ ic	individualistic
+ al + ly	individualistically
+ ity	individuality
+ ize	individualize^
+ ize + tion	individualization

I

+ ate	individuate^
+ ate + tion	individuation
industry	
+ s	industries
+ al	industrial
+ al + ly	industrially
+ ism	industrialism
+ ist	industrialist*
+ ize	industrialize^
+ tion	industrialization
+ ous	industrious
+ ous + ly	industriously
+ ness	industriousness
infant	
+ s	infants
+ e	infante
+ ile	infantile
+ ine	infantine
+ ism	infantilism
+ ity	infantility
+ ery	infantry*
+ y	infancy
infatuate	
+ s	infatuates
+ ed	infatuated
+ ing	infatuating
+ tion	infatuation*
infect	
+ s	infects
+ ed	infected
+ ing	infecting
+ ion	infection*
+ ous	infectious
+ ly	infectiously
+ ness	infectiousness
+ ive	infective
+ ity	infectivity
+ or	infector
inferior	
+ s	inferiors
+ ity	inferiority
+ ly	inferiorly
infest	
+ s	infests
+ ed	infested
+ ing	infesting
+ ant	infestant*
+ tion	infestation*
+ er	infester*
infiltrate	
+ s	infiltrates
+ ed	infiltrated
+ ing	infiltrating
+ ion	infiltration*
+ ive	infiltrative
+ or	infiltrator*
infinite	
+ ly	infinitely
+ ness	infiniteness
+ ive	infinitive*
+ al	infinitival
+ ive + ly	infinitively
+ ity	infinity*
infirmary*	
inflate	
+ s	inflates
+ ed	inflated
+ ing	inflating
+ able	inflatable*
+ er, + or	inflater, inflator
+ ion	inflation
+ ary	inflationary
+ ism	inflationism
+ ist	inflationist
inflect	
+ s	inflects
+ ed	inflected
+ ing	inflecting
+ able	inflectable
+ ion	inflection*
+ al	inflectional
+ ly	inflectionally
+ ive	inflective
influence	
+ s	influences
+ ed	influenced
+ ing	influencing
+ ent	influent*
+ al	influential
+ ly	influentially
inform (2)	
+ s	informs
+ ed	informed
+ ing	informing
+ ant	informant*
+ tion	information
+ al	informational
+ less	informationless
+ ive	informative
+ ive + ly	informatively
+ ive + ness	informativeness
+ ory	informatory
+ ory + ly	informatorily
+ ed + ly	informedly
+ er	informer*
informal	
+ ity	informality
+ ly	informally

ingredient*	
inhabit	
+ s	inhabits
+ ed	inhabited
+ ing	inhabiting
+ able	inhabitable
+ ant	inhabitant*
+ y	inhabitancy
+ tion	inhabitation
+ er	inhabiter
inherit	
+ s	inherits
+ ed	inherited
+ ing	inheriting
+ or	inheritor*
+ ess	inheritress
+ able	inheritable
+ ity	inheritability
+ ness	inheritableness
+ ance	inheritance
initial	
+ s	initials
+ ed	initialed
+ ing	initialing
+ ism	initialism
+ ize	initialize^
+ ize + tion	initialization
+ ly	initially
+ ness	initialness
initiate	
+ s	initiates
+ ed	initiated
+ ing	initiating
+ ion	initiation*
+ ive	initiative
+ or	initiator*
+ ory	initiatory
injure	
+ s	injures
+ ed	injured
+ ing	injuring
+ ous	injurious
+ ly	injuriously
+ ness	injuriousness
+ y	injury*
innocent	
+ s	innocents
+ ly	innocently
+ ence	innocence
+ y	innocency
insect	
+ s	insects
+ ary	insectary*
+ ile	insectile

insert	
+ s	inserts
+ ed	inserted
+ ing	inserting
+ er	inserter
+ ion	insertion*
+ al	insertional
inside	
+ s	insides
+ er	insider*
insist	
+ s	insists
+ ed	insisted
+ ing	insisting
+ ence	insistence
+ y	insistency*
+ ent	insistent
+ ly	insistently
inspect	
+ s	inspects
+ ed	inspected
+ ing	inspecting
+ ion	inspection*
+ ive	inspective
+ or	inspector*
+ ate	inspectorate
+ ship	inspectorship
inspire	
+ s	inspires
+ ed	inspired
+ ing	inspiring
+ tion	inspiration
+ al	inspirational
+ ly	inspirationally
+ ate + or	inspirator
+ ory	inspiratory
+ er	inspirer
install	
+ s	installs
+ ed	installed
+ ing	installing
+ er	installer*
+ tion	installation*
+ ment	installment*
instant	
+ s	instants
+ er	instanter
+ ance	instance*
+ y	instancy*
+ ate	instantiate^
+ tion	instantiation
+ ly	instantly
+ ness	instantness
+ ous	instantaneous

+ ous + ly	instantaneously
+ ous + ness	instantaneousness
instead (2)	
instinct	
+ s	instincts
+ ive	instinctive
+ ly	instinctively
+ al	instinctual
institute	
+ s	institutes
+ ed	instituted
+ ing	instituting
+ er, + or	instituter, institutor
+ ion	institution*
+ al	institutional
+ ly	institutionally
+ ism	institutionism
+ ist	institutionist
+ ize	institutionalize^
+ ize + tion	institutionalization
instruct	
+ s	instructs
+ ed	instructed
+ ing	instructing
+ ion	instruction*
+ al	instructional
+ ive	instructive
+ ly	instructively
+ ness	instructiveness
+ or	instructor*
+ ess	instructress
+ ship	instructorship
+ ion	instruction
instrument	
+ s	instruments
+ al	instrumental
+ ly	instrumentally
+ ism	instrumentalism
+ ist	instrumentalist*
+ ity	instrumentality
+ tion	instrumentation*
insult	
+ s	insults
+ ed	insulted
+ ing	insulting
+ ly	insultingly
+ er	insulter
insure	
+ s	insures
+ ed	insured
+ ing	insuring
+ able	insurable
+ ity	insurability
+ ance	insurance*
+ er	insurer*

integrate	
+ s	integrates
+ ed	integrated
+ ing	integrating
+ able	integrable
+ able + ity	integrability
+ al	integral*
+ al + ity	integrality
+ ly	integrally
+ ion	integration*
+ ist	integrationist
+ ive	integrative
+ or	integrator*
+ ity	integrity
intellect	
+ s	intellects
+ ion	intellection
+ ive	intellective
+ ive + ly	intellectively
+ al	intellectual
+ al + ity	intellectuality
+ al + ly	intellectually
+ ness	intellectualness
+ ism	intellectualism
+ ist	intellectualist
+ ic	intellectualistic
+ ize	intellectualize^
+ ize + tion	intellectualization
+ er	intellectualizer
+ ence	intelligence
+ ence + er	intelligencer
+ ible	intelligible
+ ible + ly	intelligibly
+ ible + ity	intelligibility
intelligent	
+ ent + ly	intelligently
+ ent + al	intelligential
intend	
+ s	intends
+ ed	intended
+ ing	intending
+ er	intender
+ ance	intendance
+ ant	intendant
+ ed + ly	intendedly
+ ed + ness	intendedness
+ ment	intendment
+ t	intent
+ tion	intention*
+ al	intentional
+ al + ly	intentionally
+ ity	intentionality
+ t + ly	intently
+ t + ness	intentness

intense	
+ ly	intensely
+ ness	intenseness
+ ify	intensify^
+ ify + tion	intensification
+ ion	intension
+ al	intensional
+ al + ly	intensionally
+ ity	intensity*
+ ive	intensive
+ ive + ly	intensively
+ ive + ness	intensiveness

intercourse	

interest	
+ s	interests
+ ed	interested
+ ing	interesting
+ ed + ly	interestedly
+ ing + ly	interestingly
+ ness	interestingness

interfere	
+ s	interferes
+ ed	interfered
+ ing	interfering
+ er	interferer
+ ence	interference
+ al	interferential

intermediate	
+ s	intermediates
+ ed	intermediated
+ ing	intermediating
+ y	intermediacy
+ ary	intermediary*
+ ly	intermediately
+ ness	intermediateness
+ ion	intermediation

intern	
+ s	interns
+ ed	interned
+ ing	interning
+ ship	internship

international	
+ ism	internationalism
+ ist	internationalist
+ ize	internationalize^
+ tion	internationalization
+ ly	internationally
+ ity	internationality

interpret	
+ s	interprets
+ ed	interpreted
+ ing	interpreting
+ able	interpretable
+ ity	interpretability
+ tion	interpretation*
+ al	interpretational
+ ate + ive	interpretative
+ ate + ive + ly	interpretatively
+ er	interpreter*
+ ive	interpretive
+ ive + ly	interpretively

interrogate	
+ s	interrogates
+ ed	interrogated
+ ing	interrogating
+ ee	interrogatee*
+ ion	interrogation*
+ al	interrogational
+ ive	interrogative
+ ly	interrogatively
+ or	interrogator*
+ ory	interrogatory*

interrupt	
+ s	interrupts
+ ed	interrupted
+ ing	interrupting
+ er	interrupter*
+ ible	interruptible
+ ion	interruption*
+ ive	interruptive

interval	
+ s	intervals
+ ic	intervallic

interview	
+ s	interviews
+ ed	interviewed
+ ing	interviewing
+ ee	interviewee*
+ er	interviewer*

intimate	
+ ly	intimately
+ ness	intimateness

into	

intrigue	
+ s	intrigues
+ ed	intrigued
+ ing	intriguing
+ ly	intriguingly
+ er	intriguer
+ ant	intriguant*

introduce	
+ s	introduces
+ ed	introduced
+ ing	introducing
+ er	introducer
+ tion	introduction*
+ ory	introductory
+ ly	introductorily

I

intrude

+ s	intrudes
+ ed	intruded
+ ing	intruding
+ er	intruder*
+ sion	intrusion*
+ ive	intrusive
+ ly	intrusively
+ ness	intrusiveness

invade

+ s	invades
+ ed	invaded
+ ing	invading
+ sion	invasion*
+ ive	invasive
+ ly	invasively
+ ness	invasiveness

invent

+ s	invents
+ ed	invented
+ ing	inventing
+ ion	invention*
+ ive	inventive
+ ive + ly	inventively
+ ness	inventiveness
+ or	inventor*
+ ory	inventory^
+ al	inventorial
+ al + ly	inventorially

invert

+ s	inverts
+ ed	inverted
+ ing	inverting
+ er	inverter
+ ible	invertible

invest

+ s	invests
+ ed	invested
+ ing	investing
+ able	investable
+ ment	investment*
+ or	investor*
+ ure	investiture*

investigate

+ s	investigates
+ ed	investigated
+ ing	investigating
+ ion	investigation*
+ al	investigational
+ ive	investigative
+ or	investigator*
+ ory	investigatory

invisible

+ s	invisibles
+ ity	invisibility
+ ly	invisibly
+ ness	invisibleness

invite

+ s	invites
+ ed	invited
+ ing	inviting
+ ee	invitee
+ er	inviter
+ ion	invitation*
+ al	invitational
+ ory	invitatory*

involve

+ s	involves
+ ed	involved
+ ing	involving
+ ly	involvedly
+ er	involver
+ ment	involvement*

inward*

irate

+ ly	irately
+ ness	irateness

Ireland

+ ish	Irelandish

Irish

+ ly	Irishly

iron

+ s	irons
+ ed	ironed
+ ing	ironing
+ er	ironer*
+ ness	ironness
+ bind + ed	ironbound
+ hand + ed	ironhanded
+ hand + ed + ly	ironhandedly
+ hand + ed + ness	ironhandedness
+ heart + ed	ironhearted
+ master	ironmaster*
+ side	ironside
+ stone	ironstone
+ ware	ironware
+ weed	ironweed
+ wood	ironwood
+ work	ironwork

irony

+ s	ironies
+ ic	ironic
+ ly	ironically
+ ness	ironicalness
+ ist	ironist

irresponsible

irrigate

+ s	irrigates
+ ed	irrigated

I

+ ing irrigating
+ ion irrigation
+ or irrigator*

irritate

+ s irritates
+ ed irritated
+ ing irritating
+ ing + ly irritatingly
+ able irritable
+ ness irritableness
+ able + ly irritably
+ ity irritability*
+ ant irritant*
+ ion irritation*
+ ive irritative

is

+ n't isn't

island (2)

+ s islands
+ er islander*

isolate

+ s isolates
+ ed isolated
+ ing isolating
+ able isolable
+ ion isolation*
+ ism isolationism
+ ist isolationist*
+ or isolator

Israel

+ ite Israelite*

issue

+ s issues
+ ed issued
+ ing issuing
+ able issuable
+ ly issuably
+ ance issuance
+ ant issuant
+ er issuer

it

+ 'd it'd
+ 'll it'll
+ s its
+ 's it's
+ self itself

Italy

+ an Italian*
+ ate Italianate^
+ ism Italianism
+ ize Italianize^
+ ic italic
+ ic + ize italicize^

itch

+ s itches
+ ed itched
+ ing itching
+ y itchy
+ er itchier
+ est itchiest
+ ness itchiness

item

+ s items
+ ize itemize^
+ tion itemization

ivy*

I

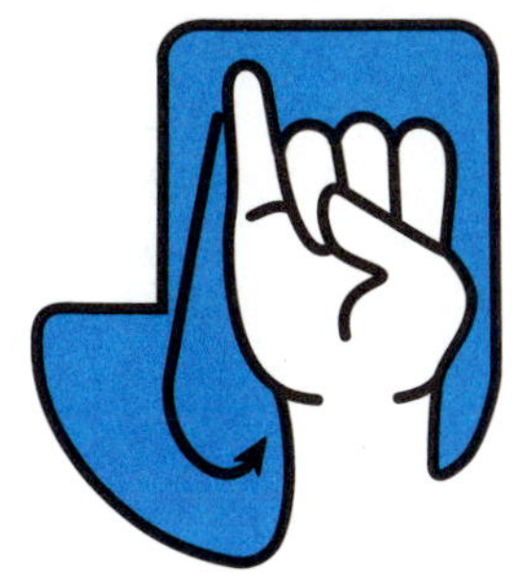

jacket^	
jack-in-the-box*	
jack-o'-lantern*	
jacks	
jail	
+ s	jails
+ ed	jailed
+ ing	jailing
+ er	jailer*
+ bird	jailbird*
+ break	jailbreak*
jam^	
janitor	
+ s	janitors
+ al	janitorial
+ ess	janitress
January* (2)	
Japan (2)	
+ ese	Japanese
+ ize	Japanize^
+ tion	Japanization
jar	
+ s	jars
+ ed	jarred
jay*	
jealous	
+ ly	jealously
+ ness	jealousness
+ y	jealousy
jeans*	
jeep*	
jell^	
jello	
jelly	
+ s	jellies
+ ed	jellied
+ ing	jellying
+ like	jellylike
+ fish	jellyfish
Jesus	
jet	
+ s	jets
+ ed	jetted
+ ing	jetting

+ line + er	jetliner*
Jew	
+ s	Jews
+ ery	Jewry*
+ ess	Jewess*
+ ish	Jewish
+ ly	Jewishly
+ ness	Jewishness
jewel	
+ s	jewels
+ ed	jeweled
+ ing	jeweling
+ er	jeweler*
+ ery	jewelry
jingle	
+ s	jingles
+ ed	jingled
+ ing	jingling
+ er	jingler
job	
+ s	jobs
+ ed	jobbed
+ ing	jobbing
+ er	jobber*
+ hold + er	jobholder*
+ less	jobless
+ ness	joblessness
jog	
+ s	jogs
+ ed	jogged
+ ing	jogging
+ er	jogger
join	
+ s	joins
+ ed	joined
+ ing	joining
+ able	joinable
+ er	joiner
+ ery	joinery
joint	
+ s	joints
+ ed	jointed
+ ing	jointing
+ ed + ly	jointedly

+ ness	jointedness
+ er	jointer
+ ly	jointly
+ ure	jointure
+ worm	jointworm*
joke	
+ s	jokes
+ ed	joked
+ ing	joking
+ ly	jokingly
+ er	joker*
journal	
+ s	journals
+ ese	journalese
+ ism	journalism
+ ist	journalist*
+ ic	journalistic
+ ly	journalistically
+ ize	journalize^
+ er	journalizer
journey	
+ s	journeys
+ ed	journeyed
+ ing	journeying
+ er	journeyer
+ man	journeyman
+ work	journeywork
joy	
+ s	joys
+ ed	joyed
+ ing	joying
+ ful	joyful
+ ful + ly	joyfully
+ ful + ness	joyfulness
+ less	joyless
+ less + ly	joylessly
+ less + ness	joylessness
+ ous	joyous
+ ous + ly	joyously
+ ous + ness	joyousness
+ ride	joyride^
+ ride + er	joyrider*
+ stick	joystick
judge	
+ s	judges
+ ed	judged
+ ing	judging
+ er	judger
+ ment	judgement*
+ ment + al	judgemental
+ ship	judgeship*
+ al	judicial
+ ly	judicially
+ ary	judiciary
+ ous	judicious
+ ous + ly	judiciously
+ ness	judiciousness
+ ate + ory	judicatory*
+ ure	judicature
juggle	
+ s	juggles
+ ed	juggled
+ ing	juggling
+ er	juggler
+ ery	jugglery
juice	
+ s	juices
+ ed	juiced
+ ing	juicing
+ er	juicer
+ y	juicy
+ y + er	juicier
+ est	juiciest
+ ly	juicily
+ ness	juiciness
+ head	juicehead
July (2)	
jumble^	
jump	
+ s	jumps
+ ed	jumped
+ ing	jumping
+ er	jumper*
+ y	jumpy
+ y + er	jumpier
+ est	jumpiest
+ ness	jumpiness
June (2)	
jungle*	
junior	
+ s	juniors
+ ate	juniorate
junk	
+ s	junks
+ ed	junked
+ ing	junking
+ y	junkie*
+ yard	junkyard*
just	
+ ice	justice*
+ ice + able	justiciable
+ ice + able + ity	justiciability
+ ice + ar	justiciar
+ ify	justify^
+ ify + able	justifiable
+ ify + able + ity	justifiability
+ ify + er	justifier*
+ tion	justification*

J

+ ive	justificative
+ ory	justificatory
+ ly	justly
+ ness	justness
juvenile	
+ ity	juvenility
+ ence	juvenescence
+ ent	juvenescent

J

kangaroo*	
karate	
+ ist	karateist
keep	
+ s	keeps
+ ed	kept
+ ing	keeping
+ er	keeper*
kerchief	
+ s	kerchiefs
+ ed	kerchiefed
ketchup (catsup)	
key	
+ s	keys
+ ed	keyed
+ ing	keying
+ less	keyless
+ board	keyboard*
+ board + er	keyboarder*
+ board + ist	keyboardist*
+ button	keybutton*
+ hole	keyhole*
+ note	keynote^
+ pad	keypad*
+ punch	keypunch^
+ stone	keystone*
+ stroke	keystroke^
+ way	keyway
+ word	keyword*
kick	
+ s	kicks
+ ed	kicked
+ ing	kicking
+ able	kickable
+ er	kicker*
+ y	kicky
+ back	kickback*
+ off	kickoff*
+ stand	kickstand*
+ up	kickup*
kid (2)	
+ s	kids
+ ed	kidded

+ ing	kidding
+ ly	kiddingly
+ y	kiddy*
+ skin	kidskin
kidnap	
+ s	kidnaps
+ ed	kidnapped
+ ing	kidnapping
+ er	kidnapper*
kill	
+ s	kills
+ ed	killed
+ ing	killing
+ ly	killingly
+ er	killer*
+ joy	killjoy*
kilometer*	
kind	
+ s	kinds
+ er	kinder
+ est	kindest
+ ly	kindly
+ ly + er	kindlier
+ ly + est	kindliest
+ ly + ness	kindliness
+ ness	kindness
+ less	kindless
+ less + ly	kindlessly
+ heart + ed	kindhearted
+ heart + **ly**	kindheartedly
+ heart + **ness**	kindheartedness
kindergarten	
+ s	kindergartens
+ er	kindergartner*
king	
+ s	kings
+ dom	kingdom*
+ ly	kingly
+ er	kinglier
+ est	kingliest
+ bird	kingbird*
+ craft	kingcraft
+ fish	kingfish

+ fish + er	kingfisher*
+ make + er	kingmaker*
+ pin	kingpin*
+ ship	kingship
+ side	kingside
kiss	
+ s	kisses
+ ed	kissed
+ ing	kissing
+ able	kissable
+ er	kisser*
kitchen (2)	
+ s	kitchens
+ ware	kitchenware
kite^	
+ s	kites
+ ed	kited
+ ing	kiting
+ like	kitelike
kitten	
+ s	kittens
+ ed	kittened
+ ing	kittening
+ y	kitty*
+ ish	kittenish
+ ly	kittenishly
+ ness	kittenishness
Kleenex	
knee	
+ s	knees
+ ed	kneed
+ ing	kneeing
+ cap	kneecap*
+ hole	kneehole*
+ pan	kneepan*
kneel	
+ s	kneels
+ ed	kneeled, knelt
+ ing	kneeling
+ er	kneeler*
knife	
+ s	knives
+ ed	knifed
+ ing	knifing
+ like	knifelike
knit	
+ s	knits
+ ed	knitted
+ ing	knitting
+ er	knitter*
+ wear	knitwear
knob	
+ s	knobs
+ ed	knobbed
+ ly	knobbly
+ y	knobby
+ er	knobbier
+ est	knobbiest
knock	
+ s	knocks
+ ed	knocked
+ ing	knocking
+ er	knocker*
+ about	knockabout*
+ down	knockdown*
+ off	knockoff*
knot	
+ s	knots
+ ed	knotted
+ ing	knotting
+ er	knotter
+ y	knotty
+ y + er	knottier
+ est	knottiest
+ grass	knotgrass
+ hole	knothole*
+ weed	knotweed
know	
+ s	knows
+ ed	knew
+ en	known
+ ing	knowing
+ ing + ly	knowingly
+ able	knowable
+ er	knower
+ age	knowledge
+ age + able	knowledgeable
+ ity	knowledgeability
+ ness	knowledgeableness
+ able + ly	knowledgeably
Kool Aid	
Korea	
+ an	Korean*
kosher^ (2)	

label	
+ s	labels
+ ed	labeled
+ ing	labeling
+ or	labolor*
labor	
+ s	labors
+ ed	labored
+ ing	laboring
+ ory	laboratory*
+ er	laborer*
+ ous	laborious
+ ly	laboriously
+ ness	laboriousness
+ ite	Laborite
+ save + ing	laborsaving
lace	
+ s	laces
+ ed	laced
+ ing	lacing
+ er	lacer
+ less	laceless
+ like	lacelike
+ y	lacy
+ y + er	lacier
+ est	laciest
lack^	
ladder	
+ s	ladders
+ like	ladderlike
lady	
+ s	ladies
+ like	ladylike
+ ship	ladyship
+ bug	ladybug*
+ finger	ladyfinger*
+ fish	ladyfish
+ love	ladylove
lake	
+ s	lakes
+ er	laker
+ front	lakefront*
+ shore	lakeshore*
+ side	lakeside*
lamb	
+ s	lambs
+ ed	lambed
+ ing	lambing
+ er	lamber
+ kill	lambkill
+ skin	lambskin
laminate	
+ s	laminates
+ ed	laminated
+ ing	laminating
+ ion	lamination*
+ or	laminator*
lamp	
+ s	lamps
+ black	lampblack
+ light	lamplight
+ light + er	lamplighter*
+ shell	lampshell
land	
+ s	lands
+ ed	landed
+ ing	landing
+ er	lander
+ less	landless
+ fall	landfall
+ fill	landfill
+ form	landform
+ hold + er	landholder
+ hold + ing	landholding
+ lady	landlady*
+ lock + ed	landlocked
+ lord	landlord
+ lord + ism	landlordism
+ mark	landmark*
+ own + er	landowner*
+ ship	landownership
+ slide	landslide*
+ s + man	landsman
+ ward	landward*
lane*	
language*	

L

lantern*	
lap	
+ s	laps
+ ed	lapped
+ ing	lapping
+ er	lapper
+ ful	lapful
+ board	lapboard*
+ dog	lapdog*
lard	
+ s	lards
+ ed	larded
+ ing	larding
+ er	larder*
+ y	lardy
large	
+ er	larger
+ est	largest
+ ly	largely
+ ness	largeness
+ heart + ed	largehearted
+ heart + ed + ness	largeheartedness
+ mouth	largemouth
lash	
+ s	lashes
+ ed	lashed
+ ing	lashing*
+ er	lasher
last	
+ s	lasts
+ ed	lasted
+ ing	lasting
+ er	laster
+ ly	lastly
+ ing + ly	lastingly
+ ness	lastingness
late	
+ er	later
+ est	latest
+ ish	latish
+ ly	lately
+ ness	lateness
+ come + er	latecomer*
later	
Latin	
+ ate	Latinate
+ an	Latinian
+ ism	Latinism
+ ist	Latinist
+ ity	latinity
+ ize	latinize^
+ tion	latinization
latitude	
+ s	latitudes
+ al	latitudinal
+ ly	latitudinally
+ an	latitudinarian
+ ism	latitudinarianism
laugh	
+ s	laughs
+ ed	laughed
+ ing	laughing
+ able	laughable
+ ness	laughableness
+ able + ly	laughably
+ er	laugher
+ ing + ly	laughingly
+ t + er	laughter
launch	
+ s	launches
+ ed	launched
+ ing	launching
+ er	launcher
+ pad	launchpad*
launder	
+ s	launders
+ ed	laundered
+ ing	laundering
+ y	laundry*
+ man	laundryman*
+ woman	laundrywoman*
+ ess	laundress
law	
+ s	laws
+ ful	lawful
+ ful + ly	lawfully
+ ful + ness	lawfulness
+ less	lawless
+ less + ly	lawlessly
+ less + ness	lawlessness
+ er	lawyer*
+ break + er	lawbreaker*
+ break + ing	lawbreaking
+ give + er	lawgiver
+ make + er	lawmaker*
+ make + ing	lawmaking
+ man	lawman*
+ suit	lawsuit*
lawn	
+ s	lawns
+ y	lawny
lawyer	
+ s	lawyers
+ ing	lawyering
+ ly	lawyerly
+ like	lawyerlike

lay	
+ s	lays
+ ed	laid
+ ing	laying
+ ic	laic
+ al	laical
+ ly	laically
+ ize	laicize ^
+ tion	laicization
+ ity	laity*
+ about	layabout*
+ away	layaway*
+ man	layman*
+ off	layoff*
+ out	layout*
+ over	layover*
+ person	layperson*
+ woman	laywoman*
layer	
+ s	layers
+ ed	layered
+ ing	layering
+ age	layerage
lazy	
+ s	lazes
+ ed	lazed
+ ing	lazing
+ er	lazier
+ est	laziest
+ ly	lazily
+ ness	laziness
+ ish	lazyish
+ bone + s	lazybones
lead (verb)	
+ s	leads
+ ed	led
+ ing	leading
+ er	leader*
+ ship	leadership
+ off	leadoff
+ man	leadman
lead (metal)	
+ en	leaden
+ ly	leadenly
+ ness	leadenness
+ less	leadless
+ y	leady
+ er	leadier
+ est	leadiest
+ work	leadwork
leaf	
+ s	leafs, leaves
+ ed	leafed, leaved
+ ing	leafing
+ age	leafage
+ less	leafless
+ let	leaflet*
+ like	leaflike
+ y	leafy
+ er	leafier
+ est	leafiest
league	
+ s	leagues
+ ed	leagued
+ ing	leaguing
+ er	leaguer*
leak	
+ s	leaks
+ ed	leaked
+ ing	leaking
+ age	leakage
+ er	leaker*
+ y	leaky
+ y + er	leakier
+ est	leakiest
+ ly	leakily
+ ness	leakiness
+ proof	leakproof
lean	
+ s	leans
+ ed	leaned
+ ing	leaning
+ ly	leanly
+ ness	leanness
leap	
+ s	leaps
+ ed	leaped
+ ing	leaping
+ er	leaper
+ frog	leapfrog^
learn	
+ s	learns
+ ed	learned
+ ing	learning
+ able	learnable
+ er	learner*
+ ly	learnedly
+ ness	learnedness
least	
+ way + s	leastways
+ wise	leastwise
leather	
+ s	leathers
+ ed	leathered
+ ing	leathering
+ like	leatherlike
+ er + n	leathern
+ y	leathery

L

+ back	leatherback
+ leaf	leatherleaf
+ neck	leatherneck
+ wood	leatherwood
leave	
+ s	leaves
+ ed	left
+ ing	leaving*
+ er	leaver
lecture	
+ s	lectures
+ ed	lectured
+ ing	lecturing
+ ship	lectureship
ledge	
+ s	ledges
+ y	ledgy
ledger*	
left	
+ ish	leftish
+ ism	leftism
+ ist	leftist
+ ward	leftward
+ y	lefty*
left	
+ over	leftover*
leg	
+ s	legs
+ ed	legged
+ ing	legging*
+ less	legless
+ y	leggy
+ er	leggier
+ est	leggiest
+ ness	leginess
+ work	legwork
legal	
+ ese	legalese
+ ism	legalism
+ ist	legalist*
+ ic	legalistic
+ al + ly	legalistically
+ ity	legality*
+ ize	legalize^
+ tion	legalization
+ ly	legally
legend	
+ s	legends
+ ary	legendary
+ ly	legendarily
+ y	legendry
legislate	
+ s	legislates
+ ed	legislated
+ ing	legislating
+ ion	legislation
+ ive	legislative
+ ly	legislatively
+ or	legislator*
+ al	legislatorial
+ ship	legislatorship*
+ ess	legislatress
+ ure	legislature*
leisure	
+ ed	leisured
+ ly	leisurely
+ ness	leisureliness
lemon	
+ s	lemons
+ y	lemony
lemonade	
lend	
+ s	lends
+ ed	lent
+ ing	lending
+ able	lendable
+ er	lender*
length	
+ s	lengths
+ en	lengthen^
+ en + er	lengthener*
+ way + s	lengthways
+ wise	lengthwise
+ y	lengthy
+ y + er	lengthier
+ est	lengthiest
+ ly	lengthily
+ ness	lengthiness
lens	
+ s	lenses
+ ed	lensed
+ less	lensless
leopard	
+ s	leopards
+ ess	leopardess
leprechaun	
+ s	leprechauns
+ ish	leprechaunish
less	
+ er	lesser
+ est	least
+ en	lessen^
lesson^	
let	
+ s	lets
+ ed	let
+ ing	letting
+ 's	let's
+ down	letdown*
+ up	letup*

letter	
+ s	letters
+ ed	lettered
+ ing	lettering
+ er	letterer*
+ form	letterform
+ head	letterhead
+ press	letterpress
+ space + ing	letterspacing
lettuce*	
level	
+ s	levels
+ ed	leveled
+ ing	leveling
+ er	leveler*
+ head + ed	levelheaded
+ head + **ness**	levelheadedness
liar*	
liberty	
+ s	liberties
+ al	liberal*
+ ly	liberally
+ al + ism	liberalism
+ al + ist	liberalist
+ ic	liberalistic
+ ity	liberality
+ ize	liberalize^
+ ize + tion	liberalization
+ ize + er	liberalizer
+ ate	liberate^
+ ate + ion	liberation
+ ion + ist	liberationist
+ ate + or	liberator
+ an	liberatarian
+ an + ism	liberatarianism
+ ine	libertine*
+ age	libertinage
+ ine + ism	libertinism
library	
+ s	libraries
+ an	librarian*
+ ship	librarianship
license	
+ s	licenses
+ ed	licensed
+ ing	licensing
+ able	licensable
+ ee	licensee*
+ er	licenser*
+ ure	licensure
+ ate	licentiate*
+ ous	licentious
+ ly	licentiously
+ ness	licentiousness

lick^	
lid	
+ s	lids
+ ed	lidded
+ ing	lidding
+ less	lidless
lie	
+ s	lies
+ ed	lied
+ ing	lying
+ ar	liar*
lie (recline)	
+ s	lies
+ ed	lay
+ en	lain
+ ing	lying
+ er	lier*
life	
+ s	lives (plural)
+ er	lifer
+ ful	lifeful
+ less	lifeless
+ ly	lifelessly
+ less + ness	lifelessness
+ like	lifelike
+ like + ness	lifelikeness
+ blood	lifeblood
+ boat	lifeboat*
+ guard	lifeguard*
+ line	lifeline*
+ long	lifelong
+ save + er	lifesaver*
+ save + ing	lifesaving
+ time	lifetime*
+ way	lifeway
+ work	lifework
lift	
+ s	lifts
+ ed	lifted
+ ing	lifting
+ able	liftable
+ er	lifter
+ gate	liftgate
light	
+ s	lights
+ ed	lighted
+ ing	lighting
+ en	lighten^
+ en + er	lightener
+ er	lighter*
+ age	lighterage
+ est	lightest
+ less	lightless
+ ly	lightly

+ ness	lightness
+ some	lightsome
+ some + ly	lightsomely
+ some + ness	lightsomeness
+ face	lightface
+ fast	lightfast
+ heart + ed	lighthearted
+ heart + ed + ly	lightheartedly
+ heart + ed + ness	lightheartedness
+ house	lighthouse*
+ plane	lightplane
+ proof	lightproof
+ ship	lightship*
+ tight	lighttight
+ weigh + t	lightweight*
+ wood	lightwood

lightning^

like	
+ s	likes
+ ed	liked
+ ing	liking
+ able	likable
+ able + ness	likableness
+ ity	likability
+ ly	likely
+ er	likelier
+ est	likeliest
+ hood	likelihood
+ en	liken^
+ ness	likeness*
+ wise	likewise

limb	
+ s	limbs
+ ed	limbed
+ ing	limbing
+ less	limbless

lime	
+ s	limes
+ ed	limed
+ ing	liming
+ light	limelight
+ stone	limestone
+ water	limewater
+ y	limey*

limit	
+ s	limits
+ ed	limited
+ ing	limiting
+ able	limitable
+ tion	limitation*
+ al	limitational
+ ive	limitative
+ ed + ly	limitedly
+ ed + ness	limitedness
+ er	limiter*
+ less	limitless
+ less + ly	limitlessly
+ less + ness	limitlessness

Lincoln	
+ a	Lincolniana

line	
+ s	lines
+ ed	lined
+ ing	lining*
+ age	lineage
+ al	lineal
+ al + ity	lineality
+ al + ly	lineally
+ ment	lineament
+ ment + al	lineamental
+ ar	linear
+ ar + ity	linearity
+ ar + ly	linearly
+ ize	linearize^
+ ize + tion	linearization
+ tion	lineation
+ er	liner*
+ back + er	linebacker*
+ back + ing	linebacking
+ breed	linebreed^
+ cut	linecut
+ man	lineman*
+ s + man	linesman*
+ up	lineup*

linguistic	
+ s	linguistics
+ al	linguistical
+ ly	lingually
+ an	linguistician
+ ist	linguist*

link	
+ s	links
+ ed	linked
+ ing	linking
+ age	linkage*
+ er	linker
+ boy	linkboy
+ man	linkman*
+ s + man	linksman*
+ up	linkup*

linoleum	
+ ate	linoleate

lion	
+ s	lions
+ ess	lioness
+ ize	lionize^
+ heart + ed	lionhearted
+ like	lionlike
+ fish	lionfish

lip

+ s	lips
+ ed	lipped
+ ing	lipping
+ less	lipless
+ like	liplike
+ y	lippy
+ er	lippier
+ est	lippiest
+ read + ing	lipreading

lipstick*

liqueur*

liquid

+ s	liquids
+ ate	liquidate^
+ ity	liquidity
+ ly	liquidly
+ ness	liquidness
+ tion	liquidation
+ ate + or	liquidator*
+ ify	liquefy^
+ able	liquefiable
+ able + ity	liquefiability
+ ify + er	liquefier*
+ ize	liquidize^
+ ent	liquescent

liquor^

list

+ s	lists
+ ed	listed
+ ing	listing
+ er	lister*
+ less	listless
+ ly	listlessly
+ ness	listlessness

listen

+ s	listens
+ ed	listened
+ ing	listening
+ able	listenable
+ er	listener*
+ ship	listenership

liter*

literate

+ ly	literately
+ ness	literateness
+ y	literacy
+ ary	literary
+ ary + ly	literarily
+ ary + ness	literariness
+ ion	literation

literature

literal

+ ly	literally
+ ness	literalness
+ ism	literalism
+ ist	literalist
+ ic	literalistic
+ ity	literality
+ ize	literalize^

litter

+ s	litters
+ ed	littered
+ ing	littering
+ er	litterer*
+ y	littery
+ bag	litterbag*
+ bug	litterbug*
+ mate	littermate*

little

+ er	littler
+ est	littlest
+ ness	littleness

live

+ s	lives
+ ed	lived
+ ing	living
+ able	livable
+ ity	liveability
+ able + ness	livableness
+ ly	lively
+ er	livelier
+ est	liveliest
+ hood	livelihood
+ ly + ly	livelily
+ ly + ness	liveliness
+ en	liven^
+ long	livelong

liver

+ s	livers
+ ish	liverish
+ ness	liverishness

lizard*

load

+ s	loads
+ ed	loaded
+ ing	loading
+ er	loader*
+ master	loadmaster*

loaf

+ s	loafs, loaves
+ ed	loafed
+ ing	loafing
+ er	loafer*

loan

+ s	loans
+ ed	loaned
+ ing	loaning
+ able	loanable

L

+ er	loaner*
+ word	loanword*
lobster	
+ s	lobsters
+ man	lobsterman*
local	
+ e	locale*
+ ism	localism
+ ite	localite*
+ ity	locality*
+ ize	localize^
+ able	localizable
+ able + ity	localizability
+ tion	localization
+ ly	locally
locate	
+ s	locates
+ ed	located
+ ing	locating
+ able	locatable
+ er, + or	locater, locator
+ ion	location*
+ ive	locative
lock	
+ s	locks
+ ed	locked
+ ing	locking
+ able	lockable
+ age	lockage
+ box	lockbox*
+ nut	locknut*
+ out	lockout*
+ step	lockstep
+ stitch	lockstitch
+ up	lockup*
locker*	
locket*	
locust*	
lodge	
+ s	lodges
+ ed	lodged
+ ing	lodging*
+ er	lodger*
+ ment	lodgment
log	
+ s	logs
+ ed	logged
+ ing	logging
+ er	logger*
+ y	logy
+ y + er	logier
+ est	logiest
+ book	logbook*
+ jam	logjam*
+ roll	logroll^
logic	
+ al	logical
+ ity	logicality
+ ly	logically
+ ness	logicalness
lollipop*	
London	
+ er	Londoner*
lone	
+ er	loner*
+ ly	lonely
+ ly + ness	loneliness
+ ly + er	lonelier
+ est	loneliest
+ ly + ly	lonelily
+ ness	loneness
lonesome	
+ ly	lonesomely
+ ness	lonesomeness
long	
+ s	longs
+ ed	longed
+ ing	longing*
+ ly	longingly
+ er	longer
+ est	longest
+ ish	longish
+ ness	longness
+ boat	longboat*
+ bow	longbow*
+ bow + man	longbowman*
+ hair	longhair
+ hair + ed	longhaired
+ hand	longhand
+ horn	longhorn
+ house	longhouse
+ line	longline
+ shore + man	longshoreman*
+ sight + ed	longsighted
+ some	longsome
+ some + ly	longsomely
+ some + ness	longsomeness
+ time	longtime
longitude	
+ al	longitudinal
+ ly	longitudinally
look	
+ s	looks
+ ed	looked
+ ing	looking
+ er	looker*
+ out	lookout*
+ up	lookup

L

loop

+ s	loops
+ ed	looped
+ ing	looping
+ er	looper
+ y	loopy
+ hole	loophole*

loose

+ s	looses
+ ed	loosed
+ ing	loosing
+ en	loosen^
+ er	looser
+ est	loosest
+ ly	loosely
+ ness	looseness

lord

+ s	lords
+ ed	lorded
+ ing	lording
+ ly	lordly
+ er	lordlier
+ est	lordliest
+ ness	lordliness
+ ship	lordship*

lose

+ s	loses
+ ed	lost
+ ing	losing
+ able	losable
+ able + ness	losableness
+ ed + ness	lostness
+ er	loser*

loss*

lot^

lotion*

lottery*

loud

+ en	louden^
+ er	louder
+ est	loudest
+ ly	loudly
+ ness	loudness
+ mouth	loudmouth*
+ mouth + ed	loudmouthed
+ speak + er	loudspeaker*

lounge

+ s	lounges
+ ed	lounged
+ ing	lounging
+ er	lounger*
+ wear	loungewear

louse

+ s	louses
+ ed	loused
+ ing	lousing

lousy

+ er	lousier
+ est	lousiest
+ ly	lousily
+ ness	lousiness

love

+ s	loves
+ ed	loved
+ ing	loving
+ able	lovable
+ able + ly	lovably
+ able + ness	lovableness
+ less	loveless
+ less + ly	lovelessly
+ less + ness	lovelessness
+ er	lover*
+ er + ly	loverly
+ ing + ly	lovingly
+ ing + ness	lovingness
+ bird	lovebird*
+ lock	lovelock*
+ make + ing	lovemaking
+ sick	lovesick
+ sick + ness	lovesickness
+ some	lovesome

lovely

+ s	lovelies
+ er	lovelier
+ est	loveliest
+ ly	lovelily
+ ness	loveliness

low

+ er	lower^
+ y	lowery
+ est	lowest
+ s	lows
+ ed	lowed
+ ing	lowing
+ ly	lowly
+ ly + er	lowlier
+ ly + est	lowliest
+ ly + ness	lowliness
+ ness	lowness
+ er + case	lowercase^
+ er + more + est	lowermost
+ ball	lowball^
+ birth + en	lowborn
+ boy	lowboy*
+ breed + ed	lowbred
+ brow	lowbrow*
+ down	lowdown
+ land	lowland
+ land + er	lowlander

L

luck

+ s	lucks
+ ed	lucked
+ ing	lucking
+ less	luckless
+ y	lucky
+ er	luckier
+ est	luckiest
+ ly	luckily
+ ness	luckiness

luggage

lumber

+ s	lumbers
+ ed	lumbered
+ ing	lumbering
+ man	lumberman*
+ yard	lumberyard*

lump

+ s	lumps
+ ed	lumped
+ ing	lumping
+ er	lumper*
+ ish	lumpish
+ ish + ly	lumpishly
+ ish + ness	lumpishness
+ y	lumpy
+ y + er	lumpier
+ est	lumpiest
+ y + ly	lumpily
+ y + ness	lumpiness

lunch

+ s	lunches
+ ed	lunched
+ ing	lunching
+ er	luncher*
+ an	luncheon*
+ room	lunchroom*
+ time	lunchtime

lung^

lust

+ s	lusts
+ ed	lusted
+ ing	lusting
+ ful	lustful
+ ful + ly	lustfully
+ ful + ness	lustfulness
+ y	lusty
+ er	lustier
+ est	lustiest
+ y + ly	lustily
+ hood	lustihood
+ y + ness	lustiness

Lutheran

+ s	Lutherans
+ ism	Lutheranism

luxury

+ s	luxuries
+ ance	luxuriance
+ ant	luxuriant
+ ly	luxuriantly
+ ate	luxuriate^
+ ous	luxurious
+ ous + ly	luxuriously
+ ness	luxuriousness

lyric

+ s	lyrics
+ al	lyrical
+ ly	lyrically
+ ness	lyricalness
+ ism	lyricism
+ ist	lyricist*

macaroni
+ s — macaronies
+ ic — macaronic

machine
+ s — machines
+ ed — machined
+ ing — machining
+ able — machinable
+ ity — machinability
+ ate — machinate^
+ or — machinator*
+ tion — machination*
+ like — machinelike
+ ery — machinery*
+ ist — machinist*

mad
+ s — mads
+ ed — madded
+ ing — madding
+ er — madder
+ est — maddest
+ en — madden^
+ ing + ly — maddeningly
+ ish — maddish
+ ly — madly
+ ness — madness
+ man — madman*

magazine
+ s — magazines
+ ist — magazinist*

magic
+ s — magics
+ ed — magicked
+ ing — magicking
+ al — magical
+ ly — magically
+ an — magician*

magnet
+ s — magnets
+ ic — magnetic
+ ly — magnetically
+ ism — magnetism
+ ite — magnetite
+ ite + ic — magnetitic
+ ize — magnetize^
+ tion — magnetization
+ er — magnetizer
+ able — magnetizable
+ o — magneto*

magnificent
+ ic — magnific
+ al — magnifical
+ al + ly — magnifically
+ ence — magnificence
+ ent + ly — magnificently

magnify
+ s — magnifies
+ ed — magnified
+ ing — magnifying
+ tion — magnification*
+ er — magnifier*

mail
+ s — mails
+ ed — mailed
+ ing — mailing*
+ able — mailable
+ ity — mailability
+ er — mailer*
+ bag — mailbag*
+ box — mailbox
+ carry + er — mailcarrier*
+ man — mailman*
+ woman — mailwoman*

main
+ s — mains
+ ly — mainly
+ frame — mainframe*
+ land — mainland
+ land + er — mainlander*
+ line — mainline^
+ line + er — mainliner
+ mast — mainmast*
+ sail — mainsail*
+ sheet — mainsheet
+ spring — mainspring
+ stay — mainstay
+ top — maintop

M

mainstream^
maintain

+ s	maintains
+ ed	maintained
+ ing	maintaining
+ able	maintainable
+ ity	maintainability
+ ance	maintainance
+ er	maintainer

majesty

+ s	majesties
+ ic	majestic
+ ly	majestically

major

+ s	majors
+ ed	majored
+ ing	majoring
+ ity	majority*
+ an	majoritarian
+ ism	majoritarianism

make

+ s	makes
+ ed	made
+ ing	making
+ able	makable
+ er	maker*
+ ready	makeready
+ up	makeup
+ weigh + t	makeweight

male

+ s	males
+ ness	maleness
+ ine	masculine
+ ity	masculinity
+ ize	masculinize^
+ tion	masculinization
+ ly	masculinely

mall*
mammal

+ s	mammals
+ an	mammalian
+ ate + ed	mammillated
+ ary	mammary
or + ary	mammillary

man

+ s	mans
+ ed	manned
+ ing	manning
+ hood	manhood
+ kind	mankind
+ ish	mannish
+ ish + ly	mannishly
+ ish + ness	mannishness
+ like	manlike
+ ly	manly
+ ly + ness	manliness
+ handle	manhandle^
+ hole	manhole*
+ hunt	manhunt*
+ serve + ant	manservant*

manage

+ s	manages
+ ed	managed
+ ing	managing
+ able	manageable
+ ity	manageability
+ ly	manageably
+ ness	manageableness
+ er	manager*
+ er + al	managerial
+ al + ly	managerially
+ ment	management
+ ment + al	managemental
+ ship	managership

mane^
manicure

+ s	manicures
+ ed	manicured
+ ing	manicuring
+ ist	manicurist*

manner

+ s	manners
+ ed	mannered
+ ism	mannerism*
+ ist	mannerist
+ ic	manneristic
+ ly	mannerly
+ ness	mannerliness
+ less	mannerless

mansion*
manual

+ s	manuals
+ ly	manually

manufacture

+ s	manufactures
+ ed	manufactured
+ ing	manufacturing
+ er	manufacturer*
+ ory	manufactory

manuscript*
many

+ fold	manyfold

map

+ s	maps
+ ed	mapped
+ ing	mapping
+ able	mapable
+ er	mapper*
+ like	maplike
+ make + er	mapmaker*

M

marble
+ s — marbles
+ ed — marbled
+ ing — marbling
+ ize — marbleize^
+ y — marbly

March (2)

march (parade)
+ s — marches
+ ed — marched
+ ing — marching
+ er — marcher*
+ like — marchlike

margarine

margin
+ s — margins
+ ed — margined
+ ing — margining
+ al — marginal
+ a — marginalia
+ ity — marginality
+ ly — marginally
+ ate — marginate^
+ tion — margination

mark
+ s — marks
+ ed — marked
+ ing — marking
+ ly — markedly
+ er — marker*
+ down — markdown
+ s + man — marksman*
+ s + woman — markswoman*
+ up — markup

market
+ s — markets
+ ed — marketed
+ ing — marketing
+ able — marketable
+ ity — marketability
+ er — marketer*
+ place — marketplace

maroon^

marriage*

marry
+ s — marries
+ ed — married*
+ ing — marrying
+ age — marriage*
+ **able** — marriageable

marshmallow
+ s — marshmallows
+ y — marshmallowy

marvel
+ s — marvels
+ ed — marveled
+ ing — marveling
+ ous — marvelous
+ ly — marvelously
+ ness — marvelousness

mash
+ s — mashes
+ ed — mashed
+ ing — mashing
+ er — masher*

mask
+ s — masks
+ ed — masked
+ ing — masking
+ able — maskable
+ er — masker*

massage
+ s — massages
+ ed — massaged
+ ing — massaging
+ er — massager*

mast
+ s — masts
+ ed — masted
+ ing — masting
+ head — masthead*

master
+ s — masters
+ ed — mastered
+ ing — mastering
+ ful — masterful
+ ful + ly — masterfully
+ ful + ness — masterfulness
+ ly — masterly
+ ly + ness — masterliness
+ ship — mastership
+ y — mastery
+ mind — mastermind^
+ piece — masterpiece*
+ work — masterwork

mat^
+ e — matte

match
+ s — matches
+ ed — matched
+ ing — matching
+ er — matcher
+ able — matchable
+ less — matchless
+ ly — matchlessly
+ board — matchboard
+ book — matchbook

+ box	matchbox
+ lock	matchlock
+ make+ er	matchmaker*
+ make + ing	matchmaking
+ stick	matchstick*
+ up	matchup
+ wood	matchwood
mate	
+ s	mates
+ ed	mated
+ ing	mating
+ in + mate	inmate
+ in + mate + s	inmates
+ s	inmates
+ mis - mate	mismate
+ mis - mate + ed	mismated
+ ed	mismated
+ mis - mate + ing	mismating
material	
+ s	materials
+ ism	materialism
+ ist	materialist*
+ ic	materialistic
+ ic + al + ly	materialistically
+ ity	materiality*
+ ize	materialize^
+ er	materializer*
+ tion	materialization*
+ ly	materially
+ ness	materialness
math	
+ s	maths
+ ic + s	mathematics
+ al	mathematical
+ ly	mathematically
+ an	mathematician*
+ tion	mathematization
matter	
+ s	matters
+ ed	mattered
+ ing	mattering
+ y	mattery
mature	
+ s	matures
+ ed	matured
+ ing	maturing
+ ate	maturate^
+ tion	maturation
+ al	maturational
+ ly	maturely
+ ity	maturity
matzo*	
maximum	
+ s	maximums
+ ize	maximize^
+ er	maximizer*
+ al	maximal
+ ly	maximally
+ ist	maximalist*
may	
+ en *or* + t	might
+ n't	mayn't
May (2)	
+ ing	Maying
+ day	Mayday
+ fly	mayfly
+ flower	mayflower*
+ pole	maypole*
+ pop	maypop
+ time	Maytime
maybe	
mayonnaise	
mayor	
+ s	mayors
+ al	mayoral
+ y	mayoralty
McDonalds	
me	
meadow	
+ s	meadows
+ land	meadowland*
meal	
+ s	meals
+ y	mealy
+ er	mealier
+ est	mealiest
+ time	mealtime
+ worm	mealworm
+ y + bug	mealybug*
+ y + mouth+ ed	mealymouthed
mean	
+ s	means
+ ed	meant
+ ing	meaning*
+ ful	meaningful
+ ful + ly	meaningfully
+ ful + ness	meaningfulness
+ less	meaningless
+ less + ly	meaninglessly
+ less + ness	meaninglessness
+ er	meaner
+ est	meanest
+ ly	meanly
+ ness	meanness
+ time	meantime
+ while	meanwhile
measles	
+ ed	measled
+ y	measly
+ er	measlier

M

+ est	measliest
measure	
+ s	measures
+ ed	measured
+ly	measuredly
+ ing	measuring
+able	measurable
+ity	measurability
+ able +ly	measurably
+ er	measurer*
+ less	measureless
+ ment	measurement*
meat	
+ s	meats
+ less	meatless
+ y	meaty
+ er	meatier
+ est	meatiest
mechanic	
+ s	mechanics
+ al	mechanical
+ ly	mechanically
+ an	mechanician*
+ ism	mechanism*
+ ist	mechanist*
+ ic	mechanistic
+ ist + ly	mechanistically
+ ize	mechanize^
+ tion	mechanization
+ er	mechanizer*
medal	
+ s	medals
+ ist	medalist*
+ ic	medallic
medic	
+ s	medics
+ al	medical
+ ly	medically
+ ate	medicate*
+ ed	medicated
+ ing	medicating
+ tion	medication*
+ able	medicable
medicine	
+ s	medicines
+ able	medicinable
+ al	medicinal
+ ly	medicinally
meditate	
+ s	meditates
+ ed	meditated
+ ing	meditating
+ or	meditator*
+ tion	meditation
+ tive	meditative
+ ly	meditatively
+ ness	meditativeness
medium	
+ s	mediums
+ ship	mediumship
meet	
+ s	meets
+ ed	met
+ ing	meeting*
+ er	meeter*
+ ly	meetly
+ ing + house	meetinghouse
melody	
+ s	melodies
+ ic	melodic
+ ly	melodically
+ ous	melodious
+ ous + ly	melodiously
+ ness	melodiousness
+ ist	melodist*
+ ize	melodize^
+ er	melodizer*
+ drama	melodrama
melon*	
melt	
+ s	melts
+ ed	melted
+ ing	melting
+ er	melter
+ able	meltable
+ ity	meltability
+ ly	meltingly
+ down	meltdown*
+ water	meltwater
member	
+ s	members
+ ed	membered
+ ship	membership
dis +	dismember
dis + member + s	dismembers
dis + member + ed	dismembered
dis + member + ing	dismembering
dis + member + ment	dismemberment
memo*	
memorize	
+ s	memorizes
+ ed	memorized
+ ing	memorizing
+ able	memorizable
+ tion	memorization
+ er	memorizer*
memory	
+ s	memories
+ able	memorable

M

+ ness	memorableness
+ able + ly	memorably
+ ity	memorability
+ al	memorial*
+ ly	memorially
+ ist	memorialist
+ ize	memorialize^
men	
+ s + wear	menswear
+ fold	menfold
mend	
+ s	mends
+ ed	mended
+ ing	mending
+ er	mender*
+ able	mendable*
meningitis	
+ ic	meningitic
+ ly	meningitically
menorah*	
menstruate	
+ s	menstruates
+ ed	menstruated
+ ing	menstruating
+ tion	menstruation
+ al	menstrual
mental	
+ ly	mentally
+ ist	mentalist*
+ ic	mentalistic
+ ism	mentalism
+ ity	mentality
+ tion	mentation
mention	
+ s	mentions
+ ed	mentioned
+ ing	mentioning
+ able	mentionable
+ er	mentioner*
menu*	
mercy	
+ s	mercies
+ ful	merciful
+ ful + ly	mercifully
+ ful + ness	mercifulness
+ less	merciless
+ less + ly	mercilessly
+ less + ness	mercilessness
mermaid*	
merry	
+ er	merrier
+ est	merriest
+ ly	merrily
+ ness	merriness
+ make + er	merrymaker*
+ make + ing	merrymaking*
mess	
+ s	messes
+ ed	messed
+ ing	messing
+ y	messy
+ y + er	messier
+ est	messiest
+ ly	messily
+ ness	messiness
message^	
met	
metal	
+ s	metals
+ ed	metaled
+ ing	metaling
+ ic	metallic*
+ ly	metallically
+ ize	metalize^
+ ware	metalware*
+ work	metalwork*
+ work + er	metalworker*
+ work + ing	metalworking*
meter	
+ s	meters
+ ed	metered
+ ic	metric*
+ al	metrical
+ ly	metrically
+ tion	metrication
+ ize	metrilize^
+ ist	metrist*
method	
+ s	methods
+ ic	methodic
+ al	methodical
+ ly	methodically
+ ness	methodicalness
+ ism	methodism
+ ist	methodist*
+ ist + ic	methodistic
+ ize	methodize^
Mexico	
+ an	Mexican*
mice	
microphone	
+ s	microphones
+ ic	microphonic*
microscope	
+ s	microscopes
+ ic	microscopic
+ al	microscopical
+ ly	microscopically

microwave*	
mid	
a +	amid
	midair
	midbrain
	midday
	midfield
	midfielder
	midland
	midline
	midmost
	midpoint
	midsection
	midships
	midshipman
	midsize
	midstream
	midsummer
	midterm
	midtown
	midway
	midweek
	midweekly
	midwife
	midwinter
	midyear
middle	
+ s	middles
+ er	middler*
midget*	
midnight	
+ ly	midnightly
might (2)	
+ y	mighty
+ er	mightier
+ est	mightiest
+ ly	mightily
+ ness	mightiness
mile	
+ s	miles
+ er	miler*
+ age	mileage*
military	
+ s	militaries
+ ance	militance
+ y	militancy
+ ant	militant*
+ ant + ly	militantly
+ ness	militantness
+ ly	militarily
+ ism	militarism*
+ ist	militarist*
+ ic	militaristic
+ ic + ly	militaristically
+ ize	militarize^

To see the way to form words with the prefix shown here, refer to the section showing the root word involved.

+ tion	militarization
+ ate	militate*
+ ate + ed	militated
+ ate + ing	militating
milk	
+ s	milks
+ ed	milked
+ ing	milking
+ er	milker*
+ y	milky
+ y + er	milkier
+ est	milkiest
+ man	milkman
mill	
+ s	mills
+ ed	milled
+ ing	milling
+ er	miller*
+ age	millage
+ pond	millpond*
+ race	millrace*
+ stone	millstone*
+ stream	millstream*
milliliter*	
millimeter*	
million	
+ s	millions
+ fold	millionfold
+ th	millionth
Milwaukee	
mince	
+ s	minces
+ ed	minced
+ ing	mincing
+ er	mincer*
+ ly	mincingly
+ meat	mincemeat
mind	
+ s	minds
+ ed	minded
+ ing	minding
+ er	minder*
+ ness	mindedness
+ ful	mindful
+ ful + ly	mindfully
+ ful + ness	mindfulness
+ less	mindless
+ less + ly	mindlessly
+ less + ness	mindlessness
mine	
+ s	mines
+ ed	mined
+ ing	mining
+ er	miner*

+ lay + er	minelayer*
+ sweep + er	minesweeper*
mine (2)	
mineral	
+ s	minerals
+ ize	mineralize^
+ able	mineralizable
+ tion	mineralization
miniature	
+ s	miniatures
+ ist	miniaturist*
+ ic	miniaturistic
+ ize	miniaturize^
+ tion	miniaturization
minimum	
+ s	minimums
+ ize	minimize^
+ tion	minimization
+ er	minimizer*
+ al	minimal
+ ist	minimalist*
+ ism	minimalism
minister	
+ s	ministers
+ ed	ministered
+ ing	ministering
+ al	ministerial*
+ ly	ministerially
+ ant	ministrant*
+ tion	ministration*
+ y	ministry*
minor	
+ s	minors
+ ity	minority*
minus	
minute*	
mirror	
+ s	mirrors
+ ed	mirrored
+ ing	mirroring
+ like	mirrorlike

mis (prefix)

> To see the way to form words with the prefix shown here, refer to the section showing the root word involved.

misact
misaddress
misadjust
misadventure
misadvise
misaim
misanalysis
misanalyze
misapplication
misapply
misassemble
misbalance
misbecome
misbehave
misbehaver
misbehavior
misbelief
misbelieve
misbeliever
misbound
misbrand
misbutton
miscalculate
miscalculation
miscall
miscaption
miscarriage
miscarry
miscatalog
mischance
mischannel
mischarge
mischoice
miscite
misclassification
misclassify
miscode
miscommunication
miscomprehension
miscomputation
miscompute
misconception
misconduct
misconnect
misconnection
misconstruction
miscopy
miscorrelation
miscount
miscut
misdate
misdeal
misdeclare
misdefine
misdescribe
misdescription
misdevelop
misdiagnose
misdiagnosis
misdirect
misdirection
misdistribution
misdivision
misdo
misdraw

miseducate
miseducation
misemphasis
misemphasize
misemploy
misemployment
misestimate
misestimation
misevaluate
misfile
misfiled
misfire
misfit
misfocus
misfortune
misfunction
misgive
misgiving
misgivings
misgovern
misgovernment
misgrade
misguidance
misguide
misguided
misguides
misguiding
mishandle
mishear
mishit
misidentification
misidentify
misimpression
misinform
misinformation
misinterpret
misjudge
miskick
misknow
mislabel
mislay
mislead
mislearn
mislike
mislocate
mislocation
mismake
mismanage
mismanagement
mismark
mismarriage
mismatch
mismate
mismotivate
misname
misorder
misorient
misorientation
mispackage
mispend
misperceive
misperception
mispicture
misplace
misplan
misplay
misposition
misprescribe
misprint
mispronounce
mispronunciation
misquotation
misquote
misread
misreference
misregister
misregistration
misrelate
misremember
misreport
misrepresent
misroute
misrule
missend
misset
misshape
misshapen
misshapenly
missort
misspell
misstate
misstatement
misstep
misstrike
misthrow
mistime
mistitle
mistrain
mistranslate
mistranslation
mistreat
mistrial
mistrust
mistruth
mistune
mistype
misusage
misuse

M

	misvalue
	misvocalization
	miswrite
mischief	
+ ous	mischievous
+ ly	mischievously
+ ness	mischievousness
miser	
+ s	misers
+ ly	miserly
+ able	miserable
+ **ness**	miserableness
+ able + ly	miserably
+ ly + ness	miserliness
+ y	misery
miss^	
Miss	
mission	
+ er	missioner*
+ ize	missionize^
+ tion	missionization
+ s	missions
+ ed	missioned
+ ing	missioning
+ ary	missionary
+ ary + s	missionaries
mistake	
+ s	mistakes
+ ed	mistook
+ en	mistaken
+ ing	mistaking
+ able	mistakable
+ ly	mistakenly
+ er	mistaker*
mister	
misunderstand	
+ s	misunderstands
+ ed	misunderstood
+ ing	misunderstanding*
mitt	
+ s	mitts
+ en	mitten*
mix	
+ s	mixes
+ ed	mixed
+ ing	mixing
+ ure	mixture*
+ er	mixer*
moan^	
mobile	
+ ity	mobility
+ ing	mobiling
+ ize	mobilize^
+ tion	mobilization
model	
+ s	models
+ ed	modeled
+ ing	modeling
+ er	modeler*
moderate	
+ s	moderates
+ ed	moderated
+ ing	moderating
+ tion	moderation
+ or	moderator*
+ ship	moderatorship*
modern	
+ ity	modernity
+ ly	modernly
+ ness	moderness
+ ism	modernism
+ ist	modernist*
+ ic	modernistic
+ ize	modernize^
+ er	modernizer*
+ tion	modernization*
modify	
+ s	modifies
+ ed	modified
+ ing	modifying
+ able	modifiable
+ ity	modifiability
+ er	modifier*
+ tion	modification*
molasses	
mold	
+ s	molds
+ ed	molded
+ ing	molding*
+ able	moldable*
+ er	molder*
+ y	moldy
+ y + er	moldier
+ est	moldiest
+ ness	moldiness
mole	
+s	moles
molecule	
+ s	molecules
+ ar	molecular
+ ary	moleculary
mom	
+ s	moms
+ y	mommy*
+ a	momma
moment	
+ s	moments
+ ary	momentary

M

+ ary + ly	momentarily
+ ness	momentariness
+ ly	momently
+ ous	momentous
+ ous + ly	momentously
+ ous + ness	momentousness
momentum*	
Monday*	
money	
+ s	monies
+ ed	monied
+ ary	monetary
+ ily	monetarily
+ ist	monetarist*
+ ize	monetize^
+ tion	monetization
+ er	moneyer*
+ bag + s	moneybags
+ lend + er	moneylender*
monkey^	
monotone	
+ s	monotones
+ ic	monotonic
+ ic + ly	monotonically
+ icity	monotonicity
+ ous	monotonous
+ ous + ly	monotonously
+ ness	monotonousness
+ y	monotony
monster	
+ s	monsters
+ ous	monstrous
+ ly	monstrously
+ ness	monstrousness
+ ity	monstrosity*
Montana	
month	
+ s	months
+ ly	monthly*
+ long	monthlong
mood	
+ s	moods
+ y	moody
+ er	moodier
+ est	moodiest
+ ly	moodily
+ ness	moodiness
moon	
+ s	moons
+ ed	mooned
+ ing	mooning
+ ish	moonish
+ ish + ly	moonishly
+ y	moony
+ like	moonlike
+ light	moonlight
+ light + ed	moonlit
+ rise	moonrise
+ shine	moonshine*
+ shine + er	moonshiner*
+ ward	moonward
moose	
moral	
+ ly	morally
+ ism	moralism*
+ ist	moralist*
+ ic	moralistic
+ ist + ly	moralistically
+ ity	morality
+ ize	moralize*
+ ed	moralized
+ ing	moralizing
+ tion	moralization
morale	
more	
+ est	most
+ over	moreover
Mormon	
+ s	Mormons
+ ism	Mormonism
morn	
morning*	
mosquito^	
moss	
+ s	mosses
+ y	mossy
+ er	mossier
+ est	mossiest
+ like	mosslike
most	
+ ly	mostly
motel*	
moth	
+ s	moths
+ like	mothlike
+ y	mothy
+ ball	mothball
+ proof	mothproof
mother	
+ s	mothers
+ ed	mothered
+ ing	mothering
+ ly	motherly
+ hood	motherhood
+ less	motherless
motivate	
+ s	motivates
+ ed	motivated

M

+ ing motivating
+ or motivator*
+ ive motivative
+ tion motivation*
+ al motivational
+ ly motivationly

motive
+ s motives
+ ed motived
+ ing motiving
+ ity motivity
+ less motiveless
+ less + ly motivelessly
+ ic motivic

motor
+ s motors
+ ed motored
+ ing motoring
+ dom motordom
+ less motorless
+ ist motorist*
+ ize motorize^
+ tion motorization
+ ic motoric
+ bike motorbike*
+ boat motorboat*
+ boat + ing motorboating
+ car motorcar*
+ man motorman*
+ way motorway*

motorcycle
+ s motorcycles
+ ist motorcyclist*

mound^

mount
+ s mounts
+ ed mounted
+ ing mounting*
+ able mountable*

mountain (2)
+ s mountains
+ eer mountaineer*
+ eer + ing mountaineering
+ side mountainside*
+ ous mountainous
+ ly mountainously
+ ness mountainousness
+ y mountainy
+ top mountaintop*

mouse
+ s mouses
+ ed moused
+ ing mousing
+ er mouser*
+ y mousy
+ ly mousily
+ ness mousiness
+ y + er mousier
+ est mousiest

mouth
+ s mouths
+ ed mouthed
+ ing mouthing
+ like mouthlike
+ ful mouthful*
+ y mouthy
+ er mouthier
+ est mouthiest
+ piece mouthpiece
+ wash mouthwash

move
+ s moves
+ ed moved
+ ing moving
+ er mover*
+ able movable
+ able + ness movableness
+ ity movability
+ less moveless
+ less + ly movelessly
+ less + ness movelessness
+ ment movement*
+ ing + ly movingly

movie
+ s movies
+ dom moviedom
+ make + er moviemaker*
+ go + er moviegoer*
+ make + ing moviemaking*
+ go + ing moviegoing

mow
+ s mows
+ ed mowed
+ ing mowing
+ er mower*

Mrs.

much
+ ness muchness

mud
+ s muds
+ ed mudded
+ ing mudding
+ y muddy*
+ y + ed muddied
+ ly muddily
+ y + ness muddiness
+ y + ing muddying

M

muff^		
muffin*		
mug		
	+ s	mugs
	+ ed	mugged
	+ ing	mugging
	+ er	mugger*
	+ ee	muggee*
	+ ful	mugful*
mule		
	+ s	mules
	+ ed	muled
	+ ing	muling
	+ e + er	muleteer*
	+ ish	mulish
	+ ly	mulishly
	+ ish + ness	mulishness*
multiple		
	+ s	multiples
multiply		
	+ s	multiplies
	+ ed	multiplied
	+ ing	multiplying
	+ er	multiplier*
	+ ic + tion	multiplication
	+ ive	multiplicative
	+ ive + ly	multiplicatively
	+ ity	multiplicity*
mumble		
	+ s	mumbles
	+ ed	mumbled
	+ ing	mumbling
	+ er	mumbler*
	+ ly	mumbly
mumps		
munch		
	+ s	munches
	+ ed	munched
	+ ing	munching
	+ er	muncher*
	+ y + s	munchies
murder		
	+ s	murders
	+ ed	murdered
	+ ing	murdering
	+ er	murderer*
	+ ee	murderee*
	+ ess	murderess*
	+ ous	murderous
	+ ly	murderously
	+ ness	murderousness
muscle		
	+ s	muscles
	+ ed	muscled
	+ ing	muscling
	+ ar	muscular
	+ ity	muscularity
	+ ly	muscularly
museum*		
mushroom^		
music		
	+ al	musical
	+ ly	musically
	+ ity	musicality
	+ ize	musicalize^
	+ tion	musicalization*
	+ an	musician*
must		
	+ n't	mustn't
mustache		
	+ s	mustaches
	+ ed	mustached
	+ o	mustachio*
	+ o + ed	mustachioed
mustard		
	+ s	mustards
	+ y	mustardy
mutter		
	+ s	mutters
	+ ed	muttered
	+ ing	muttering
	+ er	mutterer*
mutual		
	+ ism	mutualism
	+ ist	mutualist
	+ ic	mutualistic
	+ ity	mutuality
	+ ize	mutualize^
	+ tion	mutualization
	+ ly	mutually
my		
	+ en	mine
mystery		
	+ s	mysteries
	+ ic	mystic*
	+ al	mystical
	+ al + ly	mystically
	+ ism	mysticism
	+ ify	mystify^
	+ ing + ly	mystifyingly
	+ er	mystifier*
	+ tion	mystification
	+ ous	mysterious
	+ ous + ly	mysteriously
	+ ness	mysteriousness
myth		
	+ s	myths
	+ ic	mythic

M

+ al	mythical
+ ly	mythically
+ ize	mythicize^
+ er	mythicizer*
+ make + er	mythmaker*

M

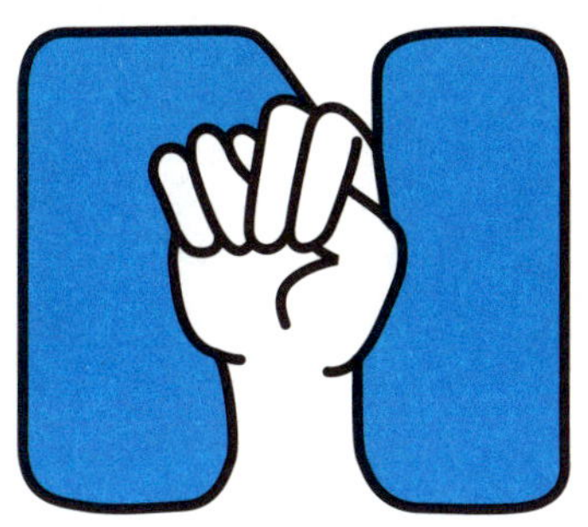

nag		
	+ s	nags
	+ ed	nagged
	+ ing	nagging
	+ ly	naggingly
	+ er	nagger*
nail		
	+ s	nails
	+ ed	nailed
	+ ing	nailing
	+ er	nailer*
	+ brush	nailbrush*
	+ head	nailhead*
naive		
	+ ly	naively
	+ ness	naiveness
	+ ity	naivete, naivety
	+ s	naiveties
naked		
	+ ly	nakedly
	+ ness	nakedness
name		
	+ s	names
	+ ed	named
	+ ing	naming
	+ er	namer*
	+ able	nameable
	+ less	nameless
	+ ly	namely
	+ ness	namelessness
	+ less + ly	namelessly
	+ plate	nameplate*
nap		
	+ s	naps
	+ ed	napped
	+ ing	napping
	+ er	napper*
	+ less	napless
napkin*		
narrow		
	+ s	narrows
	+ ed	narrowed
	+ ing	narrowing
	+ er	narrower
	+ est	narrowest
	+ ly	narrowly
	+ ness	narrowness
nasal		
	+ ity	nasality
	+ ize	nasalize
	+ s	nasalizes
	+ ed	nasalized
	+ ing	nasalizing
	+ tion	nasalization
nasty		
	+ er	nastier
	+ est	nastiest
	+ ly	nastily
	+ ness	nastiness
nation		
	+ s	nations
	+ al	national
	+ ly	nationally
	+ ism	nationalism
	+ ist	nationalist*
	+ ic	nationalistic
	+ ic + ly	nationalistically
	+ ity	nationality*
	+ ize	nationalize^
	+ ize + tion	nationalization
	+ er	nationalizer
	+ hood	nationhood
	+ wide	nationwide
native		
	+ s	natives
	+ ly	natively
	+ ness	nativeness
	+ ism	nativism
	+ ist	nativist*
	+ ic	nativistic
	+ ity	nativity
nature		
	+ s	natures
	+ al	natural
	+ ly	naturally
	+ ness	naturalness
	+ ism	naturalism
	+ ist	naturalist*

+ **ic**	naturalistic
+ **ic + ly**	naturalistically
+ **ize**	naturalize
+ **tion**	naturalization
naughty	
+ er	naughtier
+ est	naughtiest
+ ly	naughtily
+ ness	naughtiness
nausea	
+ ate	nauseate^
+ **ly**	nauseatingly
+ ous	nauseous
+ ous + ly	nauseously
+ **ness**	nauseousness
navy	
+ s	navies
+ al	naval
+ able	navigable
+ **ity**	navigability
+ **ness**	navigableness
+ **ly**	navigably
+ ate	navigate^
+ **tion**	navigation
+ **tion + al**	navigational
+ **al + ly**	navigationally
near	
+ s	nears
+ ed	neared
+ ing	nearing
+ by	nearby
+ ly	nearly
+ ness	nearness
+ sight +ed	nearsighted
neat	
+ en	neaten
+ **s**	neatens
+ **ed**	neatened
+ **ing**	neatening
+ er	neater
+ est	neatest
+ ly	neatly
+ ness	neatness
necessary	
+ s	necessaries
+ ate	necessitate^
+ **tion**	necessitation
+ ous	necessitous
+ **ly**	necessitously
+ **ness**	necessitousness
+ ity	necessity*
+ **an**	necessitarian*
+ **ism**	necessitarianism
necklace*	
nectar	
+ s	nectars
+ ous	nectarous
+ y	nectary*
nectarine*	
need	
+ s	needs
+ ed	needed
+ ing	needing
+ ful	needful
+ ful + ness	needfulness
+ n't	needn't
+ y	needy
+ **er**	needier
+ **est**	neediest
+ y + ness	neediness
+ less	needless
+ **ly**	needlessly
+ less + ness	needlessness
needle	
+ s	needles
+ ed	needled
+ ing	needling
+ like	needlelike
+ fish	needlefish
+ point	needlepoint
negative	
+ s	negatives
+ ed	negatived
+ ing	negativing
+ ly	negatively
+ ness	negativeness
+ ity	negativity
+ ism	negativism
+ ist	negativist
+ **ic**	negativistic
neglect	
+ s	neglects
+ ed	neglected
+ ing	neglecting
+ ful	neglectful
+ ful + ly	neglectfully
+ ful + ness	neglectfulness
+ er	neglecter
+ ance	negligence
+ ant	negligent
+ ant + ly	negligently
+ able	negligible
+ able + ly	negligibly
+ able + ness	negligibleness
+ **ity**	negligibility
negotiate	
+ s	negotiates

+ ed	negotiated
+ ing	negotiating
+ er	negotiator*
+ ant	negotiant*
+ able	negotiable
+ **ity**	negotiability
+ **ly**	negotiably
+ ery	negotiatory
+ tion	negotiation*
neighbor	
+ s	neighbors
+ ed	neighbored
+ ing	neighboring
+ ly	neighborly
+ **ness**	neighborliness
+ hood	neighborhood*
neither	
nephew*	
nerve	
+ s	nerves
+ ed	nerved
+ ing	nerving
+ less	nerveless
+ less + ly	nervelessly
+ less + ness	nervelessness
+ y	nervy
+ **er**	nervier
+ **est**	nerviest
+ y + ly	nervily
+ y + ness	nerviness
nervous	
+ ity	nervosity
+ ly	nervously
+ ness	nervousness
nest	
+ s	nests
+ ed	nested
+ ing	nesting
+ er	nester*
net	
+ s	nets
+ ed	netted
+ ing	netting
+ work	network^
neuter	
+ s	neuters
+ ed	neutered
+ ing	neutering
+ al	neutral
+ **ly**	neutrally
+ **ness**	neutralness
+ **ist**	neutralist*
+ **ic**	neutralistic
+ **ity**	neutrality*
+ **ize**	neutralize^
+ **er**	neutralizer*
+ **tion**	neutralization*
neutron	
+ s	neutrons
+ ic	neutronic
never	
+ more	nevermore
+ the + less	nevertheless
new	
+ er	newer
+ est	newest
+ ish	newish
+ ly	newly
+ ness	newness
+ born	newborn*
+ found	newfound
+ **wed**	newlywed*
+ speak	newspeak
+ s	news
+ **less**	newsless
+ **y**	newsy
+ y + er	newsier
+ y + est	newsiest
+ s + boy	newsboy*
+ s + break	newsbreak*
+ s + deal + er	newsdealer*
+ s + letter	newsletter*
+ s + magazine	newsmagazine*
+ s + man	newsman*
+ s + people	newspeople
+ s + person	newsperson*
+ s + print	newsprint
+ s + read + er	newsreader*
+ s + room	newsroom*
+ s + stand	newsstand*
+ s + week + ly	newsweekly*
+ s + woman	newswoman*
+ s + worth + y	newsworthy
+ s + worth **+ ness**	newsworthiness
+ s + write + ing	newswriting*
newspaper	
+ s	newspapers
+ man	newspaperman*
+ woman	newspaperwoman*
New York	
next	
nibble	
+ s	nibbles
+ ed	nibbled
+ ing	nibbling
+ er	nibbler*
nice	
+ er	nicer

N

+ est	nicest
+ ly	nicely
+ ness	niceness
+ ity	nicety*

nickel

+ s	nickels
+ ed	nickeled
+ ing	nickeling

niece*

night

+ s	nights
+ ly	nightly
+ y	nightie*
+ cap	nightcap*
+ cloth + es	nightclothes
+ club	nightclub*
+ dress	nightdress*
+ fall	nightfall
+ glow	nightglow
+ gown	nightgown*
+ life	nightlife
+ long	nightlong
+ shirt	nightshirt*
+ side	nightside
+ stand	nightstand*
+ stick	nightstick*
+ time	nighttime*
+ walk + er	nightwalker*

nip

+ s	nips
+ ed	nipped
+ ing	nipping
+ ing + ly	nippingly
+ er	nipper*
+ y	nippy
+ y + er	nippier
+ y + est	nippiest
+ **ness**	nippiness
+ y + ly	nippily

no

+ s	noes
+ body	nobody*
+ how	nohow
+ way	noway*
+ where	nowhere
+ wise	nowise

noble

+ s	nobles
+ er	nobler
+ est	noblest
+ ity	nobility
+ y	nobly
+ man	nobleman*
+ woman	noblewoman*

noise

+ s	noises
+ ed	noised
+ ing	noising
+ less	noiseless
+ less + ly	noiselessly
+ y	noisy
+ **er**	noisier
+ **est**	noisiest
+ y + ly	noisily
+ **ness**	noisiness
+ make + er	noisemaker*

nominate

+ s	nominates
+ ed	nominated
+ ing	nominating
+ er	nominator*
+ ee	nominee*
+ tion	nomination*

non (prefix)

> To see the way to form words with the prefix shown here, refer to the section showing the root word involved.

nonabstract
nonacademic
nonacceptable
nonactivated
nonactor
nonadaptive
nonadditive
nonadditivity
nonadhesive
nonadjustable
nonadmirer
nonadmission
nonadolescent
non-African
nonage
nonaggression
nonaggressive
nonagricultural
nonalcoholic
nonallergic
nonalphabetic
nonanalytic
nonanimal
nonanswer
nonappearance
nonarchitect
nonarchitecture
nonargument
nonart
nonartist
nonartistic
nonassociated
nonathlete

nonatomic
nonattached
nonattachment
nonattendance
nonattender
nonattentive
nonauditory
nonauthor
nonauthoritarian
nonauthoritative
nonautomatic
nonautomotive
nonavailability
nonbacterial
nonbank
nonbasic
nonbearing
nonbehavioral
nonbeing
nonbelief
nonbeliever
nonbetting
nonbibliographic
nonbinding
nonbiographical
nonbiological
nonbiologist
nonbiting
nonblack
nonbody
nonbook
nonbrand
nonbreakable
nonbreeder
nonbreeding
nonbuilding
nonburnable
nonbusiness
nonbuying
noncabinet
noncaking
noncallable
noncaloric
noncancelable
noncancerous
noncapital
noncapitalist
noncareer
noncarrier
noncash
non-Catholic
noncausal
noncelebration
noncellular
noncentral
noncertificated
noncertified
nonchallenging
noncharacter
nonchemical
nonchosen
non-Christian
nonchurch(goer)
noncircular
noncirculating
noncitizen
nonclass
nonclassical
nonclassified
nonclassroom
nonclinical
noncoincidence
noncollector
noncollege
noncollegiate
noncolor
noncolored
noncolorfast
noncommercial
noncommissioned
noncommital
noncommitally
noncommited
noncommitment
noncommunicating
noncommunication
noncommunicative
non-Communist
noncommunity
noncommutative
noncommutativity
noncomparability
noncomparable
noncompetition
noncompetitive
noncompetitor
noncomplex
noncomplicated
noncomposer
noncompound
noncomprehension
noncomputer
nonconceptual
nonconcern
noncondensable
nonconditioned
nonconducting
nonconduction
nonconductive
nonconductor

N

nonconference
nonconfidence
nonconfidential
nonconflicting
nonconfrontation
nonconfrontational
nonconnection
nonconscious
nonconservation
nonconservative
nonconstant
nonconstitutional
nonconstruction
nonconstructive
nonconsumer
nonconsuming
nonconsumption
nonconsumptive
noncontact
noncontagious
noncontinuous
noncontract
noncontractual
noncontributing
noncontributory
noncontrollable
noncontrolled
noncontrolling
noncontroversial
nonconventional
nonconvertible
noncooperation
noncooperationist
noncooperative
noncooperator
noncorrelation
noncounty
noncoverage
noncreative
noncreativity
noncredit
noncrime
noncriminal
noncrisis
noncritical
noncrossover
noncrushable
noncrystalline
noncultivated
noncultivation
noncultural
noncurrent
noncustomer
noncyclic
noncyclical
nondance
nondancer
nondeceptive
nondecision
nondecreasing
nondeductive
nondefense
nondegree
nondelegate
nondelinquent
nondemanding
nondemocratic
nondepartmental
nondependent
nondescriptive
nondesert
nondestructive
nondestructively
nondestructiveness
nondeterministic
nondevelopment
nondeviant
nondiabetic
nondiplomatic
nondirected
nondirectional
nondirective
nondisabled
nondisclosure
nondiscount
nondiscountable
nondiscrimination
nondiscriminatory
nondistinctive
nondividing
nondoctor
nondollar
nondominant
nondramatic
nondrinker
nondriver
nondrug
nondrying
nonearning
noneconomic
noneconomist
nonedible
noneditorial
noneducation
noneducational
noneffective
nonelastic
nonelected
nonelection
nonelective

N

nonelectric
nonelectrical
nonelectronic
nonelementary
nonemergency
nonemotional
nonemphatic
nonemployee
nonemployment
nonempty
nonending
nonenforceability
nonenforceable
nonenforcement
nonengagement
nonengineering
nonentertainment
nonequivalence
nonessential
nonestablished
nonestablishment
non-European
nonevent
nonevidence
nonexchangeable
nonexistence
nonexistent
nonexistential
nonexperimental
nonexpert
nonexplanatory
nonexplosive
nonexposed
nonfact
nonfactual
nonfaculty
nonfading
nonfamily
nonfan
nonfarm
nonfarmer
nonfat
nonfatal
nonfattening
nonfatty
nonfederal
nonfederated
nonfiction
nonfictional
nonfigurative
nonfinal
nonfinancial
nonflowering
nonflying
nonfood
nonformal
nonfossil
nonfreezing
nonfuel
nonfulfillment
nonfunctional
nonfunctioning
nongame
nongaseous
nongay
nongenetic
nongeometrical
nongovernment
nongovernmental
nongraded
nongraduate
nongranular
nongreasy
nongreen
nongrowing
nongrowth
nonhandicapped
nonhappening
nonhardy
nonharmonic
nonhereditary
nonhero
non-Hispanic
nonhistorical
nonhome
nonhospital
nonhospitalized
nonhostile
nonhuman
nonhysterical
nonimage
nonimitative
nonimplication
nonimportation
noninclusion
nonincreasing
nonindependence
non-Indian
nonindividual
nonindustrial
nonindustrialization
nonindustrialized
nonindustry
noninfected
noninfectious
noninfective
noninfested
noninflationary
noninflectional
noninfluence

N

noninformation
noninitial
noninitiate
noninjury
noninstallment
noninstitutional
noninstitutionalized
noninstructional
noninsured
nonintellectual
noninteracting
nonintercourse
noninvasive
noninvolvement
noniron
nonirrigated
nonirritant
nonirritating
nonissue
non-Jew
non-Jewish
nonjoiner
nonjudgmental
nonjudicial
nonkosher
nonlanguage
nonlawyer
nonleaded
nonleague
nonlegal
nonlibrarian
nonlibrary
nonlife
nonlineal
nonlinear
nonlinearity
nonlinguistic
nonliquid
nonliterary
nonliterate
nonliving
nonlocal
nonlogical
nonmagnetic
nonmajor
nonmanagement
nonmanagerial
nonmanual
nonmanufacturing
nonmarket
nonmatching
nonmaterial
nonmaterialistic
nonmathematical
nonmeasurable
nonmeat
nonmechanical
nonmechanistic
nonmedical
nonmeeting
nonmember
nonmembership
nonmental
nonmetal
nonmetalic
nonmetric
nonmetrical
nonmilitant
nonmilitary
nonminority
nonmolecular
nonmonetary
nonmoney
nonmoral
nonmotorist
nonmotorized
nonmoving
nonmusic
nonmusical
nonnational
nonnative
nonnatural
nonnecessity
nonnegative
nonnegotiable
nonnews
nonnormative
nonnuclear
nonnucleated
nonnumerical
nonnutritious
nonnutritive
nonobservance
nonobservant
nonobvious
nonoccupational
nonoccurrence
nonofficial
nonoperatic
nonoperating
nonoperational
nonoverlapping
nonowner
nonparalleled
nonparasitic
nonparticipant
nonparticipating
nonparticipation
nonparticipatory
nonparty

N

nonpassive
nonpast
nonpaying
nonpayment
nonperformance
nonpermissive
nonperson
nonpersonal
nonphilosopher
nonphilosophical
nonphotographic
nonphysical
nonphysician
nonplanar
nonplastic
nonplay
nonplaying
nonpoisonous
nonpolar
nonpolice
nonpolitical
nonpolitically
nonpolitician
nonpolluting
nonpoor
nonpractical
nonpracticing
nonpregnant
nonprescription
nonprint
nonproblem
nonproducing
nonproductive
nonprofessional
nonprofessionally
nonprofessorial
nonprofit
nonprogram
nonprogressive
nonpsychiatric
nonpsychiatrist
nonpsychological
nonpublic
nonpunitive
nonpurposive
nonquantitative
nonracial
nonracially
nonradioactive
nonrailroad
nonrated
nonreactive
nonreactor
nonreader
nonrealistic
nonreappointment
nonreceipt
nonrecognition
nonrecombinant
nonreducing
nonrefillable
nonreflecting
nonregulated
nonregulation
nonrelative
nonrelativistic
nonreligious
nonrenewable
nonrenewal
nonrepayable
nonrepresentation
nonrepresentative
nonresidence
nonresidency
nonresident
nonresidential
nonresistance
nonresistant
nonreturnable
nonreusable
nonreversible
nonrevolutionary
nonrioter
nonrioting
nonrotating
nonroutine
nonrubber
non-Russian
nonsalable
nonscheduled
nonschizophrenic
nonschool
nonscience
nonscientific
nonscientist
nonseasonal
nonsecure
nonselected
nonselective
nonself
non-self-governing
nonsensational
nonsense
nonsensical
nonsensically
nonsensicalness
nonsensuous
nonsentence
nonserious
nonsexual

nonshrink
nonshrinkable
nonsigner
nonsimultaneous
nonsinkable
nonskater
nonskeletal
nonskeptical
nonskier
nonslip
nonsmoker
nonsmoking
nonsocial
nonsocialist
nonsolar
nonsolution
nonspatial
nonspeaker
nonspeaking
nonspecialist
nonspecific
nonspecifically
nonspeech
nonsporting
nonstandard
nonstarter
nonstationary
nonstatistical
nonsteady
nonstick
nonstop
nonstory
nonstructural
nonstructured
nonstudent
nonsuccess
nonsugar
nonsuit
nonsupervisory
nonsupport
nonsurgical
nonswimmer
nonsyllabic
nonsymbolic
nonsystem
nonsystematic
nonsystemic
nontarget
nontaxable
nonteaching
nontechnical
nontheatrical
nonthematic
nontheoretical
nontherapeutic
nonthinking
nonthreatening
nontidal
nontitle
nontobacco
nontonal
nontotalitarian
nontraditional
nontransferable
nontypical
nonuniform
nonuniformity
nonunion
nonuniversal
nonuniversity
nonuse
nonuser
nonvanishing
nonverbal
nonverbally
nonveteran
nonviewer
nonviolence
nonviolent
nonviolently
nonviral
nonvisual
nonvocal
nonvocational
nonvolcanic
nonvoluntary
nonvoter
nonvoting
non-Western
nonwhite
nonwinning
nonwoody
nonword
nonworker
nonworking
nonwoven
nonwrite
nonyellowing
nonzero

none
noodle^
noon

+ er	nooner*
+ ing	nooning
+ day	noonday
+ hour	noonhour
+ tide	noontide
+ time	noontime

nor

norm	
+ s	norms
+ ed	normed
+ ive	normative
+ ive + ly	normatively
+ ive + ness	normativeness
normal	
+ ly	normally
+ ize	normalize^
+ **able**	normalizable
+ **tion**	normalization
+ **er**	normalizer
north	
+ er	norther
+ ern	northern
+ ner	northerner
+ er + ly	northerly*
+ ing	northing
+ ward	northward*
+ east + ward	northeastward
+ east + er	northeaster
+ east + er + n	northeastern
+ east + er + n + er	northeasterner
+ east + **ly**	northeasterly
+ west + **ly**	northwesterly
+ west + er + n	northwestern
+ west +er + n + er	northwesterner
+ west + ward	northwestward
Norway	
+ an	Norwegian*
nose	
+ s	noses
+ ed	nosed
+ ing	nosing
+ y	nosy, nosey
+ **ly**	nosily
+ **ness**	nosiness
+ **er**	nosier
+ **est**	nosiest
+ band	noseband
+ bleed	nosebleed
+ dive	nosedive
+ gay	nosegay
+ piece	nosepiece
+ wheel	nosewheel
nostril	
not (2)	
notch	
+ s	notches
+ ed	notched
+ ing	notching
+ back	notchback*
note	
+ s	notes
+ ed	noted
+ ing	noting
+ ed + ly	notedly
+ ed + ness	notedness
+ er	noter*
+ able	notable
+ **ity**	notability
+ able + ly	notably
+ able + ness	notableness
+ worth + y	noteworthy
+ worth + y + ly	noteworthily
+ worth + y + ness	noteworthiness
+ less	noteless
+ ize	notarize^
+ ize + tion	notarization*
+ ary	notary*
+ ate + tion	notation*
+ **al**	notational
+ ate	notate^
+ ice	notice^
+ ice + able	noticeable
+ ice + able + ly	noticeably
+ ify	notify^
+ ify + er	notifier*
+ ify + tion	notification*
+ book	notebook*
+ case	notecase*
+ hold + er	noteholder*
+ pad	notepad*
+ paper	notepaper*
nothing	
+ ness	nothingness
notion	
+ s	notions
+ al	notional
+ **ly**	notionally
+ **ity**	notionality
noun*	
November (2)	
now	
nuclear	
nucleus	
+ ate	necleate^
+ **tion**	nucleation
+ ate + er	nucleator
+ ic	nucleic
nude	
+ s	nudes
+ er	nuder
+ est	nudest
+ ly	nudely
+ ity	nudity
+ ism	nudism
+ ist	nudist*
+ ness	nudeness

number

+ s	numbers
+ ed	numbered
+ ing	numbering
+ able	numberable
+ er	numberer
+ less	numberless
+ ic	numeric
+ ic + al	numerical
+ ic + al + ly	numerically
+ al	numeral
+ ate	numerate^
+ **tion**	numeration
+ ary	numerary

numeral

+ s	numerals
+ ly	numerally

numerator*

nun

+ s	nuns
+ ery	nunnery*

nurse

+ s	nurses
+ ed	nursed
+ ing	nursing
+ er	nurser*
+ ery	nursery*

N

nut

+ s	nuts
+ y	nutty
+ **er**	nuttier
+ **est**	nuttiest
+ ed	nutted
+ ing	nutting
+ like	nutlike
+ pick	nutpick*
+ meg	nutmeg

nutrient*

nutrition

+ ist	nutritionist*
+ ment	nutriment*
+ al	nutritional
+ **ly**	nutritionally
+ ive	nutritive
+ ive + ly	nutritively
+ ous	nutritious
+ ous + ly	nutritiously
+ **ness**	nutritiousness

oar	
+ s	oars
+ ed	oared
+ ing	oaring
+ lock	oarlock
+ s + man	oarsman
oat	
+ s	oats
+ en	oaten
+ er	oater*
+ cake	oatcake
oatmeal	
oath	
+ s	oaths
obey	
+ s	obeys
+ ed	obeyed
+ ing	obeying
+ ent	obedient
+ ly	obediently
+ ence	obedience
+ s + ant	obeisant
+ s + ance	obeisance
object (noun)	
+ s	objects
+ ive	objective*
+ less	objectless
+ less + ness	objectlessness
+ ly	objectively
+ ive + ness	objectiveness
+ ity	objectivity
+ ism	objectivism
+ ist	objectivist
+ ic	objectivistic
object (verb)	
+ s	objects
+ ed	objected
+ ing	objecting
+ or	objector
+ or + s	objectors
+ ion	objection*
+ able	objectionable
+ ly	objectionably
+ ness	objectionableness

obligate	
+ s	obligates
+ ed	obligated
+ ing	obligating
+ ion	obligation*
+ ry	obligatory
+ ly	obligatorily
observe	
+ s	observes
+ ed	observed
+ ing	oberving
+ ing + ly	observingly
+ er	observer*
+ able	observable
+ able + ly	observably
+ ance	observance*
+ ant	observant
+ ant + ly	observantly
+ tion	observation*
+ tion + al	observational
+ ry	observatory*
obstacle	
+ s	obstacles
obstinate	
+ ly	obstinately
+ ness	obstinateness
+ y	obstinacy
obtain	
+ s	obtains
+ ed	obtained
+ ing	obtaining
+ er	obtainer*
+ able	obtainable
+ ity	obtainability
+ ment	obtainment
obvious	
+ ly	obviously
+ ness	obviousness
occupation	
+ s	occupations
+ al	occupational
+ ly	occupationally
occupy	
+ s	occupies

O

+ ed	occupied
+ ing	occupying
+ er	occupier*
+ ant	occupant*
+ y	occupancy*
occur	
+ s	occurs
+ ed	occurred
+ ing	occurring
+ ence	occurrence*
+ ent	occurrent
ocean	
+ s	oceans
+ ic	oceanic
October (2)	
octopus	
+ s	octopuses
odd	
+ s	odds
+ er	odder
+ est	oddest
+ ly	oddly
+ ness	oddness
+ ity	oddity*
+ ball	oddball*
+ ment	oddment*
odor	
+ s	odors
+ ed	odored
+ less	odorless
+ ant	odorant*
+ ize	odorize*
+ ing	odorizing
+ ous	odorous
+ ly	odorously
+ ness	odorousness
of	
off	
+ s	offs
+ ed	offed
+ ing	offing
+ spring	offspring
+ stage	offstage
+ ish	offish
+ ness	offishness
+ track	offtrack
+ beat	offbeat
+ hand	offhand
+ hand + ed	offhanded
+ hand **+ ly**	offhandedly
+ hand **+ ness**	offhandedness
+ print	offprint
+ screen	offscreen
+ set	offset
+ shoot	offshoot
+ shore	offshore
+ side	offside
offer	
+ s	offers
+ ed	offered
+ ing	offering*
+ ry	offertory*
office	
+ s	offices
+ er	officer*
+ al	official
+ ly	officially
+ dom	officialdom
+ ese	officialese
+ ism	officialism
+ ant	officiant*
+ ry	officiary*
+ ate	officiate^
+ tion	officiation
+ ine + al	officinal
+ ous	officious
+ ous **+** ly	officiously
+ ness	officiousness
often	
+ time + s	oftentimes
oil	
+ s	oils
+ ed	oiled
+ ing	oiling
+ er	oiler*
+ y	oily
+ y + er	oilier
+ y + est	oiliest
+ ly	oilily
+ ness	oiliness
+ bird	oilbird*
+ can	oilcan*
+ cloth	oilcloth*
+ man	oilman
+ seed	oilseed*
+ skin	oilskin*
+ stone	oilstone*
ointment	
+ s	ointments
okra	
old	
+ er	older
+ est	oldest
+ en	olden
olive	
+ s	olives
+ ine	olivine (stone)
olympic	
+s	olympics
+ an	olympian*

omelet	
+ s	omelets
omit	
+ s	omits
+ ed	omitted
+ ing	omitting
+ ible	omissible
+ sion	omission*
on	
+ look + er	onlooker*
+ go + ing	ongoing
+ look + ing	onlooking
+ set	onset
+ rush	onrush
+ shore	onshore
+ side	onside
+ stage	onstage
+ to	onto
+ ward	onward*
once	
one fourth	
one half	
onion	
+ s	onions
+ skin	onionskin*
only	
onto	
onward	
+ s	onwards
opaque	
+ s	opaques
+ ly	opaquely
+ ness	opaqueness
open	
+ s	opens
+ ed	opened
+ ing	opening*
+ er	opener*
+ ly	openly
+ ness	openness
+ able	openable
+ ity	openability
+ est	openest
+ hand + ed	openhanded
+ hand **+ ly**	openhandedly
+ hand **+ ness**	openhandedness
+ heart + ed	openhearted
+ heart **+ ly**	openheartedly
+ heart **+ ness**	openheartedness
+ mouth + ed	openmouthed
+ mouth **+ ly**	openmouthedly
+ mouth **+ ness**	openmouthedness
+ work	openwork*
+ work + ed	openworked

opera	
+ ic	operatic
+ ly	operatically
+ s	operas
+ go + er	operagoer*
+ go + ing	operagoing
operate	
+ s	operates
+ ed	operated
+ ing	operating
+ or	operator*
+ ant	operant*
+ ant + ly	operantly
+ ion	operation*
+ al	operational
+ ion **+ ly**	operationally
+ ism	operationalism
+ ist	operationalist
+ ic	operationalistic
+ ive	operative*
+ ive + ly	operatively
+ ive + ness	operativeness
+ or + less	operatorless
opinion (2)	
+ s	opinions
+ ed	opinioned
+ ate + ed	opinionated
+ ate **+ ly**	opinionatedly
+ ate **+ ness**	opinionatedness
+ ive	opinionative
+ ly	opinionatively
+ ive + ness	opinionativeness
opossum/possum	
+ s	opossums
opportune	
+ ly	opportunely
+ ness	opportuneness
+ ism	opportunism
+ ist	opportunist*
+ ic	opportunistic
+ ic + ly	opportunistically
+ ity	opportunity*
oppose	
+ s	opposes
+ ed	opposed
+ ing	opposing
+ able	opposable
+ ity	opposability
+ er	opposer*
+ ite	opposite*
+ ly	oppositely
+ ness	oppositeness
+ ion	opposition
+ ion + al	oppositional
+ ist	oppositionist*

O

option	
+ s	options
+ ing	optioning
+ al	optional
+ ly	optionally
or	
oral	
+ s	orals
+ ly	orally
+ ity	orality
+ ism	oralism
orange	
+ s	oranges
+ ry	orangery
+ ade	orangeade
+ wood	orangewood
orbit	
+ s	orbits
+ ed	orbited
+ ing	orbiting
+ er	orbiter*
+ al	orbital
orchard	
+ s	orchards
+ ist	orchardist*
orchestra	
+ s	orchestras
+ al	orchestral
+ ly	orchestrally
+ ate	orchestrate^
+ tion	orchestration*
+ tion + al	orchestrational
+ or	orchestrator*
order	
+ s	orders
+ ed	ordered
+ ing	ordering
+ less	orderless
+ ly	orderly*
+ ness	orderliness
+ al	ordinal*
+ ry	ordinary
+ ate	ordinate*
ordinance	
+ s	ordinances
ordinary	
+ s	ordinaries
+ ily	ordinarily
+ ness	ordinariness
ore	
+ s	ores
organize	
+ s	organizes
+ ed	organized

+ ing	organizing
+ er	organizer*
+ able	organizable
+ tion	organization*
+ al	organizational
+ ly	organizationally
orient	
+ s	orients
+ ed	oriented
+ ing	orienting
+ al	oriental
+ ly	orientally
+ ism	orientalism
+ ist	orientalist
+ ize	orientalize^
+ ate	orientate^
+ tion	orientation*
+ tion + al	orientational
+ tion + ly	orientationally
+ ee + r + ing	orienteering
origin	
+ ate	originate^
+ tion	origination
+ or	originator*
+ s	origins
+ al	original*
+ ly	originally
+ ity	originality*
+ ive	originative
+ ive + ly	originatively
ornament	
+ s	ornaments
+ ed	ornamented
+ ing	ornamenting
+ al	ornamental
+ ly	ornamentally
+ tion	ornamentation
+ ate	ornate
orphan	
+ s	orphans
+ ed	orphaned
+ ing	orphaning
+ hood	orphanhood
+ age	orphanage*
orthodontic	
+ s	orthodontics
+ ist	orthodontist*
ostrich	
+ s	ostriches
+ like	ostrichlike
other	
+ s	others
+ ness	otherness
+ where	otherwhere

+ while	otherwhile*
+ wise	otherwise
+ world	otherworld
+ world + ly	otheworldly
+ world + **ness**	otherworldliness

ought

+ n't	oughtn't

ounce

+ s	ounces

our (2)

+ s	ours
+ self	ourself
+ self + s	ourselves

out

+ age	outage*
+ er	outer
+ let	outlet
+ ing	outing*
+ most	outmost
+ side	outside*
+ ward	outward
+ side + er	outsider*
+ side + er + ness	outsiderness
+ ward + ness	outwardness
+ ward + ly	outwardly
+ back	outback

out (Used as a prefix)

> To see the way to form words with the prefix shown here, refer to the section showing the root word involved.

outachieve
outact
outbalance
outboard
outbound
outbox
outbrag
outbrave^
outbreak
outbreed
outbuilding
outcatch
outcharge
outclass
outclimb
outcoach
outcompete
outcount
outcome
outcrop^
outcross
outcry
outdated
outdistance^
outdo^
outdoor*
outdance
outdebate
outdeliver
outdesign
outdoorsman
outdoorsmanship
outdoorsy
outdraw*
outdrawn
outdress
outdrew
outdrink
outdrive
outearn
outeat
outercoat
outermost
outerwear
outface^
outfall
outfeet
outfield
outfight
outfigure
outfish
outfit^
outflow^
outfly
outfoot
outfox^
outgain
outgas^
outgeneral^
outgiving
outgo
outgoing
outgoingness
outgrow
outgrown
outgrows
outgrowth
outguess
outguessed
outguesses
outguessing
outgun^
outhaul^
outhear
outhit
outhouse
outhunt
outinfluence
outintrigue
outjump
outkick
outkill

O

outland
outlandish
outlandishly
outlandishness
outlast
outlaw^
outlay^
outleap
outlearn
outlier
outline^
outlive^
outlook
outlying
outman
outmarch
outmatch^
outmuscle
outnumber^
outorganize
outpass
outpatient
outperform
outpitch
outplacement
outplay
outpoint^
outpopulate
outpost
outpour
outpouring
outpray
outprice
outproduce
outpromise
outpull^
outpunch
output
outrace^
outrange^
outrate
outreach^
outridden
outride^
outrider
outright
outrival
outroar
outrow
outrun^
outrush
outsail
outscheme
outscoop
outscore
outsell^
outset
outshine^
outshoot^
outshout
outsight
outsing
outsit
outsize
outskate
outskirt
outsmart^
outsparkle
outspeak
outspeed
outspend^
outspoken
outspokenly
outspokenness
outspread^
outstand^
outstandingly
outstare^
outstation
outstay^
outstretch^
outstrip^
outswim
outtake
outtalk^
outthink^
outthrow
outtrade
outturn
outvote
outwait
outwalk
outwatch
outwear^
outweigh^
outwit^
outwork^
outworn
outworned
outworns
outwrestle
outwrite
outyell
outyield

outfit
outline
oval

+ s	ovals

O

+ ly ovally
+ ness ovalness

oven

+ s ovens
+ proof ovenproof
+ bird ovenbird

over

+ s overs
+ ed overed
+ ing overing
+ age overage
+ age + s overages

over (prefix)

To see the way to form words with the prefix shown here, refer to the section showing the root word involved.

overall*
overalled
overachiever
overact
overaction
overactive
overactivity
overarm
overbalance
overbear^
overbearingly
overbite
overblown
overboard
overbook^
overbought
overbuild
overbuilds
overbuilt
overbuilding
overburden^
overbuy^
overcall^
overcapitalize
overcapitalization
overcharge
overcloud^
overcost
overcome^
overcommit^
overcommitment
overcrowd^
overdetermined
overdevelop^
overdevelopment
overdo^
overdominance
overdominant
overdraw^
overdress^
overdrive^
overeat^
overeaten
overexpose^
overexposure
overextend^
overextension
overfeed^
overfill^
overfish^
overflight
overflow^
overfly^
overglaze^
overgrown
overgrowth
overhand
overhanded
overhang^
overhaul
overhead
overhear^
overheat^
overissue^
overissuance
overjoy
overkill^
overland
overlap^
overlay^
overleaf
overleap
overleaps
overlearn^
overlook^
overlord
overlordship
overman
overmaster^
overmatch^
overnight
overpass^
overpersuade^
overpersuasion
overplaid
overplaided
overplay^
overplus
overpopulate^
overpopulation
overpopulationed
overpower^
overpoweringly
overpressure
overprice^
overprint^

O

overproof
overproportion
overproportionate
overproportionately
overqualified
overreach
overrepresented
overrepresentation
override^
overridden
overripe
overrule^
overrun^
oversea
overseas
oversee^
oversensitive
oversensitiveness
oversensitivity
overset
oversets
oversetting
oversexed
overshadow^
overshirt
overshoe
overshoot^
oversight
oversimple
oversimply
oversimplify
oversimplification
oversize
oversized
overskirt
oversleep^
oversold
oversoul
overspend^
overspill
overspread
overstate^
overstatement
overstay^
overstep^
overstory
overstuff^
oversubscribe^
overtake^
overtaken
overtax^
overthrow^
overthrown
overtime
overtone
overtop
overtrade^
overtrick
overturn^
overvalue^
overvaluation
overview
overwear
overweary
overweigh
overweight
overwinter^
overwork^
overwrite^
overwritten

overalls		
overwhelm		
	+ s	overwhelms
	+ ed	overwhelmed
	+ ing	overwhelming
	+ ly	overwhelmingly
owe		
	+ s	owes
	+ ed	owed
	+ ing	owing
owl		
	+ s	owls
	+ ish	owlish
	+ ly	owlishly
	+ ness	owlishness
own		
	+ s	owns
	+ ed	owned
	+ ing	owning
	+ er	owner*
	+ ship	ownership
oxygen		
	+ ic	oxygenic
	+ less	oxygenless
	+ ate	oxygenate^
	+ or	oxygenator
	+ tion	oxygenation
oyster		
	+ s	oysters
	+ catch + er	oystercatcher*
	+ ed	oystered
	+ ing	oystering
	+ man	oysterman

O

pacific
+ ly — pacifically
+ ify — pacify^
+ able — pacifiable
+ tion — pacification
+ ism — pacifism
+ ify + ist — pacificist*
+ ist + ly — pacifistically

pacifier
+ s — pacifiers

pack
+ s — packs
+ ed — packed
+ ing — packing
+ er — packer*
+ able — packable*
+ ity — packability
+ t — packet
+ board — packboard*
+ horse — packhorse*
+ man — packman
+ sack — packsack*
+ saddle — packsaddle*
+ thread — packthread*
+ ing + house — packinghouse*

package
+ s — packages
+ ed — packaged
+ ing — packaging
+ er — packager

pad
+ s — pads
+ ed — padded
+ ing — padding

paddle
+ s — paddles
+ ed — paddled
+ ing — paddling
+ er — paddler*
+ ball — paddleball
+ board — paddleboard
+ boat — paddleboat
+ fish — paddlefish

page
+ s — pages
+ ed — paged
+ ing — paging
+ er — pager*

pageant
+ s — pageants
+ ry — pageantry
+ ry + s — pageantries

pail
+ s — pails
+ ful — pailful*

pain
+ s — pains
+ ed — pained
+ ing — paining
+ ful — painful
+ ful + er — painfuller
+ ful + ly — painfully
+ ful + ness — painfulness
+ ful + est — painfullest
+ less — painless
+ less + ly — painlessly
+ less + ness — painlessness
+ kill + er — painkiller*
+ kill + ing — painkilling
+ s + take + ing — painstaking
+ s + take **+ ly** — painstakingly

paint
+ s — paints
+ ed — painted
+ ing — painting*
+ er — painter*
+ er + ly — painterly
+ er **+ ness** — painterliness
+ brush — paintbrush*

pair
+ s — pairs
+ ed — paired
+ ing — pairing*

pajama
+ s — pajamas

P

pal
+ s pals
+ ed palled
+ ing palling
+ ly pally
+ ship palship
palace
+ s palaces
pale
+ s pales
+ ed paled
+ ing paling
+ er paler
+ est palest
+ ly palely
+ ness paleness
+ ish palish
+ face paleface*
pamphlet
+ s pamphlets
+ e + er pamphleteer^
pan
+ s pans
+ ed panned
+ ing panning
+ ful panful*
+ fish panfish
+ fry panfry^
+ handle panhandle^
+ handle + er panhandler*

pancake
+ s pancakes
+ ed pancaked
+ ing pancaking
panda
+ s pandas
panel
+ s panels
+ ed panelled
+ ing panelling
+ ist panelist*
panic
+ s panics
+ ed panicked
+ ing panicking
+ y panicky
pansy
+ s pansies
pant
+ s pants
+ ed panted
+ ing panting
+ y panty*
+ dress pantdress*
+ suit pantsuit*

panther
+ s panthers
panty
+ s panties
panty hose
paper
+ s papers
+ ed papered
+ ing papering
+ er paperer*
+ y papery
+ ness paperiness
+ back paperback^
+ board paperboard*
+ bind + ed paperbound
+ boy paperboy*
+ hang + er paperhanger*
+ hang + ing paperhanging
+ make + er papermaker*
+ make + ing papermaking
+ weight paperweight
+ work paperwork*
parachute
+ s parachutes
+ ed parachuted
+ ing parachuting
+ ic parachutic
+ ist parachutist*
parade
+ s parades
+ ed paraded
+ ing parading
+ er parader*
paradise
+ al paradisal
+ ic paradisaic
+ ic + al paradisaical
+ ic + al + ly paradisaically
+ ic + al paradisiacal
+ ic + al + ly paradisiacally
paradox
+ s paradoxes
+ al paradoxical
+ ly paradoxically
+ ity paradoxicality
+ ness paradoxicalness
paragraph
+ s paragraphs
+ ed paragraphed
+ ing paragraphing
+ ic paragraphic
+ er paragrapher*
parakeet
+ s parakeets

parallel	
+ s	parallels
+ ed	paralleled
+ ing	paralleling
+ ism	parallelism
paramedic	
+ al	paramedical
paranoid	
+ s	paranoids
+ a	paranoia
+ ic	paranoic
+ ly	paranoically
+ al	paranoidal
paraprofessional	
+ s	paraprofessionals
parasite	
+ s	parasites
+ ic	parasitic
+ al	parasitical
+ ly	parasitically
+ ism	parasitism
+ ize	parasitize^
+ tion	parasitization
paratrooper	
+ s	paratroopers
pardon	
+ s	pardons
+ ed	pardoned
+ ing	pardoning
+ able	pardonable
+ able + ly	pardonably
+ able + ness	pardonableness
+ er	pardoner*
pare	
+ s	pares
+ ed	pared
+ ing	paring*
+ er	parer*
parent	
+ s	parents
+ ed	parented
+ ing	parenting
+ al	parental
+ ly	parentally
+ hood	parenthood
parenthesis	
+ s	parentheses
+ ize + s	parenthesizes
+ ed	parenthesized
+ ing	parenthesizing
Paris	
+ an	Parisian*
park	
+ s	parks
+ ed	parked
+ ing	parking
+ like	parklike
+ land	parkland*
+ way	parkway*
parliament	
+ s	parliaments
+ ry	parliamentary
+ an	parliamentarian*
parrot	
+ s	parrots
+ ed	parroted
+ ing	parroting
parsnip	
+ s	parsnips
part	
+ s	parts
+ ed	parted
+ ing	parting
+ al	partial
+ly	partially
+ ity	partiality*
+ ible	partible
+ tion	partition^
+ tion + ist	partitionist*
+ way	partway
+ ive	partative
+ ive + ly	partatively
participate	
+ s	participates
+ ed	participated
+ ing	participating
+ ant	participant*
+ tion	participation
+ al	participational
+ ry	participatory
particle	
+ s	particles
+ board	particleboard*
particular	
+ s	particulars
+ ism	particularism
+ ist	particularist*
+ ic	particularistic
+ ity	particularity
+ ize	particularize^
+ tion	particularization
+ ly	particularly
+ ate	particulate*
partner	
+ s	partners
+ ed	partnered
+ ing	partnering
+ ship	partnership*

P

party	
+ s	parties
+ ed	partied
+ ing	partying
pass	
+ s	passes
+ ed	passed
+ ing	passing
+ ing + ly	passingly
+ ing + ness	passingness
+ able	passable
+ ly	passably
+ age	passage^
+ ant	passant
+ ive	passive
+ ate	passivate^
+ ate + tion	passivation
+ ism	passivism
+ ist	passivist
+ ive + ly	passively
+ t	past
+ t + time	pastime*
+ ness	pastness
passenger	
+ s	passengers
passion	
+ less	passionless
+ al	passional
+ ate	passionate
+ ly	passionately
+ ness	passionateness
+ ist	Passionist*
im +	impassion^
Passover (2)	
paste	
+ s	pastes
+ ed	pasted
+ ing	pasting
+ ies	pasties
+ ness	pastiness
+ y	pasty
+ board	pasteboard*
+ down	pastedown*
+ up	pasteup*
pastrami	
pastry	
+ s	pastries
pasture	
+ s	pastures
+ ed	pastured
+ ing	pasturing
+ age	pasturage*
+ land	pastureland*
pat	
+ s	pats
+ ed	patted
+ ing	patting
+ y	patty
patch	
+ s	patches
+ ed	patched
+ ing	patching
+ y	patchy
+ er	patchier
+ est	patchiest
+ ly	patchily
+ ness	patchiness
+ work	patchwork*
path	
+ s	pathes
+ way	pathway*
patient	
+ s	patients
+ ly	patiently
+ ence	patience
patio	
+ s	patios
patriot	
+ s	patriots
+ ic	patriotic
+ ly	patriotically
+ ism	patriotism
patrol	
+ s	patrols
+ ed	patrolled
+ ing	patrolling
+ er	patroller*
+ man	patrolman
pattern	
+ s	patterns
+ ed	patterned
+ ing	patterning
+ less	patternless
pause	
+ s	pauses
+ ed	paused
+ ing	pausing
pave	
+ s	paves
+ ed	paved
+ ing	paving
+ ment	pavement*
+ er	paver
paw	
+ s	paws
+ ed	pawed
+ ing	pawing
pay	
+ d	paid

+ ed	payed
+ ing	paying
+ able	payable
+ ee	payee*
+ er	payer*
+ ment	payment*
+ back	payback*
+ check	paycheck*
+ day	payday*
+ load	payload*
+ master	paymaster*
+ off	payoff*
+ out	payout*
+ roll	payroll*
pea	
+ s	peas
+ like	pealike
peace	
+ able	peacable
+ able + ly	peaceably
+ able + ness	peaceableness
+ ful	peaceful
+ ful + ly	peacefully
+ ful + ness	peacefulness
+ keep + ing	peacekeeping
+ keep + er	peacekeeper*
+ make + er	peacemaker*
+ make + ing	peacemaking*
+ time	peacetime*
peach	
+ s	peaches
+ y	peachy
+ er	peachier
+ est	peachiest
peacock	
+ s	peacocks
+ ish	peacockish
+ y	peacocky
peak	
+ s	peaks
+ ed	peaked
+ ing	peaking
+ ed + ness	peakedness
peanut	
+ s	peanuts
pear	
+ s	pears
pebble	
+ s	pebbles
+ ed	pebbled
+ ing	pebbling
+ y	pebbly
pecan	
+ s	pecans

peck	
+ s	pecks
+ ed	pecked
+ ing	pecking
+ y	pecky
+ er	pecker*
+ er + wood	peckerwood*
peculiar	
+ ly	peculiarly
+ ity	peculiarity*
peddle	
+ s	peddles
+ ed	peddled
+ ing	peddling
+ er	peddler*
peek	
+ s	peeks
+ ed	peeked
+ ing	peeking
peel (2)	
+ s	peels
+ ed	peeled
+ ing	peeling
+ er	peeler*
pen	
+ s	pens
+ ed	penned
+ ing	penning
+ hold+ er	penholder*
+ knife	penknife*
+ man	penman
+ man + ship	penmanship*
penalty	
+ s	penalties
+ ize	penalize^
pencil	
+ s	pencils
+ ed	pencilled
+ ing	pencilling*
+ er	penciller*
pendulum	
+ ar	pendular
+ ous	pendulous
+ ness	pendulousness
penetrate	
+ s	penetrates
+ ed	penetrated
+ ing	penetrating
+ ing + ly	penetratingly
+ ive	penetrative
+ ive + ly	penetratively
+ ive + ness	penetrativeness
+ able	penetrable
+ ity	penetrability

P

+ ant	penetrant
+ ion	penetration
penguin	
+ s	penguins
penis	
+ s	penises
pennant	
+ s	pennants
penny	
+ s	pennies
+ weigh + t	pennyweight
+ worth	pennyworth*
ten +	tenpenny
two +	twopenny
people	
+ s	peoples
+ ed	peopled
+ ing	peopling
+ less	peopleless
+ hood	peoplehood*
pepper	
+ s	peppers
+ ed	peppered
+ ing	peppering
+ y	peppery
+ box	pepperbox*
+ corn	peppercorn*
+ tree	peppertree*
peppermint	
+ s	peppermints
per	
perceive	
+ s	perceives
+ ed	perceived
+ ing	perceiving
+ able	perceivable
+ ly	perceivably
+ er	perceiver*
+ t	percept
+ able	perceptible
+ ity	perceptibility
+ t **+ ly**	perceptibly
+ tion	perception*
+ tion + al	perceptional
+ ive	perceptive
+ ive + ly	perceptively
+ ive + ness	perceptiveness
+ t + al	perceptual
+ t + al + y	perceptually
percent	
+ s	percents
+ age	percentage*
+ ile	percentile*
perch	
+ s	perches

+ ed	perched
+ ing	perching
percolate	
+ s	percolates
+ ed	percolated
+ ing	percolating
+ or	percolator*
perfect	
+ s	perfects
+ ed	perfected
+ ing	perfecting
+ tion	perfection*
+ tion + ist	perfectionist*
+ ism	perfectism
+ ist	perfectist*
+ er	perfecter*
+ ness	perfectness
+ ible	perfectible
+ ity	perfectibility
+ ive	perfective
+ ive + ly	perfectively
+ ive + ness	perfectiveness
+ ly	perfectly
perform	
+ s	performs
+ ed	performed
+ ing	performing
+ able	performable
+ ity	performability
+ er	performer*
+ ance	performance*
+ ry	performatory
+ ive	performative
perfume	
+ s	perfumes
+ ed	perfumed
+ ing	perfuming
+ er	perfumer*
+ ry	perfumery
+ ive	perfurmative
perhaps	
perimeter	
+ s	perimeters
period	
+ s	periods
+ ic	periodic
+ al	periodical
+ ly	periodically
+ icity	periodicity
+ ize **+ tion**	periodization
periscope	
+ s	periscopes
+ ic	periscopic*
permanent	
+ s	permanents

P

+ ence	permanence
+ ence + y	permanency
+ ly	permanently
+ ness	permanentness
permit	
+ s	permits
+ ed	permitted
+ ing	permitting
+ ible	permissible
+ ly	permissibly
+ ible + ness	permissibleness
+ sion	permission
+ ive	permissive
+ ive + ly	permissively
+ ive + ness	permissiveness
perpendicular	
+ s	perpendiculars
+ y	perpendiculary
+ ness	perpendicularness
+ ity	perpendicularity
perpetual	
+ ly	perpetually
+ ate	perpetuate^
+ or	perpetuator
+ tion	perpetuation
+ ity	perpetuity
persecute	
+ s	persecutes
+ ed	persecuted
+ ing	persecuting
+ ion	persecution
+ ee	persecutee
+ or	persecutor*
+ or + y	persecutory
persist	
+ s	persists
+ ed	persisted
+ ing	persisting
+ er	persister*
+ ence	persistence
+ ence + y	persistency
+ ent	persistent
+ ly	persistently
person	
+ s	persons
+ able	personable
+ able + ness	personableness
+ age	personage
+ al	personal
+ ly	personally
+ hood	personhood
+ ism	personalism
+ ist	personalist
+ ist + ic	personalistic

+ ize	personalize^
+ ize + tion	personalization
+ ate	personate^
+ ate + ion	personation
+ ify	personify^
+ ify + tion	personification
personality	
perspective	
+ s	perspectives
+ ly	perspectively
+ al	perspectival
perspire	
+ s	perspires
+ ed	perspired
+ ing	perspiring
+ tion	perspiration
+ or + y	perspiratory
persuade	
+ s	persuades
+ ed	persuaded
+ ing	persuading
+ able	persuadable
+ er	persuader*
+ s+ ible	persuasible
+ sion	persuasion
+ ive	persuasive
+ ly	persuasively
+ ness	persuasiveness
pervert	
+ s	perverts
+ ed	perverted
+ ing	perverting
+ ly	perversely
+ ness	perverseness
+ ive	perversive
+ ed + ly	pervertedly
+ ed + ness	pervertedness
pest	
+ s	pests
+ hole	pesthole*
+ house	pesthouse*
+ er + ous	pestiferous
+ ous + ly	pestiferously
+ ous + ness	pestiferousness
+ ence	pestilence
+ ent	pestilent
+ ent + ly	pestilently
+ ent + al	pestilential
+ ent + al + ly	pestilentially
pet	
+ s	pets
+ ed	petted
+ ing	petting
+ er	petter*

Philadelphia

philosophy

+ s	philosophies
+ er	philosopher*
+ ic	philosophic
+ al	philosophical
+ ly	philosophically
+ ize	philosophize^
+ ize + er	philosophizer*

phobia

+ s	phobias
+ c	phobic

phone

+ s	phones
+ ed	phoned
+ ing	phoning
ear +	earphone

photo

+ s	photos

photograph

+ s	photographs
+ ed	photographed
+ ing	photographing
+ er	photographer*
+ y	photography
+ ic	photographic
+ ly	photographically

phrase

+ s	phrases
+ ed	phrased
+ ing	phrasing
+ al	phrasal
+ ly	phrasally
+ make + er	phrasemaker*
+ make + ing	phrasemaking*

physical

+ ly	physically
+ ness	physicalness
+ ism	physicalism*
+ ist	physicalist*
+ ic	physicalistic
+ ity	physicality

physics

+ an	physician*
+ ist	physicist*

piano

+ s	pianos
+ ist	pianist*
+ ic	pianistic*
+ ly	pianistically

piccolo

+ s	piccolos
+ ist	piccoloist*

pick (2)

+ s	picks
+ ed	picked
+ ing	picking
+ er	picker*
+ y	picky
+ y + er	pickier
+ est	pickiest
+ ing + s	pickings
+ ax	pickax
+ lock	picklock
+ off	pickoff
+ pocket	pickpocket
+ proof	pickproof
+ up	pickup

pickle

+ s	pickles
+ ed	pickled
+ ing	pickling

picnic

+ s	picnics
+ ed	picnicked
+ ing	picnicking
+ y	picnicky

picture

+ s	pictures
+ ed	pictured
+ ing	picturing
+ al	pictorial
+ ly	pictorially
+ al + ness	pictorialness
+ al + ism	pictorialism
+ al + ist	pictorialist
+ al + ize	pictorialize^
+ al + ize + tion	pictorialization
+ ize	picturize^
+ ize **+ tion**	picturization

pie

+ s	pies
+ crust	piecrust*
+ plant	pieplant*

piece

+ s	pieces
+ ed	pieced
+ ing	piecing
+ meal	piecemeal
+ wise	piecewise
+ work	piecework

pier

+ s	piers

pierce

+ s	pierces
+ ed	pierced
+ ing	piercing
+ ly	piercingly

P

pig	
+ s	pigs
+ ed	pigged
+ ing	pigging
+ ry	piggery*
+ ish	piggish
+ ish + ly	piggishly
+ ish + ness	piggishness
+ y	piggy
+ er	piggier
+ est	piggiest
+ y + back	piggyback^
+ head + ed	pigheaded
+ head **+ ness**	pigheadedness
+ head **+ ly**	pigheadedly
+ pen	pigpen*
+ skin	pigskin*
+ stick	pigstick*
+ stick + er	pigsticker*
+ tail	pigtail
+ tail + ed	pigtailed
+ weed	pigweed
pigeon	
+ s	pigeons
+ hole	pigeonhole^
+ hole + er	pigeonholer
+ ite	pigeonite*
+ wing	pigeonwing*
piglet	
+ s	piglets
pile	
+ s	piles
+ ed	piled
+ ing	piling*
+ ate	pileate
+ ate + ed	pileated
+ less	pileless
+ up	pileup*
pilgrim	
+ s	pilgrims
+ age	pilgrimage^
pill	
+ s	pills
+ ed	pilled
+ ing	pilling
+ box	pillbox*
pillow	
+ s	pillows
+ ed	pillowed
+ ing	pillowing
+ case	pillowcase*
pilot	
+ s	pilots
+ ed	pilotted
+ ing	pilotting
+ age	pilotage
+ less	pilotless
pimple	
+ s	pimples
+ ed	pimpled
+ ly	pimply
pin	
+ s	pins
+ ed	pinned
+ ing	pinning
(and compound words as follows:)	
	pinball
	pinbone
	pinfeather
	pinfish
	pinhead
	pinheaded
	pinheadedness
	pinhole
	pinpoint
	pinpoints
	pinpointed
	pinpointing
	pinsetter
	pinspotter
	pinstripe
	pintail
	pinup
	pinweed
	pinwheel
	pinwork
	pinworm
pinafore	
+ s	pinafores
+ ed	pinafored
pinch	
+ s	pinches
+ ed	pinched
+ ing	pinching
+ er	pincher*
pine	
+ s	pines
+ ed	pined
+ ing	pining*
+ y	piny
+ al	pineal*
+ ry	pinery*
+ cone	pinecone
+ drop + s	pinedrops
+ land	pineland
+ wood	pinewood
pineapple	
+ s	pineapples

ping-pong

pink

+ s	pinks
+ ed	pinked
+ ing	pinking
+ y	pinkie*
+ ish	pinkish
+ ish + ness	pinkishness
+ ly	pinkly
+ eye	pinkeye
+ root	pinkroot

pint

+ s	pints

pioneer

+ s	pioneers
+ ed	pioneered
+ ing	pioneering

pipe

+ s	pipes
+ ed	piped
+ ing	piping
+ less	pipeless
+ like	pipelike
+ er	piper*
+ fish	pipefish
+ line	pipeline
+ stone	pipestone

pirate

+ s	pirates
+ ed	pirated
+ ing	pirating
+ ic + al	piratical
+ ic + **ly**	piratically
+ y	piracy

pitch (2)

+ s	pitches
+ ed	pitched
+ ing	pitching
+ er	pitcher*
+ er + s	pitchers
+ man	pitchman
+ out	pitchout
+ stone	pitchstone
+ woman	pitchwoman

pitchfork

+ s	pitchforks
+ ed	pitchforked
+ ing	pitchforking

Pittsburgh

pity

+ s	pities
+ ed	pitied
+ ing	pitying
+ ing + ly	pityingly

pixie

+ s	pixies
+ ish	pixieish
+ ness	pixiness
+ ed	pixilated
+ tion	pixilation

pizza (2)

+ s	pizzas

place

+ s	places
+ ed	placed
+ ing	placing
+ able	placeable
+ less	placeless
+ less + ly	placelessly
+ ment	placement*
+ er	placer*
+ hold + er	placeholder
+ kick	placekick
+ man	placeman

plagiarize

+ s	plagiarizes
+ ed	plagiarized
+ ing	plagiarizing
+ ism	plagiarism
+ ist	plagiarist*
+ ic	plagiaristic*
+ y	plagiary

plague

+ s	plagues
+ ed	plagued
+ ing	plaguing
+ er	plaguer*
+ y	plaguey
+ ly	plaguily

plaid

+ s	plaids
+ ed	plaided

plain

+ ly	plainly
+ ness	plainness
+ s	plains
+ s + man	plainsman
+ cloth + e + s	plainclothes
+ cloth + e +s + man	plainclothesman
+ song	plainsong
+ speak + en	plainspoken
+ speak + en + ness	plainspokenness

plan

+ s	plans
+ ed	planned
+ ing	planning
+ er	planner*
+ less	planless

+ less + ly	planlessly
+ less + ness	planlessness
plane	
+ s	planes
+ ed	planed
+ ing	planing
+ er	planer*
+ load	planeload
+ ish	planish
+ ish + er	planisher*
planet	
+ s	planets
+ ry	planetary
plant	
+ s	plants
+ ed	planted
+ ing	planting*
+ er	planter*
+ able	plantable
+ like	plantlike
+ tion	plantation*
plaster	
+ s	plasters
+ ed	plastered
+ ing	plastering
+ er	plasterer*
+ y	plastery
+ board	plasterboard*
+ work	plasterwork*
plastic	
+ s	plastics
+ ly	plastically
+ ity	plasticity
+ ize	plasticize^
+ ize + tion	plasticization*
+ ize + er	plasticizer*
plate	
+ s	plates
+ ed	plated
+ ing	plating
+ ful	plateful
+ er	plater*
+ like	platelike
+ y	platy
+ make + er	platemaker*
+ make + ing	platemaking
plateau	
+ s	plateaus
platter	
+ s	platters
+ ful	platterful
play	
+ s	plays
+ ed	played
+ ing	playing
+ able	playable
+ ity	playability
+ er	player*
+ ful	playful
+ ful + ly	playfully
+ ful + ness	playfulness
+ act	playact
+ back	playback
+ book	playbook
+ boy	playboy
+ fellow	playfellow
+ field	playfield
+ girl	playgirl
+ go + er	playgoer
+ ground	playground
+ house	playhouse
+ land	playland
+ list	playlist
+ make + er	playmaker
+ mate	playmate
+ pen	playpen
+ room	playroom
+ suit	playsuit
+ thing	plaything
+ time	playtime
+ ware	playware
please	
+ s	pleases
+ ed	pleased
+ ing	pleasing
+ ing + ly	pleasingly
+ ing + ness	pleasingness
+ ance	pleasance
+ ant	pleasant
+ ant + ly	pleasantly
+ ant + ness	pleasantness
+ ry	pleasantry*
+ ure	pleasure*
+ ure + ed	pleasured
+ ure + ing	pleasuring
+ ure + able	pleasurable
+ able + ity	pleasurability
+ able + ly	pleasurably
+ able + ness	pleasurableness
+ less	pleasureless
pledge	
+ s	pledges
+ ed	pledged
+ ing	pledging
+ er	pledger*
+ ee	pledgee*
plenty	
+ ful	plentiful

+ ful + ly	plentifully
+ ful + ness	plentifulness
+ ous	plenteous
+ ous + ly	plenteously
+ ous + ness	plenteousness
+ ry	plenary
+ ish	plenish^
+ re + plenty + ish	replenish
pliers	
plow	
+ s	plows
+ ed	plowed
+ ing	plowing
+ er	plower*
+ able	plowable
+ back	plowback
+ boy	plowboy
+ man	plowman
+ share	plowshare
plug	
+ s	plugs
+ ed	plugged
+ ing	plugging
+ er	plugger*
plum	
+ s	plums
+ like	plumlike
plural	
+ s	plurals
+ ly	plurally
+ ism	pluralism
+ ist	pluralist
+ ic	pluralistic
+ ic + ly	pluralistically
+ ity	plurality
+ ize	pluralize^
+ ize + tion	pluralization
plus	
+ s	pluses
+ age	plussage
non +	nonplus
non + plus + es	nonpluses
non + plus + ed	nonplussed
non + plus + ing	nonplussing
pneumonia	
+ ic	pneumonic
pocket	
+ s	pockets
+ ed	pocketed
+ ing	pocketing
+ ful	pocketful*
+ able	pocketable
+ book	pocketbook
+ knife	pocketknife

poem	
+ s	poems
poet	
+ s	poets
+ ess	poetess*
+ ic	poetic
+ al	poetical
+ ly	poetically
+ ness	poeticalness
+ ism	poeticism
+ ize	poeticize*
+ ize + er	poeticizer*
poetry	
point	
+ s	points
+ ed	pointed
+ ing	pointing
+ er	pointer*
+ ly	pointedly
+ ness	pointedness
+ less	pointless
+ y	pointy
+ y + er	pointier
+ est	pointiest
+ al + ism	pointillism
+ al + ist	pointillist*
+ al **+ ic**	pointillistic
poison	
+ s	poisons
+ ed	poisoned
+ ing	poisoning*
+ er	poisoner*
+ ous	poisonous
+ ly	poisonously
poke	
+ s	pokes
+ ed	poked
+ ing	poking
+ er	poker*
+ y	poky
+ ly	pokily
+ ness	pokiness
Poland (2)	
+ ish	Polish
pole	
+ s	poles
+ ed	poled
+ ing	poling
+ less	poleless
+ ax	poleax
+ cat	polecat
+ ar	polar
+ ity	polarity
+ ize	polarize^

+ ize + tion	polarization
+ ize + able	polarizable
+ ize + ity	polarizability
police	
+ s	polices
+ ed	policed
+ ing	policing
+ man	policeman
+ woman	policewoman
policy	
+ s	policies
+ holder	policyholder*
polish	
+ s	polishes
+ ed	polished
+ ing	polishing
+ er	polisher*
polite	
+ er	politer
+ est	politest
politic	
+ s	politics
+ al	political
+ ly	politically
+ an	politician*
+ ity	polity*
+ ize	politicize^
+ ize + tion	politicization
+ al + ize	politicalize^
+ al + ize + tion	politicalization
+ k	politick^
+ er	politicker*
pollute	
+ s	pollutes
+ ed	polluted
+ ing	polluting
+ er	polluter*
+ tion	pollution
+ ive	pollutive
poncho	
+ s	ponchos
pond	
+ s	ponds
+ ed	ponded
+ ing	ponding
+ weed	pondweed
ponder	
+ s	ponders
+ ed	pondered
+ ing	pondering
+ er	ponderer*
+ able	ponderable*
+ ous	ponderous
+ ous + ly	ponderously
+ ous + ness	ponderousness
pony	
+ s	ponies
+ ed	ponied
+ ing	ponying
+ tail	ponytail*
pool	
+ s	pools
+ ed	pooled
+ ing	pooling
+ room	poolroom
+ side	poolside
poor	
+ er	poorer
+ est	poorest
+ ly	poorly
+ ness	poorness
+ ish	poorish
+ house	poorhouse
pop	
+ s	pops
+ ed	popped
+ ing	popping
popcorn	
popsicle	
+ s	popsicles
popular	
+ ly	popularly
+ ity	popularity
+ ize	popularize^
+ ize + tion	popularization
+ ize + er	popularizer*
+ ist	populist*
+ ism	populism*
populate	
+ s	populates
+ ed	populated
+ ing	populating
+ tion	population*
+ al	populational
+ ous	populous
+ ly	populously
+ ness	populousness
porch	
+ s	porches
porcupine	
+ s	porcupines
pork	
+ y	porky
+ y + er	porkier
+ y + est	porkiest
+ er	porker*
porpoise	
+ s	porpoises

P

port

+ s	ports
+ ed	ported
+ ing	porting
+ able	portable*
+ able + ly	portably
+ age	portage^
+ ity	portability
+ al	portal*
+ ive	portative
+ er	porter*
+ hole	porthole*
+ ly	portly
+ ly + er	portlier
+ ly + est	portliest
+ ess	portress
+ able + s	portables

position

+ s	positions
+ ed	positioned
+ ing	positioning
+ al	positional
+ ly	positionally

positive

+ s	positives
+ ly	positively
+ ness	positiveness
+ ism	positivism*
+ ist	positivist*
+ ic	positivistic
+ ity	positivity*

possible (2)

+ ly	possibly
+ ity	possibility*

post

+ s	posts
+ ed	posted
+ ing	posting*
+ al	postal
+ age	postage
+ bag	postbag
+ box	postbox
+ boy	postboy
+ card	postcard
+ hole	posthole
+ man	postman
+ mark	postmark
+ master	postmaster
+ mistress	postmistress
+ paid	postpaid
+ script	postscript

post (prefix)

To see the way to form words with the prefix shown here, refer to the section showing the root word involved.

post abortion
post accident
post adolescent
post arrest
post atomic
post attack
post bachelor
post base
post biblical
post burn
post capitalist
post Christian
post civilization
post civilized
post college
post collegiate
post colonial
post conception
post consonantal
post convention
post crisis
post crystallization
post deadline
post debate
post delivery
post dive
post drug
post editing
post educational
post election
post embryonic
post embryonal
post emergency
post exercise
post experience
post experimental
post explosion
post exposure
post fault
post flight
post freeze
post game
post graduation
post harvest
post heat
post hospital
post human
post independence
post industrial
post infection
post isolation
post landing
post launch

post	liberation
post	literate
post	marital
post	mating
post	midnight
post	presidential
post	primary
post	prison
post	race
post	recession
post	retirement
post	revolutionary
post	riot
post	romantic
post	romanticism
post	season
post	secondary
post	stimulation
post	stimulatory
post	stimulus
post	strike
post	surgical
post	teen
post	treatment
post	trial
post	vaccinal
post	war
post	workshop
post	classical
post	date
post	doctoral
post	emergence
post	face
post	form
post	graduate
post	impressionism
post	modern
post	modernist
post	modernism
post	operative
post	position
post	positional
post	positionally
post	positive
post	positively
post	test

poster

+ s	posters

postpone

+ s	postpones
+ ed	postponed
+ ing	postponing
+ able	postponable*
+ er	postponer*
+ ment	postponement*

posture

+ s	postures
+ ed	postured
+ ing	posturing
+ al	postural

pot

+ s	pots
+ ed	potted
+ ing	potting
+ y	potty*
+ y + ed	pottied
+ y + ing	pottying
+ belly	potbelly*
+ belly + ed	potbellied
+ boil	potboil
+ boil + er	potboiler*
+ boy	potboy*

potato

+ s	potatoes

pouch

+ s	pouches
+ ed	pouched
+ ing	pouching
+ y	pouchy
+ er	pouchier
+ y + s	pouchies

pound

+ s	pounds
+ ed	pounded
+ ing	pounding
+ er	pounder*
+ age	poundage

pour

+ s	pours
+ ed	poured
+ ing	pouring
+ able	pourable*
+ er	pourer*

pout

+ s	pouts
+ ed	pouted
+ ing	pouting
+ er	pouter*
+ y	pouty

powder

+ s	powders
+ ed	powdered
+ ing	powdering
+ er	powderer*
+ er + y	powdery

power

+ s	powers
+ ed	powered
+ ing	powering
+ ful	powerful

P

+ ful + ly	powerfully
+ less	powerless
+ less + ly	powerlessly
+ less + ness	powerlessness
+ boat	powerboat
+ house	powerhouse
pox	
+ s	poxes
+ ed	poxed
+ ing	poxing
practice	
+ ed	practiced
+ ing	practicing*
+ er	practicer*
+ al	practical
+ al + ness	practicalness*
+ ity	practicality*
+ able + ity	practicability*
+ able + ly	practicably
+ able + ness	practicableness
+ tion + er	practitioner*
praise	
+ s	praises
+ ed	praised
+ ing	praising
+ er	praiser*
+ worth + y	praiseworthy
+ worth + **ly**	praiseworthily
+ worth + **ness**	praiseworthiness
pray	
+ s	prays
+ ed	prayed
+ ing	praying
+ er	prayer*
+ ful	prayerful
+ ful + ly	prayerfully
+ ful + ness	prayerfulness

pre (prefix)

> To see the way to form words with the prefix shown here, refer to the section showing the root word involved.

preadmission
preadult
preagricultural
preannounce
prearrange
prearrangement
preassign
prebattle
precivilization
preclear
preclearance
precode
precollege
precolonial
precommitment
precompute
preconsonantal
preconsonantally
preconstruct
preconvention
precool
precrash
precut
predawn
predefine
predelivery
predemocratic
predeparture
predesignate
predesignation
predevelopment
predinner
predischarge
prediscovery
predive
predrill
preedit
preelectric
preemployment
preerect
preestablish
preexperiment
prefight
prefile
prefinance
prefire
preflame
preformulate
prefreshman
pregame
preharvest
preheadache
prehiring
pre-Hispanic
preholiday
prehuman
preindustrial
preinterview
preinvasion
prelaunch
prelife
preliterary
prelogical
prelunch
preluncheon
premanufacture
premarket
premarketing
premarriage

premeal
premeasure
premedicate
premeet
premix
premodern
premodification
premodify
premold
premoral
prenoon
prenotification
prenotify
prenumber
preopening
preoperational
preorder
prepast
prepill
preplan
prepresidential
preprice
preprimary
preprimer
preproduction
preprogram
prepublication
prepunch
prepurchase
prequalification
prequalify
prerace
prerecession
prerehearsal
prerelease
prerequire
preretirement
prereturn
prereview
prerevolution
prerevolutionary
prerinse
preriot
prerock
preromantic
presale
preschedule
prescreen
preseason
presentence
presentencing
preservice
preshow
presleep
preslice
presong
presort
prespecify
presplit
prestamp
prestorage
prestrike
prestructure
presweeten
pretape
pretechnological
pretelevision
pretermination
pretest
pretheatre
pretournament
pretrain
pretravel
pretreat
pretreatment
pretrial
pretrim
pretype
preunification
preuniversity
prewar
prewash
prewhaling
prework
prewrap
preadaptation
preadapted
preadaptive
preadolescence
preatomic
prebiological
precalculus
precancerous
preclinical
preconception
precondition
preconscious
preconsciously
precook
precritical
predate
predestine
predestinarian
predestinarianism
predestinate^
predestination
predestinator
predetermination

P

predetermine^
predispose
predoctoral
predominate
predominately
predominance
predominancy
predominant
predominantly
predomination
preemergence
preemergent
preexistence
preexistent
prefiguration
prefigurative
prefiguratively
prefigurativeness
prefigure^
prefigurement
preform^
preformation
prefrontal
prehistorian
prehistoric
prehistorical
prehistorically
prejudge^
prejudger
prejudgment
premarital
premaritally
premature
prematurely
prematureness
prematurity
premed
premedical
premeditate
premeditated
premeditatedly
premeditation
premeditative
premenstrual
premenstrually
prename
prenominate
prenomination
preoccupy^
preoccupancy
preoccupation
preorbital
prepay^
prepayment
preplant
preponderancy
preponderance
preponderantly
preponderate
preponderation
preposition
prepositional
prepositionally
preprint
preprocess
preprofessional
prerecord
preregister^
preregistration
preschool
preschooler
prescientific
prescore
preselect
presell
preset
presignify
prestress
presuppose
presupposition
presuppositional
pretax
preteen
preview
prevocational
prewriting

preach

+ s	preaches
+ ed	preached
+ ing	preaching
+ er	preacher*
+ ly	preachingly
+ ify	preachify^
+ ment	preachment
+ y	preachy
+ y + er	preachier
+ est	preachiest
+ y + ly	preachily
+ ness	preachiness

precious

+ ly	preciously
+ ness	preciousness

precipitate

+ s	precipitates
+ ed	precipitated
+ ing	precipitating
+ able	precipitable
+ ance	precipitance

P

+ ant	precipitant*
+ ance + y	precipitancy
+ ant + ly	precipitantly
+ ant + ness	precipitantness
+ or	precipitator*
+ ive	precipitative
+ ly	precipitately
+ ness	precipitateness
+ ion	precipitation
+ ous	precipitous
+ ous + ly	precipitously
+ ous + ness	precipitousness
+ able	precipitable
precise	
+ ly	precisely
+ ness	preciseness
+ an	precisian*
+ an + ism	precisianism
+ ion	precision
+ ion + ist	precisionist*
predicate	
+ s	predicates
+ ive	predicative
+ or + y	predicatory
+ ment	predicament*
+ ed	predicated
+ ing	predicating
+ ion	predication
+ able	predicable
predict	
+ s	predicts
+ ed	predicted
+ ing	predicting
+ able	predictable
+ ity	predictability
+ able + ly	predictably
+ ness	predictableness
+ ive	predictive
+ ive + ly	predictively
+ or	predictor*
+ ion	prediction*
prefer	
+ s	prefers
+ ed	preferred
+ ing	preferring
+ er	preferrer*
+ able	preferable
+ able + ly	preferably
+ ity	preferability
+ ence	preference*
+ al	preferential
+ al + ly	preferentially
+ ment	preferment*

prefix	
+ s	prefixes
+ al	prefixal
pregnant	
+ ly	pregnantly
+ y	pregnancy
prejudice	
+ s	prejudices
+ ed	prejudiced
+ ing	prejudicing
+ al	prejudicial
+ ly	prejudicially
+ ness	prejudicialness
+ ous	prejudicious
premier	
+ s	premiers
+ e	premiere
+ e + s	premieres
+ ed	premiered
+ ing	premiering
prepare	
+ s	prepares
+ ed	prepared
+ ing	preparing
+ er	preparer*
+ tion	preparation*
+ ive	preparative
+ ly	preparatively
+ ate + or	preparator*
+ ate **+ ly**	preparatorily
+ ness	preparedness
Presbyterian	
+ y	Presbytery
+ er	Presbyter*
prescribe	
+ s	prescribes
+ ed	prescribed
+ ing	prescribing
+ er	prescriber*
+ t	prescript
+ tion	prescription*
+ ive	prescriptive
+ ly	prescriptively
+ tion + s	prescriptions
prescription	
+ s	prescriptions
presence	
present	
+ s	presents
+ ly	presently
+ ness	presentness
+ ism	presentism
present (verb)	
+ s	presents

+ ed	presented
+ ing	presenting
+ er	presenter*
+ able	presentable
+ ity	presentability
+ ly	presentably
+ ness	presentableness
+ tion	presentation*
+ al	presentational
+ ee	presentee
+ ment	presentment*

preserve

+ s	preserves
+ ed	preserved
+ ing	preserving
+ tion	preservation
+ ist	preservationist*
+ ive	preservative*
+ able	preservable*
+ ity	preservability
+ er	preserver*

president

+ s	presidents
+ al	presidential
+ ly	presidentially
+ ship	presidentship*

press

+ s	presses
+ ed	pressed
+ ing	pressing
+ ly	pressingly
+ er	presser*
+ ure	pressure*
+ ure + less	pressureless
+ ize	pressurize^
+ ize + tion	pressurization

pretend

+ s	pretends
+ ed	pretended
+ ing	pretending
+ er	pretender*
+ sion	pretension*
+ sion + less	pretensionless
+ ous	pretentious
+ ous + ly	pretentiously
+ ness	pretentiousness
+ ed + ly	pretendedly

pretty

+ s	pretties
+ ed	prettied
+ ing	prettying
+ ly	prettily
+ ness	prettiness
+ ify	prettify^
+ ify **+ tion**	prettification*

pretzel

+ s	pretzels

prevent

+ s	prevents
+ ed	prevented
+ ing	preventing
+ able	preventable
+ ity	preventability
+ er	preventer*
+ ate + ive	preventative*
+ ive	preventive
+ ive + ly	preventively
+ ive + ness	preventiveness
+ ion	prevention*

price

+ s	prices
+ ed	priced
+ ing	pricing
+ er	pricer*
+ less	priceless
+ less + ly	pricelessly
+ y	pricey
+ y + er	pricier
+ est	priciest

pride

+ ed	prided
+ ing	priding
+ ful	prideful
+ ful + ly	pridefully
+ ful + ness	pridefulness

priest

+ s	priests
+ ess	priestess*
+ hood	priesthood
+ ly	priestly
+ ness	priestliness

primary

+ s	primaries
+ ly	primarily

prime

+ s	primes
+ ed	primed
+ ing	priming
+ ly	primely
+ ness	primeness
+ er	primer*
+ ive	primative*
+ ive + ly	primatively
+ ive + ness	primativeness
+ ity	primitivity
+ ism	primitivism
+ ist	primitivist
+ ic	primitivistic
+ a	prima
+ o	primo

P

prime minister	
+ s	prime ministers
+ al	prime ministerial
+ y	prime ministry
+ ship	prime ministership*
prince	
+ s	princes
+ ship	princeship*
+ ly	princely
+ er	princelier
+ est	princeliest
+ dom	princedom
+ ness	princeliness
+ ing	princeling
princess	
+ s	princesses
principal	
+ s	principals
+ ly	principally
+ ship	principalship
+ ity	principality*
principle	
+ s	principles
+ ed	principled
print	
+ s	prints
+ ed	printed
+ ing	printing
+ able	printable
+ ity	printability
+ er	printer*
+ er + y	printery*
+ less	printless
+ make + ing	printmaking
+ make + er	printmaker*
+ out	printout
prior	
+ ate	priorate
+ ess	prioress*
+ y	priory
+ ship	priorship*
+ ly	priorly
+ ize	prioritize^
+ ize + tion	prioritization*
+ ity	priority*
+ or	prioritor*
prison	
+ s	prisons
+ er	prisoner*
private	
+ s	privates
+ y	privacy
+ ly	privately
+ ness	privateness

+ ee + er	privateer*
+ tion	privation*
+ ism	privatism*
+ ive	privative*
+ ive + ly	privatively
+ ize	privatize^
+ ize + tion	privatization
prize	
+ s	prizes
+ ed	prized
+ ing	prizing
+ er	prizer*
+ fight	prizefight
+ fight + er	prizefighter*
+ fight + ing	prizefighting
+ win + ing	prizewinning
+ win + er	prizewinner*
pro	
+ s	pros
+ act + ive	proactive
+ choice	prochoice
+ grade	prograde
+ nuclear	pronuclear
+ rate	prorate
+ long	prolong
+ long + s	prolongs
+ long + ed	prolonged
+ long + ing	prolonging
+ long + er	prolonger
+ long + tion	prolongation
probable	
+ ity	probability*
+ ism	probabilism*
+ ist	probabilist*
+ ic	probabilistic
+ y	probably
problem	
+ s	problems
+ ic	problematic
+ ly	problematically
proceed	
+ s	proceeds
+ ed	proceeded
+ ing	proceeding*
+ ure	procedure
+ al	procedural
+ ly	procedurally
process	
+ s	processes
+ ed	processed
+ ing	processing*
+ ible	processible*
+ ity	processibility*
+ ion	procession*
+ al	processional*

P

+ ly	processionally
+ or	processor*
proclaim	
+ s	proclaims
+ ed	proclaimed
+ ing	proclaiming
+ er	proclaimer*
+ tion	proclamation*
procrastinate	
+ s	procrastinates
+ ed	procrastinated
+ ing	procrastinating
+ ion	procrastination*
+ or	procrastinator*
produce	
+ s	produces
+ ed	produced
+ ing	producing
+ er	producer*
+ ible	producible*
+ t	product*
+ tion	production*
+ al	productional
+ ive	productive
+ ly	productively
+ ness	productiveness
+ ity	productivity
profane	
+ s	profanes
+ ed	profaned
+ ing	profaning
+ tion	profanation*
+ or + y	profanatory*
+ ly	profanely
+ ness	profaneness*
+ ity	profanity*
profess	
+ s	professes
+ ed	professed
+ ing	professing
+ or	professor*
+ ion	profession*
+ ion + al	professional
+ ion **+ ly**	professionally
+ ed + ly	professedly
+ ion **+ ism**	professionalism
+ ion **+ ize**	professionalize^
+ ion **+ ize** + tion	professionalization
+ or + al	professorial
+ or **+ ly**	professorially
+ ate	professorate
+ ship	professorship*
profile	
+ s	profiles
+ ed	profiled
+ ing	profiling*
+ er	profiler*
profit	
+ s	profits
+ ed	profitted
+ ing	profitting
+ able	profitable
+ ity	profitability
+ ness	profitableness
+ ly	profitably
+ ee + er	profiteer*
+ **er** + ing	profiteering
+ **er** + ed	profiteered
+ less	profitless
profound	
+ ly	profoundly
+ ness	profoundness
+ ity	profundity*
program	
+ s	programs
+ ed	programmed
+ ing	programming*
+ able	programmable*
+ ity	programmability
+ ic	programmatic
+ ly	programmatically
+ er	programmer*
progress	
+ s	progresses
+ ed	progressed
+ ing	progressing
+ion	progression*
+ al	progressional
+ ive	progressive
+ ly	progressively
+ ness	progressiveness
+ ism	progressivism
+ ist	progressivist*
+ ic	progressivistic
prohibit	
+ s	prohibits
+ ed	prohibited
+ ing	prohibiting
+ ion	prohibition
+ ist	prohibitionist*
+ ive	prohibitive*
+ ly	prohibitively
+ ness	prohibitiveness
+ ory	prohibitory
project (noun)	
+ s	projects
+ ed	projected
+ ing	projecting

P

+ ile	projectile*
+ ion	projection*
+ ist	projectionist*
+ ive	projective
+ ly	projectively
+ or	projector*
project (verb)	
+ s	projects
prologue	
+ s	prologues
+ ize	prologize^
promise	
+ s	promises
+ ed	promised
+ ing	promising
+ ee	promisee*
+ or	promisor*
+ ly	promisingly
+ ory	promissory
promote	
+ s	promotes
+ ed	promoted
+ ing	promoting
+ able	promotable*
+ ity	promotability*
+ er	promoter*
+ ion	promotion*
+ al	promotional*
+ ive	promotive
+ ness	promotiveness*
pronoun (2)	
+ s	pronouns
+ al	pronominal
pronounce	
+ s	pronounces
+ ed	pronounced
+ ing	pronouncing
+ able	pronounceable*
+ ity	pronounceability
+ er	pronouncer*
+ ly	pronouncedly
+ ment	pronouncement*
+ tion	pronunciation*
+ al	pronunciational
proof	
+ s	proofs
+ ed	proofed
+ ing	proofing
+ er	proofer*
+ like	prooflike
+ read	proofread*
+ read + ing	proofreading
+ read + er	proofreader*
+ room	proofroom*

propaganda	
+ ist	propagandist*
+ ic	propagandistic*
+ ize	propagandize^
+ er	propagandizer*
proper	
+ ly	properly
+ ness	properness*
property	
+ s	properties
+ ed	propertied
+ less	propertyless
prophecy	
+ s	prophecies
+ ed	prophecied
+ ing	prophecying*
+ er	prophecier*
+ t	prophet*
+ t + ess	prophetess*
+ ic	prophetic
+ al	prophetical
+ ly	prophetically
proportion	
+ s	proportions
+ ed	proportioned
+ ing	proportioning
+ al	proportional
+ ly	proportionally
+ able	proportionable*
+ able + ly	proportionably
+ ity	proportionality
+ ate	proportionate^
+ ate + ly	proportionately
prose	
+ s	proses
+ ed	prosed
+ ing	prosing*
+ er	proser*
+ y	prosy
+ y + er	prosier
+ y + est	prosiest
+ y + ly	prosily
+ y + ness	prosiness
+ ic	prosaic
+ ic + ly	prosaically
+ ism	prosaism
+ ist	prosaist*
+ ate + er	prosateur
prostitute	
+ s	prostitutes
+ ed	prostituted
+ ing	prostituting
+ ion	prostitution*
+ or	prostitutor*

protect	
+ s	protects
+ ed	protected
+ ing	protecting
+ or	protector*
+ or + ship	protectorship*
+ ive	protective
+ ly	protectively
+ ness	protectiveness
+ ant	protectant*
+ ion	protection*
+ ist	protectionist*
+ ism	protectionism*
+ al	protectoral*
+ ate	protectorate*
+ ory	protectory*
+ ess	protectress*
Protestant	
+ s	Protestants
proton	
+ s	protons
+ ic	protonic
+ ate	protonate^
+ tion	protonation
proud	
+ ly	proudly
+ ful	proudful
+ heart + ed	proudhearted
prove	
+ s	proves
+ ed	proved
+ ing	proving
+ able	provable
+ able + ness	provableness
+ er	prover*
+ en	proven
+ en + ly	provenly
proverb	
+ s	proverbs
+ al	proverbial
+ ly	proverbially
provide	
+ s	provides
+ ed	provided
+ ing	providing
+ ent	provident
+ ent + ly	providently
+ ent + al	providential
+ ent **+ ly**	providentially
+ er	provider*
+ ence	providence
prune	
+ s	prunes
+ ed	pruned
+ ing	pruning
+ er	pruner*
psychiatry	
+ ist	psychiatrist*
+ ic	psychiatric
+ ly	psychiatrically
psychology	
+ s	psychologies
+ ist	psychologist*
pteranodon	
+ s	pteranodons
public	
+ ness	publicness
+ ly	publicly
+ an	publican*
+ tion	publication*
+ ist	publicist*
+ ize	publicize^
+ ish	publish^
+ able	publishable
+ er	publisher*
publicity	
pudding	
+ s	puddings
puddle	
+ s	puddles
+ ed	puddled
+ ing	puddling
+ er	puddler*
puff	
+ s	puffs
+ ed	puffed
+ ing	puffing
+ er	puffer*
+ ery	puffery
+ y	puffy
+ ness	puffiness
pull	
+ s	pulls
+ ed	pulled
+ ing	pulling
+ er	puller*
+ back	pullback
+ out	pullout
+ over	pullover
pulse	
+ s	pulses
+ ed	pulsed
+ ing	pulsing
+ er	pulser*
+ ant	pulsant
+ ate	pulsate*
+ ate + ing	pulsating
+ ile	pulsatile
+ tion	pulsation
+ ate + or	pulsator*

pump
+ s pumps
+ ed pumped
+ ing pumping
+ er pumper*
pumpkin
+ s pumpkins
+ seed pumpkinseed
pun
+ s puns
+ ed punned
+ ing punning
+ y punny
+ er punnier
+ est punniest
punch
+ es punches
+ ed punched
+ ing punching
+ less punchless
+ ball punchball
+ board punchboard
punctuate
+ s punctuates
+ ed punctuated
+ ing punctuating
+ or punctuator*
+ tion punctuation*
punish
+ s punishes
+ ed punished
+ ing punishing
+ able punishable
+ ity punishability
+ er punisher*
+ ment punishment*
+ tion punition*
+ ive punitive*
+ ly punitively
+ ness punitiveness
pupil
+ s pupils
+ age pupilage
puppet
+ s puppets
+ r + y puppetry
+ ee + er puppeteer*
puppy
+ s puppies
+ ish puppyish
+ like puppylike
purchase
+ s purchases
+ ed purchased
+ ing purchasing
+ er purchaser*
+ able purchasable
pure
+ ly purely
+ ness pureness
+ ify purify^
+ ify **+ tion** purification
+ ity purity
+ er purer
+ est purest
+ ee puree^
+ ist purist*
+ ic puristic
+ ify **+ or** purificator*
+ ify **+ ory** purificatory
+ ify + er purifier*
purple
+ s purples
+ ed purpled
+ ing purpling
+ ly purply
+ ish purplish
purpose
+ s purposes
+ ed purposed
+ ing purposing
+ ful purposeful
+ ful + ly purposefully
+ ful + ness purposefulness
+ less purposeless
+ less + ly purposelessly
+ less + ness purposelessness
+ ly purposely
+ ive purposive
+ ive + ly purposively
+ ive + ness purposiveness
purr
+ s purrs
+ ed purred
+ ing purring*
+ ing + ly purringly
purse
+ s purses
+ ed pursed
+ ing pursing
+ like purselike
+ er purser*
pursue
+ s pursues
+ ed pursued
+ ing pursuing
+ ant pursuant
+ ance pursuance
+ er pursuer*
+ t pursuit*

P

push

+ s	pushes
+ ed	pushed
+ ing	pushing
+ er	pusher*
+ ful	pushful
+ ful + ness	pushfulness
+ y	pushy
+ y + er	pushier
+ est	pushiest
+ ly	pushily
+ ness	pushiness
+ ball	pushball
+ cart	pushcart
+ chair	pushchair
+ down	pushdown
+ over	pushover

put

+ s	puts
+ out	putout

puzzle

+ s	puzzles
+ ed	puzzled
+ ing	puzzling
+ er	puzzler*
+ ment	puzzlement
+ ing + ly	puzzlingly

P

quake

+ s	quakes
+ ed	quaked
+ ing	quaking

Quaker

+ s	Quakers
+ ish	Quakerish
+ ism	Quakerism*
+ ly	Quakerly

qualification

+ s	qualifications

qualify

+ s	qualifies
+ ed	qualified
+ ing	qualifying
+ ly	qualifiedly
+ able	qualifiable*

quality

+ s	qualities
+ ive	qualitative
+ ly	qualitatively

quantity

+ s	quantities
+ ed	quanted
+ ify	quantify^
+ ify + er	quantifier*
+ ify + ing	quantifying
+ ify + able	quantifyable*
+ ify **+ tion**	quantification
+ ify **+ al**	quantificational
+ ify **+ ly**	quantificationally
+ ate	quantitate^
+ ate + ion	quantitation
+ ive	quantitative
+ ive + ly	quantitatively
+ ive + ness	quantitativeness
+ al	quantal
+ m	quantum
+ a	quanta
+ ize	quantize^
+ ize + ion	quantization*
+ ize + er	quantizier*

quarrel

+ s	quarrels
+ ed	quarreled
+ ing	quarreling*
+ er	quarreler*
+ some	quarrelsome
+ some + ly	quarrelsomely
+ some + ness	quarrelsomeness

quart

+ s	quarts
+ an	quartan
+ ic	quartic
+ ile	quartile
+ t	quartet

quarter

+ s	quarters
+ age	quarterage
+ ing	quartering*
+ ly	quarterly*
+ en	quartern
+ back	quarterback
+ deck	quarterdeck
+ final	quarterfinal
+ master	quartermaster
+ saw + ed	quartersawed
+ staff	quarterstaff*

queen

+ ed	queened
+ ing	queening
+ ly	queenly
+ ness	queenliness
+ ship	queenship
+ side	queenside

queer

+ s	queers
+ ed	queered
+ ing	queering*
+ ish	queerish
+ ly	queerly
+ ness	queerness*

question

+ s	questions
+ ed	questioned
+ ing	questioning

+ er	questioner*
+ able	questionable*
+ ly	questionably
+ ness	questionableness
+ ary	questionary
+ less	questionless
quick	
+ er	quicker
+ est	quickest
+ ly	quickly
+ ness	quickness
+en	quicken*
+ y	quickie*
+ sand	quicksand
+ set	quickset
+ silver	quicksilver
+ step	quickstep
quiet	
+ s	quiets
+ ed	quieted
+ ing	quieting
+ ly	quietly
+ ness	quietness
+ er	quieter*
+ ism	quietism*
+ ist	quietist*
+ ic	quietistic*
quit	
+ s	quits
+ ed	quitted
+ ing	quitting
+ er	quitter*
+ ance	quittance
quite	
quiz	
+ s	quizzes
+ ed	quizzed
+ ing	quizzing*
+ er	quizzer*
+ ic + al	quizzical
+ **ly**	quizzically
+ **ity**	quizzicality
quote	
+ s	quotes
+ ed	quoted
+ ing	quoting
+ able	quotable
+ tion	quotation*
quotient	
+ s	quotients

Q

rabbi

+ s	rabbis
+ ate	rabbinate
+ ic	rabbinic*
+ al	rabbinical
+ ly	rabbinically
+ ism	rabbinism*

rabbit

+ s	rabbits
+ y	rabbity
+ ed	rabbited
+ ing	rabbiting
+ er	rabbiter*
+ ery	rabbitry*

raccoon

+ s	raccoons

race

+ s	races
+ ed	raced
+ ing	racing
+ er	racer*
+ al	racial
+ al + ly	racially
+ al + ism	racialism*
+ al + ist	racialist*
+ al **+ ic**	racialistic
+ ism	racism
+ course	racecourse
+ horse	racehorse
+ mate	racemate
+ track	racetrack
+ way	raceway

rack

+ s	racks
+ ed	racked
+ ing	racking*
+ ful	rackful*
+ er	racker*
+ ing + ly	rackingly

racket (racquet)

+ s	rackets
+ ed	racketed
+ ing	racketing*
+ e + er	racketeer*

radar

radio

+ s	radios
+ ed	radioed
+ ing	radioing
+ man	radioman
+ act + ive	radioactive
+ act + **ly**	radioactively
+ act + **ity**	radioactivity
+ biology	radiobiology
+ biology + **al**	radiobiological
+ biology + ist	radiobiologist
+ chemistry	radiochemistry
+ chemistry + ist	radiochemist
+ chemistry + **al**	radiochemical
+ ecology	radioecology
+ ecology + **al**	radioecological
+ ecology + ist	radioecologist
+ element	radioelement
+ label	radiolabel
+ locate + tion	radiolocation
+ phone	radiophone
+ protect + ive	radioprotective
+ protect + ion	radioprotection
+ sense + ive	radiosensitive
+ therapy	radiotherapy

radish

+ s	radishes

radius

+ s	radiuses
+ al	radial
+ an	radian

raft

+ s	rafts
+ ed	rafted
+ ing	rafting
+ er	rafter*
+ s + man	raftsman

rag

+ s	rags
+ ed	ragged
+ ing	ragging
+ ly	raggedly
+ ness	raggedness

rage	
+ s	rages
+ ed	raged
+ ing	raging
out +	outrage
rail	
+ s	rails
+ ed	railed
+ ing	railing*
+ er	railer*
+ bird	railbird
+ bus	railbus
+ car	railcar
+ head	railhead
+ road	railroad^
+ way	railway
rain	
+ s	rains
+ ed	rained
+ ing	raining*
+ y	rainy
+ y + er	rainier
+ y + est	rainiest
+ bird	rainbird
+ coat	railcoat
+ drop	raindrop
+ fall	rainfall
+ make + ing	rainmaking
+ proof	rainproof
+ storm	rainstorm
+ wash	rainwash
+ water	rainwater
+ wear	rainwear
rainbow (2)	
+ s	rainbows
raise	
+ s	raises
+ ed	raised
+ ing	raising*
+ er	raiser*
raisin	
+ s	raisins
rake	
+ s	rakes
+ ed	raked
+ ing	raking*
+ er	raker*
+ ish	rakish
+ ly	rakishly
+ ness	rakishness
+ hell	rakehell
ram	
+ s	rams
+ ed	rammed
+ ing	ramming*
+ er	rammer*
+ s + horn	ramshorn
ramp	
+ s	ramps
ran (2)	
ranch	
+ s	ranches
+ ed	ranched
+ ing	ranching*
+ er	rancher*
+ man	ranchman
+ hand	ranchhand
range	
+ s	ranges
+ ed	ranged
+ ing	ranging*
+ er	ranger*
+ y	rangy
+ y + er	rangier
+ y + est	rangiest
+ hand	rangehand
rape	
+ s	rapes
+ ed	raped
+ ing	raping
+ er	raper*
+ ist	rapist*
+ ous	rapacious
+ **ous** + ly	rapaciously
+ **ous** + ness	rapaciousness
+ seed	rapeseed
rapid	
+ ly	rapidly
+ ness	rapidness
+ ity	rapidity
rare	
+ ly	rarely
+ ness	rareness*
+ er	rarer
+ est	rarest
+ ify	rarefy*
+ ify + ed	rarefied*
+ ify + ing	rarefying
+ ity	rarity*
rash	
+ s	rashes
+ ly	rashly
+ ness	rashness
rat	
+ s	rats
+ ed	ratted
+ ing	ratting*
+ y	ratty
+ y + er	rattier
+ y + est	rattiest

+ er ratter*
+ like ratlike*
+ fish ratfish
+ line ratline
+ tail rattail
+ trap rattrap

rate
+ s rates
+ ed rated
+ ing rating*
+ er rater*
+ pay + er ratepayer

rather

rattle
+ s rattles
+ ed rattled
+ ing rattling*
+ er rattler*
+ ing + ly rattlingly
+ ly rattly
+ brain rattlebrain
+ brain + ed rattlebrained
+ snake rattlesnake
+ trap rattletrap

raw
+ ly rawly
+ ness rawness
+ er rawer
+ est rawest
+ hide rawhide
+ bone + ed rawboned

ray
+ s rays
+ ed rayed
+ ing raying
+ less rayless
+ less + ness raylessness

razor
+ s razors
+ back razorback

re (prefix)

To see the way to form words with the prefix shown here, refer to the section showing the root word involved.

reaccept
reacquaint
react
reactivate
reactivation
readdress
readjust
readjustment
readmission
readmit
readopt
reaffirm
reaffirmation
reaffix
reanalysis
reanalyze
reanimate
reanimation
reappear
reappearance
reapplication
reapply
reappoint
reappointment
reapprove
reargue
reargument
rearrange
rearrangement
rearrest
reassemblage
reassemble
reassembly
reassess
reassessment
reassign
reassignment
reassume
reassurance
reassure^
reassuringly
reattach
reattachment
reattempt
reawaken
rebalance
rebaptism
rebaptize
rebid
rebind
rebirth
reblend
rebloom
reboard
rebody
reboil
rebook
rebore
reborn
rebottle
rebound
rebranch
rebuild
reburial
rebury
rebuy

R

recalculate
recalculation
recall^
recallability
recallable
recaller
recanalization
recanalize
recanalized
recanalizes
recap
recapitalization
recapitalize
recapitalized
recapitalizes
recapture
recentralization
recertification
recertify
rechallenge
rechannel
recharge
recheck
recirculate
recirculation
reclassification
reclassify
reclosure
recodification
recodify
recoin
recoinage
recollect
recolonization
recolonize
recolor
recombinant
recombination
recombinational
recombine
recommence
recommencement
recommission
recommit
recommital
recommitment
recompose
recomputation
recompute
reconcentrate
reconcentration
reconception
reconceptualize
recondense
recondition
reconfirm
reconnect
reconnection
reconquer
reconsider
reconstitute
reconstruct
recontact
recontour
reconversion
reconvert
reconvince
recopy
recork
recount
recover
recross
recrystalization
recrystalize
recurved
recut
recycle
redate
rededicate
rededication
redefine
redefinition
redeliver
redelivery
redeposit
redescribable
redescribe^
redesign
redetermination
redetermine
redevelop
redigestion
redirect
rediscount
rediscover
rediscovery
rediscuss
redispose
redisposition
redissolve
redistribute
redistrict
redivide
redivision
redo
redouble
redoubtable
redraw

R

redream
redrill
reduplicate
reduplicated
reduplicating
reecho
reedit
reeducate
reelect
reembroider
reemerge
reemergence
reemission
reemit
reemphasis
reemploy
reenergize
reengage
reengineer
reenter
reequip
reequipment
reerect
reescalate
reescalation
reestablish
reestablishment
reestimate
reevaluate
reevaluation
reexamination
reexamine
reexperience
reexplore
reexport
reexportation
reface
refashion
refeed
refeel
refence
refight
refigure
refile
refill
refinance
refind
refit
refix
refloat
reflow
refold
reform
reformulate
reformulation
refortification
refortify
refound
refoundation
reframe
refreeze
refresh
refry
refuel
refurnish
regain
regather
regenerate
regive
reglaze
regrade
regrant
regreen
regrind
regroup
regrow
regrowth
rehandle
rehang
rehear
reheat
rehinge
rehire
rehospitalization
rehospitalize
rehouse
rehumanize
rehypnotize
reidentify
reimage
reimagine
reimplantation
reimport
reimportation
reimpression
reindustrialization
reindustrialize
reinfestation
reinhabit
reinitiate
reinjure
reinjury
reinsert
reinsertion
reinspect
reinspection
reinstall
reinstallation

R

reinstate
reinstitute
reinstitutionalization
reinsurance
reinsure
reintegrate
reinterview
reintroduce
reintroduction
reinvade
reinvasion
reinvent
reinvest
reinvestigate
reinvestigation
reissue
rejacket
rejudge
rejuggle
rekey
rekeyboard
reknit
relabel
relaunch
relay
relearn
relend
relicense
relicensure
relight
relink
relive
reload
relocate
relock
remake
remap
remark
remarket
remarriage
remarry
remaster
rematch
remate
rematerialize
remeasure
remeasurement
remeet
remelt
remilitarization
remilitarize
remix
remobilization
remobilize
remodel
remodify
remold
remonetization
remonetize
remotivate
remotivation
remount
renail
rename
renationalization
renationalize
renature
renest
renew
renominate
renumber
reobserve
reoccupation
reoccupy
reoccur
reoccurrence
reoffer
reoil
reopen
reoperate
reoperation
reorchestrate
reorchestration
reorder
reorganize
reorient
reorientate
reorientation
reoutfit
repack
repackage
repaint
repaper
repassage
repattern
repave
repay
repeople
rephotograph
rephrase
replan
replant
replate
replay
repledge
repolarize
repolish
repopularize

R

repopulate
repopulation
reposition
repot
repower
repressurize
reprice
reprint
reprocess
reproduce
reprogram
republish
repump
repunctuation
repurchase
repurify
rerack
reraise
reread
rerecord
reregister
reregistration
reremind
rerepeat
rereview
reroof
reroute
rerun
resail
resale
resample
resaw
rescale
reschedule
reschool
rescore
rescreen
resculpt
reseal
reseason
reseat
resection
resecure
resee
reseed
resell
reseller
resend
resensitize
resentence
reservice
resettle
resettlement
resew
reshape
reshave
reship
reshoe
reshoot
reshow
resight
resite
resitting
resize
resocialization
resocialize
resolder
resole
resolidification
resolidify
resound
respecification
respecify
respell
respiritualize
respot
respray
restack
restage
restamp
restandardization
restandardize
restart
restate
restimulate
restimulation
restock
restore
restrengthen
restress
restrike
restructure
restudy
restuff
restyle
resummon
resupply
resurface
resuspend
resystematize
retable
retackle
retag
retake
retarget
retaste
reteach
reteam

R

	retell
	retell
	retest
	retexture
	rethink
	rethread
	retie
	retighten
	retime
	retool
	retouch
	retrace
	retrain
	retransfer
	retransform
	retransformation
	retranslate
	retrial
	retry
	retune
	retype
	reunify
	reunion
	reunite
	reuse
	revaccinate
	revaccination
	revalue
	revitalize
	revote
	rewake
	rewaken
	rewarm
	rewash
	reweave
	reweigh
	rewet
	rewind
	rewire
	reword
	rewrap
	rewrite
	rezone
reach	
+ s	reaches
+ ed	reached
+ ing	reaching
+ able	reachable
+ er	reacher*
read	
+ s	reads
+ able	readable*
+ ity	readability*
+ ness	readableness*
+ ly	readably
+ er	reader*
+ ship	readership
+ out	readout
+ ed	read
ready	
+ ly	readily
+ s	readies
+ ed	readied*
+ ing	readying*
+ ness	readiness*
real (2)	
+ ness	realness
+ ism	realism*
+ ist	realist*
+ ic	realistic
+ ic + ly	realistically
+ ity	reality*
+ y	really
realize	
+ s	realizes
+ ed	realized
+ ing	realizing*
+ tion	realization*
+ able	realizable*
+ er	realizer*
reap	
+ s	reaps
+ ed	reaped
+ ing	reaping
+ er	reaper*
+ hook	reaphook
rear	
+ s	rears
+ ed	reared
+ ing	rearing*
+ er	rearer*
+ guard	rearguard
+ most	rearmost
+ view	rearview
+ ward	rearward
reason	
+ s	reasons
+ ed	reasoned
+ ing	reasoning*
+ able	reasonable*
+ ity	reasonability*
+ able + ly	reasonably
+ ness	reasonableness*
+ less	reasonless
+ less + ly	reasonlessly
rebel	
+ s	rebels
+ ed	rebelled

R

+ ing rebelling*
+ ion rebellion*
+ ous rebellious
+ ly rebelliously
+ ness rebelliousness

receive
+ s receives
+ ed received
+ ing receiving*
+ able receivable*
+ er receiver*
+ ship receivership*
+ t receipt*
+ ive receptive*
+ ness receptiveness
+ tion reception*
+ ist receptionist*
+ ity receptivity
+ al receptical*
+ or receptor*
+ ent recipient*

recent
+ ly recently
+ ness recentness

recess
+ s recesses
+ ed recessed
+ ing recessing*
+ ion recession*
+ ary recessionary*
+ al recessional*
+ ive recessive*
+ ly recessively
+ ness recessiveness

recipe
+ s recipes

recognize
+ s recognizes
+ ed recognized
+ ong recognizing*
+ tion recognition*
+ ance recognizance*
+ able recognizable*
+ ity recognizability*
+ ly recognizably
+ er recognizer*

recommend
+ s recommends
+ ed recommended
+ ing recommending*
+ able recommendable*
+ ory recommendatory*
+ tion recommendation*

record
+ s records
+ ed recorded
+ ing recording*
+ able recordable*
+ tion recordation*
+ er recorder*
+ ist recordist*

recruit
+ s recruits
+ ed recruited
+ ing recruiting*
+ er recruiter*
+ ment recruitment*

rectangle
+ s rectangles
+ ar rectangular*
+ ity rectangularity*
+ ly rectangularly

red
+ er redder
+ est reddest
+ en redden*
+ en + ed reddened
+ en + ing reddening*
+ ish reddish
+ ish + ness reddishness*
+ ness redness*
+ ly redly
+ bird redbird
+ bone redbone
+ breast redbreast
+ brick redbrick
+ cap redcap
+ coat redcoat
+ ear redear
+ eye redeye
+ fish redfish
+ head redhead
+ head + ed redheaded
+ horse redhorse
+ leg redleg
+ line redline
+ root redroot
+ shirt redshirt
+ skin redskin
+ start redstart
+ top redtop
+ wing redwing

reduce
+ s reduces
+ ed reduced
+ ing reducing*
+ er reducer*

R

+ ible	reducible*
+ ity	reducibility*
+ ly	reducibly
+ ant	reductant*
+ tion	reduction*
+ al	reductional
+ ism	reductionism*
+ ist	reductionist*
+ ic	reductionistic*
+ ive	reductive*

reef

+ s	reefs
+ ed	reefed
+ ing	reefing*
+ y	reefy
+ er	reefer*

reel

+ s	reels
+ ed	reeled
+ ing	reeling

refer

+ s	refers
+ ed	referred
+ ing	referring
+ al	referral*
+ able	referable*
+ er	referrer*
+ ee	referee*
+ ence	reference*
+ ent	referent*
+ ent + al	referential*
+ ity	referentiality*
+ ent **+ ly**	referentially

reflect

+ s	reflects
+ ed	reflected
+ ing	reflecting
+ ance	reflectance
+ ion	reflection*
+ al	reflectional
+ ive	reflective
+ ly	reflectively
+ ness	reflectiveness
+ or	reflector*
+ ize	reflectorize^
+ ize + tion	reflectorization

reflex

+ s	reflexes
+ ed	reflexed
+ ion	reflexion*
+ ive	reflexive*
+ ly	reflexively
+ ness	reflexiveness*
+ ity	reflexivity*

refrigerate

+ s	refrigerates
+ ed	refrigerated
+ ing	refrigerating
+ or	refrigerator*
+ tion	refrigeration
+ ant	refrigerant*

refuse

+ s	refuses
+ ed	refused
+ ing	refusing*
+ al	refusal*
+ er	refuser*

region (2)

+ s	regions
+ al	regional*
+ ism	regionalism*
+ ist	regionalist*
+ ic	regionalistic*
+ ize	regionalize^
+ ly	regionally

register

+ s	registers
+ ed	registered
+ ing	registering
+ able	registrable
+ ant	registrant*
+ ar	registrar*
+ tion	registration*
+ y	registry*

regress

+ s	regresses
+ ed	regressed
+ ing	regressing
+ or	regressor*
+ ion	regression*
+ ive	regressive
+ ly	regressively
+ ness	regressiveness

regret

+ s	regrets
+ ed	regretted
+ ing	regretting
+ ful	regretful*
+ ful + ly	regretfully
+ ful + ness	regretfulness*
+ able	regrettable*
+ able + ly	regrettably

regular

+ s	regulars
+ ity	regularity
+ ize	regularize^
+ ize + tion	regularization*
+ ly	regularly
+ ate	regulate*

+ ed	regulated
+ ing	regulating*
+ ive	regulative*
+ ory	regulatory*
+ tion	regulation*
+ or	regulator*
rehabilitate	
+ s	rehabilitates
+ ed	rehabilitated
+ ing	rehabilitating*
+ tion	rehabilitation*
+ or	rehabilitator*
+ ive	rehabilitative*
rehearse	
+ s	rehearses
+ ed	rehearsed
+ ing	rehearsing*
+ al	rehearsal*
+ er	rehearser*
reign	
+ s	reigns
+ ed	reigned
+ ing	reigning
reindeer	
+ s	reindeers
reinforce	
+ s	reinforces
+ ed	reinforced
+ ing	reinforcing
+ able	reinforceable
+ ment	reinforcement*
reject	
+ s	rejects
+ ed	rejected
+ ing	rejecting
+ ly	rejectingly
+ or	rejector*
+ ive	rejective*
+ ee	rejectee*
+ tion	rejection*
relate	
+ s	relates
+ ed	related
+ ing	relating*
+ able	relatable*
+ er	relater*
+ ed + ly	relatedly
+ ness	relatedness
+ tion	relation*
+ al	relational
+ al + ly	relationally
+ ship	relationship*
relative	
+ s	relatives
+ ly	relatively
+ ism	relativism*
+ ist	relativist*
+ ic	relativistic
+ ity	relativity*
+ ize	relativize^
relax	
+ s	relaxes
+ ed	relaxed
+ ing	relaxing
+ ant	relaxant*
+ tion	relaxation*
relay	
+ s	relays
+ ed	relayed
+ ing	relaying
release	
+ s	releases
+ ed	released
+ ing	releasing*
+ er	releaser*
+ able	releasable*
relieve	
+ s	relieves
+ ed	relieved
+ ing	relieving*
+ f	relief*
+ able	relievable*
+ er	reliever*
+ ly	relievedly
religion	
+ s	religions
+ less	religionless
+ ist	religionist*
+ ous	religious
+ ity	religiousity*
+ ly	religiously
+ ness	religiousness*
rely	
+ s	relies
+ ed	relied
+ ing	relying*
+ able	reliable*
+ ity	reliability*
+ ness	reliableness*
+ able + ly	reliably
+ ance	reliance*
+ ant	reliant*
+ ant + ly	reliantly
remain	
+ s	remains
+ ed	remained
+ ing	remaining*
+ er	remainder*

R

remedy	
+ s	remedies
+ ed	remedied
+ ing	remedying*
+ less	remediless*
+ able	remediable*
+ al	remedial*
+ ly	remedially
+ ate	remediate*
+ ate + ed	remediated
+ ate + ing	remediating*
+ tion	remediation*
remember	
+ s	remembers
+ ed	remembered
+ ing	remembering*
+ able	rememberable*
+ ity	rememberability*
+ er	rememberer*
+ ance	remembrance*
+ ance + er	remembrancer*
remind	
+ s	reminds
+ ed	reminded
+ ing	reminding*
+ er	reminder*
+ ful	remindful
reminisce	
+ s	reminisces
+ ed	reminisced
+ ing	reminiscing*
+ er	reminiscer*
+ ence	reminiscence*
+ ent	reminiscent*
+ ly	reminiscently
+ al	reminiscial
remote	
+ er	remoter
+ est	remotest
+ ly	remotely
+ ness	remoteness*
remove	
+ s	removes
+ ed	removed
+ ing	removing*
+ er	remover*
+ al	removal
+ able	removable*
+ ity	removability*
+ ness	removableness*
+ ly	removably
rent	
+ s	rents
+ ed	rented
+ ing	renting*
+ al	rental*
+ able	rentable*
+ ity	rentability*
+ er	renter*
repair	
+ s	repairs
+ ed	repaired
+ ing	repairing*
+ able	repairable*
+ ity	repairability*
+ er	repairer*
+ able	reparable*
+ tion	reparation*
+ ive	reparative
+ man	repairman
repeat	
+ s	repeats
+ ed	repeated*
+ ing	repeating*
+ er	repeater*
+ ed + ly	repeatedly
+ able	repeatable*
+ ity	repeatability
+ tion	repetition*
+ al	repetitional*
+ ous	repetitious
+ ous + ly	repetitiously
+ ous + ness	repetitiousness
+ ive	repetitive*
+ ive + ly	repetitively
+ ive + ness	repetitiveness*
repel	
+ s	repels
+ ed	repelled
+ ing	repelling*
+ er	repeller*
+ y	repellency*
+ ent	repellent*
+ ent + ly	repellently
replace	
+ s	replaces
+ ed	replaced
+ ing	replacing*
+ able	replaceable*
+ er	replacer*
+ ment	replacement*
reply	
+ s	replies
+ ed	replied
+ ing	replying*
+ er	replier*
report	
+ s	reports
+ ed	reported

+ ing	reporting*
+ er	reporter*
+ able	reportable*
+ age	reportage*
+ ly	reportedly
+ al	reportorial*
+ ly	reportorially
represent	
+ ed	represented
+ s	represents
+ ing	representing*
+ er	representer*
+ able	representable*
+ tion	representation*
+ tion + al	representational*
+ tion **+ ly**	representationally
+ ism	representationalism*
+ ist	representationalist*
+ ive	representative*
+ ive + ly	representatively
+ ness	representativeness*
reptile	
+ s	reptiles
+ an	reptilian*
republic	
+ s	republics
+ an	republican*
+ ism	republicanism*
+ ize	republicanize^
repute	
+ s	reputes
+ ed	reputed
+ ing	reputing*
+ ed + ly	reputedly
+ able	reputable*
+ ity	reputability*
+ able + ly	reputably
+ tion	reputation*
+ al	reputational*
request	
+ s	requests
+ ed	requested
+ ing	requesting*
+ er	requester*
+ or	requestor*
require	
+ s	requires
+ ed	required
+ ing	requiring*
+ ment	requirement*
+ ite	requisite*
+ ness	requisiteness*
+ tion	requisition*
rescue	
+ s	rescues
+ ed	rescued
+ ing	rescuing*
+ er	rescuer*
research	
+ s	researches
+ ed	researched
+ ing	researching*
+ able	researchable*
+ er	researcher*
+ ist	researchist*
resent	
+ s	resents
+ ed	resented
+ ing	resenting*
+ ful	resentful*
+ ful + ly	resentfully
+ ment	resentment*
reserve (2)	
+ s	reserves
+ ed	reserved
+ ing	reserving*
+ tion	reservation*
+ ly	reservedly
+ ness	reservedness*
+ ist	reservist*
reside	
+ s	resides
+ ed	resided
+ ing	residing*
+ er	resider*
+ ent	resident*
+ ence	residence*
+ y	residency*
+ al	residential*
+ ly	residentially
resign	
+ s	resigns
+ ed	resigned
+ ing	resigning*
+ ly	resignedly
+ ness	resignedness*
+ er	resigner*
+ tion	resignation*
resist	
+ s	resists
+ ed	resisted
+ ing	resisting*
+ ance	resistance*
+ ant	resistant*
+ er	resister*
+ ible	resistible*
+ ible + ity	resistibility*
+ ive	resistive*
+ ly	resistively
+ ness	resistiveness*

R

+ ive + ity	resistivity*
+ less	resistless*
+ less + ness	resistlessness*
+ or	resistor*
resource	
+ s	resources
+ ful	resourceful*
+ ful + ly	resourcefully
+ ful + ness	resourcefulness*
respect	
+ s	respects
+ ed	respected
+ ing	respecting*
+ er	respecter*
+ able	respectable*
+ able + ness	respectableness*
+ ity	respectability*
+ ful	respectful*
+ ful + ly	respectfully
+ ful + ness	respectfulness*
+ ive	respective*
+ ive + ness	respectiveness*
responsible	
+ ness	responsibleness*
+ y	responsibly
+ ity	responsibility*
rest	
+ s	rests
+ ed	rested
+ ing	resting*
+ er	rester*
+ ful	restful*
+ ful + ness	restfulness*
+ ive	restive*
+ ive + ness	restiveness*
restaurant	
+ s	restaurants
+ er	restauranteur*
restless	
+ ly	restlessly
+ ness	restlessness*
restrain	
+ s	restrains
+ ed	restrained
+ ing	restraining*
+ ly	restrainedly
+ t	restraint*
restroom	
+ s	restrooms
result (2)	
+ s	results
+ ful	resultful*
+ less	resultless*
+ ant	resultant*
+ ly	resultantly

retard	
+ s	retards
+ ed	retarded
+ ing	retarding*
+ er	retarder*
+ ant	retardant*
+ ate	retardate*
+ tion	retardation*
retire	
+ s	retires
+ ed	retired
+ ing	retiring*
+ ee	retiree*
+ ant	retirant*
+ ed + ly	retiredly
+ ed + ness	retiredness*
+ ment	retirement*
+ ing + ly	retiringly
+ ing + ness	retiringness*
retreat	
+ s	retreats
+ ed	retreated
+ ing	retreating*
+ er	retreater*
+ ant	retreatant*
retrospect	
+ s	retrospects
+ tion	retrospection*
+ ive	retrospective*
+ ly	retrospectively
return	
+ s	returns
+ ed	returned
+ ing	returning*
+ er	returner*
+ able	returnable*
+ ee	returnee*
reveal	
+ s	reveals
+ ed	revealed
+ ing	revealing*
+ ing + ly	revealingly
+ ment	revealment*
+ tion	revelation*
+ or	revelator*
+ ory	revelatory
revenge	
+ s	revenges
+ ed	revenged
+ ing	revenging*
+ ful	revengeful*
+ ful + ly	revengefully
+ ful + ness	revengefulness*
+ er	revenger*

reverse

+s	reverses
+ ed	reversed
+ ing	reversing*
+ al	reversal*
+ ly	reversely
+ ible	reversible*
+ ity	reversibility*
+ ion	reversion*
+ ion + al	reversional*
+ ary	reversionary*
+ ion + er	reversioner*
+ t	revert*
+ t + ed	reverted
+ t + ing	reverting*
+ t + ible	revertible*
+ t + er	reverter*
+ ant	revertant*

review

+ s	reviews
+ ed	reviewed
+ ing	reviewing*
+ er	reviewer*

revise

+ s	revises
+ ed	revised
+ ing	revising*
+ er	reviser*
+ or	revisor*
+ al	revisal*
+ ion	revision*
+ able	revisable*
+ ism	revisionism*
+ ist	revisionist*
+ ary	revisionary*

revolt

+ s	revolts
+ ed	revolted
+ ing	revolting*
+ ly	revoltingly

revolve

+ s	revolves
+ ed	revolved
+ ing	revolving*
+ er	revolver*
+ able	revolvable*
+ tion	revolution*
+ ist	revolutionist*
+ ary	revolutionary*
+ ly	revolutionarily
+ ness	revolutionariness*
+ ize	revolutionize*
+ ize + ed	revolutionized
+ ize + ing	revolutionizing*
+ ize + er	revolutionizer*

reward

+ s	rewards
+ ed	rewarded
+ ing	rewarding*
+ ly	rewardingly

rhinoceros

+ s	rhinoceroses

rhubarb

rhyme (2)

+ s	rhymes
+ ed	rhymed
+ ing	rhyming*
+ less	rhymeless*
+ er	rhymer*

rhythm

+ s	rhythms
+ ic	rhythmic*
+ al	rhythmical*
+ ly	rhythmically
+ icity	rhythmicity*
+ ist	rhythmist*
+ ize	rhythmize^
+ ize + tion	rhythmization*

ribbon

+ s	ribbons
+ ed	ribboned
+ ing	ribboning*
+ like	ribbonlike
+ fish	ribbonfish

rice

+ s	rices
+ er	ricer*

rich

+ s	riches
+ er	richer
+ est	richest
+ ness	richness*
+ ly	richly
+ en	richen^

rid

+ s	rids
+ ed	ridded
+ ing	ridding*
+ ance	riddance*

riddle

+ s	riddles
+ ed	riddled
+ ing	riddling*
+ er	riddler*

ride

+ s	rides
+ ed	rode
+ ing	riding*
+ en	ridden

+ able rideable*
+ er rider*
+ er + less riderless
+ er + ship ridership*

ridicule

+ s ridicules
+ ed ridiculed
+ ing ridiculing*
+ ous ridiculous
+ ly ridiculously
+ ness ridiculousness*

rifle

+ s rifles
+ ed rifled
+ ing rifling*
+ ry riflery*
+ bird riflebird
+ man rifleman

right

+ s rights
+ ed righted
+ ing righting*
+ ness rightness*
+ er righter*
+ ful rightful*
+ ful + ly rightfully
+ ful + ness rightfulness*
+ ism rightism*
+ ist rightist*
+ ous righteous
+ ous + ly righteously
+ ous + ness righteousness*
+ ly rightly
+ ward rightward

ring

+ s rings
+ ed ringed
+ ing ringing*
+ like ringlike
+ er ringer*
+ ing + ly ringingly
+ bark ringbark
+ bone ringbone
+ lead + er ringleader
+ master ringmaster
+ neck ringneck
+ side ringside
+ tail ringtail
+ tail + ed ringtailed
+ worm ringworm

rinse

+ s rinses
+ ed rinsed
+ ing rinsing*
+ er rinser*

riot

+ s riots
+ ed rioted
+ ing rioting*
+ er rioter*
+ ous riotous*
+ ly riotously
+ ness riotousness*

rip

+ s rips
+ ed ripped
+ ing ripping*
+ er ripper*
+ saw ripsaw
+ stop ripstop

ripe

+ er riper
+ est ripest
+ ly ripely
+ ness ripeness*
+ en ripen*
+ ed ripened
+ ing ripening*
+ en + er ripener*

rise

+ s rises
+ ed rose
+ en risen
+ ing rising*
+ er riser*

risk

+ s risks
+ ed risked
+ ing risking*
+ er risker*
+ y risky*
+ y + er riskier
+ est riskiest
+ ness riskiness

rival

+ s rivals
+ ed rivaled
+ ing rivaling*
+ ry rivalry*
+ ous rivalrous

river

+ s rivers
+ bank riverbank
+ bed riverbed
+ boat riverboat
+ front riverfront
+ ine riverine
+ side riverside

R

+ ward	riverward
+ weed	riverweed
roach	
+ s	roaches
+ ed	roached
+ ing	roaching*
road	
+ s	roads
+ less	roadless*
+ ity	roadability*
+ bed	roadbed
+ block	roadblock
+ hold + ing	roadholding
+ house	roadhouse
+ y	roadie*
+ runner	roadrunner*
+ side	roadside
+ stead	roadstead*
+ way	roadway
+ work	roadwork
+ worth + y	roadworthy
+ worth + **ness**	roadworthiness
roam	
+ s	roams
+ ed	roamed
+ ing	roaming*
+ er	roamer*
roar	
+ s	roars
+ ed	roared
+ ing	roaring*
+ er	roarer*
+ ly	roaringly
roast	
+ s	roasts
+ ed	roasted
+ ing	roasting*
+ er	roaster*
rob	
+ s	robs
+ ed	robbed
+ ing	robbing*
+ er	robber*
+ ery	robbery*
robe	
+ s	robes
+ ed	robed
+ ing	robing*
robin	
+ s	robins
robot	
+ s	robots
+ ic	robotic*
+ ism	robotism*
+ ize	robotize^
+ tion	robotization*
rock	
+ s	rocks
+ ed	rocked
+ ing	rocking*
+ er	rocker*
+ like	rocklike
+ y	rocky*
+ y + er	rockier
+ est	rockiest
+ ness	rockiness*
+ bound	rockbound
+ fall	rockfall
+ fish	rockfish
+ rose	rockrose
+ weed	rockweed
rocket	
+ s	rockets
+ ed	rocketed
+ ing	rocketing*
+ ry	rocketry*
rodent	
+ s	rodents
rodeo	
+ s	rodeos
role	
+ s	roles
roll	
+ s	rolls
+ ed	rolled
+ ing	rolling*
+ er	roller*
+ back	rollback
+ out	rollout
+ over	rollover
+ top	rolltop
romance	
+ s	romances
+ ed	romanced
+ ing	romancing*
+ er	romancer*
romantic	
+ ly	romantically
+ ism	romanticism*
+ ist	romanticist*
+ ize	romanticize^
+ ize + tion	romanticization*
Rome	
+ an	Roman*
+ ism	Romanism*
+ ize	romanize^
+ tion	romanization*
roof	
+ s	roofs
+ ed	roofed

R

+ ing	roofing*
+ less	roofless*
+ like	rooflike
+ er	roofer*
+ line	roofline
+ top	rooftop
room	
+ s	rooms
+ ed	roomed
+ ing	rooming*
+ er	roomer*
+ ful	roomful*
+ mate	roommate*
+ y	roomy
+ y + er	roomier
+ est	roomiest
roost	
+ s	roosts
+ ed	roosted
+ ing	roosting*
rooster	
+ s	roosters
root	
+ s	roots
+ ed	rooted
+ ing	rooting*
+ less	rootless*
+ less +ness	rootlessness*
+ like	rootlike
+ age	rootage*
+ ed + ness	rootedness*
+ hold	roothold
+ stock	rootstock
+ y	rooty*
rope	
+ s	ropes
+ ed	roped
+ ing	roping*
+ er	roper*
+ ery	ropery*
+ y	ropey*
+ y + er	ropier
+ y + est	ropiest
+ ness	ropiness*
+ dance + er	ropedancer
+ dance + ing	ropedancing
+ walk	ropewalk
+ walk + er	ropewalker
+ way	ropeway
rose	
+ s	roses
+ y	rosy*
+ y + er	rosier
+ y + est	rosiest
+ y + ness	rosiness*
+ ate	roseate*
+ ly	roseately
+ ery	rosary*
+ bay	rosebay
+ bush	rosebush
+ fish	rosefish
+ water	rosewater
+ wood	rosewood
rot	
+ s	rots
+ ed	rotted
+ ing	rotting*
+ en	rotten
+ er	rotter*
rotate	
+ s	rotates
+ ed	rotated
+ ing	rotating*
+ ion	rotation*
+ able	rotatable*
+ ive	rotative*
+ ly	rotatively
+ al	rotational*
+ or	rotator*
+ ory	rotatory*
rough	
+ s	roughs
+ er	rougher*
+ est	roughest
+ ly	roughly
+ ish	roughish
+ ness	roughness*
+ age	roughage*
+ en	roughen^
+ house	roughhouse
+ leg	roughleg
+ neck	roughneck
+ ride + er	roughrider
round	
+ s	rounds
+ ed	rounded
+ ing	rounding*
+ ly	roundly
+ ness	roundness*
+ ed + ness	roundedness*
+ ish	roundish
+ er	rounder*
+ head + ed	roundheaded
+ house	roundhouse
+ s + man	roundsman
+ up	roundup
+ wood	roundwood
+ worm	roundworm

R

route

+ s	routes
+ ed	routed*
+ ing	routing*
+ man	routeman
+ way	routeway

routine

+ s	routines
+ ly	routinely
+ ize	routinize^
+ ize + tion	routinization*

row

+ s	rows
+ ed	rowed
+ ing	rowing*
+ boat	rowboat
+ lock	rowlock

royal

+ s	royals
+ ly	royally
+ ism	royalism*
+ ist	royalist*
+ t + y	royalty*

rub

+ s	rubs
+ ed	rubbed
+ ing	rubbing*

rubber

+ y	rubbery*

rubella

rude

+ er	ruder
+ est	rudest
+ ly	rudely
+ ness	rudeness*

rug

+ s	rugs

ruin

+ s	ruins
+ ed	ruined
+ ing	ruining*
+ ate	ruinate^
+ er	ruiner*
+ ate + tion	ruination*
+ ous	ruinous*
+ ly	ruinously
+ ness	ruinousness*

rule

+ s	rules
+ ed	ruled
+ ing	ruling*
+ er	ruler*
+ less	ruleless*
+ ship	rulership*

rummage

+ s	rummages
+ ed	rummaged
+ ing	rummaging*
+ er	rummager*

rumor

+ s	rumors
+ ed	rumored
+ ing	rumoring*

run (2)

+ s	runs
+ ed	ran
+ ing	running*
+ less	runless
+ er	runner*
+ y	runny*
+ about	runabout
+ around	runaround
+ away	runaway
+ back	runback
+ down	rundown
+ way	runway

rush

+ s	rushes
+ ed	rushed
+ ing	rushing*
+ er	rusher*
+ ee	rushee*

Russia

+ ify	Russify
+ ify + ed	Russified
+ ify + ing	Russifying*
+ ify + tion	Russification*
+ an	Russian*
+ ness	Russianness*
+ ize	Russianize^
+ ize + tion	Russianization*

rust

+ s	rusts
+ ed	rusted
+ ing	rusting*
+ proof	rustproof
+ y	rusty*
+ y + er	rustier
+ est	rustiest
+ ly	rustily
+ ness	rustiness*

rye

+ s	ryes
+ bread	ryebread
+ grass	ryegrass

R

Sabbath	
+ an	Sabbatarian*
+ ism	Sabbatarianism*
+ ic	sabbatic*
+ al	sabbatical*
sack	
+ s	sacks
+ ed	sacked
+ ing	sacking*
+ er	sacker*
+ ful	sackful*
+ cloth	sackcloth
sacred	
+ ly	sacredly
+ ness	sacredness*
sad	
+ er	sadder
+ est	saddest
+ en	sadden^
+ ly	sadly
+ ness	sadness*
saddle	
+ s	saddles
+ ed	saddled
+ ing	saddling*
+ less	saddleless
+ er	saddler*
+ ery	saddlery*
+ bag	saddlebag
+ bow	saddlebow
+ cloth	saddlecloth
+ tree	saddletree
safe	
+ er	safer
+ est	safest
+ ly	safely
+ ness	safeness*
+ t + y	safety*
+ crack + er	safecracker
+ guard	safeguard
+ keep + ing	safekeeping
+ light	safelight
said	
sail	
+ s	sails
+ ed	sailed
+ ing	sailing*
+ er	sailer*
+ or	sailor*
+ able	sailable*
+ board	sailboard
+ boat	sailboat
+ cloth	sailcloth
+ fish	sailfish
+ plane	sailplane
saint	
+ s	saints
+ ly	saintly
+ dom	saintdom*
+ like	saintlike
+ ed	sainted
+ hood	sainthood*
+ ness	saintliness*
salad	
+ s	salads
salami	
+ s	salamis
sale	
+ s	sales
+ girl	salesgirl
+ lady	saleslady
+ man	salesman
+ man + ship	salesmanship
+ people	salespeople
+ person	salesperson
+ room	salesroom
+ woman	saleswoman
salt	
+ s	salts
+ ed	salted
+ ing	salting*
+ y	salty*
+ er	saltier
+ est	saltiest
+ like	saltlike
+ less	saltless*

+ ness	saltness*
+ y + ness	saltiness*
+ shaker	saltshaker
+ water	saltwater
+ work + s	saltworks
+ box	saltbox
salute	
+ s	salutes
+ ed	saluted
+ ing	saluting*
+ er	saluter*
+ ary	salutary*
+ ly	salutarily
+ ness	salutariness*
+ tion	salutation*
+ ate + ory	salutatory*
+ an	salutatorian*
+ er + ous	salutiferous
same	
sample	
+ s	samples
+ ed	sampled
+ ing	sampling*
+ er	sampler*
sand	
+ s	sands
+ ed	sanded
+ ing	sanding*
+ er	sander*
+ y	sandy*
+ est	sandiest
+ bag	sandbag
+ bank	sandbank
+ bar	sandbar
+ box	sandbox
+ glass	sandglass
+ hill	sandhill
+ hog	sandhog
+ lot	sandlot
+ man	sandman
+ paper	sandpaper^
+ pile	sandpile
+ soap	sandsoap
+ stone	sandstone
+ storm	sandstorm
+ worm	sandworm
sandal	
+ s	sandals
+ ed	sandaled
sandwich	
+ s	sandwiches
+ ed	sandwiched
+ ing	sandwiching*
sang	

sanitary	
+ an	sanitarian
+ ize	sanitize^
+ ize + tion	sanitization
+ tion	sanitation
sank (2)	
Santa Claus	
sarcasm	
+ s	sarcasms
+ ic	sarcastic
+ ly	sarcastically
sat	
satellite	
+ s	satellites
satisfy	
+ s	satisfies
+ ed	satisfied
+ ing	satisfying
+ tion	satisfaction
+ ory	satisfactory
+ ory + ly	satisfactorily
+ ness	satisfactoriness
+ able	satisfiable
+ ing + ly	satisfyingly
Saturday	
+ s	Saturdays
sauce	
+ s	sauces
+ ed	sauced
+ ing	saucing*
+ er	saucer*
+ y	saucy*
+ ly	saucily
+ ness	sauciness*
+ er + like	saucerlike
+ y + er	saucier
+ est	sauciest
+ boat	sauceboat
+ box	saucebox
+ pan	saucepan
sausage	
+ s	sausages
save	
+ s	saves
+ ed	saved
+ ing	saving*
+ able	savable*
+ er	saver*
saviour	
saw (noun)	
+ s	saws
+ ed	sawed
+ ing	sawing*
+ like	sawlike
+ er	sawer*

+ bone + s	sawbones
+ dust	sawdust
+ fish	sawfish
+ fly	sawfly
+ horse	sawhorse
+ log	sawlog
+ tooth	sawtooth
saw (verb)	
say	
+ s	says
+ ed	said
+ ing	saying*
+ er	sayer*
+ able	sayable*
scale	
+ s	scales
+ ed	scaled
+ ing	scaling*
+ less	scaleless
+ like	scalelike
+ able	scalable*
+ ar	scalar*
+ er	scaler*
+ y	scaly*
scare	
+ s	scares
+ ed	scared
+ ing	scaring*
+ er	scarer*
+ y	scary*
+ y + er	scarier
+ est	scariest
+ ly	scarily
+ crow	scarecrow
scarf	
+ s	scarfs
+ ed	scarfed
+ pin	scarfpin
+ skin	scarfskin
scatter	
+ s	scatters
+ ed	scattered
+ ing	scattering*
+ er	scatterer*
+ ly	scatteringly
+ tion	scatteration*
+ brain	scatterbrain
+ brain + ed	scatterbrained
+ good	scattergood
+ gram	scattergram
+ gun	scattergun
+ shot	scattershot
scene	
+ s	scenes
+ ic	scenic*
+ ery	scenery*
schedule	
+ s	schedules
+ ed	scheduled
+ ing	scheduling*
+ er	scheduler*
scheme	
+ s	schemes
+ ed	schemed
+ ing	scheming*
+ ism	schematism*
+ ize	schematize^
+ ize + tion	schematization*
+ er	schemer*
+ ic	schematic*
+ ly	schematically
schizophrenic	
+ ly	schizophrenically
school	
+ s	schools
+ ed	schooled
+ ing	schooling*
+ bag	schoolbag
+ book	schoolbook
+ boy	schoolboy
+ child	schoolchild
+ fellow	schoolfellow
+ girl	schoolgirl
+ house	schoolhouse
+ man	schoolman
+ master	schoolmaster
+ mate	schoolmate
+ room	schoolroom
+ teach + er	schoolteacher
+ time	schooltime
+ work	schoolwork
science	
+ s	sciences
+ al	sciential
+ ic	scientific
+ ly	scientifically
+ ism	scientism*
+ ist	scientist*
+ ize	scientize^
scissor	
+ s	scissors
+ ed	scissored
+ ing	scissoring*
+ tail	scissortail
scold	
+ s	scolds
+ ed	scolded
+ ing	scolding*
+ er	scolder*

S

scoop
+ s scoops
+ ed scooped
+ ing scooping*
+ ful scoopful*

scoot
+ s scoots
+ ed scooted
+ ing scooting*
+ er scooter*

score
+ s scores
+ ed scored
+ ing scoring*
+ er scorer*
+ less scoreless
+ board scoreboard
+ card scorecard
+ keep + er scorekeeper

scorpion
+ s scorpions

Scot
+ s Scots
+ man Scotsman
+ woman Scotswoman
+ y Scottie*
+ ish Scottish
+ ism Scotticism*

scout
+ s scouts
+ ed scouted
+ ing scouting
+ er scouter*
+ master scoutmaster*

scramble
+ s scrambles
+ ed scrambled
+ ing scrambling
+ er scrambler*

scrape
+ s scrapes
+ ed scraped
+ ing scraping*
+ er scraper*

scratch
+ s scratches
+ ed scratched
+ ing scratching*
+ er scratcher*
+ y scratchy*
+ y + er scratchier
+ est scratchiest
+ ness scratchiness
+ board scratchboard

scream
+ s screams
+ ed screamed
+ ing screaming*
+ er screamer*
+ ly screamingly

screen
+ s screens
+ ed screened
+ ing screening*
+ able screenable*
+ er screener*
+ land screenland
+ play screenplay
+ write + er screenwriter

screw
+ s screws
+ ed screwed
+ ing screwing*
+ er screwer*
+ like screwlike
+ y screwy*
+ y + er screwier
+ est screwiest
+ ness screwiness*
+ ball screwball
+ up screwup
+ worm screwworm
+ drive + er screwdriver
+ drive + er + s screwdrivers

script
+ s scripts
+ ed scripted
+ ing scripting*
+ ure scripture*
+ ure + al scriptural
+ ure **+ ly** scripturally
+ write + er scriptwriter

scrub
+ s scrubs
+ ed scrubbed
+ ing scrubbing*
+ er scrubber*
+ y scrubby*
+ y + er scrubbier
+ est scrubbiest
+ land scrubland
+ woman scrubwoman

sculpt
+ s sculpts
+ ed sculpted
+ ing sculpting
+ or sculptor*
+ ure sculpture^
+ ess sculptress*

S

+ al	sculptural
+ ly	sculpturally
sea	
+ s	seas
+ bag	seabag
+ bed	seabed
+ bird	seabird
+ board	seaboard
+ boot	seaboot
+ bear + en	seaborne
+ coast	seacoast
+ floor	seafloor
+ food	seafood
+ front	seafront
+ go + ing	seagoing
+ man	seaman
+ man + like	seamanlike
+ man + ly	seamanly
+ man + ship	seamanship
+ mark	seamark
+ mount	seamount
+ piece	seapiece
+ plane	seaplane
+ ward	seaward
+ port	seaport
+ quake	seaquake
+ water	seawater
+ train	seatrain
+ wall	seawall
+ way	seaway
+ worth + y	seaworthy
+ worth + **ness**	seaworthiness
+ shore	seashore
+ sick	seasick
+ sick + ness	seasickness
+ weed	seaweed
+ side	seaside
seal	
+ s	seals
+ ed	sealed
+ ing	sealing*
+ ant	sealant*
+ er	sealer*
+ skin	sealskin
seam	
+ s	seams
+ ed	seamed
+ ing	seaming*
+ y	seamy
+ y + er	seamier
+ y + est	seamiest
+ ness	seaminess
search	
+ s	searches
+ ed	searched
+ ing	searching*
+ able	searchable*
+er	searcher*
+ ly	searchingly
+ less	searchless
+ light	searchlight
seashell	
+ s	seashells
season	
+ s	seasons
+ ed	seasoned
+ ing	seasoning*
+ less	seasonless*
+ ity	seasonality*
+ er	seasoner*
+ able	seasonable*
+ able + ly	seasonably
+ al	seasonal*
+ al + ly	seasonally
seat	
+ s	seats
+ ed	seated
+ ing	seating*
+ er	seater*
+ mate	seatmate
second	
+ s	seconds
+ ed	seconded
+ ing	seconding*
+ ly	secondly
+ ary	secondary*
+ ary + ly	secondarily
+ ness	secondariness*
+ hand	secondhand
secret	
+ s	secrets
+ ly	secretly
+ y	secrecy*
+ ive	secretive*
+ ive + ly	secretively
+ ness	secretiveness*
secretary (2)	
+ s	secretaries
+ al	secretarial*
+ ship	secretaryship*
section	
+ s	sections
+ ed	sectioned
+ ing	sectioning*
+ al	sectional*
+ ly	sectionally
+ ism	sectionalism*
secure	
+ s	secures
+ ed	secured

S

+ ing	securing*
+ ly	securely
+ ness	secureness
+ ity	security*
+ er	securer*
+ ment	securement*

see

+ s	sees
+ ed	saw
+ en	seen
+ ing	seeing

seed

+ s	seeds
+ ed	seeded
+ ing	seeding*
+ er	seeder*
+ ness	seediness*
+ y	seedy*
+ y + er	seedier
+ est	seediest
+ ly	seedily
+ bed	seedbed
+ cake	seedcake
+ eat + er	seedeater
+ s + man	seedsman
+ time	seedtime

seek

+ s	seeks
+ ed	sought
+ ing	seeking*
+ er	seeker*

seem

+ s	seems
+ ed	seemed
+ ing	seeming*
+ ing + ly	seemingly
+ ly	seemly*
+ ness	seemliness*
+ er	seemlier
+ est	seemliest

seesaw

+ s	seesaws
+ ed	seesawed
+ ing	seesawing*

segment

+ s	segments
+ ed	segmented
+ ing	segmenting*
+ al	segmental*
+ ly	segmentally
+ tion	segmentation*

seldom

select

+ s	selects
+ ed	selected
+ ing	selecting*
+ ive	selective*
+ ly	selectively
+ ive + ness	selectiveness*
+ ity	selectivity*
+ ness	selectness*
+ ee	selectee*
+ tion	selection*
+ or	selector*
+ man	selectman

self

+ s	selves
+ ed	selved
+ ing	selving*
+ dom	selfdom*
+ hood	selfhood*
+ less	selfless
+ less + ly	selflessly
+ less + ness	selflessness*
+ ness	selfness*
+ same	selfsame

self (used as a prefix)

To see the way to form words with the prefix shown here, refer to the section showing the root word involved.

self-acceptance
self-accusation
self-accusatory
self-adjusting
self-admitted
self-admittedly
self-advancement
self-advertisement
self-advertiser
self-affirmation
self-assessment
self-assignment
self-betterment
self-cancel
self-care
self-characterization
self-charging
self-classification
self-command
self-confirming
self-constituted
self-consuming
self-created
self-creation
self-critical
self-criticism
self-damning
self-deceit
self-deceiver
self-deceiving
self-deception

self-deceptive
self-defeating
self-dependence
self-dependent
self-described
self-description
self-descriptive
self-development
self-differentiation
self-directed
self-directing
self-direction
self-directive
self-dissatisfaction
self-doubt
self-doubting
self-educated
self-education
self-evaluate
self-evaluation
self-exclusion
self-exhibition
self-existence
self-existent
self-explaining
self-explanatory
self-extinction
self-finance
self-formed
self-generated
self-generating
self-give
self-guided
self-hate
self-hating
self-hatred
self-healing
self-help
self-humbling
self-hypnosis
self-improvement
self-initiated
self-instructed
self-interpretation
self-interview
self-isolation
self-labeled
self-locking
self-maintenance
self-management
self-mastery
self-motivated
self-motivating
self-negating

self-operating
self-operative
self-oriented
self-pleasing
self-policing
self-praise
self-preoccupation
self-preoccupied
self-preserving
self-proclaimed
self-produced
self-professed
self-promoted
self-promotion
self-protection
self-protective
self-protectiveness
self-punishing
self-punishment
self-raised
self-recrimination
self-reformation
self-regulation
self-restraining
self-restraint
self-ridicule
self-selected
self-selection
self-set
self-surrender
self-therapy
self-transformation
self-understanding
self-worship
self-worshipper
self-abuse
self-acting
self-activity
self-actualize
self-actualization
self-addressed
self-adjustment
self-admiration
self-affected
self-analysis
self-analytical
self-applauding
self-applause
self-appointed
self-assembly
self-assumption
self-aware
self-awareness
self-belt

self-belted
self-betrayal
self-binder
self-born
self-centered
self-centeredly
self-centeredness
self-closing
self-collected
self-colored
self-composed
self-composedly
self-composedness
self-conceit
self-concept
self-conception
self-concern
self-concerned
self-confessed
self-confession
self-confidence
self-confident
self-confidently
self-confrontation
self-congratulation
self-congratulatory
self-conscious
self-consciously
self-consciousness
self-consistency
self-consistent
self-content
self-contented
self-contentedness
self-contentment
self-control
self-controlled
self-correcting
self-corrective
self-culture
self-dealing
self-dedication
self-defense
self-defensive
self-definition
self-denial
self-denying
self-destroyer
self-destruct
self-destruction
self-destructive
self-destructiveness
self-determination
self-determined
self-determining
self-determinism
self-devoted
self-devotedly
self-devotedness
self-devoting
self-devotion
self-discovery
self-distributing
self-distrust
self-distrustful
self-dramatization
self-dramatizing
self-drive
self-elected
self-employed
self-employment
self-energizing
self-enforcing
self-esteem
self-evidence
self-evident
self-evidently
self-examination
self-excited
self-explanatory
self-exploration
self-expression
self-expressive
self-feed
self-feeds
self-fed
self-feeding
self-feeder
self-feeling
self-fertile
self-fertilization
self-fertilized
self-fertilizing
self-flattering
self-flattery
self-forgetful
self-forgetfulness
self-forgetting
self-forgettingly
self-fruitful
self-fruitfulness
self-given
self-glorification
self-glorifying
self-glory
self-governance
self-governed
self-governing

S

self-government
self-hardening
self-heal
self-identification
self-image
self-importance
self-important
self-inclusive
self-incriminating
self-incrimination
self-instructional
self-insurance
self-insured
self-insurer
self-interest
self-interested
self-interestedness
self-involved
self-justification
self-justifying
self-knowing
self-knowledge
self-limited
self-limiting
self-liquidating
self-loader
self-loading
self-love
self-made
self-mailer
self-mailing
self-moved
self-observation
self-opinion
self-opinionated
self-opinionatedness
self-organization
self-partiality
self-perception
self-pity
self-pitying
self-pityingly
self-pleased
self-preservation
self-pride
self-published
self-purification
self-question
self-questioning
self-rating
self-realization
self-realizationist
self-recognition
self-recording

self-reflection
self-reflective
self-registering
self-regulating
self-reliance
self-reliant
self-respect
self-respecting
self-revealing
self-revelation
self-rewarding
self-righteous
self-righteousness
self-rising
self-rule
self-ruling
self-satisfaction
self-satisfied
self-sealing
self-searching
self-seeker
self-seeking
self-selected
self-selection
self-serve
self-service
self-serving
self-starter
self-starting
self-stick
self-stimulation
self-stimulatory
self-study
self-styled
self-suggestion
self-support
self-supported
self-supporting
self-surrender
self-taught
self-tolerance
self-treatment
self-trust
self-will
self-willed
self-willedly
self-willedness
self-worth

selfish

+ ly	selfishly
+ ness	selfishness

sell

+ s	sells
+ ed	sold

S

+ ing	selling*
+ er	seller*
+able	sellable*
+ out	sellout
+ out + s	sellouts
semester	
+ s	semesters
+ al	semestral
seminary	
+ s	seminaries
+ an	seminarian*
+ ist	seminarist*
senate	
+ s	senates
+ or	senator*
+ or + al	senatorial*
+ an	senatorian*
+ ship	senatorship*
send	
+ s	sends
+ ed	sent
+ ing	sending*
+ er	sender*
senior	
+ s	seniors
+ ity	seniority*
sense	
+ s	senses
+ ed	sensed
+ ing	sensing*
+ ate	sensate*
+ ate + ly	sensately
+ tion	sensation*
+ tion + al	sensational*
+ tion **+ ly**	sensationally
+ tion **+ ism**	sensationalism*
+ tion **+ ist**	sensationalist*
+ tion **+ ic**	sensationalistic
+ tion **+ ize**	sensationalize^
+ tion **+ ize + tion**	sensationalization*
+ ful	senseful
+ less	senseless*
+ less + ly	senselessly
+ less + ness	senselessness*
+ ible	sensible*
+ ity	sensibility*
+ ible + ly	sensibly
+ ible + ness	sensibleness*
+ ize	sensitize^
+ ize + tion	sensitization*
+ or	sensor*
+ or **+ al**	sensorial*
+ ory	sensory*
+ al	sensual*
+ al + ly	sensually
+ al + ness	sensualness*
+ al + ism	sensualism*
+ al + ize	sensualize^
+ al + ize + tion	sensualization*
+ ous	sensuous
+ ous + ly	sensuously
+ ous + ness	sensuousness*
+ ous + ity	sensuosity*
sensitive	
+ ly	sensitively
+ ness	sensitiveness*
+ ity	sensitivity*
sentence	
+ s	sentences
+ ed	sentenced
+ ing	sentencing*
+ al	sentential*
+ ous	sententious
+ ly	sententiously
+ ness	sententiousness*
separate	
+ s	separates
+ ed	separated
+ ing	separating*
+ or	separator*
+ able	separable*
+ able + ly	separably
+ ity	separability*
+ able + ness	separableness*
+ ly	separately
+ ness	separateness*
+ tion	separation*
+ tion + ist	separationist*
+ ism	separatism*
+ ist	separatist*
+ ic	separatistic*
+ ive	separative*
September (2)	
sequence	
+ s	sequences
+ ed	sequenced
+ ing	sequencing*
+ er	sequencer*
+ y	sequency*
+ t	sequent*
+ al	sequential*
+ ly	sequentially
sequin	
+ s	sequins
+ ed	sequined
sergeant	
+ s	sergeants
+ y	sergeancy*
+ y	sergeanty*

S

series

+ al	serial*
+ ly	serially
+ ism	serialism*
+ ist	serialist*
+ ate	seriate^
+ ate + ly	seriately
+ ize	serialize^
+ ize + **tion**	serialization*

serious

+ ly	seriously
+ ness	seriousness*

servant

+ s	servants
+ hood	servanthood*
+ less	servantless

serve

+ s	serves
+ ed	served
+ ing	serving*
+ er	server*
+ ice	service^
+ ice + er	servicer*
+ ice + able	serviceable*
+ ice **+ ity**	serviceability*
+ ice **+ ly**	serviceably
+ ice + able + ness	serviceableness*
+ ice + man	serviceman
+ ice + woman	servicewoman
+ ite	Servite*
+ ite + or	servitor*
+ ile	servile*
+ ile + ly	servilely
+ ile + ness	servileness*
+ ile + ity	servility*

set

+ s	sets
+ ing	setting*
+ er	setter*
+ back	setback
+ line	setline
+ off	setoff
+ out	setout
+ screw	setscrew
+ up	setup

settle

+ s	settles
+ ed	settled
+ ing	settling*
+ er	settler*
+ ee	settee*
+ ment	settlement*

several

+ ly	severally
+ fold	severalfold*

sew

+ s	sews
+ ed	sewed
+ en	sewn
+ ing	sewing*
+ able	sewable*
+ ity	sewability*

sewer

+ s	sewers
+ age	sewerage*

sex

+ s	sexes
+ ed	sexed
+ ing	sexing*
+ ism	sexism*
+ ist	sexist*
+ less	sexless
+ less + ly	sexlessly
+ less + ness	sexlessness*
+ al	sexual
+ ly	sexually
+ ity	sexuality*
+ al + ize	sexualize^
+ y	sexy
+ er	sexier
+ est	sexiest

shade

+ s	shades
+ ed	shaded
+ ing	shading*
+ less	shadeless
+ er	shader*
+ y	shady
+ y + er	shadier
+ est	shadiest
+ ly	shadily
+ ness	shadiness*

shadow

+ less	shadowless
+ like	shadowlike
+ y	shadowy
+ ly	shadowily
+ ness	shadowiness

shake

+ s	shakes
+ ed	shook
+ en	shaken
+ able	shakable*
+ er	shaker*
+ down	shakedown
+ out	shakeout

Shakespeare

+ an	Shakespearean

shall (2)

+ en	should

shallow

+ s	shallows
+ ly	shallowly
+ ness	shallowness*

shame

+ s	shames
+ ed	shamed
+ ing	shaming*
+ face + ed	shamefaced
+ face + ed + ly	shamefacedly
+ face + ed + ness	shamefacedness
+ ful	shameful
+ ful + ly	shamefully
+ ful + ness	shamefulness*
+ less	shameless
+ less + ly	shamelessly
+ less +ness	shamelessness*

shampoo

+ s	shampoos
+ ed	shampooed
+ ing	shampooing*
+ er	shampooer*

shape

+ s	shapes
+ ed	shaped
+ ing	shaping*
+ er	shaper*
+ able	shapable*
+ less	shapeless
+ less + ly	shapelessly
+ less + ness	shapelessness*
+ ly	shapely*
+ ly + er	shapelier
+ est	shapeliest
+ ly + ness	shapeliness*
+ en	shapen*
mis + shape + en	misshapen

share

+ s	shares
+ ed	shared
+ ing	sharing*
+ er	sharer*
+ able	shareable*
+ ity	shareability*
+ crop	sharecrop
+ crop + er	sharecropper
+ hold + ing	shareholding
+ hold + er	shareholder

shark

+ s	sharks
+ like	sharklike
+ skin	sharkskin

sharp

+ s	sharps
+ ly	sharply
+ ness	sharpness
+ en	sharpen^
+ en + er	sharpener*
+ er	sharper
+ est	sharpest
+ y	sharpie*
+ shoot + er	sharpshooter

shave

+ s	shaves
+ ed	shaved
+ ing	shaving*
+ er	shaver*

she

shears

sheep

+ ish	sheepish
+ ly	sheepishly
+ ness	sheepishness
+ dog	sheepdog
+ fold	sheepfold
+ herd	sheepherd
+ herd + er	sheepherder
+ herd + ing	sheepherding
+ s + head	sheepshead
+ shear + s	sheepshears
+ shear + er	sheepshearer*
+ shear + ing	sheepshearing*
+ skin	sheepskin

sheet

+ s	sheets
+ ed	sheeted
+ ing	sheeting*
+ er	sheeter*

shelf

+ ed	shelved
+ ing	shelving*
+ ful	shelfful*
+ like	shelflike

shell

+ s	shells
+ y	shelly*
+ ed	shelled
+ ing	shelling*
+ er	sheller*
+ fish	shellfish
+ fish + ry	shellfishery
+ proof	shellproof
+ work	shellwork

shelter

+ s	shelters
+ ed	sheltered

S

+ ing	sheltering*
+ less	shelterless
+ er	shelterer*
+ belt	shelterbelt
shepherd	
+ s	shepherds
+ ing	shepherding*
+ ed	shepherded
+ ess	shepherdess*
shh	
shield	
+ s	shields
+ ed	shielded
+ ing	shielding*
+ er	shielder*
shine	
+ s	shines
+ ed	shined
+ ing	shining*
+ er	shiner*
+ y	shiny
+ y + er	shinier
+ est	shiniest
+ ness	shininess*
+ en or ed	shone
ship	
+ s	ships
+ ed	shipped
+ ing	shipping*
+ able	shippable*
+ ment	shipment*
+ er	shipper*
+ board	shipboard
+ bear + en	shipborne
+ build + er	shipbuilder
+ build + ing	shipbuilding
+ fit + er	shipfitter
+ lap	shiplap
+ load	shipload
+ man	shipman
+ master	shipmaster
+ own + er	shipowner
+ shape	shipshape
+ side	shipside
+ way	shipway
+ worm	shipworm
+ wreck	shipwreck^
+ yard	shipyard
shirt	
+ s	shirts
+ ing	shirting*
+ dress	shirtdress
+ front	shirtfront
+ make + er	shirtmaker

+ sleeve	shirtsleeve
+ tail	shirttail
+ waist	shirtwaist
shiver	
+ s	shivers
+ ed	shivered
+ ing	shivering*
+ y	shivery
shock	
+ s	shocks
+ ed	shocked
+ ing	shocking*
+ able	shockable*
+ er	shocker*
+ ly	shockingly
+ proof	shockproof
shoe	
+ s	shoes
+ ed	shoed
+ ing	shoeing*
+ less	shoeless
+ black	shoeblack
+ horn	shoehorn
+ lace	shoelace
+ make + er	shoemaker
+ string	shoestring
shoot	
+ s	shoots
+ ed	shot
+ ing	shooting*
+ er	shooter*
shop	
+ s	shops
+ ed	shopped
+ ing	shopping*
+ er	shopper*
+ keep + er	shopkeeper
+ lift	shoplift^
+ lift + er	shoplifter
+ talk	shoptalk
+ wear + en	shopworn
shore	
+ s	shores
+ ed	shored
+ ing	shoring*
short	
+ s	shorts
+ ed	shorted
+ ish	shortish
+ age	shortage*
+ en	shorten^
+ en + er	shortener*
+ ly	shortly
+ ness	shortness*

+ y	shorty*
+ bread	shortbread
+ cake	shortcake
+ change	shortchange^
+ change + er	shortchanger*
+ come + ing	shortcoming*
+ cut	shortcut*
+ fall	shortfall*
+ grass	shortgrass*
+ hair	shorthair*
+ hand	shorthand
+ hand + ed	shorthanded
+ hand + ed + ly	shorthandedly
+ horn	shorthorn*
+ list	shortlist
+ sight + ed	shortsighted
+ sight + ed + ly	shortsightedly
+ sight + ed + ness	shortsightedness*
+ stop	shortstop*
+ wave	shortwave*

shot

+ s	shots
+ gun	shotgun

should (2)

shoulder

+ s	shoulders
+ ed	shouldered
+ ing	shouldering*

shout

+ s	shouts
+ ed	shouted
+ ing	shouting*
+ er	shouter*

shovel

+ s	shovels
+ er	shoveler*
+ ed	shoveled
+ ing	shoveling*
+ ful	shovelful*

show

+ s	shows
+ ed	showed
+ en	shown
+ ing	showing*
+ y	showy
+ est	showiest
+ boat	showboat
+ case	showcase
+ down	showdown
+ man	showman
+ man + ship	showmanship
+ piece	showpiece
+ place	showplace
+ room	showroom
+ stop + er	showstopper

shower

+ s	showers
+ ed	showered
+ ing	showering*
+ y	showery

shrimp

+ s	shrimps
+ y	shrimpy
+ er	shrimper*

shrink (2)

+ s	shrinks
+ ed	shrank
+ ed	shrunk
+ en	shrunken
+ er	shrinker*
+ able	shrinkable*
+ age	shrinkage*

shut

+ s	shuts
+ ing	shutting*
+ er	shutter*
+ er + less	shutterless
+ er + bug	shutterbug
+ down	shutdown
+ off	shutoff
+ out	shutout

shy

+ er	shier
+ est	shiest
+ ly	shyly
+ ness	shyness*
+ s	shies
+ ed	shied
+ ing	shying*

sick

+ er	sicker
+ est	sickest
+ en	sicken^
+ ing + ly	sickeningly
+ y	sickie*
+ ish	sickish
+ ish + ly	sickishly
+ ish + ness	sickishness
+ ly	sickly
+ ly + er	sicklier
+ ly + est	sickliest
+ ly + ed	sicklied
+ ly + ness	sickliness
+ ness	sickness*
+ o	sicko*
+ bed	sickbed
+ room	sickroom

S

side

+ s	sides
+ ed	sided
+ ing	siding*
+ arm	sidearm
+ band	sideband
+ board	sideboard
+ car	sidecar
+ dress	sidedress
+ dress + ing	sidedressing
+ hill	sidehill
+ kick	sidekick
+ light	sidelight
+ line	sideline
+ line + er	sideliner
+ long	sidelong
+ man	sideman
+ piece	sidepiece
+ show	sideshow
+ slip	sideslip
+ spin	sidespin
+ split + ing	sidesplitting
+ step	sidestep
+ track	sidetrack
+ walk	sidewalk
+ wall	sidewall
+ ward	sideward
+ way	sideway
+ way + s	sideways
+ wind + er	sidewinder
+ wise	sidewise

sift

+ s	sifts
+ ed	sifted
+ ing	sifting
+ er	sifter*

sigh

+ s	sighs
+ ed	sighed
+ ing	sighing*
+ er	sigher*

sight

+ s	sights
+ ed	sighted
+ ing	sighting*
+ less	sightless
+ less + ly	sightlessly
+ less + ness	sightlessness*
+ ly	sightly
+ see	sightsee

sign

+ s	signs
+ ed	signed
+ ing	signing*
+ er	signer*
+ ory	signatory
+ ure	signature*
+ ify	signify*
+ ance	significance*
+ ance + y	significancy*
+ ant	signficant
+ ant + ly	significantly
+ tion	signification*
+ ive	significative*
+ ic	signific*
+ post	signpost

signal

+ s	signals
+ ed	signaled
+ ing	signaling*
+ er	signaler*
+ ize	signalize^
+ ize + tion	signalization*
+ ly	signally
+ man	signalman
+ ment	signalment*

silent

+ s	silents
+ ly	silently
+ ness	silentness
+ ence	silence^
+ er	silencer*

silly

+ s	sillies
+ er	sillier
+ est	silliest
+ ly	sillily
+ ness	silliness*

silver

+ s	silvers
+ ed	silvered
+ er	silverer*
+ ing	silvering*
+ y	silvery
+ ly	silverly
+ y + ness	silveriness
+ en	silvern
+ berry	silverberry
+ fish	silverfish
+ side	silverside*
+ ware	silverware
+ weed	silverweed

similar

+ ly	similarly
+ ity	similarity*

simple

+ er	simpler
+ est	simplest
+ ness	simpleness*
+ ly	simply

S

+ icity simplicity*
+ ify simplify^
+ ify + tion simplification*
+ ify + er simplifier*
+ ism simplism*
+ **ic** simplistic*
+ **ic** + ly simplistically
+ mind + ed simpleminded

simultaneous
+ ly simultaneously
+ ness simultaneousness*
+ ity simultaneity

sin
+ s sins
+ ed sinned
+ ing sinning*
+ er sinner*
+ ful sinful
+ ful + ly sinfully
+ ful + ness sinfulness*
+ less sinless
+ less + ly sinlessly
+ less + ness sinlessness*

since

sing
+ s sings
+ ed sang
+ en sung
+ ing singing*
+ er singer*
+ able singable*
+ song singsong

single
+ s singles
+ ed singled
+ ing singling*
+ ness singleness*
+ ly singly

sink (2)
+ s sinks
+ ed sank
+ en sunk
+ ed + en sunken
+ able sinkable*
+ age sinkage*
+ er sinker*
+ hole sinkhole

sip
+ s sips
+ ed sipped
+ ing sipping*
+ er sipper*

sir
+ s sirs

siren
+ s sirens

sister (2)
+ s sisters
+ ly sisterly
+ hood sisterhood*
- in - law sister-in-law

sit
+ s sits
+ ed sat
+ ing sitting*
+ er sitter*

site
+ s sites
+ ed sited
+ ing siting*

situate
+ s situates
+ ed situated
+ ing situating
+ tion situation*
+ al situational
+ ly situationally

size
+ s sizes
+ ed sized
+ ing sizing*
+ able sizable
+ ly sizably
+ ness sizableness

skate
+ s skates
+ ed skated
+ ing skating*
+ er skater*
+ board skateboard
+ board + er skateboarder
+ board + ing skateboarding

skeleton
+ s skeletons
+ al skeletal
+ ly skeletally
+ ize skeletonize^
+ ize + er skeletonizer*

skeptic
+ s skeptics
+ ism skepticism*
+ al skeptical*
+ ly skeptically

sketch
+ s sketches
+ ed sketched
+ ing sketching*
+ er sketcher*

S

+ y	sketchy
+ y + er	sketchier
+ y + est	sketchiest
+ ly	sketchily
+ ness	sketchiness*
+ book	sketchbook
+ pad	sketchpad
ski	
+ s	skis
+ ed	skied
+ ing	skiing*
+ er	skier*
skill	
+ s	skills
+ ful	skillful
+ ful + ly	skillfully
+ ful + ness	skillfulness*
+ less	skilless
+ less + ness	skillessness*
+ ed	skilled
skillet	
+ s	skillets
skin	
+ s	skins
+ ed	skinned
+ ing	skinning*
+ er	skinner*
+ ful	skinful
+ head	skinhead
+ tight	skintight
skinny	
+ er	skinnier
+ est	skinniest
skip	
+ s	skips
+ ed	skipped
+ ing	skipping
+ er	skipper*
+ able	skippable
skirt	
+ s	skirts
+ ed	skirted
+ ing	skirting*
+ er	skirter*
skull	
+ s	skulls
+ ed	skulled
+ cap	skullcap*
skunk	
+ s	skunks
+ ed	skunked
+ ing	skunking*
sky	
+ s	skies
+ ed	skyed
+ bear + en	skyborne
+ cap	skycap
+ dive	skydive*
+ dive + ing	skydiving
+ dive + ed	skydove
+ hook	skyhook
+ light	skylight
+ light + ed	skylighted
+ line	skyline
+ rocket	skyrocket
+ sail	skysail
+ walk	skywalk
+ ward	skyward
+ way	skyway
+ write	skywrite
+ write + er	skywriter
+ write + s	skywrites
+ write + en	skywritten
+ write + ed	skywrote
+ write + ing	skywriting
+ scrape + er	skyscraper
+ scrape + er + s	skyscrapers
slack	
+ s	slacks
+ ed	slacked
+ ing	slacking*
+ er	slacker*
+ ly	slackly
+ ness	slackness*
slang	
+ s	slangs
+ y	slangy
+ ly	slangily
+ ness	slangness
slap	
+ s	slaps
+ ed	slapped
+ ing	slapping
slave	
+ s	slaves
+ ed	slaved
+ ing	slaving*
+ er	slaver*
+ ery	slavery*
+ hold + er	slaveholder
sled	
+ s	sleds
+ ed	sledded
+ ing	sledding
+ er	sledder*
sleep	
+ s	sleeps
+ ed	slept
+ ing	sleeping*
+ like	sleeplike

S

+ er	sleeper*
+ less	sleepless
+ less + ly	sleeplessly
+ less + ness	sleeplessness*
+ y	sleepy*
+ y + er	sleepier
+ y + est	sleepiest
+ ly	sleepily
+ ness	sleepiness
+ walk	sleepwalk
+ walk + er	sleepwalker
+ wear	sleepwear
+ y + head	sleepyhead
sleeve	
+ s	sleeves
+ ed	sleeved
+ less	sleeveless
sleigh	
+ s	sleighs
+ ed	sleighed
+ ing	sleighing*
slice	
+ s	slices
+ ed	sliced
+ ing	slicing*
+ er	slicer*
slide	
+ s	slides
+ ed	slid
+ ing	sliding*
+ er	slider*
+ way	slideway
slight	
+ ly	slightly
+ ness	slightness*
+ s	slights
+ed	slighted
+ ing	slighting*
+ ing + ly	slightingly
+ er	slighter
+ est	slightest
slim	
+ ly	slimly
+ ness	slimness*
+ er	slimmer
+ est	slimmest
+ s	slims
+ ed	slimmed
+ ing	slimming*
slip	
+ s	slips
+ ed	slipped
+ er + y	slippery
+ er + ist	slipperiest
+ ing	slipping*
+ age	slippage*
+ y	slippy*
+ est	slippiest
+ y + er	slippier
+ case	slipcase
+ cover	slipcover
+ form	slipform
+ knot	slipknot
+ over	slipover
+ sole	slipsole
+ stick	slipstick
+ stream	slipstream
+ up	slipup
+ ware	slipware
+ way	slipway
slipper	
+ s	slippers
slop	
+ s	slops
+ ed	slopped
+ ing	slopping*
+ work	slopwork
+ y	sloppy
+ y + er	sloppier
+ y + est	sloppiest
+ **ly**	sloppily
+ **ness**	sloppiness*
slope	
+ s	slopes
+ ed	sloped
+ ing	sloping*
slow	
+ s	slows
+ ed	slowed
+ ing	slowing*
+ ish	slowish
+ er	slower
+ est	slowest
+ ly	slowly
+ ness	slowness*
slug	
+ s	slugs
+ ed	slugged
+ ing	slugging*
+ er	slugger*
+ ish	sluggish
+ ly	sluggishly
+ ness	sluggishness
small	
+ er	smaller
+ est	smallest
+ ish	smallish
+ ness	smallness

S

+ hold + er	smallholder
+ hold + ing	smallholding
+ mind + ed	smallminded
+ scale	smallscale
+ word	smallword
+ time	smalltime
smart	
+ s	smarts
+ ed	smarted
+ ing	smarting
+ en	smarten^
+ ness	smartness
+ ly	smartly
+ y	smartie
smell	
+ s	smells
+ ed	smelled
+ ing	smelling*
+ er	smeller*
+ y	smelly
+ y + er	smellier
+ est	smelliest
smile	
+ s	smiles
+ ed	smiled
+ ing	smiling*
+ less	smileless
smog	
+ s	smogs
+ less	smogless
+ y	smoggy
+ er	smoggier
+ est	smoggiest
smoke	
+ s	smokes
+ ed	smoked
+ ing	smoking
+ able	smokeable
+ less	smokeless
+ like	smokelike
+ er	smoker*
+ house	smokehouse
+ stack	smokestack
+ proof	smokeproof
+ y	smoky
+ y + ly	smokily
+ y + ness	smokiness
+ y + er	smokier
+ y + est	smokiest
smooth	
+ s	smoothes
+ ed	smoothed
+ ing	smoothing*
+ ly	smoothly
+ ness	smoothness*

+ en	smoothen*
+ en + ed	smoothened
+ en + ing	smoothening*
+ y	smoothie*
+ bore	smoothbore
snack	
+ s	snacks
+ ed	snacked
+ ing	snacking*
snag	
+ s	snags
+ ed	snagged
+ ing	snagging*
+ y	snaggy*
snail	
+ s	snails
+ like	snaillike
snake	
+ s	snakes
+ ed	snaked
+ ing	snaking*
+ like	snakelike
+ y	snaky*
+ ly	snakily
+ bird	snakebird
+ bite	snakebite
+ root	snakeroot
+ skin	snakeskin
+ weed	snakeweed
snap	
+ s	snaps
+ ed	snapped
+ ing	snapping*
+ er	snapper*
+ ly	snappily
+ ness	snappiness*
+ ish	snappish
+ ish + ly	snappishly
+ ish + ness	snappishness*
+ y	snappy*
+ y + er	snappier
+ est	snappiest
+ back	snapback
+ dragon	snapdragon
+ shoot + er	snapshooter
+ shoot	snapshot
snatch	
+ s	snatches
+ ed	snatched
+ ing	snatching
+ er	snatcher*
sneak	
+ s	sneaks
+ ed	sneaked
+ ing	sneaking

S

+ ing + ly	sneakingly
+ y	sneaky
+ y + er	sneakier
+ y + est	sneakiest
+ ly	sneakily
+ ness	sneakiness
sneaker	
+ s	sneakers
+ ed	sneakered
sneeze	
+ s	sneezes
+ ed	sneezed
+ ing	sneezing*
+ er	sneezer*
+ y	sneezy*
+ weed	sneezeweed
sniff	
+ s	sniffs
+ ed	sniffed
+ ing	sniffing*
+ er	sniffer*
+ ish	sniffish
+ ish + ly	sniffishly
+ ish + ness	sniffishness*
+ y	sniffy*
+ y + ly	sniffily
+ ness	sniffiness
snip	
+ s	snips
+ ed	snipped
+ ing	snipping*
+ er	snipper*
+ y	snippy*
+ y + er	snippier
+ y + est	snippiest
+ er + snap + er	snippersnapper
+ t	snippet*
+ t + y	snippety*
snob	
+ s	snobs
+ ery	snobbery*
+ ish	snobbish
+ ly	snobbishly
+ ness	snobbishness*
+ ism	snobbism*
+ y	snobby*
+ er	snobbier
+ est	snobbiest
snore	
+ s	snores
+ ed	snored
+ ing	snoring*
+ er	snorer*
snow	
+ s	snows
+ ed	snowed
+ ing	snowing
+ y	snowy
+ y + ly	snowily
+ ness	snowiness
+ y + er	snowier
+ est	snowiest
+ ball	snowball^
+ bank	snowbank
+ belt	snowbelt
+ berry	snowberry
+ bird	snowbird
+ blink	snowblink
+ blow + er	snowblower
+ bind + ed	snowbound
+ brush	snowbrush
+ cap	snowcap
+ drift	snowdrift
+ drop	snowdrop
+ fall	snowfall
+ field	snowfield
+ flake	snowflake
+ make + er	snowmaker
+ make + ing	snowmaking
+ man	snowman
+ melt	snowmelt
+ mobile	snowmobile^
+ pack	snowpack
+ plow	snowplow
+ shoe	snowshoe^
+ like	snowlike
+ storm	snowstorm
+ suit	snowsuit
so	
soap	
+ s	soaps
+ ed	soaped
+ ing	soaping*
+ er	soaper*
+ y	soapy*
+ y + er	soapier
+ est	soapiest
+ bark	soapbark
+ berry	soapberry
+ box	soapbox
+ stone	soapstone
soccer	
social	
+ s	socials
+ able	sociable*
+ able + ly	sociably
+ ism	socialism*
+ ist	socialist*
+ ic	socialistic*
+ ite	socialite*

S

+ ize	socialize^
+ tion	socialization*
+ er	socializer*
+ ly	socially
+ ness	sociableness*
+ able + ity	sociability*
+ ic + ly	socialistically
social work	
+ er	social worker*
society	
+ s	societies
+ al	societal
+ ly	societally
sock	
+ s	socks
+ ed	socked
+ ing	socking*
+ less	sockless*
socket	
+ s	sockets
+ ed	socketed
+ ing	socketing*
soda	
+ s	sodas
sofa	
+ s	sofas
soft	
+ ly	softly
+ ness	softness*
+ ish	softish
+ en	soften^
+ en + er	softener*
+ y	softy*
+ heart + ed	softhearted
+ heart + ed + ly	softheartedly
+ heart + ed + ness	softheartedness
+ head	softhead
+ cover	softcover
+ bind + ed	softbound
+ ball	softball
+ back	softback
+ ware	software
+ wood	softwood
soil	
+ s	soils
+ ed	soiled
+ ing	soiling*
+ age	soilage*
+ less	soilless*
+ ure	soilure*
solar	
+ ize	solarize^
+ tion	solarization*

sold	
solder	
+ s	solders
+ ed	soldered
+ ing	soldering*
+ ity	solderability*
+ er	solderer*
soldier	
+ s	soldiers
+ ed	soldiered
+ ing	soldiering*
+ ship	soldiership*
+ ly	soldierly
+ y	soldiery
sole	
+ s	soles
+ ed	soled
+ ing	soling*
+ ness	soleness*
+ ly	solely
solid	
+ ly	solidly
+ s	solids
+ ness	solidness*
+ ify	solidify^
+ tion	solidification*
+ ity	solidarity*
+ ist	solidarist*
+ ic	solidaristic*
+ ism	solidarism*
solution	
+ s	solutions
solve	
+ s	solves
+ ed	solved
+ ing	solving*
+ er	solver*
+ able	solvable*
some	
+ body	somebody
+ day	someday
+ deal	somedeal
+ how	somehow
+ one	someone
+ place	someplace
+ thing	something
+ time	sometime
+ time + s	sometimes
+ way	someway
+ what	somewhat
+ when	somewhen
+ where	somewhere
+ where + s	somewheres

S

somersault

+ s	somersaults
+ ed	somersaulted
+ ing	somersaulting*

son

+ s	sons
+ hood	sonhood*
+ y	sonny*

song

+ s	songs
+ like	songlike
+ ful	songful*
+ ful + ly	songfully
+ ful + ness	songfulness
+ less	songless
+ less + ly	songlessly
+ bird	songbird
+ book	songbook
+ write + er	songwriter
+ write + ing	songwriting

soon

+ er	sooner

sophisticate

+ s	sophisticates
+ ed	sophisticated
+ ly	sophisticatedly
+ ing	sophisticating*
+ tion	sophistication*

sophomore

+ s	sophomores
+ ic	sophomoric

sore

+ s	sores
+ ly	sorely
+ ness	soreness*
+ head	sorehead*
+ head + ed	soreheaded

sorry

+ er	sorrier
+ est	sorriest
+ ness	sorriness
+ ly	sorrily
+ w	sorrow*
+ w + er	sorrower
+ ful	sorrowful
+ ful + ly	sorrowfully
+ ful + ness	sorrowfulness*

sort

+ s	sorts
+ ed	sorted
+ ing	sorting*
+ er	sorter*
+ tion	sortition*

soul

+ s	souls
+ ed	souled
+ ful	soulful
+ ful + ly	soulfully
+ ful + ness	soulfulness*
+ less	soulless
+ less + ly	soullessly
+ less + ness	soullessness*

sound

+ s	sounds
+ ed	sounded
+ ing	sounding*
+ ly	soundly
+ ness	soundness*
+ able	soundable*
+ er	sounder*
+ less	soundless
+ less + ly	soundlessly
+ board	soundboard
+ box	soundbox
+ proof	soundproof
+ stage	soundstage

soup

+ s	soups
+ y	soupy
+ ed	souped
+ ing	souping*
+ er	soupier
+ est	soupiest
+ spoon	soupspoon

sour

+ s	sours
+ ed	soured
+ ing	souring*
+ ly	sourly
+ ness	sourness*
+ ish	sourish

source

+ s	sources
+ ed	sourced
+ ing	sourcing*
+ less	sourceless
+ book	sourcebook

south

+ bound	southbound
+ east	southeast
+ east + er	southeaster
+ east + er + ly	southeasterly
+ east + er + n	southeastern
+ east + er + n + more + est	southeasternmost
+ east + ward	southeastward
+ east + ward + s	southeastwards
+ er	souther
+ er + ly	southerly*
+ er + n	southern
+ **n** + more + est	southernmost

S

+ **n** + ness	southernness
+ **n** + er	Southerner
+ **n** + ism	Southernism
+ er + n + wood	southernwood
+ ing	southing
+ land	southland
+ paw	southpaw
+ ward	southward*
+ west	southwest
+ west + er	southwester
+ west + er + ly	southwesterly
+ west + er + n	southwestern
+ west + **n** + most	southwesternmost
+ west + **n** + er	southwesterner
+ west + ward	southwestward
+ west + ward + s	southwestwards

space

+ s	spaces
+ ed	spaced
+ ing	spacing*
+ er	spacer*
+ less	spaceless
+ ward	spaceward
+ al	spacial*
+ ous	spacious
+ ly	spaciously
+ ness	spaciousness
+ band	spaceband
+ craft	spacecraft
+ flight	spaceflight
+ man	spaceman
+ port	spaceport
+ ship	spaceship
+ woman	spacewoman

spaghetti

+ s	spaghettis
+ like	spaghettilike

Spain

+ ish	Spanish
+ ness	Spanishness
+ d	Spaniard

spank

+ s	spanks
+ ed	spanked
+ ing	spanking*
+ er	spanker*

spark

+ s	sparks
+ ed	sparked
+ ing	sparking*
+ er	sparker*
+ y	sparky
+ y + er	sparkier

sparkle

+ s	sparkles
+ ed	sparkled
+ er	sparkler*
+ ing	sparkling*

sparrow

+ s	sparrows
+ like	sparrowlike
+ grass	sparrowgrass

spatula

+ s	spatulas
+ ate	spatulate*

speak

+ s	speaks
+ ed	spoke
+ en	spoken
+ ing	speaking*
+ er	speaker*
+ ship	speakership
+ er + phone	speakerphone
+ ed + **man**	spokesman
+ ed + **woman**	spokeswoman
+ ed + **person**	spokesperson

spear

+ s	spears
+ ed	speared
+ ing	spearing*
+ er	spearer*
+ fish	spearfish
+ head	spearhead^
+ man	spearman

special

+ s	specials
+ ly	specially
+ ness	specialness*
+ ism	specialism*
+ ist	specialist*
+ ity	speciality*
+ ize	specialize^
+ tion	specialization*
+ t + y	specialty*

specific

+ s	specifics
+ ify	specify^
+ tion	specification*
+ ity	specificity*
+ er	specifier*
+ able	specifiable*

speech

+ s	speeches
+ ify	speechify^
+ less	speechless
+ less + ly	speechlessly
+ less + ness	speechlessness

S

speed	
+ s	speeds
+ ed	sped-or speeded
+ ing	speeding*
+ er	speeder*
+ y	speedy
+ y + er	speedier
+ est	speediest
+ o	speedo*
+ ball	speedball
+ boat	speedboat
+ light	speedlight
+ up	speedup
+ way	speedway
+ well	speedwell
spell	
+ s	spells
+ ed	spelled
+ ing	spelling*
+ er	speller*
+ bind	spellbind
+ bind + s	spellbinds
+ bind + ing	spellbinding
+ bind + ed	spellbound
spend	
+ s	spends
+ ed	spent
+ ing	spending*
+ able	spendable*
+ er	spender*
spice	
+ s	spices
+ ed	spiced
+ ing	spicing*
+ er	spicer*
+ ery	spicery*
+ ly	spicily
+ ness	spiciness
+ y	spicy
+ y + er	spicier
+ est	spiciest
+ bush	spicebush
spider	
+ s	spiders
+ y	spidery
+ web	spiderweb*
spill	
+ s	spills
+ ed	spilled
+ ing	spilling*
+ t	spilt
+ able	spillable*
+ er	spiller*
+ over	spillover
+ way	spillway

spin	
+ s	spins
+ ed	spun
+ ing	spinning*
+ er + s	spinners*
+ less	spinless
+ out	spinout
spinach	
spine	
+ s	spines
+ ed	spined
+ al	spinal*
+ ly	spinally
+ like	spinelike*
+ y	spiny*
+ er	spinier
+ est	spiniest
+ ness	spininess*
+ less	spineless
+ less + ly	spinelessly
+ less + ness	spinelessness*
spirit	
+ s	spirits
+ ed	spirited
+ ed + ly	spiritedly
+ ed + ness	spiritedness*
+ less	spiritless*
+ less + ly	spiritlessly
+ less + ness	spiritlessness*
+ ing	spiriting*
+ ism	spiritism*
+ ic	spiritistic*
+ al	spiritual*
+ al + ly	spiritually
+ al + ness	spiritualness
+ al + ism	spiritualism*
+ al + ist	spiritualist*
+ al + **ic**	spiritualistic*
+ ity	spirituality*
+ ize	spiritualize^
+ tion	spiritualization*
+ t + y	spiritualty
+ ous	spiritous-or-spirituous
spit	
+ s	spits
+ ed	spat
+ ing	spitting*
+ er	spitter*
+ fire	spitfire
spite	
+ s	spites
+ ed	spited
+ ing	spiting*
+ ful	spiteful

+ ful + ly spitefully
+ ful + ness spitefulness*

splash

+ s splashes
+ ed splashed
+ ing splashing*
+ er splasher*
+ y splashy*
+ y + er splashier
+ est splashiest
+ ly splashily
+ ness splashiness*
+ board splashboard
+ down splashdown

splice

+ s splices
+ ed spliced
+ ing splicing*
+ er splicer*

splinter

+ s splinters
+ ed splintered
+ ing splintering*
+ y splintery*

split

+ s splits
+ ing splitting

spoil

+ s spoils
+ ed spoiled
+ ing spoiling*
+ er spoiler*
+ age spoilage*
+ able spoilable*
+ s + man spoilsman

sponge

+ s sponges
+ ed sponged
+ ing sponging*
+ er sponger*
+ y spongy
+ ness sponginess*
+ y + er spongier
+ est spongiest

spook

+ s spooks
+ ed spooked
+ y spooky*
+ y + er spookier
+ est spookiest
+ ish spookish*
+ ery spookery*
+ ly spookily
+ ness spookiness*

spool

+ s spools
+ ed spooled
+ ing spooling*

spoon

+ s spoons
+ ed spooned
+ er spooner*
+ ing spooning*
+ ful spoonful*
+ y spoony
+ y + er spoonier
+ y + est spooniest

sport

+ s sports
+ ful sportful
+ ful + ly sportfully
+ ful + ness sportfulness*
+ ing sporting*
+ ing + ly sportingly
+ y sporty*
+ y + er sportier
+ est sportiest
+ ly sportily
+ ness sportiness*
+ ive sportive*
+ ive + ly sportively
+ ive + ness sportiveness
+ fish + er + man sportfisherman
+ fish + ing sportfishing
+ s + man sportsman
+ s + man + like sportsmanlike
+ s + man + ly sportsmanly
+ s + man + ship sportsmanship
+ s + wear sportswear
+ s + woman sportswoman
+ s + write + er sportswriter

spot

+ s spots
+ ed spotted
+ ing spotting*
+ able spotable*
+ less spotless
+ less + ly spotlessly
+ less + ness spotlessness*
+ er spotter*
+ y spotty*
+ y + er spottier
+ est spottiest
+ ly spottily
+ ness spottiness*
+ light spotlight

sprain

+ s sprains

S

+ ed	sprained
+ ing	spraining*
spray	
+ s	sprays
+ ed	sprayed
+ ing	spraying*
+ er	sprayer*
spread	
+ s	spreads
+ ing	spreading
+ er	spreader*
+ able	spreadable*
+ ity	spreadability
spring	
+ s	springs
+ ed	sprang
+ en	sprung
+ ing	springing*
+ er	springer*
+ y	springy
+ y + er	springier
+ est	springiest
+ ly	springily
+ ness	springiness*
+ board	springboard
+ head	springhead
+ house	springhouse
+ lock	springlock
+ tail	springtail
+ tide	springtide
+ time	springtime
+ water	springwater
+ wood	springwood
sprinkle	
+ s	sprinkles
+ ed	sprinkled
+ ing	sprinkling*
+ er	sprinkler*
+ er + ed	sprinklered
spurt	
+ s	spurts
+ ed	spurted
+ ing	spurting*
spy	
+ s	spies
+ ed	spied
+ ing	spying*
+ glass	spyglass
squad	
+ s	squads
+ ed	squadded
+ ing	squadding*
square	
+ s	squares
+ ed	squared

+ ing	squaring*
+ ly	squarely
+ ish	squarish
+ ish + ly	squarishly
+ ish + ness	squarishness*
squash	
+ s	squashes
+ ed	squashed
+ ing	squashing*
+ er	squasher*
+ y	squashy
+ y + er	squashier
+ est	squashiest
+ ly	squashily
+ ness	squashiness
squeal	
+ s	squeals
+ ed	squealed
+ ing	squealing*
+ er	squealer*
squeeze	
+ s	squeezes
+ ed	squeezed
+ ing	squeezing*
+ er	squeezer*
+ able	squeezable*
+ ity	squeezability*
squid	
+ s	squids
+ ed	squidded
+ ing	squidding*
squirm	
+ s	squirms
+ ed	squirmed
+ ing	squirming*
+ er	squirmer*
+ y	squirmy*
squirrel	
+ s	squirrels
+ ed	squirrelled
+ ing	squirrelling*
+ y	squirrelly*
stab	
+ s	stabs
+ ed	stabbed
+ ing	stabbing*
+ er	stabber*
stack	
+ s	stacks
+ ed	stacked
+ ing	stacking*
+ er	stacker*
+ able	stackable*
stadium	
+ s	stadiums

staff

+ s	staffs
+ ed	staffed
+ ing	staffing*
+ er	staffer*

stage

+ s	stages
+ ed	staged
+ ing	staging*
+ able	stageable*
+ ful	stageful*
+ er	stager*
+ ly	stagily
+ ness	staginess
+ y	stagey-or-stagy
+ y + er	stagier
+ est	stagiest
+ coach	stagecoach
+ craft	stagecraft
+ hand	stagehand
+ strike + ed	stagestruck

stain

+ s	stains
+ ed	stained
+ ing	staining*
+ able	stainable*
+ ity	stainability*
+ er	stainer*
+ -less	stainless
+ -less + ly	stainlessly

stair

+ s	stairs
+ case	staircase
+ way	stairway
+ well	stairwell

stale

+ s	stales
+ ed	staled
+ ing	staling*
+ er	staler*
+ est	stalest
+ y	staley*
+ ness	staleness*
+ mate	stalemate

stall

+ s	stalls
+ ed	stalled
+ ing	stalling

stamp

+ s	stamps
+ ed	stamped
+ ing	stamping
+ er	stamper
+ less	stampless

stand

+ s	stands
+ ed	stood
+ ing	standing*
+ er	stander*
+ ee	standee*
+ a + way	standaway
+ by	standby
+ by + s	standbys
+ off	standoff
+ off + ish	standoffish
+ off + ish + ly	standoffishly
+ off + ish + ness	standoffishness
+ pat	standpat
+ pipe	standpipe
+ point	standpoint
+ still	standstill

standard

+ s	standards
+ ize	standardize^
+ tion	standardization*
+ bear + er	standardbearer
+ bred	standardbred

staple

+ s	staples
+ ed	stapled
+ ing	stapling*
+ er	stapler*

star

+ s	stars
+ ed	starred
+ ing	starring*
+ y	starry
+ er	starrier
+ est	starriest
+ ness	starriness
+ less	starless
+ less + ness	starlessness
+ dom	stardom
+ ward	starward*
super +	superstar*
+ board	starboard
+ fish	starfish
+ flower	starflower
+ gaze	stargaze^
+ light	starlight
+ light + ed	starlit

stare

+ s	stares
+ ed	stared
+ ing	staring*
+ er	starer*

start

+ s	starts
+ ed	started

S

+ ing	starting*
+ er	starter*
startle	
+ s	startles
+ ed	startled
+ ing	startling*
+ ly	startlingly
+ ness	startlingness*
+ er	startler*
starve	
+ s	starves
+ ed	starved
+ ing	starving
+ tion	starvation*
+ ling	starveling*
state	
+ s	states
+ ed	stated
+ ed + ly	statedly
+ ing	stating*
+ ant	statant*
+ able	statable or stateable*
+ hood	statehood*
+ less	stateless
+ ly	stately
+ ness	stateliness
+ ment	statement*
+ ism	statism*
+ ist	statist*
+ ive	stative
+ er	stater*
+ or	stator*
+ craft	statecraft*
+ house	statehouse*
+ room	stateroom*
+ side	stateside
+ s + man	statesman
+ s + man + ly	statesmanly
+ s + man + like	statesmanlike
+ s + man + ship	statesmanship*
+ wide	statewide
+ s + woman	stateswoman
station	
+ s	stations
+ ed	stationed
+ ing	stationing
+ master	stationmaster
stationary	
stationery	
statistics	
+ al	statistical
+ ly	statistically
+ an	statistician*

statue	
+ s	statues
+ ary	statuary
stay	
+ s	stays
+ ed	stayed
+ ing	staying
+ er	stayer*
+ sail	staysail
stead	
+ s	steads
+ ed	steaded
+ ing	steading*
+ y	steady
+ er	steadier
+ est	steadiest
+ ly	steadily
+ ness	steadiness*
+ y + s	steadies
+ y + ed	steadied
+ y + ing	steadying*
+ fast	steadfast
+ fast + ly	steadfastly
+ fast + ness	steadfastness
steak	
+ s	steaks
steal	
+ s	steals
+ ed	stole
+ en	stolen
+ ing	stealing*
+ able	stealable*
+ er	stealer*
+ th	stealth*
+ y	stealthy
+ y + er	stealthier
+ est	stealthiest
+ y + ly	stealthily
+ ness	stealthiness*
steam	
+ s	steams
+ ed	steamed
+ ing	steaming*
+ er	steamer*
+ est	steamiest
+ y + er	steamier
+ y	steamy*
+ ly	steamily
+ ness	steaminess
+ boat	steamboat
+ fit + er	steamfitter
+ roll + er	steamroller
+ ship	steamship

steel	
+ s	steels
+ ed	steeled
+ ing	steeling
+ y	steely or steelie*
+ y + er	steelier
+ est	steeliest
+ ness	steeliness
+ head	steelhead
+ work	steelwork
+ work + er	steelworker
+ yard	steelyard
steep	
+ s	steeps
+ ed	steeped
+ ing	steeping*
+ ly	steeply
+ ness	steepness
+ er	steeper*
+ est	steepest
+ en	steepen*
+ en + ed	steepened
+ en + ing	steepening*
stegosaurus	
stem	
+ s	stems
+ ed	stemmed
+ ing	stemming
+ er	stemmer
+ less	stemless
+ y	stemmy
+ y + er	stemmier
+ est	stemmiest
+ ware	stemware
step	
+ s	steps
+ ed	stepped
+ ing	stepping*
+ er	stepper*
+ like	steplike
+ brother	stepbrother
+ child	stepchild
+ daughter	stepdaughter
+ father	stepfather
+ ladder	stepladder
+ mother	stepmother
+ parent	stepparent
+ sister	stepsister
+ son	stepson
+ wise	stepwise
stereo	
+ s	stereos
stethoscope	
+ s	stethoscopes
+ ic	stethoscopic

stew	
+ s	stews
+ ed	stewed
+ ing	stewing*
+ pan	stewpan
stick	
+ s	sticks
+ ed	stuck
+ ing	sticking
+ er	sticker
+ ful	stickful
+ ness	stickiness
+ y	sticky
+ y + er	stickier
+ est	stickiest
+ ly	stickily
+ ball	stickball
+ handle	stickhandle^
+ man	stickman
+ pin	stickpin
+ seed	stickseed
+ tight	sticktight
+ weed	stickweed
+ work	stickwork
still	
+ s	stills
+ ed	stilled
+ ing	stilling*
+ ness	stillness
+ y	stilly
+ birth	stillbirth
+ birth + en	stillborn
+ man	stillman
+ room	stillroom
stimulus	
+ ate	stimulate^
+ tion	stimulation*
+ or	stimulator*
+ ory	stimulatory
+ ant	stimulant*
sting	
+ s	stings
+ ed	stung
+ ing	stinging*
+ ly	stingingly
+ er	stinger*
+ less	stingless
stingy	
+ er	stingier
+ est	stingiest
+ ly	stingily
+ ness	stinginess
stink	
+ s	stinks
+ ed	stank

+ en	stunk
+ ing	stinking*
+ er	stinker*
+ y	stinky*
+ bug	stinkbug
+ horn	stinkhorn
+ pot	stinkpot
+ stone	stinkstone
+ weed	stinkweed
+ wood	stinkwood
stir	
+ s	stirs
+ ed	stirred
+ ing	stirring
+ er	stirrer*
+ about	stirabout
+ fry	stir-fry
stitch	
+ s	stitches
+ ed	stitched
+ ing	stitching*
+ er	stitcher*
+ ery	stitchery*
stock	
+ s	stocks
+ ed	stocked
+ ing	stocking*
+ er	stocker*
+ ish	stockish
+ ist	stockist*
+ y	stocky*
+ y + er	stockier
+ est	stockiest
+ ly	stockily
+ ness	stockiness*
+ breed + er	stockbreeder
+ fish	stockfish
+ hold + er	stockholder
+ keep + er	stockkeeper
+ man	stockman
+ pile	stockpile
+ pot	stockpot
+ proof	stockproof
+ room	stockroom
+ take + ing	stocktaking
+ yard	stockyard
stocking	
+ s	stockings
+ ed	stockinged
stole	
stomach	
+ s	stomachs
+ ed	stomached
+ ing	stomaching*

+ er	stomacher*
+ ic	stomachic*
+ al	stomachal*
+ ic + al	stomachical*
+ y	stomachy
+ ache	stomachache
+ ache + s	stomachaches
stone	
+ s	stones
+ ed	stoned
+ ing	stoning
+ er	stoner
+ y	stony
+ y + er	stonier
+ est	stoniest
+ ly	stonily
+ ness	stoniness
+ crop	stonecrop
+ cut + er	stonecutter*
+ fish	stonefish
+ wall	stonewall
+ wall + er	stonewaller
+ ware	stoneware
+ work	stonework
stop	
+ s	stops
+ ed	stopped
+ ing	stopping*
+ er	stopper*
+ able	stoppable*
+ age	stoppage*
+ light	stoplight
+ over	stopover
+ watch	stopwatch
store	
+ s	stores
+ ed	stored
+ ing	storing*
+ front	storefront
+ house	storehouse
+ keep + er	storekeeper
+ room	storeroom
+ ship	storeship
+ wide	storewide
storm	
+ s	storms
+ ed	stormed
+ ing	storming*
+ y	stormy
+ est	stormiest
+ er	stormier
+ ly	stormily
+ ness	storminess*

story	
+ s	stories
+ ed	storied
+ ing	storying*
+ board	storyboard
+ book	storybook
+ tell + er	storyteller
stove	
+ s	stoves
+ pipe	stovepipe
straddle	
+ s	straddles
+ ed	straddled
+ ing	straddling*
+ er	straddler*
straight	
+ er	straighter
+ est	straightest
+ ly	straightly
+ ness	straightness*
+ ish	straightish
+ en	straighten^
+ en + er	straightener*
+ a + way	straightaway
+ breed + ed	straightbred
+ edge	straightedge
+ for + ward	straightforward*
+ for + ward + ly	straightforwardly
+ for + ward + ness	straightforwardness
+ way	straightway
strange	
+ er	stranger*
+ est	strangest
+ ly	strangely
+ ness	strangeness*
straw	
+ s	straws
+ y	strawy
+ flower	strawflower
+ hat	strawhat
strawberry (2)	
+ s	strawberries
stray	
+ s	strays
+ ed	strayed
+ ing	straying
+ er	strayer*
stream	
+ s	streams
+ ed	streamed
+ ing	streaming
+ er	streamer*
+ bed	streambed
+ line	streamline^
+ line + er	streamliner
+ side	streamside
street	
+ s	streets
+ car	streetcar
+ light	streetlight
+ walk + er	streetwalker
+ wise	streetwise
strength	
+ en	strengthen^
stress	
+ s	stresses
+ ed	stressed
+ ing	stressing
+ or	stressor*
+ ful	stressful
+ ful + ly	stressfully
+ ful + ness	stressfulness*
+ less	stressless
+ less + ly	stresslessly
+ less + ness	stresslessness*
stretch	
+ s	stretches
+ ed	stretched
+ ing	stretching*
+ able	stretchable*
+ ity	stretchability*
strict	
+ ly	strictly
+ ness	strictness*
+ ure	stricture*
strike	
+ s	strikes
+ ed	struck
+ en	stricken
+ ing	striking*
+ ing + ly	strikingly
+ er	striker*
+ bound	strikebound
+ break + er	strikebreaker
+ out	strikeout
+ over	strikeover*
string	
+ s	strings
+ ed	strung
+ ing	stringing*
+ less	stringless
+ er	stringer*
+ y	stringy*
+ y + er	stringier
+ est	stringiest
+ board	stringboard
+ course	stringcourse
+ piece	stringpiece

strip

+ s	strips
+ ed	stripped
+ ing	stripping*
+ er	stripper*
+ able	strippable*
+ tease	striptease
film +	filmstrip

stripe

+ s	stripes
+ ed	striped
+ ing	striping*
+ less	stripeless
+ er	striper*
+ est	stripiest
+ y	stripy*
+ y + er	stripier

strive

+ s	strives
+ ed	strove
+ en	striven
+ ing	striving*
+ er	striver*

stroke

+ s	strokes
+ ed	stroked
+ ing	stroking
+ er	stroker*

strong

+ er	stronger
+ est	stongest
+ ish	strongish
+ ly	strongly
+ th	strength*
+ box	strongbox
+ hold	stronghold
+ man	strongman

structure

+ s	structures
+ ed	structured
+ ing	structuring*
+ al	structural*
+ ly	structurally
+ ism	structuralism*
+ ist	structuralist*
+ ize	structuralize^
+ less	structureless
+ less + ness	structurelessness*

struggle

+ s	struggles
+ ed	struggled
+ ing	struggling
+ er	struggle*

stubborn

+ ly	stubbornly
+ ness	stubbornness*

study

+ s	studies
+ ed	studied
+ ing	studying*
+ ed + ness	studiedness*
+ ed + ly	studiedly
+ ous	studious
+ ous + ly	studiously
+ ous + ness	studiousness*
+ ent	student
+ ent + s	students
+ ent + ship	studentship*

stuff

+ s	stuffs
+ ed	stuffed
+ ing	stuffing*
+ er	stuffer*
+ y	stuffy*
+ y + er	stuffier
+ est	stuffiest
+ ly	stuffily
+ ness	stuffiness

stump

+ age	stumpage*
+ y	stumpy*
+ s	stumps
+ ed	stumped
+ ing	stumping*

stung

stupid

+ ly	stupidly
+ ness	stupidness*
+ ity	stupidity*

style

+ s	styles
+ ed	styled
+ ing	styling*
+ ish	stylish
+ ish + ly	stylishly
+ ish + ness	stylishness*
+ **ic**	stylistic*
+ **ic** + ly	stylistically
+ er	styler*
+ ist	stylist*
+ less	styleless
+ less + ness	stylelessness*
+ ize	stylize^
+ ize + **tion**	stylization*

S

sub (prefix)

To see the way to form words with the prefix shown here, refer to the section showing the root word involved.

subacute
subacutely
subadolescent
subaerial
subalternate
subalternately
subarea
subassembly
subatmospheric
subatomic
subaverage
subbase
subbasement
subblock
subbranch
subcabinet
subcategorization
subcategorize
subcategory
subceiling
subcellar
subcellular
subcenter
subcentral
subcentrally
subchapter
subchaser
subchief
subclass
subclassification
subclimax
subclinical
subclinically
subcluster
subcode
subcollection
subcollege
subcollegiate
subcolony
subcommission
subcommittee
subcommunity
subcompact
subcomponent
subcondensation
subconscious
subconsciously
subconsciousness
subcontinent
subcontinental
subcontract
subcontractor
subcool
subcounty
subcritical
subcrustal
subcultural
subculturally
subculture
subcurative
subdecision
subdepartment
subdevelopment
subdialect
subdirector
subdistrict
subdividable
subdivide
subdivider
subdivision
subdivisions
subdominant
subeconomic
subeconomy
subedit
subeditor
subeditorial
subemployed
subemployment
subentry
suberect
subfamily
subfield
subfile
subfix
subfossil
subframe
subfreezing
subgeneration
subgoal
subgovernment
subgrade
subgroup
subhuman
subhumid
subimprint
subindustry
subinterval
subirrigation
subjoin
subkingdom
sublanguage
sublet
sublets
subletting
sublevel
sublibrarian

S

sublicense
subline
sublingual
subliterary
subliterate
subliterature
sublot
submachine gun
submanager
submarginal
submarginally
submarket
submicroscopically
submicroscopic
submillimeter
subminiature
subminimal
subminimum
subminister
submultiple
subnational
subnetwork
subnormal
subnormality
subnormally
subnuclear
suboceanic
suborder
suborganization
subpanel
subparagraph
subparallel
subpart
subpolar
subpolitical
subpopulation
subprincipal
subproblem
subprocess
subproduct
subprofessional
subprogram
subproject
subregion
subring
subsample
subsatellite
subscale
subscience
subsea
subsecretary
subsection
subsector
subsense

subsentence
subseries
subset
subsite
subsocial
subsociety
subsoil
subspace
subspecialist
subspecialize
subspecialty
subspecific
substandard
substate
substation
substructure
subsurface
subsystem
subtask
subteen
subtemperate
subtest
subtheme
subtherapeutic
subtitle
subtopic
subtotal
subtreasury
subtribe
subunit
subvariety
subverbal
subviral
subvisible
subvisual
subvocal
subvocalization
subvocalize
subvocalized
subvocalizes
subvocalizing
subvocally
subwriter
subzero
subzone

subject

+ s	subjects
+ ed	subjected
+ ing	subjecting*
+ ion	subjection*
+ ify	subjectify
+ ify + **tion**	subjectification
+ less	subjectless

S

+ ive	subjective*
+ ly	subjectively
+ ness	subjectiveness*
+ ity	subjectivity*
+ ism	subjectivism*
+ ist	subjectivist*
+ ic	subjectivistic*
+ ize	subjectivize^
+ ize + tion	subjectization*
submarine	
+ s	submarines
+ ed	submarined
+ ing	submarining*
+ er	submariner*
subscribe	
+ s	subscribes
+ ed	subscribed
+ ing	subscribing*
+ ion	subscription*
+ t	subscript*
substance	
+ s	substances
+ less	substanceless
+ al	substantial
+ al + ly	substantially
+ ity	substantiality*
+ al + ness	substantialness*
+ ive	substantive*
+ ive + ly	substantively
+ ive + ness	substantiveness*
+ ize	substantivize^
+ ive + al	substantival
+ ive + ly	substantivally
+ ate	substantiate^
+ tion	substantiation*
+ ate + ive	substantiative*
substitute	
+ s	substitutes
+ ed	substituted
+ ing	substituting*
+ ion	substitution*
+ al	substitutional*
+ ly	substitutionally
+ ary	substitutionary*
subtle	
+ er	subtler
+ est	subtlest
+ ness	subtleness*
+ ly	subtly
+ t + y	subtilty or subtlety*
subtract	
+ s	subtracts
+ ed	subtracted
+ ing	subtracting*
+ ion	subtraction*
+ or	subtractor*
+ ive	subtractive*
subway (2)	
+ s	subways
+ ed	subwayed
+ ing	subwaying*
succeed	
+ s	succeeds
+ ed	succeeded
+ ing	succeeding*
+ er	succeeder*
success	
+ s	successes
+ ful	successful
+ ful + ly	successfully
+ ful + ness	successfulness*
+ ion	succession*
+ ion + al	successional*
+ ion **+ ly**	successionally
+ or	successor*
+ ive	successive*
+ ive + ly	successively
+ ive + ness	successiveness*
such	
+ like	suchlike
suck	
+ s	sucks
+ ed	sucked
+ ing	sucking*
+ er	sucker^
sucker	
+ s	suckers
sudden	
+ ly	suddenly
+ ness	suddenness
suffer	
+ s	suffers
+ ed	suffered
+ ing	suffering*
+ er	sufferer*
+ ance	sufferance*
+ ness	sufferableness
+ ly	sufferably
+ able	sufferable*
suffix	
+ s	suffixes
+ ed	suffixed
+ ing	suffixing*
+ tion	suffixation*
+ al	suffixal*
sugar	
+ s	sugars
+ ed	sugared

S

+ ing	sugaring*
+ y	sugary
+ berry	sugarberry
+ cane	sugarcane
+ house	sugarhouse
+ plum	sugarplum
suggest	
+ s	suggests
+ ed	suggested
+ ing	suggesting*
+ er	suggester*
+ ion	suggestion*
+ ible	suggestible*
+ ity	suggestibility*
+ ive	suggestive*
+ ive + ly	suggestively
+ ness	suggestiveness*
suicide	
+ s	suicides
+ ed	suicided
+ ing	suiciding*
+ al	suicidal*
+ ly	suicidally
suit	
+ s	suits
+ ed	suited
+ ing	suiting*
+ or	suitor*
+ er	suiter*
+ e	suite*
sum	
+ s	sums
+ ed	summed
+ ing	summing*
+ able	summable*
+ ity	summability*
+ tion	summation*
+ al	summational*
+ ive	summative*
summary	
+ s	summaries
+ ize	summarize^
+ tion	summarization
+ ly	summarily
summer	
+ s	summers
+ ed	summered
+ ing	summering*
+ y	summery
+ time	summertime
summon	
+ s	summons
+ s + s	summonses
+ ed	summoned
+ ing	summoning*
+ er	summoner*
sun	
+ s	suns
+ ed	sunned
+ ing	sunning*
+ -less	sunless
+ y	sunny
+ est	sunniest
+ er	sunnier
+ bake + ed	sunbaked
+ bath	sunbath
+ bath + ed	sunbathed
+ beam	sunbeam
+ belt	sunbelt
+ bird	sunbird
+ bonnet	sunbonnet
+ bow	sunbow
+ burn	sunburn^
+ dew	sundew
+ down	sundown
+ down + er	sundowner
+ dress	sundress
+ drop + s	sundrops
+ fast	sunfast
+ fish	sunfish
+ flower	sunflower
+ lamp	sunlamp
+ light + ed	sunlit
+ light	sunlight
+ rise	sunrise
+ roof	sunroof
+ screen	sunscreen
+ seek + er	sunseeker
+ set	sunset
+ shade	sunshade
+ shine	sunshine
+ spot	sunspot
+ strike + ed	sunstroke
+ strike + en	sunstruck
+ suit	sunsuit
+ tan	suntan
+ up	sunup
+ ward	sunward
sundae	
+ s	sundaes
Sunday	
+ s	Sundays
sunrise	
+s	sunrises
sunset	
+ s	sunsets
super	
+ able + ly	superably

+ able + ness superableness
+ able superable

super (prefix)

To see the way to form words with the prefix shown here, refer to the section showing the root word involved.

superachiever
superactivity
superadd
superaddition
superambitious
superathlete
superbad
superbank
superbear
superblack
superblock
superboard
superbomb
superbomber
superbright
supercabinet
supercalendar
supercar
supercargo
supercarrier
supercautious
supercenter
supercharge
supercharger
superchip
superchurch
supercity
supercivilization
supercivilized
superclass
superclean
superclub
supercomfortable
supercompetitive
superconduct
superconductive
superconductivity
superconductor
superconfident
superconservative
supercontinent
superconvenient
supercool
supercop
supercountry
supercriminal
supercurrent
supercute
superdominant
supereffective
superelevate
superelevation
superexpress
superfamily
superfan
superfast
superfine
superfirm
superfix
superfluid
superfluidity
supergalaxy
supergene
supergiant
supergood
supergovernment
supergraphics
supergroup
supergrowth
superheat
superheater
superhero
superheroine
superhigh frequency
superhighway
superhit
superhuman
superhumanly
superhumanness
superindividual
superinfect
superinfection
superintellectual
superintelligence
superintelligent
superintend
superintensity
superlarge
superlife
superlight
superliner
superluxurious
superluxury
supermale
superman
supermarket
supermasculine
supermilitant
supermind
superminister
supermodel
supermodern
supermom
supernation

S

supernational
supernatural
supernaturalism
supernaturalist
supernaturalistic
supernaturally
supernaturalness
supernature
supernormal
supernumerary
supernumeries
supernutrition
superorder
superparcisitism
superpark
superperson
superphysical
superplane
superplastic
superplasticity
superplayer
superpolite
superport
superpower
superpowered
superpowerful
superpowers
superprize
superpro
superprofessional
superquality
superrace
superreal
superrealism
superregional
superrich
superroad
superromantic
superromanticism
supersafe
supersalesman
superscale
superschool
superscout
superscript
superscription
supersecrecy
supersecret
supersell
superseller
supersensible
supersensitive
supersensitively
supersensitiveness
supersensitivity
supersensory
superserviceable
supersexuality
supersharp
supershow
supersinger
supersize
supersized
supersmooth
supersoft
supersonic
supersonically
supersonics
supersophisticated
superspecial
superspecialist
superspecialization
superspecialized
superspokesman
superspy
superstar
superstardom
superstate
superstation
superstimulate
superstock
superstore
superstraight
superstrength
superstrike
superstrong
supersubstantial
supersubtle
supersubtlety
supersurgeon
supersystem
supertanker
supertax
superterrific
superthick
superthin
superthriller
supertight
supertrick
superwave
superweapon
superwide
superwife
superwoman

superintendent

+ s	superintendents
+ ence	superintendence
+ y	superintendency

S

superman
superstition

+ s	superstitions
+ ous	superstitious
+ ly	superstitiously

supervise

+ s	supervises
+ ed	supervised
+ ing	supervising*
+ ion	supervision*
+ or	supervisor*
+ ory	supervisory*

supper

+ s	suppers

supplement

+ s	supplements
+ ed	supplemented
+ ing	supplementing*
+ tion	supplementation*
+ al	supplemental*
+ ary	supplementary*

supply

+ s	supplies
+ ed	supplied
+ ing	supplying*
+ er	supplier*

support

+ s	supports
+ ed	supported
+ ing	supporting*
+ er	supporter*
+ able	supportable*
+ ity	supportability*
+ ive	supportive
+ ness	supportiveness*

suppose

+ s	supposes
+ ed	supposed
+ ing	supposing*
+ able	supposable*
+ able + ly	supposably
+ ed + ly	supposedly
+ tion	supposition*
+ al	suppositional*
+ ous	suppositious
+ ite + ous	supposititious

suppress

+ s	suppresses
+ ed	suppressed
+ ing	suppressing*
+ ant	suppressant*
+ ible	suppressible*
+ ity	suppressibility*
+ ive	suppressive*
+ ness	suppressiveness*
+ ion	suppression*
+ or	suppressor*

sure

+ er	surer
+ est	surest
+ ness	sureness*
+ ly	surely
+ t + y	surety*
+ ship	suretyship
+ fire	surefire
+ foot + ed	surefooted
+ foot + ly	surefootly
+ foot + ed + ness	surefootedness

surface

+ s	surfaces
+ ed	surfaced
+ ing	surfacing*
+ er	surfacer*

surgery

+ s	surgeries
+ an	surgeon*
+ al	surgical*
+ ly	surgically

surprise

+ s	surprises
+ ed	surprised
+ ing	surprising*
+ ly	surprisingly
+ al	surprisal*
+ er	surpriser*

surrender

+ s	surrenders
+ ed	surrendered
+ ing	surrendering*

surround

+ s	surrounds
+ ed	surrounded
+ ing	surrounding*

survive

+ s	survives
+ ed	survived
+ ing	surviving*
+ or	survivor*
+ al	survival*
+ ist	survivalist*
+ able	survivable*
+ ity	survivability*
+ ship	survivorship*

suspect

+ s	suspects
+ ed	suspected
+ ing	suspecting*
+ ion	suspicion^

+ ous	suspicious
+ ly	suspiciously
+ ness	suspiciousness*
suspend	
+ s	suspends
+ ed	suspended
+ ing	suspending*
+ sion	suspension*
+ ive	suspensive*
+ ly	suspensively
+ or	suspensor*
+ ory	suspensory*
+ er	suspender*
+ ence	suspense
+ ence + ful	suspenseful*
+ er + s	suspenders
swallow	
+ s	swallows
+ ed	swallowed
+ ing	swallowing*
+ able	swallowable*
+ er	swallower*
swam	
swan	
+ s	swans
+ ed	swanned
+ ing	swanning*
+ ery	swannery*
sway	
+ s	sways
+ ed	swayed
+ ing	swaying*
+ er	swayer*
+ back	swayback
+ back + ed	swaybacked
sweat	
+ s	sweats
+ ed	sweated
+ ing	sweating
+ y	sweaty
+ y + er	sweatier
+ est	sweatiest
+ ly	sweatily
+ ness	sweatiness
+ band	sweatband
+ box	sweatbox
+ pant + s	sweatpants
+ shirt	sweatshirt*
+ shop	sweatshop*
sweater	
+ s	sweaters
Swede	
+ s	Swedes
Sweden	
+ ish	Swedish

sweep	
+ s	sweeps
+ ed	swept
+ ing	sweeping*
+ er	sweeper*
+ y	sweepy
+ y + er	sweepier
+ est	sweepiest
+ back	sweepback
+ ed + back	sweptback
sweet	
+ s	sweets
+ en	sweeten^
+ y	sweetie*
+ ly	sweetly
+ ness	sweetness*
+ ing	sweetening*
+ ish	sweetish
+ ish + ly	sweetishly
+ meat	sweetmeat*
+ shop	sweetshop
sweetheart	
swell	
+ s	swells
+ en	swollen
+ ed	swelled
+ ing	swelling*
+ head	swellhead
+ head + ed	swellheaded
swift	
+ s	swifts
+ ly	swiftly
+ ness	swiftness
swim	
+ s	swims
+ ed	swam
+ en	swum
+ ing	swimming*
+ er	swimmer*
+ able	swimmable*
+ ing + ly	swimmingly
+ y	swimmy*
+ y + er	swimmier
+ y + est	swimmiest
+ ly	swimmily
+ suit	swimsuit
swing	
+ s	swings
+ ed	swinged or swang
+ en	swung
+ ing	swinging
+ er	swinger*
+ ing + ly	swingingly
+ able	swingable*

+ able + ly	swingably
+ ly	swingly
+ y + er	swingier
+ y	swingy*
swipe	
+ s	swipes
+ ed	swiped
+ ing	swiping*
side +	sideswipe
switch	
+ s	switches
+ ed	switched
+ ing	switching*
+ er	switcher*
+ able	switchable
+ back	switchback
+ blade	switchblade
+ board	switchboard
+ man	switchman
+ yard	switchyard
swollen	
sword	
+ s	swords
+ like	swordlike
+ s + man	swordsman
+ s + man + ship	swordsmanship
+ fish	swordfish
+ play	swordplay
+ play + er	swordplayer
+ tail	swordtail
syllable	
+ s	syllables
+ ic	syllabic*
+ ly	syllabically
+ ary	syllabary*
+ **ic** + tion	syllabification*
+ ed	syllabled
+ ing	syllabling*
+ ate	syllabicate^
+ ify	syllabify^
symbol	
+ s	symbols
+ ize	symbolize^
+ ize + tion	symbolization*
+ ism	symbolism*
+ ist	symbolist*
+ ist + ic	symbolistic*
+ ed	symboled
+ ing	symboling*
+ ic	symbolic*
+ ly	symbolically
sympathy	
+ s	sympathies
+ ic	sympathetic*
+ ly	sympathetically
+ ize	sympathize^
+ ize + er	sympathizer*
symptom	
+ s	symptoms
+ ic	symptomatic*
+ ly	symptomatically
+ less	symptomless
synagogue	
+ s	synagogues
+ al	synagogal
synonym	
+ s	synonyms
+ ic	synonymic*
+ al	synonymical*
+ ity	synonymity*
+ ist	synonymist*
+ ize	synonymize^
+ y	synonymy*
+ ous	synonymous*
+ ous + ly	synonymously
snytax	
+ ic	snytactic*
syrup	
+ s	syrups
+ y	syrupy
system (2)	
+ s	systems
+ less	systemless
+ ic	systemic
+ ly	systemically
+ ate + ic	systematic
+ ate **+ al**	systematical*
+ ate **+ ly**	systematically
+ ic + ness	systematicness
+ ism	systematism
+ ist	systematist
+ ate + ize	systematize^
+ ate + ize + tion	systematization
+ ate + ize + er	systematizer
+ ize	systemize^
+ ize + tion	systemization

S

table

+ s	tables
+ ed	tabled
+ ing	tabling*
+ ful	tableful*
+ t	tablet*
+ ure	tablature*
+ cloth	tablecloth
+ land	tableland
+ mate	tablemate
+ spoon	tablespoon
+ spoon + ful	tablespoonful
+ top	tabletop
+ ware	tableware

tack

+ s	tacks
+ ed	tacked
+ ing	tacking*
+ er	tacker*
+ ify	tackify^
+ ify + er	tackifier*
+ y	tacky*
+ ly	tackily
+ ness	tackiness*
+ y + er	tackier
+ est	tackiest
+ board	tackboard

tackle

+ s	tackles
+ ed	tackled
+ ing	tackling*
+ er	tackler*

taco

+ s	tacos

tag

+ s	tags
+ ed	tagged
+ ing	tagging*
+ along	tagalong
+ board	tagboard

tail

+ s	tails
+ ed	tailed
+ ing	tailing*
+ er	tailer*
+ back	tailback
+ board	tailboard
+ bone	tailbone
+ coat	tailcoat
+ coat + ed	tailcoated
+ gate	tailgate^
+ light	taillight
+ piece	tailpiece
+ race	tailrace
+ spin	tailspin
+ water	tailwater

tailor

+ s	tailors
+ ed	tailored
+ ing	tailoring*

take

+ s	takes
+ ed	took
+ en	taken
+ ing	taking*
+ er	taker*
+ down	takedown
+ off	takeoff
+ over	takeover

tale

+ s	tales
+ bear + er	talebearer
+ bear + ing	talebearing

talent

+ s	talents
+ ed	talented
+ less	talentless

talk

+ s	talks
+ ed	talked
+ ing	talking*
+ er	talker*
+ ive	talkative*
+ ly	talkatively
+ ness	talkativeness*
+ y	talkie* or talky*

tall

+ er	taller

+ est	tallest
+ ness	tallness*
+ ish	tallish
+ boy	tallboy
tambourine	
+ s	tambourines
tame	
+ s	tames
+ ed	tamed
+ ing	taming*
+ er	tamer*
+ est	tamest
+ ly	tamely
+ ness	tameness*
+ able	tameable*
+ less	tameless
tan	
+ s	tans
+ ed	tanned
+ ing	tanning*
+ er	tanner*
+ est	tannest
+ er + y	tannery*
+ ish	tannish
+ age	tannage*
+ ic	tannic
+ yard	tanyard
tangerine	
+ s	tangerines
tank	
+ s	tanks
+ ed	tanked
+ ing	tanking*
+ er	tanker*
+ age	tankage*
tantrum (2)	
+ s	tantrums
tap	
+ s	taps
+ ed	tapped
+ ing	tapping*
+ er	tapper*
tape	
+ s	tapes
+ ed	taped
+ ing	taping*
tar	
+ s	tars
+ ed	tarred
+ ing	tarring*
tarantula	
+ s	tarantulas
+ e	tarantulae
tardy	
+ s	tardies
+ ly	tardily
+ ness	tardiness*
+ er	tardier
+ est	tardiest
target	
+ s	targets
+ ed	targeted
+ ing	targeting*
+ able	targetable*
tart	
+ s	tarts
+ ish	tartish
+ ly	tartly
task	
+ s	tasks
+ ed	tasked
+ ing	tasking*
+ master	taskmaster*
taste	
+ s	tastes
+ ed	tasted
+ ing	tasting*
+ ful	tasteful
+ ful + ly	tastefully
+ ful + ness	tastefulness*
+ less	tasteless
+ less + ly	tastelessly
+ less + ness	tastelessness*
+ er	taster*
+ y	tasty
+ y + er	tastier
+ est	tastiest
+ ly	tastily
+ y + ness	tastiness
+ make + er	tastemaker
tattle	
+ s	tattles
+ ed	tattled
+ ing	tattling*
+ er	tattler*
+ tale	tattletale*
taught	
tax	
+ s	taxes
+ ed	taxed
+ ing	taxing*
+ able	taxable*
+ er	taxer*
+ tion	taxation*
+ pay + er	taxpayer
+ pay + er + s	taxpayers
+ pay + ing	taxpaying
+ ly	taxingly

taxi	
+ s	taxis
+ ed	taxied
+ ing	taxiing*
+ man	taximan
tea	
+ s	teas
+ like	tealike
+ cup	teacup
+ spoon	teaspoon
+ spoon + ful	teaspoonful
+ house	teahouse
+ time	teatime
+ room	tearoom
+ pot	teapot
teach	
+ s	teaches
+ ed	taught
+ ing	teaching*
+ er	teacher*
+ able	teachable*
+ ly	teachably
+ ness	teachableness*
team	
+ s	teams
+ ed	teamed
+ ing	teaming*
+ mate	teammate*
+ work	teamwork
tear (rip)	
+ s	tears
+ ed	tore
+ en	torn
+ ing	tearing*
+ down	teardown
tear (cry)	
+ s	tears
+ y	teary*
+ y + er	tearier
+ ful	tearful
+ ful + ly	tearfully
+ ful +ness	tearfulness*
+ drop	teardrop
+ stain	tearstain
+ stain + ed	tearstained
tease	
+ s	teases
+ ed	teased
+ ing	teasing*
+ ly	teasingly
+ er	teaser*
technical	
+ ly	technically
+ ity	technicality*
+ ize	technicalize^
+ ize + tion	technicalization*
+ an	technician*
technology	
+ s	technologies
+ al	technological*
+ ly	technologically
+ ize	technologize^
teddy bear	
+ s	teddy bears
teen	
+ s	teens
+ er	teener*
+ th	teenth
+ age	teenage
+ age + d	teenaged
+ age + er	teenager
teeter totter	
+ s	teeter totters
teeth	
+ e	teethe*
+ ing	teething*
telegram	
+ s	telegrams
+ ed	telegrammed
+ ing	telegramming*
telegraph	
+ s	telegraphs
+ ed	telegraphed
+ ing	telegraphing*
+ er	telegrapher*
+ y	telegraphy*
+ ic	telegraphic*
+ ic + **ly**	telegraphically
+ ist	telegraphist*
+ ese	telegraphese
telephone	
+ s	telephones
+ ed	telelphoned
+ ing	telephoning*
+ er	telephoner*
+ ic	telephonic*
+ ist	telephonist*
+ y	telephony*
telescope	
+ s	telescopes
+ ing	telescoping*
+ ed	telescoped
+ ic	telescopic*
+ ly	telescopically
television	
+ s	televisions
+ ize	televise^

+ or	televisor*
+ al	televisual*
tell	
+ s	tells
+ ed	told
+ ing	telling*
+ er	teller*
+ ing + ly	tellingly
+ tale	telltale*
temper	
+ s	tempers
+ ed	tempered
+ ing	tempering*
+ ment	temperament*
+ ment + al	temperamental*
+ ment **+ ly**	temperamentally
+ ure	temperature*
+ ate	temperate*
+ ate + ly	temperately
+ ness	temperateness*
+ er	temperer*
+ ance	temperance*
temple	
+ s	temples
+ ed	templed
temporary	
+ s	temporaries
+ ly	temporarily
+ ness	temporariness*
tempt	
+ s	tempts
+ ed	tempted
+ ing	tempting*
+ ly	temptingly
+ able	temptable*
+ tion	temptation*
+ er	tempter*
+ ess	temptress*
tend	
+ s	tends
+ ing	tending
+ ed	tended
+ ous	tendentious
+ ous + ly	tendentiously
+ ous + ness	tendentiousness
+ ance	tendance
+ y	tendency*
tent	
+ s	tents
+ ed	tented
+ ing	tenting*
+ age	tentage*
+ er	tenter*
tepee	
+ s	tepees
term	
+ s	terms
+ ed	termed
+ ing	terming*
+ er	termer*
+ al	terminal*
+ ly	terminally
+ ate	terminate^
+ able	terminable*
+ able + ness	terminableness*
+ able + y	terminably
+ tion	termination*
+ tion + al	terminational*
+ ive	terminative*
+ ive + ly	terminatively
+ ate + or	terminator*
+ less	termless
termite	
+ s	termites
terrible	
+ y	terribly
+ ness	terribleness*
terrific	
+ ly	terrifically
territory	
+ s	territories
+ al	territorial*
+ ly	territorially
+ ity	territoriality*
+ ism	territorialism*
+ ist	territorialist*
terror	
+ s	terrors
+ ify	terrify^
+ ify **+ ly**	terrifyingly
+ less	terrorless
+ ist	terrorist*
+ ism	terrorism*
+ ize	terrorize^
test	
+ s	tests
+ ed	tested
+ ing	testing*
+ able	testable*
+ ity	testability*
+ ee	testee*
+ er	tester*
+ y	testy*
+ y + er	testier
+ y + est	testiest
+ ly	testily'
+ ness	testiness*
testify	
+ s	testifies

+ er	testifier*
+ y	testimony*
+ al	testimonial*
Texas	
+ an	Texan*
texture	
+ s	textures
+ ed	textured
+ ing	texturing*
+ ize	texturize^
+ al	textural
+ ly	texturally
than	
thank	
+ s	thanks
+ ed	thanked
+ ing	thanking*
+ ful	thankful
+ ful + ly	thankfully
+ ful + ness	thankfulness*
+ less	thankless
+ less + ly	thanklessly
+ less + ness	thanklessness*
+ worth + y	thankworthy
+ s + give + ing	Thanksgiving
that	
the (2)	
theater	
+ s	theaters
+ al	theatrical*
+ ism	theatricalism*
+ ity	theatricality
+ ly	theatrically
+ ic + **ize**	theatricalize^
+ ic	theatric*
+ ize + tion	theatricalization*
their	
+ s	theirs
them	
+ selve + s	themselves
theme	
+ s	themes
+ ic	thematic
+ ly	thematically
then	
theory	
+ s	theories
+ ize	theorize^
+ tion	theorization*
+ er	theorizer*
+ al	theoretical*
+ ly	theoretically
+ ist	theorist*
+ an	theoretician*

therapy	
+ s	therapies
+ ic	therapeutic*
+ ly	therapeutically
+ ist	therapist*
+ ure + ist	therapeutist*
there	
+ about + s	thereabouts
+ after	thereafter
+ at	thereat
+ by	thereby
+ from	therefrom
+ for	therefor
+ fore	therefore
+ in	therein
+ in + after	thereinafter
+ in + to	thereinto
+ of	thereof
+ on	thereon
+ 's	there's
+ to	thereto
+ to + fore	theretofore
+ un + to	thereunto
+ under	thereunder
+ upon	thereupon
+ with	therewith
+ with + al	therewithal
thermometer	
+ s	thermometers
+ ic	thermometric*
+ ly	thermometrically
+ y	thermometry
these	
they	
thick	
+ ly	thickly
+ ness	thickness*
+ ish	thickish
+ en	thicken^
+ en + er	thickener*
+ en + ing	thickening*
+ est	thickest
+ head	thickhead
+ head + ed	thickheaded
thief	
+ s	thieves
+ ery	thievery*
+ ed	thieved
+ ing	thieving*
+ ish	thievish
+ ly	thievishly
+ ness	thievishness*

T

thigh

+ s	thighs
+ ed	thighed
+ bone	thighbone*

thimble

+ s	thimbles
+ ful	thimbleful*

thin

+ er	thinner*
+ est	thinnest
+ s	thins
+ ed	thinned
+ ing	thinning*
+ ish	thinnish
+ ly	thinly
+ ness	thinness*

thing

+ s	things
+ ness	thingness*

think

+ s	thinks
+ ed	thought
+ ing	thinking*
+ er	thinker*
+ able	thinkable
+ ly	thinkably
+ ness	thinkableness*

third

+ ly	thirdly
+ s	thirds
+ hand	thirdhand

thirst

+ s	thirsts
+ ed	thirsted
+ ing	thirsting*
+ er	thirster
+ y	thirsty*
+ ly	thirstily
+ ness	thirstiness*
+ y + er	thirstier

this

thong

+ s	thongs
+ ed	thonged

thorn

+ s	thorns
+ ed	thorned
+ less	thornless
+ like	thornlike
+ y	thorny*
+ er	thornier
+ est	thorniest
+ ness	thorniness*

thorough

+ ly	thoroughly
+ ness	thoroughness*
+ bred	thoroughbred
+ go + ing	thoroughgoing

those

though

thought

+ s	thoughts
+ ful	thoughtful*
+ ful +ly	thoughtfully
+ ful + ness	thoughtfulness*
+ less	thoughtless*
+ less + ly	thoughtlessly
+ less + ness	thoughtlessness*
+ way	thoughtway

thousand

+ s	thousands
+ fold	thousandfold*
+ th	thousandth*

thread

+ s	threads
+ ed	threaded
+ ing	threading*
+ er	threader*
+ less	threadless*
+ like	threadlike
+ y	thready*
+ ness	threadiness*
+ bare	threadbare
+ bare + ness	threadbareness
+ worm	threadworm

threat

+ s	threats
+ en	threaten^
+ **ing** + ly	threateningly
+ er	threatener*

thrill

+ s	thrills
+ ed	thrilled
+ ing	thrilling
+ er	thriller*

throat

+ s	throats
+ ed	throated
+ ing	throating*
+ y	throaty*
+ er	throatier
+ ness	throatiness*
+ ly	throatily

throb

+ s	throbs
+ ed	throbbed
+ ing	throbbing*
+ er	throbber*

T

throne	
+ s	thrones
+ ed	throned
+ ing	throning*
through	
+ out	throughout
+ put	throughput
+ way	throughway*
throw	
+ s	throws
+ ed	threw
+ en	thrown
+ ing	throwing*
+ er	thrower*
+ away	throwaway
thrust	
+ s	thrusts
+ ing	thrusting*
+ er	thruster*
+ ful	thrustful
thumb	
+ s	thumbs
+ ed	thumbed
+ ing	thumbing*
+ hole	thumbhole
+ nail	thumbnail
+ print	thumbprint
+ tack	thumbtack
thunder	
+ s	thunders
+ ed	thundered
+ ing	thundering*
+ ing + ly	thuneringly
+ er	thunderer*
+ ous	thunderous
+ ous + ly	thunderously
+ bird	thunderbird
+ clap	thunderclap
+ cloud	thundercloud
+ head	thunderhead
+ shower	thundershower
+ stone	thunderstone
+ storm	thunderstorm
+ strike	thunderstrike^
+ strike + en	thunderstroke
Thursday	
+ s	Thursdays
ticket	
+ s	tickets
+ ed	ticketed
+ ing	ticketing*
tickle	
+ s	tickles
+ ed	tickled
+ ing	tickling*
+ er	tickler*
+ ish	ticklish
+ ly	ticklishly
+ ness	ticklishness*
tide	
+ s	tides
+ al	tidal*
+ ly	tidally
+ less	tideless
+ ing	tiding*
+ ed	tided
+ land	tideland
+ mark	tidemark
+ water	tidewater
+ way	tideway
tie	
+ s	ties
+ ed	tied
+ ing	tying*
+ break + er	tiebreaker
+ pin	tiepin
tiger	
+ s	tigers
+ ish	tigerish
+ ly	tigerishly
+ ness	tigerishness*
+ like	tigerlike
tight	
+ s	tights
+ en	tighten^
+ ly	tightly
+ ness	tightness*
+ rope	tightrope
+ wire	tightwire
tile	
+ s	tiles
+ ed	tiled
+ ing	tiling*
+ er	tiler*
till	
timber	
+ s	timbers
+ ed	timbered
+ ing	timbering*
+ head	timberhead
+ land	timberland
+ line	timberline
+ man	timberman
+ work	timberwork
time	
+ s	times
+ ed	timed
+ ing	timing
+ er	timer*

+ less	timeless
+ less + ly	timelessly
+ less + ness	timelessness*
+ ly	timely
+ ly + er	timelier
+ est	timeliest
+ less	timeless
+ ness	timeliness*
+ keep + er	timekeeper
+ keep + ing	timekeeping
+ piece	timepiece
+ save + ing	timesaving
+ serve + er	timeserver
+ table	timetable
+ work	timework
+ wear + en	timeworn
timid	
+ ity	timidity*
+ ly	timidly
+ ness	timidness*
tin	
+ s	tins
+ ed	tinned
+ ing	tinning*
+ er	tinner*
+ y	tinny*
+ y + er	tinnier
+ est	tinniest
+ ly	tinnily
+ ness	tinniness*
+ horn	tinhorn
+ plate	tinplate
+ stone	tinstone
+ ware	tinware
+ work	tinwork
+ type	tintype
tiny	
+ er	tinier
+ est	tiniest
+ ly	tinily
+ ness	tininess*
tip	
+ s	tips
+ ed	tipped
+ ing	tipping*
+ er	tipper*
+ y	tippy*
+ y + er	tippier
+y + est	tippiest
tiptoe	
+ s	tiptoes
+ ed	tiptoed
+ ing	tiptoeing*
tire	
+ s	tires
+ ed	tired
+ ing	tiring*
+ less	tireless
+ less + ly	tirelessly
+ less + ness	tirelessness*
+ ly	tiredly
+ ness	tiredness
+ some	tiresome
+ some + ly	tiresomely
+ some + ness	tiresomeness*
tissue	
+ s	tissues
+ y	tissuey
+ ar	tissular
title	
+ s	titles
+ ed	titled
+ ing	titling*
+ ist	titlist*
+ hold + er	titleholder
to	
toad	
+ s	toads
+ y	toady^
+ y + ism	toadyism
+ eat + er	toadeater
+ fish	toadfish
+ stone	toadstone
toast	
+ s	toasts
+ ed	toasted
+ ing	toasting*
+ er	toaster*
+ y	toasty*
+ y + er	toastier
+ est	toastiest
+ master	toastmaster
tobacco	
+ s	tobaccos
toboggan	
+ s	toboggans
+ ed	tobagganed
+ ing	tobagganing*
+ er	tobogganer*
+ ist	tobogganist*
today	
toe	
+ s	toes
+ ed	toed
+ ing	toeing*
+ hold	toehold
+ less	toeless

T

+ nail	toenail
+ plate	toeplate
+ piece	toepiece
together	
+ ness	togetherness
toil	
+ s	toils
+ ed	toiled
+ ing	toiling*
+ er	toiler*
+ ful	toilful
+ ful + ly	toilfully
+ some	toilsome
+ some + ly	toilsomely
+ some + ness	toilsomeness
+ wear + en	toilworn
toilet	
+ s	toilets
+ ry	toiletry*
told	
tolerate	
+ s	tolerates
+ ed	tolerated
+ ing	tolerating*
+ ant	tolerant
+ ant + ly	tolerantly
+ ness	tolerantness*
+ ance	tolerance*
+ able	tolerable*
+ able + ly	tolerably
+ ity	tolerability*
+ tion	toleration*
+ or	tolerator*
tomato	
+ s	tomatoes
+ y	tomatoey
tomb	
+ s	tombs
+ less	tombless
tomorrow	
ton	
+ s	tons
+ age	tonnage*
+ er	tonner*
tone	
+ s	tones
+ ed	toned
+ ing	toning*
+ al	tonal*
+ ly	tonally
+ al + ity	tonality*
+ less	toneless
+ less + ly	tonelessly
+ less + ness	tonelessness*
+ icity	tonicity*
+ ic	tonic*
+ er	toner*
+ t + ic	tonetic*
+ ic + ly	tonetically
+ y	tony
+ y + er	tonier
+ y + est	toniest
tongs	
tongue	
+ s	tongues
+ ed	tongued
+ ing	tonguing*
+ like	tonguelike
+ less	tongueless
tonight	
tonsil	
+ s	tonsils
tonsillectomy	
+ s	tonsillectomies
too	
took	
tool	
+ s	tools
+ ed	tooled
+ ing	tooling*
+ box	toolbox
+ head	toolhead
+ hold + er	toolholder
+ house	toolhouse
+ make + er	toolmaker
+ make + ing	toolmaking
+ room	toolroom
tooth	
+ ed	toothed
+ y	toothy
+ er	toothier
+ est	toothiest
+ ly	toothily
+ less	toothless
+ some	toothsome
+ some + ly	toothsomely
+ some + ness	toothsomeness*
+ ache	toothache*
+ pick	toothpick
toothbrush	
+ s	toothbrushes
+ ing	toothbrushing*
toothpaste	
+ s	toothpastes
top	
+ s	tops
+ ed	topped
+ ing	topping*

T

+ ful	topful*
+ less	topless
+ er	topper*
+ kick	topkick
+ knot	topknot
+ mast	topmast
+ most	topmost
+ side	topside
+ soil	topsoil
+ spin	topspin
+ stitch	topstitch
+ work	topwork
topic	
+ s	topics
+ al	topical*
+ ly	topically
+ ity	topicality*
torch	
+ s	torches
+ ed	torched
+ ing	torching*
+ bear + er	torchbearer
+ light	torchlight
tornado	
+ s	tornadoes
+ ic	tornadic
tortilla	
+ s	tortillas
tortoise	
+ s	tortoises
+ shell	tortoiseshell
torture	
+ s	tortures
+ ed	tortured
+ ing	torturing*
+ er	torturer*
+ ous	tortuous
+ ous + ly	tortuously
toss	
+ s	tosses
+ ed	tossed
+ ing	tossing*
+ pot	tosspot
total	
+ s	totals
+ ed	totaled
+ ing	totaling
+ ity	totality*
+ ize	totalize^
+ ize + er	totalizer
+ ize + tion	totalization
+ ly	totally
+ ism	totalism
+ ist	totalist
+ an	totalitarian
+ an + ism	totalitarianism
+ an + ize	totalitarianize^
touch	
+ s	touches
+ ed	touched
+ ing	touching*
+ ing + ly	touchingly
+ able	touchable*
+ er	toucher*
+ y	touchy
+ y + er	touchier
+ est	touchiest
+ y + ly	touchily
+ ness	touchiness*
+ back	touchback
+ down	touchdown
+ hole	touchhole
+ line	touchline
+ mark	touchmark
+ stone	touchstone
+ wood	touchwood
tough	
+ s	toughs
+ ed	toughed
+ en	toughen^
+ en + ing	toughening
+ **ing**	toughing*
+ ly	toughly
+ ness	toughness*
+ y	toughy*
tour	
+ s	tours
+ ed	toured
+ ing	touring*
+ ism	tourism*
+ ist	tourist*
+ ic	touristic*
+ ly	touristically
+ y	touristy
tournament	
+ s	tournaments
tow	
+ s	tows
+ ed	towed
+ ing	towing*
+ age	towage*
+ boat	towboat
+ line	towline
+ path	towpath
+ rope	towrope
toward	
+ s	towards

towel

+ s	towels
+ ed	toweled
+ ing	toweling*

tower

+ s	towers
+ ed	towered
+ ing	towering*
+ ly	toweringly
+ like	towerlike*

town

+ s	towns
+ ship	township
+ s + folk	townsfolk
+ s + man	townsman
+ s + people	townspeople
+ s + woman	townswoman

toy (2)

+ s	toys
+ ed	toyed
+ ing	toying*
+ er	toyer*
+ like	toylike

trace

+ s	traces
+ ed	traced
+ ing	tracing*
+ er	tracer*
+ ery	tracery*
+ est	traceriest
+ able	traceable*
+ ity	traceability*
+ less	traceless
+ less + ly	tracelessly

track

+ s	tracks
+ ed	tracked
+ ing	tracking*
+ er	tracker*
+ less	trackless
+ age	trackage*
+ lay + er	tracklayer
+ lay + ing	tracklaying
+ man	trackman
+ side	trackside
+ suit	tracksuit
+ walk + er	trackwalker
+ way	trackway

tractor

+ s	tractors

trade

+ s	trades
+ ed	traded
+ ing	trading*
+ er	trader*
+ able	tradable*
+ mark	trademark
+ s + man	tradesman
+ s + people	tradespeople

tradition (2)

+ s	traditions
+ al	traditional*
+ ly	traditionally
+ ism	traditionalism*
+ ist	traditionalist*
+ ic	traditionalistic*
+ less	traditionless
+ ize	traditionalize^
+ ary	traditionary*

traffic

+ s	trafficks
+ ed	trafficked
+ ing	trafficking*
+ er	trafficker*
+ able	trafficable*
+ ity	trafficability*

tragic

+ al	tragical
+ ly	tragically
+ y	tragedy*
+ an	tragedian

trail

+ s	trails
+ ed	trailed
+ ing	trailing*
+ er	trailer*
+ head	trailhead
+ side	trailside

trailer

+ s	trailers
+ ed	trailered
+ ing	trailering*
+ ist	trailerist*
+ ship	trailership*

train

+ s	trains
+ ed	trained
+ ing	training*
+ er	trainer*
+ ee	trainee*
+ ee + ship	traineeship*
+ able	trainable*
+ ity	trainability*
+ bear + er	trainbearer
+ load	trainload
+ man	trainman

trait

+ s	traits

traitor	
+ s	traitors
+ ous	traitorous
+ ly	traitorously
+ ess	traitoress*
trample	
+ s	tramples
+ ed	trampled
+ ing	trampling*
+ er	trampler*
trampoline	
+ s	trampolines
+ ing	trampolining*
+ ist	trampolinist*
tranquil	
+ ly	tranquilly
+ ness	tranquilness
+ ize	tranquilize^
+ er	tranquilizer*
+ ity	tranquility*
transfer	
+ s	transfers
+ ed	transferred
+ ing	transferring*
+ al	transferal*
+ er	transferrer*
+ ee	transferee*
+ ence	transference*
+ ence + al	transferential*
transform	
+ s	transforms
+ ed	transformed
+ ing	transforming*
+ er	transformer*
+ able	transformable*
+ ive	transformative*
+ tion	transformation*
+ al	transformational*
+ ly	transformationally
+ ist	transformationalist*
translate	
+ s	translates
+ ed	translated
+ ing	translating*
+ or	translator*
+ able	translatable*
+ ity	translatability*
+ ion	translation*
+ al	translational*
+ ive	translative*
+ ory	translatory*
transparency	
+ s	transparencies

transparent	
+ ly	transparently
+ ness	transparentness*
+ ize	transparentize^
transport	
+ s	transports
+ ed	transported
+ ing	transporting*
+ er	transporter*
+ tion	transportation*
+ al	transportational*
+ able	transportable*
+ ity	transportability*
trap	
+s	traps
+ ed	trapped
+ ing	trapping*
+ er	trapper*
+ door	trapdoor
+ nest	trapnest
trapeze	
+ s	trapezes
+ ist	trapezist*
trash	
+ s	trashes
+ ed	trashed
+ er	trasher*
+ ing	trashing*
+ y	trashy
+ ness	trashiness*
+ y + er	trashier
+ est	trashiest
+ man	trashman
travel	
+ s	travels
+ ed	traveled
+ ing	traveling*
+ er	traveler*
tray	
+ s	trays
+ ful	trayful*
treasure	
+ s	treasures
+ ed	treasured
+ ing	treasuring*
+ er	treasurer*
+ ship	treasurership*
+ able	treasurable*
+ y	treasury*
treat	
+ s	treats
+ ed	treated
+ ing	treating*
+ er	treater*

+ able	treatable
+ ity	treatability
+ ment	treatment*
+ y	treaty*
tree	
+ s	trees
+ less	treeless
+ like	treelike
+ ed	treed
+ ing	treeing*
+ top	treetop
tremendous	
+ ly	tremendously
+ ness	tremendousness
triangle	
+ s	triangles
+ ar	triangular*
+ ity	triangularity*
+ ly	triangularly
+ ate	triangulate^
+ tion	triangulation*
tribe	
+ s	tribes
+ s + man	tribesman
tribute	
+ s	tributes
+ ary	tributary*
triceratops	
trick	
+ s	tricks
+ ed	tricked
+ ing	tricking*
+ ish	trickish
+ ish + ly	trickishly
+ ish + ness	trickishness*
+ s + y	tricksy
+ s **+ er**	tricksier
+ s **+ est**	tricksiest
+ s **+ ness**	tricksiness*
+ ery	trickery*
+ er	trickster* or-tricker*
+ y	tricky
+ y + er	trickier
+ y + est	trickiest
+ y + ly	trickily
+ y + ness	trickiness*
tricycle	
+ s	tricycles
+ ed	tricycled
+ er	tricycler*
+ ing	tricycling*
trike	
+ s	trikes
+ ed	triked
+ er	triker*
+ ing	triking*
trillion	
+ s	trillions
+ th	trillionth*
trim	
+ s	trims
+ ed	trimmed
+ ing	trimming*
+ er	trimmer*
+ est	trimmest
+ ly	trimly
+ ness	trimness*
trip	
+ s	trips
+ ed	tripped
+ ing	tripping*
+ ly	trippingly
+ er	tripper*
triple	
+ s	triples
+ ed	tripled
+ ing	tripling*
+ ate	triplicate^
+ tion	triplication*
+ ity	triplicity*
+ ly	triply
+ t	triplet*
triumph	
+ s	triumphs
+ ed	triumphed
+ ing	triumphing*
+ al	triumphal*
+ ant	triumphant
+ ly	triumphantly
+ ism	triumphalism*
+ ist	triumphalist*
trombone	
+ s	trombones
+ ist	trombonist*
troop	
+ s	troops
+ ed	trooped
+ ing	trooping*
+ er	trooper*
+ ship	troopship*
trophy	
+ s	trophies
trot	
+ s	trots
+ ed	trotted
+ ing	trotting*
+ er	trotter*
trouble	
+ s	troubles
+ ed	troubled

T

+ ing	troubling*
+ some	troublesome
+ some + ly	troublesomely
+ some + ness	troublesomeness*
+ ous	troublous
+ ous + ly	troublously
+ ous + ness	troublousness*
+ make + er	troublemaker
+ make + ing	troublemaking
+ shoot + er	troubleshooter
trouser	
+ s	trousers
truck	
+ s	trucks
+ ed	trucked
+ ing	trucking*
+ er	trucker*
+ age	truckage*
+ line	truckline
+ load	truckload
+ man	truckman
+ master	truckmaster
true	
+ s	trues
+ ed	trued
+ ing	truing*
+ ness	trueness*
+ er	truer*
+ est	truest
+ ly	truly
+ th	truth*
+ ful	truthful
+ ful + ly	truthfully
+ born	trueborn
+ love	truelove
trumpet	
+ s	trumpets
+ ed	trumpeted
+ ing	trumpeting*
+ er	trumpeter*
+ like	trumpetlike
trunk	
+ s	trunks
+ ed	trunked
+ ful	trunkful*
trust	
+ s	trusts
+ ed	trusted
+ ing	trusting*
+ able	trustable*
+ ity	trustability*
+ er	truster*
+ ee	trustee^
+ ee + ship	trusteeship*
+ ful	trustful
+ ful + ly	trustfully
+ ful + ness	trustfulness*
+ less	trustless
+ y	trusty*
+ y + er	trustier
+ y + est	trustiest
+ worth + y	trustworthy
+ worth + ily	trustworthily
+ worth + **ness**	trustworthiness
try	
+ s	tries
+ ed	tried
+ ing	trying
+ ly	tryingly
+ al	trial*
+ out	tryout*
tub	
+ s	tubs
+ like	tublike
+ able	tubbable*
+ ful	tubful*
+ er	tubber*
+ y	tubby*
+ y + er	tubbier
tuba	
+ s	tubas
+ ist	tubaist*
tube	
+ s	tubes
+ ed	tubed
+ ing	tubing*
+ like	tubelike
+ less	tubeless
Tuesday	
+ s	Tuesdays
tug	
+ s	tugs
+ ed	tugged
+ ing	tugging*
+ boat	tugboat
tulip	
+ s	tulips
+ wood	tulipwood
tumble	
+ s	tumbles
+ ed	tumbled
+ ing	tumbling*
+ er	tumbler*
+ ful	tumbleful
+ down	tumbledown
+ weed	tumbleweed
tumor	
+ s	tumors

+ al	tumoral*
+ like	tumorlike
+ ous	tumorous
tuna	
+ s	tunas
tune	
+ s	tunes
+ ed	tuned
+ ing	tuning*
+ er	tuner*
+ ful	tuneful
+ ful + ly	tunefully
+ ful + ness	tunefulness*
tunnel	
+ s	tunnels
+ ed	tunneled
+ ing	tunneling*
+ er	tunneler*
+ like	tunnellike
turkey	
+ s	turkeys
turn	
+ s	turns
+ ed	turned
+ ing	turning*
+ able	turnable*
+ er	turner*
+ er + y	turnery*
+ about	turnabout
+ around	turnaround
+ buckle	turnbuckle
+ coat	turncoat
+ down	turndown
+ key	turnkey
+ off	turnoff
+ out	turnout
+ over	turnover
+ spit	turnspit
+ stone	turnstone
+ table	turntable
+ up	turnup
turnip	
+ s	turnips
turquoise	
turtle	
+ s	turtles
+ ing	turtling*
+ back	turtleback
+ head	turtlehead
+ neck	turtleneck*
+ neck + ed	turtlenecked
tutor	
+ s	tutors
+ ed	tutored
+ ing	tutoring*
+ er	tutorer*
+ age	tutorage*
+ ess	tutoress*
+ al	tutorial*
+ ship	tutorship*
twice	
twig	
+ s	twigs
+ ed	twigged
+ ing	twigging*
+ y	twiggy*
twin	
+ s	twins
+ ed	twinned
+ ing	twinning*
+ship	twinship*
+ born	twinborn
twine	
+ s	twines
+ ed	twined
+ ing	twining*
+ y	twiny*
+ er	twiner*
twirl	
+ s	twirls
+ ed	twirled
+ ing	twirling*
+ er	twirler*
+ y	twirly*
twist	
+ s	twists
+ ed	twisted
+ ing	twisting*
+ er	twister*
+ y	twisty*
type	
+ s	types
+ ed	typed
+ ing	typing*
+ er	typer*
+ able	typeable*
+ y	typey*
+ y + er	typier
+ est	typiest
+ ist	typist*
+ ify	typify^
+ al	typical*
+ ly	typically
+ ity	typicality*
+ ness	typicalness*
+ face	typeface
+ script	typescript
+ set	typeset
+ set + er	typesetter

typewriter

+ s typewriters

tyrannosaurus rex

T

ugly

+ er	uglier
+ est	ugliest
+ ify	uglify^
+ ness	ugliness*
+ ly	uglily

umbrella

+ s	umbrellas
+ ed	umbrellaed
+ ing	umbrellaing*

umpire

+ s	umpires
+ ed	umpired
+ ing	umpiring*

uncle

+ s	uncles

under (prefix) (2)

To see the way to form words with the prefix shown here, refer to the section showing the root word involved.

underachieve^
underact^
underactive
underage
underappreciated
underarm
underbelly
underbid
underbody
underbred
underbrush
undercapitalized
undercarriage
undercharge
underclass
underclassman
underclothes
undercoat
undercool
undercount
undercover
undercurrent
undercut
underdeveloped
underdevelopment
underdone
undereducated
underemphasis
underemphasized
underemployed
underemployment
underestimate
underexpose
underfeed
underfinanced
underfoot
underfur
underglaze
undergraduate
underground
undergrowth
underinflate
underinflated
underinsured
underlay
underlaid
underlying
underlie
underline
underlip
undermanned
undermine
undermost
underpants
underpart
underpass
underpay
underpin
underplay
underpopulated
underpowered
underprepared
underprice
underproduction
underproof
underpublicized
underrate
underreact
underreport
underrepresented

U

underrun
underscore
undersea
undersell
underserved
undersexed
undershirt
undershoot
undershorts
undershot
underside
undersigned
undersized
underskirt
underspin
understaffed
understate
understatement
understated
understatedly
understock
understrength
understudy
undersupply
undersurface
underthrust
undertone
undertow
undertrick
underused
undervaluation
undervalue
underwater
underwear
underweight
underwing
underworld
underwork

understand

+ s	understands
+ ed	understood
+ ing	understanding*
+ ing + ly	understandingly
+ able	understandable*
+ ity	understandability*
+ able + ly	understandably

un (prefix)

To see the way to form words with the prefix shown here, refer to the section showing the root word involved.

unable
unacademic
unacademically
unacceptability
unacceptable
unacceptably
unaccepted
unaccompanied
unaccountable
unaccountability
unaccountably
unaccounted
unachieved
unacquainted
unactable
unacted
unactorish
unadaptable
unadapted
unaddressed
unadjusted
unadmired
unadmitted
unadoptable
unadult
unadventurous
unadvertised
unadvised
unadvisedly
unaffected
unaffectedly
unaffectedness
unaffecting
unaffectionate
unaffectionately
unafraid
unaggressive
unaging
unaided
unair-conditioned
unalike
unalterability
unalterable
unalterableness
unalterably
unaltered
unambitious
unamended
un-American
unamusing
unanalyzable
unanalyzed
unanchor
unannounced
unanswerability
unanswerable
unanswerably
unanswered
unapologetic
unapologetically

unapologizing
unappetizing
unappetizingly
unappreciated
unappreciation
unappreciative
unapproachability
unapproachable
unapproachably
unapproved
unarguable
unarguably
unarm
unarticulated
unartistic
unashamed
unashamedly
unasked
unassembled
unassigned
unassisted
unassociated
unassuming
unassumingness
unathletic
unattached
unattended
unattractive
unattractively
unattractiveness
unauthorized
unautomated
unavailability
unavailable
unavailing
unavailingly
unavailingness
unaverage
unavoidable
unavoidably
unawakened
unawarded
unaware
unawarely
unawareness
unawares
unbacked
unbalance^
unbandage^
unbanned
unbaptized
unbar^
unbarbered
unbearable
unbearably
unbeatable
unbeaten
unbeautiful
unbeautifully
unbecoming
unbecomingly
unbecomingness
unbeknown
unbeknownst
unbelief
unbelievable
unbelievably
unbeliever
unbelieving
unbelievingly
unbeloved
unbelted
unbend
unbendable
unbending
unbends
unbeseeming
unbiblical
unbidden
unbind
unbinding
unbinds
unbitted
unbitten
unbitter
unblended
unblessed
unblinded
unblinking
unblinkingly
unblock^
unblooded
unblushing
unblushingly
unbodied
unbonneted
unbookish
unborn
unbought
unbouncy
unbound
unbounded
unboundedness
unbowed
unbox^
unbraid^
unbranched
unbranded

U

unbreakable
unbreathable
unbred
unbridged
unbriefed
unbright
unbrilliant
unbroken
unbruised
unbrushed
unbuckle^
unbuild
unbuildable
unbuilding
unbuilds
unbuilt
unbundle^
unburden^
unburied
unburnable
unburned
unburnt
unbusinesslike
unbusy
unbuttered
unbutton^
uncage^
uncalculated
uncalculating
uncalled
uncalled-for
uncanceled
uncap
uncapitalized
uncaptioned
uncapturable
uncared-for
uncaring
uncarpeted
uncase
uncataloged
uncatchable
uncatchy
uncaught
uncaused
uncelebrated
unceremonious
unceremoniously
unceremoniousness
uncertain
uncertainly
uncertainness
uncertainty
uncertified
unchain^
unchallengeable
unchallenged
unchallenging
unchancy
unchangeability
unchangeable
unchangeableness
unchangeably
unchanged
unchanging
unchangingly
unchangingness
unchanneled
uncharacteristic
uncharacteristically
uncharge^
uncharming
uncharted
unchartered
uncheckable
unchecked
unchewable
unchewed
unchildlike
unchristian
unchurch
unchurched
unchurches
unchurchly
uncirculated
uncivil
uncivility
uncivilized
unclaimed
unclarified
unclarity
unclassical
unclassifiable
unclassified
unclean
uncleaned
uncleanliness
uncleanly
uncleanness
unclear
uncleared
unclimbable
unclimbableness
unclip
unclose^
unclothe
unclothed
unclouded

uncloudedly
uncoated
uncoating
uncoded
uncoined
uncollected
uncollectible
uncolored
uncombed
uncombined
uncomely
uncomfortable
uncomfortably
uncomic
uncommercial
uncommercialized
uncommitted
uncommon
uncommonly
uncommonness
uncommunicable
uncompassionate
uncompelling
uncompetitive
uncompetitiveness
uncomplaining
uncomplainingly
uncompleted
uncomplicated
uncompounded
uncomprehended
uncomprehending
uncomprehendingly
uncompromisable
uncompromising
uncompromisingly
uncomputerized
unconcealed
unconcern
unconcerned
unconcernedly
unconcernedness
unconditional
unconditionally
unconditioned
unconfessed
unconfirmed
unconfused
unconnected
unconquerable
unconquerably
unconquered
unconscious
unconsciously
unconsciousness
unconsidered
unconstitutional
unconstitutionality
unconstitutionally
unconstructed
unconsumed
uncontainable
uncontainerized
uncontested
uncontracted
uncontrollable
uncontrollably
uncontrolled
uncontroversial
uncontroversially
unconventional
unconventionality
unconventionally
unconverted
unconvinced
unconvincing
unconvincingly
unconvincingness
uncooked
uncool
uncooled
uncooperative
uncork
uncorked
uncorrectable
uncorrected
uncountable
uncounted
uncouple^
uncourageous
uncover^
uncracked
uncrazy
uncreated
uncreative
uncredited
uncrippled
uncritical
uncritically
uncropped
uncross
uncrossable
uncrowded
uncrown
uncrushable
uncrystallized
uncuffed
uncultured

U

uncured
uncurious
uncurl^
uncurrent
uncurtained
uncustomarily
uncustomary
uncut
uncute
undamaged
undanceable
undated
undebatable
undebatably
undeceive^
undecidable
undecided
undeciding
undeclared
undecorated
undedicated
undefeated
undefended
undefinable
undefined
undelegated
undeliverable
undelivered
undemanding
undemocratic
undemonstrative
undemonstratively
undemonstrativeness
undeniable
undeniableness
undeniably
undescribable
undeserved
undeserving
undesignated
undesigning
undesirability
undesirable
undesirableness
undesirably
undesired
undetectable
undetected
undeterminable
undetermined
undeveloped
undeviating
undeviatingly
undiagnosed
undid
undifferentiated
undigested
undigestible
undimmed
undiplomatic
undiplomatically
undirected
undischarged
undisclosed
undiscouraged
undiscoverable
undiscovered
undiscriminating
undiscussed
undisguised
undisguisedly
undissolved
undistinguished
undistorted
undistracted
undistributed
undisturbed
undivided
undo
undoctored
undoing
undone
undotted
undouble^
undoubtable
undoubted
undoubtedly
undoubting
undpendable
undrained
undramatic
undramatically
undramatized
undrape^
undraw
undrawing
undrawn
undreamed
undress^
undrilled
undrinkable
undrunk
undulled
unduplicated
undutiful
undutifully
undutifulness
undyed

undying
uneager
unearmarked
unearned
unearth^
unearthliness
unearthly
unease
uneasily
uneasiness
uneasy
uneatable
uneaten
unecological
uneconomic
unedited
uneducable
uneducated
unelaborated
unelectable
unelected
unelectrified
unembarrassed
unemotional
unemotionally
unemphatic
unemphatically
unemployability
unemployable
unemployed
unemployment
unencouraging
unending
unendingly
unenforceable
unenforced
un-English
unenthusiastic
unenthusiastically
unenvious
unequal
unequalled
unequally
unescapable
unessential
un-European
unevaluated
uneven
unevenly
unevenness
uneventful
uneventfully
unexamined
unexampled
unexcelled
unexceptionable
unexceptional
unexcited
unexciting
unexitable
unexpected
unexpectedly
unexpectedness
unexpired
unexplainable
unexploded
unexposed
unexpressed
unexpressive
unfading
unfadingly
unfailing
unfailingly
unfair
unfairly
unfairness
unfaith
unfaithful
unfaithfully
unfaithfulness
unfaked
unfalsifiable
unfamiliar
unfamiliarity
unfamiliarly
unfamous
unfancy
unfashionable
unfashionably
unfasten^
unfathered
unfavorable
unfavorableness
unfavorably
unfavorite
unfeeling
unfeelingly
unfeelingness
unfelt
unfeminine
unfenced
unfertile
unfertilized
unfilled
unfindable
unfinished
unfired
unfit

U

unfitted
unfitting
unfittingly
unfittingness
unfix
unfixed
unflashy
unflattering
unflatteringly
unfleshed
unflyable
unfocused
unfold^
unfoldment
unfond
unforced
unforeseeable
unforeseen
unforgettable
unforgettably
unforgivable
unforgiving
unforgivingness
unforked
unformed
unformulated
unforthcoming
unfortified
unfortunate
unfortunately
unfossiliferous
unfounded
unframed
unfree
unfreedom
unfreeze
unfreezing
unfrequented
unfriended
unfriendliness
unfriendly
unfrozen
unfruitful
unfruitfully
unfruitfulness
unfulfilled
unfunny
unfurnished
unfussily
unfussy
ungenerosity
ungenerous
ungenerously
ungentle
ungentlemanly
ungerminated
ungifted
unglazed
unglue^
ungodliness
ungodly
ungotten
ungovernable
ungraceful
ungracefully
ungracefulness
ungracious
ungraciously
ungraciousness
ungraded
ungrammatical
ungrammaticality
ungraspable
ungrateful
ungratefully
ungratefulness
ungrounded
ungrouped
unguard^
unguardedly
unguardedness
unguided
unhand^
unhandily
unhandiness
unhandsome
unhandsomely
unhandy
unhappily
unhappiness
unhappy
unharmed
unharvested
unhatched
unhealed
unhealthful
unhealthily
unhealthiness
unhealthy
unheard
unheard-of
unheated
unhelpful
unhelpfully
unheroic
unhesitating
unhesitatingly
unhinge^

U

unhip
unhistorical
unhitch^
unholy
unhonored
unhood^
unhook^
unhoped
unhopeful
unhorse
unhorsed
unhorsing
unhoused
unhumorous
unhurried
unhurriedly
unhurt
unhysterical
unhysterically
unidentifiable
unidentified
unidiomatic
unignorable
unimaginable
unimaginably
unimaginative
unimaginatively
unimpaired
unimportant
unimpressed
unimpressive
unimproved
unindustrialized
uninfected
uninflated
uninflected
uninfluenced
uninformative
uninformatively
uninformed
uninhabitable
uninhabited
uninitiate
uninjured
uninspected
uninspired
uninspiring
uninstructed
uninstructive
uninsurable
uninsured
unintegrated
unintellectual
unintelligence
unintelligent
unintelligently
unintelligibility
unintelligible
unintelligibleness
unintelligibly
unintended
unintentional
unintentionally
uninterest
uninterested
uninteresting
uninterrupted
uninterruptedly
uninterruptedness
uninventive
uninvited
uninviting
uninvolved
unironically
unirradiated
unirrigated
unissued
unjoined
unjointed
unjust
unjustifiable
unjustifiably
unjustified
unjustly
unjustness
unkept
unkind
unkindliness
unkindly
unkindness
unknit^
unknow
unknowable
unknowing
unknowingly
unknowledgeable
unknown
unkosher
unlabeled
unlace^
unladylike
unlaid
unlash^
unlaundered
unlawful
unlawfully
unlawfulness
unlay

U

unlaying
unleaded
unlearn^
unlettered
unliberated
unlicked
unlikable
unlike
unlikelihood
unlikeliness
unlikely
unlikeness
unlimited
unlimitedly
unlink^
unlisted
unlistenable
unlit
unliterary
unlivable
unlive
unlived
unliving
unload^
unlocalized
unlock^
unloose
unloosen
unloosened
unloosing
unlovable
unloved
unloveliness
unlovely
unloving
unluckily
unluckiness
unlucky
unlyrical
unmade
unmagnified
unmake
unmaking
unman
unmanageable
unmanageably
unmanliness
unmanly
unmanned
unmannered
unmanneredly
unmannerliness
unmapped
unmarked
unmarketable
unmarried
unmasculine
unmask^
unmatchable
unmatched
unmeaning
unmeant
unmeasurable
unmeasured
unmechanized
unmedicated
unmeet
unmelodious
unmelodiously
unmelodiousness
unmemorable
unmemorably
unmentionable
unmerciful
unmercifully
unmerry
unmet
unmilitary
unmilled
unmindful
unmistakable
unmistakably
unmixed
unmodernized
unmodified
unmoral
unmotivated
unmounted
unmovable
unmoved
unmusical
unnail^
unnameable
unnamed
unnatural
unnaturally
unnaturalness
unnecessarily
unnecessary
unneeded
unnegotiable
unnerve^
unnewsworthy
unnoticeable
unnoticed
unnumbered
unobjectionable
unobservable

U

unobserved
unobtainable
unoccupied
unofficial
unofficially
unopenable
unopened
unopposed
unordered
unorganized
unoriginal
unown
unoxygenated
unpack^
unpaged
unpainted
unpaired
unparalled
unparasitized
unpardonable
unpassable
unpave
unpeople
unpeopled
unpeopling
unperceived
unperceiving
unperceptive
unperfect
unperformable
unperformed
unperson
unpersuaded
unpersuasive
unpick^
unpile^
unpin^
unplaced
unplanned
unplayable
unpleasant
unpleasantly
unpleasantness
unpleased
unpleasing
unplowed
unplug^
unpoetic
unpolarized
unpoliced
unpolished
unpolitical
unpolluted
unpopular
unpopularity
unpractical
unpredictability
unpredictable
unpredictably
unpregnant
unprejudiced
unpremeditated
unprepared
unpreparedness
unpressed
unpressured
unpretending
unpretentious
unpretentiously
unpretentiousness
unpretty
unprincipled
unprincipledness
unprintable
unprocessed
unproduced
unproductive
unprofessed
unprofession
unprofitable
unprofitableness
unprofitably
unprogrammable
unprogrammed
unprogressive
unpromising
unpromisingly
unpronounceable
unpronounced
unprotected
unprovable
unproved
unproven
unprovided
unpruned
unpublicized
unpublishable
unpublished
unpunctual
unpunctuality
unpunished
unqualified
unqualifiedly
unquantifiable
unquestionable
unquestionably
unquestioned
unquestioning

unquestioningly
unquiet
unquietly
unquietness
unquote
unraised
unreachable
unreached
unread
unreadable
unreadiness
unready
unreal
unrealism
unrealistic
unrealistically
unreality
unrealizable
unrealized
unreason
unreasonable
unreasonableness
unreasonably
unreasoned
unreasoning
unreceptive
unrecognizable
unrecognizably
unrecognized
unreconstructed
unrecorded
unrecoverable
unrecovered
unreel^
unreflective
unreformed
unrefrigerated
unregenerate
unregenerated
unregulated
unrehearsed
unreinforced
unrelated
unrelaxed
unreliability
unreliable
unrelieved
unrelievedly
unremembered
unremovable
unrepeatable
unreported
unrepresentative
unrepresentativeness
unrepresented
unreserve
unreserved
unreservedly
unreservedness
unresistant
unrespectable
unrest
unrestful
unrestored
unrestrained
unrestrainedly
unrestrainness
unrestraint
unreturnable
unrevealed
unreviewed
unrevised
unrevolutionary
unrewarded
unrewarding
unrhymed
unrhythmic
unrhythmical
unridable
unriddle^
unrifled
unrighteous
unrighteously
unrighteousness
unripe
unripened
unripeness
unrivaled
unroll^
unromantic
unromantically
unromanticized
unroof^
unroofed
unround
unrushed
unsaddle^
unsafe
unsaid
unsalable
unsalted
unsanitary
unsatisfactorily
unsatisfactoriness
unsatisfactory
unsatisfied
unsaved
unsay

U

unsayable
unscalable
unscheduled
unscholarly
unschooled
unscientific
unscientifically
unscramble^
unscrambler
unscreened
unscrew^
unscripted
unscriptural
unseal^
unseam^
unsearchable
unsearchably
unseasonable
unseasonableness
unseasonably
unseasoned
unseat^
unseaworthy
unsecured
unseeded
unseemliness
unseemly
unseen
unsegmented
unselected
unselective
unself-conscious
unself-consciously
unself-consciousness
unselfish
unselfishly
unselfishness
unsell
unselling
unsells
unsensational
unsensitized
unseparated
unserious
unserved
unserviceable
unset
unsettle^
unsettledness
unsettlement
unsettlingly
unsew
unsewed
unsewn
unsex
unsexed
unsexing
unsexual
unsexy
unshaded
unshakable
unshakably
unshaken
unshaped
unshapely
unshapen
unshared
unsharp
unshaven
unshelled
unship^
unshockable
unshowy
unsight^
unsightliness
unsightly
unsigned
unsinkable
unsized
unskilled
unskillful
unskillfully
unskillfulness
unsmart
unsmiling
unsmoothed
unsnap^
unsociability
unsociable
unsociableness
unsociably
unsocial
unsocially
unsoiled
unsold
unsolvable
unsolved
unsophisticated
unsophistication
unsorted
unsound
unsounded
unsoundly
unsoundness
unsown
unspeak
unspeakable
unspeakably

U

unspeaking
unspeaks
unspecialized
unspecifiable
unspecific
unspecified
unspent
unspiritual
unsplit
unspoiled
unspoilt
unspoke
unspoken
unspotted
unsprayed
unsprung
unstained
unstandardized
unstartling
unstated
unsteadily
unsteadiness
unsteady
unstep^
unstick
unsticking
unsticks
unstitch
unstoned
unstop^
unstoppable
unstoppably
unstopper
unstressed
unstring
unstringing
unstrings
unstructured
unstrung
unstuck
unstudied
unstuffy
unstylish
unsubstantial
unsubstantially
unsubstantiated
unsubtle
unsubtly
unsuccess
unsuccessful
unsuccessfully
unsuitability
unsuitable
unsuitably
unsuited
unsung
unsupervised
unsupportable
unsupported
unsure
unsurprised
unsurprising
unsurprisingly
unsuspected
unsuspecting
unsuspicious
unsweetened
unsympathetic
unsympathetically
unsystematic
unsystematically
unsystematized
untagged
untalented
untamable
untamed
untanned
untapped
untaught
unteach
unteachable
unteaching
untechnical
untempered
untended
untestable
untested
unthink
unthinkability
unthinkable
unthinkably
unthinking
unthinkingly
unthought
unthread^
unthreatening
unthrone^
untie^
untimeliness
untimely
untiring
untiringly
untitled
untogether
untold
untouchability
untouchable
untouched

U

untoward
untowardliness
untowardly
untraceable
untracked
untraditional
untraditionally
untrained
untransformed
untranslatability
untranslatable
untranslated
untraveled
untreated
untried
untrimmed
untroubled
untrue
untrusting
untrustworthy
untruth
untruthful
untruthfully
untruthfulness
untune
untutored
untwine^
untwist^
untwistedly
untypical
untypically
ununderstandable
unusable
unused
unusual
unusually
unusualness
unvaccinated
unvalved
unvaried
unvarying
unverbalized
unversed
unvisited
unvocal
unvoice^
unwanted
unwarlike
unwashed
unwashedness
unwaxed
unwearied
unweariedly
unweathered
unweave
unweaves
unweaving
unwed
unweeded
unweighed
unweight
unweights
unwelcome
unwell
unwhite
unwholesome
unwholesomely
unwilled
unwilling
unwillingly
unwillingness
unwind
unwinding
unwinds
unwinnable
unwisdom
unwise
unwisely
unwish^
unwitting
unwittingly
unwomanly
unwon
unworkability
unworkable
unworked
unworldliness
unworldly
unworn
unworried
unworthily
unworthiness
unworthy
unwound
unwounded
unwoven
unwovened
unwrap^
unwreathe
unwreathed
unwreathing
unwritten
unyielding
unyieldingly
unyoung
unzip^

uniform

+ s	uniforms
+ ed	uniformed
+ ing	uniforming*
+ ly	uniformly
+ ness	uniformness
+ ity	uniformity*

union

+ s	unions
+ ism	unionism*
+ ist	unionist*
+ ize	unionize^
+ tion	unionization*

unit

+ s	units
+ age	unitage*
+ ify	unify^
+ ify + **tion**	unification*
+ ity	unity*
+ ize	unitize^
+ ize + tion	unitization*
+ ive	unitive*

unite

+ s	unites
+ ed	united
+ ing	uniting*
+ er	uniter*

United States

universe

+ s	universes
+ al	universal*
+ ly	universally
+ ness	universalness*
+ ism	universalism*
+ ist	universalist*
+ ic	universalistic*
+ ize	universalize^
+ tion	universalization*

university

+ s	universities

unless

until

up

+ s	ups
+ ed	upped
+ ing	upping*
+ er	upper*
+ ish	uppish
+ ly	uppishly
+ ish + ness	uppishness*
+ ity	uppity*
+ ity + ness	uppitiness*

up (prefix)

To see the way to form words with the prefix shown here, refer to the section showing the root word involved.

upbeat
upbringing
upbuild
upcoming
update
updo
upend
upfield
upgrade
upgrowth
uphill
uphold
upkeep
upland
uplift
upmanship
upmarket
upraise
uprear
upright
uprightly
uprightness
uprise
upriver
uproaring
uproar
uproared
uproot
uprush
upscale
upset
upshot
upside
upspring
upstage
upstairs
upstanding
upstart
upstate
upstream
upstroke
upsweep
upswept
upswing
uptake
upthrow
upthrust
uptight
uptime
uptown
upturn
upward
upwell

	upwind
	uppercase
	upperclassman
	uppercut
	uppermost
	upperpart
upon	
urge	
+ s	urges
+ ed	urged
+ ing	urging*
+ er	urger*
+ y	urgency*
+ ent	urgent
+ ly	urgently
urine	
+ s	urines
+ al	urinal*
+ ary	urinary*
+ ate	urinate^
+ tion	urination
+ ous	urinous
+ analysis	urinalysis
us	
use (2)	
+ able	usable or useable*
+ ity	usability*
+ able + ness	usableness*
+ able + ly	usably
+ age	usage*
+ ance	usance*
+ ed	used
+ ing	using*
+ s	uses
+ ful	useful
+ ful + ly	usefully
+ ful + ness	usefulness*
+ less	useless
+ less + ly	uselessly
+ less + ness	uselessness*
+ er	user*
+ ary	usury*
+ ary + er	usurer*
+ ary + ous	usurious*
+ ous + ly	usuriously
+ ous + ness	usuriousness*
usual	
+ ly	usually
+ ness	usualness

vacant	
+ s	vacants
+ y	vacancy*
+ ly	vacantly
+ ness	vacantness*
+ ate	vacate^
vacation	
+ s	vacations
+ ed	vacationed
+ ing	vacationing*
+ er	vacationer*
+ ist	vacationist*
+ land	vacationland
vaccine	
+ s	vaccines
+ al	vaccinal*
+ ate	vaccinate^
+ or	vaccinator*
+ tion	vaccination*
vacuum	
+ s	vacuums or vacua
+ ed	vacuumed
+ ing	vacuuming*
+ ity	vacuity*
+ ous	vacuous
+ ly	vacuously
+ ness	vacuousness*
+ ize	vacuumize^
+ pack + ed	vacuum-packed
vagina	
+ s	vaginas or vaginae
+ al	vaginal*
+ ly	vaginally
vague	
+ er	vaguer*
+ est	vaguest
+ ly	vaguely
+ ness	vagueness*
vain	
+ ly	vainly
+ ness	vainness*
+ ity	vanity*
+ glory	vainglory
+ glory + ous	vainglorious

valentine	
+ s	valentines
valley	
+ s	valleys
value	
+ s	values
+ ed	valued
+ ing	valuing*
+ ate	valuate^
+ or	valuator*
+ tion	valuation*
+ al	valuational*
+ less	valueless
+ less + ness	valuelessness*
+ er	valuer*
+ able	valuable*
+ able + ness	valuableness*
+ ly	valuably
vampire	
+ s	vampires
+ ism	vampirism*
van	
+ s	vans
+ ed	vanned
+ ing	vanning*
vane	
+ s	vanes
+ ed	vaned
vanilla	
+ s	vanillas
vanish	
+ s	vanishes
+ ed	vanished
+ ing	vanishing*
+ ly	vanishingly
+ er	vanisher*
vapor	
+ s	vapors
+ ed	vapored
+ ing	vaporing
+ er	vaporer*
+ ish	vaporish
+ ish + ness	vaporishness

+ ize	vaporize^
+ able	vaporizable
+ tion	vaporization
+ er	vaporizer
+ ous	vaporous
+ ly	vaporously
+ ous + ness	vaporousness
vary	
+ s	varies
+ ed	varied
+ ing	varying*
+ ing + ly	varyingly
+ able	variable*
+ able + ity	variability*
+ able + ness	variableness*
+ able + ly	variably
+ ance	variance*
+ ant	variant*
+ ate	variate*
+ tion	variation*
+ tion + al	variational*
+ tion **+ ly**	variationally
+ er	varier*
+ al	varietal*
+ ity	variety*
+ ous	various
+ ous + ly	variously
+ ous + ness	variousness*
vase	
+ s	vases
vaseline	
+ s	vaselines
+ ed	vaselined
+ ing	vaselining*
vast	
+ ly	vastly
+ ness	vastness
veal	
+ s	veals
+ ed	vealed
+ ing	vealing*
+ er	vealer*
+ y	vealy
vegetable	
+ s	vegetables
+ ar + an	vegetarian*
+ ism	vegetarianism*
+ ly	vegetably
+ al	vegetal*
vehicle	
+ s	vehicles
+ ar	vehicular
vein	
+ s	veins
+ ed	veined
+ ing	veining*
+ er	veiner*
+ stone	veinstone
+ y	veiny
vent	
+ s	vents
+ ed	vented
+ ing	venting*
+ less	ventless
+ age	ventage*
+ er	venter*
+ ate	ventilate^
+ tion	ventilation*
+ ate + or	ventilator*
+ ory	ventilatory
venture	
+ s	ventures
+ ed	ventured
+ ing	venturing*
+ er	venturer*
+ some	venturesome
+ some + ly	venturesomely
+ some + less	venturesomeless*
verb	
+ s	verbs
+ less	verbless
+ al	verbal*
+ al + ly	verbally
+ ism	verbalism*
+ ist	verbalist*
+ ize	verbalize^
+ tion	verbalization*
+ er	verbalizer*
+ age	verbiage
+ age + tion	verbigeration*
+ ify	verbify^
+ ous	verbose
+ ous + ly	verbosely
+ ous + ness	verboseness*
+ ous + ity	verbosity*
+ ile	verbile
verse	
+ s	verses
+ ed	versed
+ er	verser*
+ t	verset*
+ ing	versing*
+ ify	versify^
+ tion	versification*
+ ify + er	versifier*
+ ic + ar	versicular
+ ion	version*
+ ion + al	versional*
+ man	verseman

vertical

+ ity	verticality*
+ ly	vertically
+ ness	verticalness*

very

vessel

+ s	vessels

vest

+ s	vests
+ ed	vested
+ ing	vesting*
+ ee	vestee*
+ er	vester*
+ ary	vestiary*
+ like	vestlike
+ ment	vestment*
+ al	vestmental*
+ ary	vestry*
+ ure	vesture^

veteran

+ s	veterans

veterinarian

+ s	veterinarians
+ ary	veterinary*

vibrate

+ s	vibrates
+ ed	vibrated
+ ing	vibrating*
+ ion	vibration*
+ al	vibrational*
+ less	vibrationless
+ or	vibrator*
+ ory	vibratory*

vice

+ s	vices

victim

+ s	victims
+ ize	victimize^
+ tion	victimization*
+ er	victimizer*
+ less	victimless

victor

+ s	victors
+ y	victory*
+ ous	victorious
+ ly	victoriously
+ ness	victoriousness

video

+ s	videos
+ cassette	videocassette*

videotape

+ s	videotapes
+ ed	videotaped
+ ing	videotaping*

view

+ s	views
+ ed	viewed
+ ing	viewing*
+ able	viewable*
+ er	viewer*
+ ship	viewership*
+ less	viewless
+ less + ly	viewlessly
+ y	viewy
+ find + er	viewfinder
+ point	viewpoint

vigor

+ ous	vigorous
+ ly	vigorously
+ ness	vigorousness*
+ ish	vigorish

village

+ s	villages
+ er	villager*
+ ery	villagery

vine

+ s	vines
+ ed	vined
+ ing	vining*
+ ery	vinery*
+ y	viny
+ y + er	vinier
+ est	viniest
+ dress + er	vinedresser
+ yard	vineyard
+ yard + ist	vineyardist

vinegar

+ s	vinegars
+ y	vinegary
+ ist	vinegarist*

violent

+ ly	violently
+ ence	violence*
+ ate	violate^
+ tion	violation*
+ or	violator*
+ ive	violative*

violet

+ s	violets

violin

+ s	violins
+ ist	violinist*
+ ic	violinistic*

virgin

+ s	virgins
+ al	virginal
+ ist	virginalist*
+ ity	virginity*

V

virus

+ s	viruses
+ al	viral
+ ly	virally

visible

+ ly	visibly
+ ness	visibleness*
+ ive	visive
+ al	visual*
+ al + ly	visually
+ ize	visualize^
+ er	visualizer*
+ tion	visualization*
+ ity	visibility*

vision

+ al	visional*
+ ly	visionally
+ s	visions
+ ed	visioned
+ ing	visioning*
+ ary	visionary*
+ ness	visionariness
+ less	visionless

visit

+ s	visits
+ ed	visited
+ ing	visiting*
+ or	visitor*
+ able	visitable*
+ ant	visitant*
+ tion	visitation*
+ or + al	visitatorial

vital

+ s	vitals
+ ly	vitally
+ ism	vitalism
+ ist	vitalist
+ ic	vitalistic
+ ity	vitality*
+ ize	vitalize^
+ tion	vitalization

vitamin

+ s	vitamins

vocabulary

+ s	vocabularies

vocation

+ s	vocations
+ al	vocational
+ ly	vocationally
+ ism	vocationalism*
+ ist	vocationalist*

voice

+ s	voices
+ ed	voiced
+ ing	voicing*
+ er	voicer*
+ al	vocal*
+ ly	vocally
+ ism	vocalism*
+ ist	vocalist*
+ ity	vocality*
+ ic	vocalic*
+ ic + ly	vocalically
+ ize	vocalize^
+ ize + tion	vocalization*
+ ize + er	vocalizer*
+ ive	vocative*
+ ive + ly	vocatively
+ ous	vociferous
+ ous + ly	vociferously
+ ous + ness	vociferousness*
+ ate	vociferate*
+ ate + tion	vociferation*
+ ate + or	vociferator*
+ ant	vociferant*
+ less	voiceless
+ less + ly	voicelessly
+ print	voiceprint

volcano

+ s	volcanos
+ ic	volcanic*
+ ly	volcanically
+ icity	volcanicity*
+ ism	volcanism*

volleyball

+ s	volleyballs

volume

+ s	volumes
+ ed	volumed
+ ing	voluming*
+ ous	voluminous
+ ly	voluminously
+ ness	voluminousness*
+ ity	voluminousity*

volunteer

+ s	volunteers
+ ed	volunteered
+ ing	volunteering*
+ ism	volunteerism*
+ ary	voluntary*
+ ly	voluntarily
+ ary + ism	voluntaryism*
+ ist	voluntaryist*
+ ness	voluntariness*

vomit

+ s	vomits
+ ed	vomited

V

+ ing	vomiting*
+ er	vomiter*
+ ory	vomitory*
vote	
+ s	votes
+ ed	voted
+ ing	voting*
+ er	voter*
+ less	voteless
vow	
+ s	vows
+ ed	vowed
+ ing	vowing*
+ er	vower*
+ ive	votive*
+ ly	votively
+ ness	votiveness*
vowel	
+ s	vowels
+ ize	vowelize^
voyage	
+ s	voyages
+ ed	voyaged
+ ing	voyaging*
+ er	voyager*
vulture	
+ s	vultures
+ ish	vulturish
+ ine	vulturine*
+ ous	vulturous

V

waddle
+ s waddles
+ ed waddled
+ ing waddling*
+ er waddler*

wade
+ s wades
+ ed waded
+ ing wading*
+ er wader*
+ able wadable or wadeable*

waffle
+ s waffles
+ ed waffled
+ ing waffling*

wag
+ s wags
+ ed wagged
+ ing wagging*

wagon
+ s wagons
+ er wagoner*

wail
+ s wails
+ ed wailed
+ ing wailing*
+ er wailer*
+ ful wailful
+ ful + ly wailfully

waist
+ s waists
+ ed waisted
+ band waistband
+ coat waistcoat
+ line waistline

wait
+ s waits
+ ed waited
+ ing waiting*
+ or waitor*
+ ess waitress*

wake
+ s wakes
+ ed woke or waked
+ ed + en woken
+ ing waking*
+ er waker*
+ ful wakeful
+ ful + ly wakefully
+ ful + ness wakefulness
+ less wakeless
+ less + ness wakelessness
+ en waken*

walk
+ s walks
+ ed walked
+ ing walking*
+ er walker*
+ about walkabout
+ out walkout
+ over walkover
+ way walkway

wall
+ s walls
+ ed walled
+ ing walling*
+ board wallboard
+ flower wallflower
+ paper wallpaper^

wallet
+ s wallets

walnut
+ s walnuts

walrus
+ s walruses

wander
+ s wanders
+ ed wandered
+ ing wandering*
+ er wanderer*

want
+ s wants
+ ed wanted
+ ing wanting*

war
+ s wars
+ ed warred

+ ing	warring*
+ less	warless
+ less + ness	warlessness*
+ like	warlike
+ or	warrior*
+ lord	warlord
+ lord + ism	warlordism
+ bonnet	warbonnet
+ head	warhead
+ path	warpath
+ plane	warplane
+ ship	warship
+ time	wartime
ward	
+ s	wards
+ ed	warded
+ ing	warding
+ er	warder*
+ er + ship	wardership
+ en	warden
+ en + ship	wardenship
+ ship	wardship
+ ess	wardress
+ room	wardroom
-ward	
for +	forward*
up +	upward*
north +	northward*
after +	afterward*
earth +	earthward*
river +	riverward*
ware	
+ s	wares
+ ed	wared
+ ing	waring
+ house	warehouse^
+ house + er	warehouser
+ house + man	warehouseman
+ room	wareroom
-ware	
silver +	silverware
table +	tableware
warm	
+ s	warms
+ ed	warmed
+ ing	warming*
+ er	warmer*
+ est	warmest
+ ish	warmish
+ ly	warmly
+ ness	warmness*
+ th	warmth
+ heart + ed	warmhearted
+ heart + **ly**	warmheartedly
warn	
+ s	warns
+ ed	warned
+ ing	warning*
+ ing + ly	warningly
+ er	warner*
wart	
+ s	warts
+ ed	warted
+ y	warty
+ hog	warthog
was (2)	
wash	
+ s	washes
+ ed	washed
+ ing	washing*
+ er	washer*
+ y	washy
+ y + er	washier
+ y + est	washiest
+ ity	washability*
+ able	washable*
+ board	washboard
+ bowl	washbowl
+ cloth	washcloth
+ house	washhouse
+ out	washout
+ rag	washrag
+ room	washroom
+ stand	washstand
+ tub	washtub
+ up	washup
+ woman	washwoman
+ er + man	washerman
+ er + woman	washerwoman
Washington	
+ an	Washingtonian*
wasp	
+ s	wasps
+ ish	waspish
+ ly	waspishly
+ ness	waspishness
+ like	wasplike
waste	
+ s	wastes
+ ed	wasted
+ ing	wasting*
+ age	wastage
+ er	waster*
+ ful	wasteful
+ ful + ly	wastefully
+ ful + ness	wastefulness*
+ basket	wastebasket
+ land	wasteland

W

+ paper	wastepaper
+ water	wastewater

watch

+ s	watches
+ ed	watched
+ ing	watching*
+ er	watcher*
+ able	watchable*
+ ful	watchful
+ ful + ly	watchfully
+ ful + ness	watchfulness
+ band	watchband
+ case	watchcase
+ dog	watchdog
+ eye	watcheye
+ make + er	watchmaker
+ make + ing	watchmaking
+ man	watchman
+ tower	watchtower
+ word	watchword

water

+ s	waters
+ ed	watered
+ ing	watering
+ er	waterer*
+ ish	waterish
+ ish + ness	waterishness
+ y	watery
+ y + ly	waterily
+ y + ness	wateriness*
+ less	waterless
+ less + ly	waterlessly
+ less + ness	waterlessness*
+ bear + en	waterborne
+ color	watercolor
+ cool + er	watercooler
+ course	watercourse
+ craft	watercraft
+ fall	waterfall
+ flood	waterflood
+ front	waterfront
+ leaf	waterleaf
+ line	waterline
+ log	waterlog
+ man	waterman
+ man + ship	watermanship
+ mark	watermark
+ melon	watermelon
+ power	waterpower
+ proof	waterproof
+ side	waterside
+ ski + ing	waterskiing
+ tight	watertight
+ way	waterway
+ weed	waterweed
+ wheel	waterwheel
+ work + s	waterworks
+ wear + en	waterworn

wave

+ s	waves
+ ed	waved
+ ing	waving*
+ less	waveless
+ less + ly	wavelessly
+ er	waver*
+ y	wavy*
+ y + er	wavier
+ est	waviest
+ ly	wavily
+ ness	waviness
+ like	wavelike
+ form	waveform
+ guide	waveguide
+ long + th	wavelength

waver

+ s	wavers
+ ed	wavered
+ ing	wavering*

wax

+ s	waxes
+ ed	waxed
+ ing	waxing*
+ er	waxer*
+ en	waxen
+ work	waxwork

way

+ s	ways
+ less	wayless
+ ward	wayward*
+ ward + ly	waywardly
+ ward + ness	waywardness*
+ going	waygoing
+ laid	waylaid
+ lay	waylay
+ lay + ing	waylaying
+ side	wayside
+ wear + en	wayworn

we

weak

+ er	weaker
+ est	weakest
+ ly	weakly
+ ness	weakness*
+ ish	weakish
+ ly	weakly
+ ly + ness	weakliness
+ en	weaken^
+ en + er	weakener*
+ heart + ed	weakhearted

wealth		
	+ y	wealthy
	+ ly	wealthily
	+ ness	wealthiness
	+ er	wealthier
	+ y + s	wealthies
weapon		
	+ s	weapons
	+ less	weaponless
	+ ery	weaponry
wear		
	+ s	wears
	+ ed	wore
	+ en	worn
	+ ing	wearing*
	+ er	wearer*
	+ able	wearable*
	+ ity	wearability*
weary		
	+ s	wearies
	+ ed	wearied
	+ ing	wearying*
	+ some	wearisome
	+ some + ly	wearisomely
	+ some + ness	wearisomeness*
	+ ly	wearily
	+ ness	weariness*
	+ ful	weariful
	+ ful + ly	wearifully
	+ ful + ness	wearifulness*
	+ less	weariless
	+ less + ly	wearilessly
	+ er	wearier
	+ est	weariest
weather		
	+ s	weathers
	+ ed	weathered
	+ ing	weathering
	+ able + ity	weatherability
	+ ly	weatherly
	+ ize	weatherize
	+ tion	weatherization
	+ board	weatherboard
	+ glass	weatherglass
	+ man	weatherman
	+ proof	weatherproof
	+ proof + ness	weatherproofness
	+ wear + en	weatherworn
weave		
	+ s	weaves
	+ ed	wove or weaved
	+ en	woven
	+ ing	weaving*
	+ er	weaver*
	+ bird	weaverbird

web		
	+ s	webs
	+ ed	webbed
	+ ing	webbing*
	+ like	weblike
	+ y	webby*
	+ fed	webfed
	+ foot	webfoot
wed		
	+ s	weds
	+ ed	wedded
	+ ing	wedding*
Wednesday		
	+ s	Wednesdays
wee		
weed		
	+ s	weeds
	+ ed	weeded
	+ ing	weeding*
	+ er	weeder*
	+ y	weedy*
	+ ness	weediness
week		
	+ ly	weekly*
	+ day	weekday*
	+ end	weekend^
	+ end + er	weekender*
	+ night	weeknight*
weep		
	+ s	weeps
	+ ed	wept
	+ ing	weeping*
	+ er	weeper*
	+ y	weepy*
weigh		
	+ s	weighs
	+ ed	weighed
	+ ing	weighing*
	+ able	weighable*
	+ er	weigher*
	+ t	weight*
	+ t + ed	weighted
	+ less	weightless
	+ less + ly	weightlessly
	+ less + ness	weightlessness*
	+ y	weighty
	+ t **+ er**	weightier
	+ t **+ est**	weightiest
	+ t **+ ly**	weightily
	+ t **+ ness**	weightiness*
weird		
	+ ly	weirdly
	+ ness	weirdness
	+ y	weirdy*
	+ o	weirdo*

wiener

+ s	wieners

welcome

+ s	welcomes
+ ed	welcomed
+ ing	welcoming*
+ er	welcomer*
+ ly	welcomely
+ ness	welcomeness*

weld

+ s	welds
+ ed	welded
+ ing	welding*
+ er	welder*
+ able	weldable*
+ ment	weldment*

well

+ s	wells
+ ed	welled
+ ing	welling*
+ advise + ed	well-advised
+ appoint + ed	well-appointed
+ away	well-away
+ be + ing	well-being
+ birth + en	well-born
+ breed + ed	well-bred
+ condition + ed	well-conditioned
+ define + ed	well-defined
+ dispose + ed	well-disposed
+ do + en	well-done
+ favor + ed	well-favored
+ fix + ed	well-fixed
+ found	well-found
+ found + ed	well-founded
+ ground + ed	well-grounded
+ handle + ed	well-handled
+ heel + ed	well-heeled
+ inform + ed	well-informed
+ intend + tion + ed	well-intentioned
+ knit	well-knit
+ knew + en	well-known
+ mean + ing	well-meaning
+ off	well-off
+ order + ed	well-ordered
+ read	well-read
+ round + ed	well-rounded
+ set	well-set
+ speak + en	well-spoken
+ spring	well-spring
+ take + en	well-taken
+ think + ed	well-thought-of
+ time + ed	well-timed
+ to + do	well-to-do
+ turn + ed	well-turned
+ wish + er	well-wisher
+ wish + ing	well-wishing
+ wear + ed	well-worn

went (see go)

were (2)

west

+ er	wester^
+ er + ly	westerly*
+ er + en	western*
+ n + er	westerner*
+ n + more + est	westernmost
+ ize	westernize^
+ ize + tion	westernization*
+ ing	westing*
+ ward	westward*
+ north + west	west-northwest
+ south + west	west-southwest

wet

+ er	wetter
+ est	wettest
+ s	wets
+ ed	wetted or wet
+ ing	wetting*
+ ly	wetly
+ ness	wetness*
+ able	wettable*
+ ity	wettability*
+ er	wetter*
+ ish	wettish
+ back	wetback
+ land	wetland
+ blanket	wet-blanket
+ nurse	wet-nurse

whale

+ s	whales
+ ed	whaled
+ ing	whaling*
+ er	whaler*
+ back	whaleback
+ boat	whaleboat
+ bone	whalebone

wharf

+ s	wharves or wharfs
+ age	wharfage*
+ master	wharfmaster

what

+ ever	whatever
+ not	whatnot
+ so + ever	whatsoever

wheat

+ s	wheats
+ en	wheaten*

wheel

+ s	wheels
+ ed	wheeled

+ ing	wheeling*
+ er	wheeler*
+ y	wheelie*
+ er + deal + er	wheeler-dealer
+ base	wheelbase
+ chair	wheelchair
+ horse	wheelhorse
+ man	wheelman
+ work	wheelwork
+ s + man	wheelsman

wheelbarrow

+ s	wheelbarrows
+ ed	wheelbarrowed
+ ing	wheelbarrowing

when

+ as	whenas
+ ever	whenever
+ so + ever	whensoever
+ ence	whence

where

+ about	whereabout*
+ as	whereas
+ at	whereat
+ by	whereby
+ fore	wherefore
+ from	wherefrom
+ in	wherein
+ in + to	whereinto
+ of	whereof
+ on	whereon
+ so + ever	wheresoever
+ through	wherethrough
+ to	whereto
+ un + to	whereunto
+ upon	whereupon
+ ever	wherever
+ with	wherewith
+ with + al	wherewithal

whether

whew

which

+ ever	whichever
+ so + ever	whichsoever

while

+ s	whiles
+ ed	whiled
+ ing	whiling*

whine

+ s	whines
+ ed	whined
+ ing	whining*
+ ly	whiningly
+ er	whiner*
+ y	whiny*

whip

+ s	whips
+ ed	whipped
+ ing	whipping*
+ er	whipper*
+ like	whiplike
+ y	whippy
+ y + er	whippier
+ est	whippiest
+ lash	whiplash
+ saw	whipsaw^
+ stitch	whipstitch^
+ stock	whipstock
+ worm	whipworm
+ er + snap + er	whippersnapper

whirl

+ s	whirls
+ ed	whirled
+ ing	whirling*
+ er	whirler
+ y	whirly*
+ pool	whirlpool
+ wind	whirlwind

whiskey

+ s	whiskeys

whisper

+ s	whispers
+ ed	whispered
+ ing	whispering*
+ ly	whisperingly
+ er	whisperer*
+ y	whispery

whistle

+ s	whistles
+ ed	whistled
+ ing	whistling*
+ er	whistler*
+ able	whistleable*

white

+ s	whites
+ er	whiter*
+ est	whitest
+ ish	whitish
+ ed	whited
+ ing	whiting*
+ ness	whiteness
+ en	whiten^
+ en + er	whitener*
+ y	whitey*
+ face	whiteface
+ fish	whitefish
+ fly	whitefly
+ out	whiteout
+ throat	whitethroat
+ wall	whitewall

+ wash	whitewash^
+ wing	whitewing
+ wood	whitewood
who	
+ ever	whoever
whole	
+ ness	wholeness
+ some	wholesome
+ some + ly	wholesomely
+ some + ness	wholesomeness*
+ heart + ed	wholehearted
+ heart + ed + ly	wholeheartedly
+ sale	wholesale
+ sale + ed	wholesaled
+ sale + ing	wholesaling
whom	
+ m	whom
+ ever	whomever
+ so + ever	whomsoever
+ s	whose
+ s + so + ever	whosesoever
+ so + ever	whosoever
why	
wicked	
+ ly	wickedly
+ ness	wickedness
wide	
+ er	wider
+ est	widest
+ ly	widely
+ ness	wideness*
+ ish	widish
+ th	width*
+ en	widen^
+ en + er	widener
+ awake	wideawake
+ band	wideband
+ mouth + ed	widemouthed
+ spread	widespread
widow	
+ s	widows
+ ed	widowed
+ ing	widowing*
+ er	widower*
+ hood	widowhood
+ er + hood	widowerhood
wife	
+ s	wives
+ hood	wifehood
+ like	wifelike
+ ly	wifely*
+ ness	wifeliness*
wig	
+ s	wigs
+ ed	wigged

+ ing	wigging*
wiggle	
+ s	wiggles
+ ed	wiggled
+ ing	wiggling*
+ er	wiggler*
+ ly	wiggly*
+ wag	wigwag
wild	
+ er	wilder
+ est	wildest
+ ish	wildish
+ ly	wildly
+ ing	wilding*
+ ness	wildness*
+ ment	wilderment*
+ er + ness	wilderness*
+ cat	wildcat^
+ fire	wildfire
+ flower	wildflower
+ land	wildland
+ life	wildlife
+ wood	wildwood
will	
+ s	wills
+ ed	willed
+ ing	willing*
+ ing + ly	willingly
+ ing + ness	willingness*
+ ful	willful
+ ful + ly	willfully
+ ful + ness	willfulness*
+ power	willpower
win	
+ s	wins
+ ed	won
+ ing	winning*
+ ing + ly	winningly
+ er	winner*
wind (verb)	
+ s	winds
+ ed	wound
+ ing	winding*
+ er	winder*
+ up	windup
wind	
+ s	winds
+ ing	winding*
+ age	windage
+ y	windy
+ er	windier
+ est	windiest
+ bag	windbag
+ blow + en	windblown
+ bear + en	windborne

+ break	windbreak
+ break + er	windbreaker
+ burn	windburn
+ burn + ed	windburned
+ chill	windchill
+ fall	windfall
+ flower	windflower
+ pipe	windpipe
+ proof	windproof
+ row	windrow
+ screen	windscreen
+ shield	windshield
+ storm	windstorm
+ sweep + ed	windswept
+ ward	windward
+ way	windway

windmill

+ s	windmills
+ ed	windmilled
+ ing	windmilling*

window

+ s	windows
+ less	windowless

wine

+ s	wines
+ ed	wined
+ ing	wining*
+ ery	winery*
+ y	winy
+ y + er	winier
+ est	winiest
+ glass	wineglass
+ grow + er	winegrower
+ press	winepress
+ shop	wineshop
+ skin	wineskin

wing

+ s	wings
+ ed	winged
+ ing	winging*
+ er	winger*
+ less	wingless
+ less + ness	winglessness*
+ like	winglike
+ back	wingback
+ man	wingman
+ over	wingover
+ spread	wingspread
+ tip	wingtip

wink

+ s	winks
+ ed	winked
+ ing	winking*
+ er	winker*

winter

+ s	winters
+ ed	wintered
+ ing	wintering*
+ er	winterer*
+ ize	winterize^
+ ize + er	winterizer*
+ ize + tion	winterization*
+ ly	winterly
+ y	wintry
+ y + er	wintrier
+ est	wintriest
+ ness	wintriness*
+ tide	wintertide
+ time	wintertime

wipe

+ s	wipes
+ ed	wiped
+ ing	wiping
+ er	wiper*
+ out	wipeout

wire

+ s	wires
+ ed	wired
+ ing	wiring*
+ like	wirelike
+ er	wirer*
+ y	wiry
+ y + er	wirier
+ est	wiriest
+ ly	wirily
+ ness	wiriness*
+ able	wirable*
+ less	wireless
+ draw	wiredraw
+ draw + er	wiredrawer
+ draw + en	wiredrawn
+ hair	wirehair
+ hair + ed	wirehaired
+ man	wireman
+ tap	wiretap^
+ way	wireway
+ work	wirework
+ worm	wireworm

wise

+ er	wiser
+ est	wisest
+ ly	wisely
+ ness	wiseness*
+ dom	wisdom
+ s	wises
+ ed	wised
+ ing	wising*

W

wish	
+ s	wishes
+ ed	wished
+ ing	wishing*
+ er	wisher*
+ ful	wishful
+ ful + ly	wishfully
+ ful + ness	wishfulness*
+ y + wash + y	wishy-washy
wit (2)	
+ s	wits
+ ed	witted
+ ing	witting*
+ ing + ly	wittingly
+ y	witty
+ er	wittior
+ est	wittiest
+ **ly**	wittily
+ less	witless
+ less + ly	witlessly
+ less +ness	witlessness*
+ y + ness	wittiness*
+ ism	witticism*
witch	
+ s	witches
+ ed	witched
+ ing	witching*
+ like	witchlike
+ y	witchy*
+ ery	witchery*
+ craft	witchcraft
with	
+ al	withal
+ in	within
+ in + door + s	withindoors
+ out	without
+ out + door + s	withoutdoors
withdraw	
+ s	withdraws
+ en	withdrawn
+ ness	withdrawnness*
+ ed	withdrew
+ ing	withdrawing*
+ al	withdrawal*
+ able	withdrawable*
witness	
+ s	witnesses
+ ed	witnessed
+ ing	witnessing
wives	
wolf	
+ s	wolves
+ ed	wolved
+ ing	wolving*
+ like	wolflike
+ er	wolfer*
+ ish	wolfish
+ ly	wolfishly
+ ness	wolfishness*
woman	
+ ly	womanly
+ ly + ness	womanliness*
+ less	womanless
+ hood	womanhood
+ ish	womanish
+ ish + ly	womanishly
+ ish + ness	womanishness*
+ ize	womanize^
+ ize + er	womanizer*
+ like	womanlike
+ power	womanpower
women	
+ folk	womenfolk*
+ kind	womenkind
won	
wonder	
+ s	wonders
+ ed	wondered
+ ing	wondering*
+ er	wonderer*
+ ful	wonderful
+ ful + ly	wonderfully
+ ful + ness	wonderfulness*
+ ment	wonderment*
+ ous	wondrous
+ ous + ly	wondrously
+ ous + ness	wondrousness*
+ land	wonderland
+ work	wonderwork*
won't	
wood	
+ s	woods
+ ed	wooded
+ en	wooden
+ ly	woodenly
+ en + ness	woodenness
+ s + y	woodsy
+ y	woody*
+ er	woodier
+ est	woodiest
+ y + ness	woodiness
+ en + head	woodenhead
+ en+ head + ed	woodenheaded
+ en + ware	woodenware
+ block	woodblock
+ craft	woodcraft
+ cut	woodcut^
+ land	woodland*
+ land + er	woodlander
+ lot	woodlot

+ man	woodman
+ note	woodnote
+ peck + er	woodpecker
+ pile	woodpile
+ s + man	woodsman
+ wind	woodwind
+ work	woodwork

wool

+ s	wools
+ en	woolen* or woollen*
+ ed	wooled
+ er	wooler
+ y	wooly or woolly or woolie
+ y + s	woollies
+ y + er	woollier
+ est	wooliest
+ ness	woolliness
+ gather + ing	woolgathering
+ gather + er	woolgatherer
+ man	woolman
+ pack	woolpack
+ sack	woolsack
+ shed	woolshed
+ skin	woolskin
+ sort + er	woolsorter

word

+ s	words
+ ed	worded
+ ing	wording*
+ less	wordless
+ less + ly	wordlessly
+ less + ness	wordlessness*
+ y	wordy
+ er	wordier
+ est	wordiest
+ y + ly	wordily
+ y + ness	wordiness*
+ age	wordage*
+ book	wordbook
+ play	wordplay

work

+ s	works
+ ed	worked
+ ing	working*
+ er	worker*
+ able	workable*
+ able + ness	workableness*
+ able + ity	workability*
+ less	workless
+ less + ness	worklessness*
+ a + day	workaday
+ bag	workbag
+ basket	workbasket
+ bench	workbench
+ boat	workboat
+ book	workbook
+ box	workbox
+ day	workday
+ folk	workfolk
+ horse	workhorse
+ man	workman
+ man + ly	workmanly
+ man + like	workmanlike
+ man + ship	workmanship
+ men	workmen
+ mate	workmate
+ out	workout*
+ people	workpeople
+ piece	workpiece
+ place	workplace
+ room	workroom
+ shop	workshop
+ station	workstation
+ table	worktable
+ up	workup
+ week	workweek
+ woman	workwoman
+ shop	workshop
+ shop + s	workshops

world

+ s	worlds
+ ly	worldly
+ wide	worldwide

worm

+ s	worms
+ ed	wormed
+ ing	worming*
+ like	wormlike
+ er	wormer*
+ y	wormy*
+ y + er	wormier
+ est	wormiest
+ hole	wormhole
+ seed	wormseed
+ wood	wormwood

worry

+ s	worries
+ ed	worried
+ ing	worrying*
+ some	worrisome
+ some + ly	worrisomely
+ some + ness	worrisomeness*
+ ly	worriedly
+ ment	worriment*
+ er	worrier*
+ wart	worrywart

W

worse

+ en	worsen^
+ er	worser*
+ est	worst

worship

+ s	worships
+ ed	worshiped
+ ing	worshiping*
+ er	worshiper*
+ ful	worshipful
+ ful + ly	worshipfully
+ ful + ness	worshipfulness*
+ less	worshipless

worth

+ ful	worthful
+ less	worthless
+ less + ly	worthlessly
+ less + ness	worthlessness*
+ y	worthy*
+ er	worthier
+ est	worthiest
+ y + ly	worthily
+ y + ness	worthiness*

would (2)

wound

+ s	wounds
+ ed	wounded
+ ing	wounding*
+ less	woundless

wow

wrap

+ s	wraps
+ ed	wrapped
+ ing	wrapping*
+ er	wrapper*
+ around	wraparound

wreath

+ s	wreaths
+ e	wreathe*
+ ed	wreathed
+ ing	wreathing*
+ y	wreathy

wreck

+ s	wrecks
+ ed	wrecked
+ ing	wrecking*
+ er	wrecker*
+ age	wreckage*

wrench

+ s	wrenches
+ ed	wrenched
+ ing	wrenching*
+ ly	wrenchingly

wrestle

+ s	wrestles
+ ed	wrestled
+ ing	wrestling*
+ er	wrestler*

wring

+ s	wrings
+ ed	wrung
+ ing	wringing*
+ er	wringer*

wrinkle

+ s	wrinkles
+ ed	wrinkled
+ ing	wrinkling*
+ y	wrinkly*

wrist

+ s	wrists
+ y	wristy
+ band	wristband*

write

+ s	writes
+ ed	wrote
+ en	written
+ ing	writing*
+ er	writer*
+ able	writable*
+ er + ly	writerly

wrong

+ s	wrongs
+ ed	wronged
+ ing	wronging
+ er	wronger*
+ est	wrongest
+ ly	wrongly
+ ness	wrongness*
+ ful	wrongful
+ ful + ly	wrongfully
+ ful + ness	wrongfulness*
+ do + er	wrongdoer
+ do + ing	wrongdoing
+ head + ed	wrongheaded
+ head + ed + ness	wrongheadedness

Xerox (2)	
+ s	Xeroxes
+ ed	Xeroxed
+ ing	Xeroxing*
+ er	Xeroxer
x-ray^	
xylophone	
+ s	xylophones
+ ist	xylophonist*

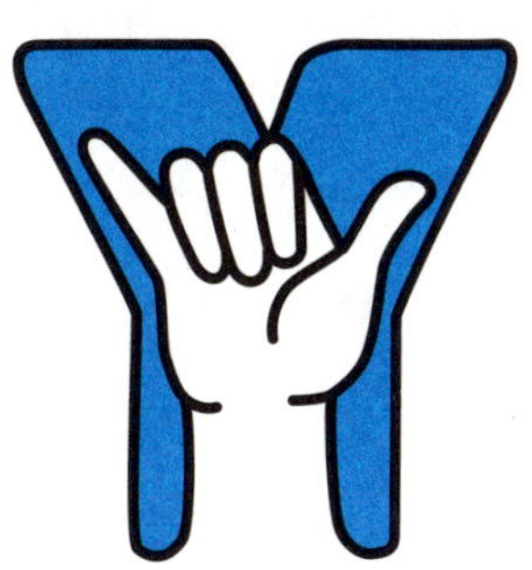

yard	
+ s	yards
+ ed	yarded
+ ing	yarding
+ age	yardage*
+ arm	yardarm*
+ bird	yardbird*
+ man	yardman
+ master	yardmaster
+ stick	yardstick*
yarn	
+ s	yarns
+ ed	yarned
+ ing	yarning*
+ er	yarner*
yawn	
+ s	yawns
+ ed	yawned
+ ing	yawning*
+ ly	yawningly
+ er	yawner*
year	
+ s	years
+ ly	yearly
+ long	yearlong
+ book	yearbook*
yeast	
+ s	yeasts
+ ed	yeasted
+ ing	yeasting*
+ y	yeasty
+ er	yeastier
+ est	yeastiest
+ ness	yeastiness*
yell	
+ s	yells
+ ed	yelled
+ ing	yelling*
+ er	yeller*
yellow	
+ s	yellows
+ ed	yellowed
+ ing	yellowing*
+ ish	yellowish
yes	
yesterday*	
yet	
yield	
+ s	yields
+ ed	yielded
+ ing	yielding*
+ er	yielder
yogurt*	
yonder	
you	
+ 'd	you'd
+ 'll	you'll
+ 're	you're
+ 've	you've
young	
+ er	younger
+ est	youngest
+ ish	youngish
+ ness	youngness
+ th	youth*
+ ful	youthful
+ ly	youthfully
+ ful + ness	youthfulness
your	
+ s	yours
+ self	yourself*
yoyo^	

zebra	
+ s	zebras
+ wood	zebrawood
zero^	
zip	
+ s	zips
+ ed	zipped
+ ing	zipping*
+ y	zippy
+ y + er	zippier
+ est	zippiest
zipper^	
zone	
+ s	zones
+ ed	zoned
+ ing	zoning*
+ al	zonal
+ ly	zonally
+ ate	zonate
+ ate + ed	zonated
+ tion	zonation*
zoo	
+ s	zoos
+ keep + er	zookeeper*
zoom^	

Products from Modern Signs Press, Inc.

Basic Tools and Techniques

Signing Exact English The Dictionary, the heart of the SEE system
Signing Exact English Interactive CD ROM with all Dictionary information and ability to print any of the illustrated signs individually or in phrases or sentences in a variety of sizes.
Teaching and Learning Signing Exact English
Student Workbook
Vocabulary Development Flash Cards
- ***Kit A***
- ***Kit B***
- ***Kit C***

Video Tapes

Curriculum Tapes
- ***Beginning Level*** – 14 lessons (workbook included)
- ***Rather Strange Stories*** (Intermediate Level) - 14 tapes
- ***Rather Ordinary Stories***
  - Basic Word Groups - 8 tapes
  - Basic Lessons - 14 tapes
  - Intermediate Lessons - 10 tapes
  - Advanced Lessons - 10 tapes

Sign With Me Produced at Boys Town National Research Hospital
- ***Building Conversation***
- ***Building Concepts***
- ***Positive Parenting***

See Me Sing Songs and Stories
The Sign for Friends David Parker
Visual Tales (available in Signed English or ASL)
- ***The Father, The Son and The Donkey***
- ***Village Stew***
- ***The Greedy Cat***
- ***The Magic Pot***
- ***The House That Jack Built***

Signed Cartoons (available in Signed English or ASL)
- ***Three Pigs***
- ***Three Bears***
- ***Casper***
- ***Animal Antics***
- ***Raggedy Ann***
- ***Jingle Bells***
- ***Pup's Christmas***
- ***Shipshape Shapes***
- ***Rudolph***
- ***Cinderella***
- ***Numbers***
- ***Red Riding Hood***
- ***Reptiles, Birds & Amphibians***

Show and Tell Stories
- Series 1 - Brown Bear, Brown Bear and This Is Me
- Series 2 - The Very Hungry Caterpillar and Goodnight Moon
- Series 3 - Nursery Rhymes

Products from Modern Signs Press, Inc.

Informational Tapes

- ***Deafness the Hidden Handicap***
- ***Growing Up with SEE***

Instructional Video Tapes in Spanish/English

Children's Collection

Coloring Books

- ***ABC's of Fingerspelling***
- ***Sign Numbers***

Storybooks Stories with illustrated signs

- ***Talking Finger Series*** - Popsicles are Cold, At Grandma's House, Little Green Monsters, I Was So Mad
- ***In Our House***
- ***Be Happy Not Sad*** (two books including coloring workbook)
- ***Grandfather Moose*** (finger rhymes)

Greeting Cards

Color Your Own Cards (in both signs and words)

- ***All Occasion***
- ***Birthday***
- ***Christmas***

Special Products

Music In Motion
Signos Para El Ingles Exacto (Signing Exact English in Spanish)
Using Affixes With Signing Exact English (Affix Reference)
Deaf Students Can Be Great Readers (Research)
Pledge of Allegiance Poster
Signs Everywhere (showing signs for cities and states)
Sign with Kids A curriculum for teaching hearing kids sign language (see below)
Signing Bear "Honey"
Cosmo Gets An Ear All about a boy and his hearing aid
Sign with Your Baby (early communication for hearing babies)
One Mother's Story
Rubber Stamps
Sign Language T-Shirts (with alphabet on front)
Sign Language Tote Bags (with alphabet on one side)

Products from Modern Signs Press, Inc.

FOR MORE INFORMATION ON OTHER PRODUCTS
MAIL – PHONE – FAX
TO REQUEST A FREE CATALOG

Modern Signs Press, Inc.
P.O. Box 1181
Los Alamitos, CA 90720

562/596-8548 V
562/493-4168 V/TDD
562/795-6614 FAX
email: modsigns@modernsignspress.com
website: www.modernsignspress.com